P9-AQE-145

# Managing Enterprise Content: A Unified Content Strategy

## Content Highlights:

This book describes how to:

- Identify key business needs for a unified content strategy
- Zero in on the causes of the real "pain" the organization suffers in creating and managing content
- Identify the potential return on investment (ROI) for a unified content strategy
- Analyze content and model it for effective reuse
- Design metadata for reuse, retrieval, and tracking
- Design workflow to support your unified content strategy
- Identify the right types of technology to support the strategy
- Help your staff adopt a unified content strategy
- Implement a unified content strategy, following a phased approach

Today's businesses are overwhelmed with the need to create more content, more quickly, customized for more customers and for more media than ever before. *Managing Enterprise Content: A Unified Content Strategy* provides the concepts, strategies, guidelines, processes, and technological options that will prepare enterprise content managers and authors to meet the increasing demands of creating, managing, and distributing content.

This book shows readers how to escape from The Content Silo Trap, which isolates authors, increases the cost of content creation, results in disparate processes and technology, and prevents businesses from effectively meeting customers' information needs.

—*Ann Rockley*

"This book is very thorough—it covers issues that arise when you first start looking at identifying the usefulness of a content management strategy in your organization, and takes you through the entire evaluation, design, implementation and follow up. It contains more than the theory. I've read in other books—it gives some concrete examples, and tells me what questions I need to answer or get answered at various steps in the process of moving toward a unified content management approach. It takes a practical approach to the issues involved instead of just focusing on the more philosophical benefits."

—**Heather Searl, Manager,** *Technical Communications, MDS Sciex*

"With Ann Rockley's extensive background in applying these principles and practices, she presents a clear, common-sense approach to single sourcing theory and implementation. She is an acknowledged expert in the single sourcing arena. She is known for her encyclopedic knowledge of almost every tool available to produce or manage content in a single sourced environment."

—**Jan Shelton, Sr. Technical Writer,** *MetaSolv Software, Inc.*

New Riders

www.newriders.com

# Managing Enterprise Content:
## A Unified Content Strategy

Ann Rockley

Pamela Kostur

Steve Manning

New Riders

1249 Eighth Street, Berkeley, California 94710
An Imprint of Peachpit, a division of Pearson Education

## Managing Enterprise Content: A Unified Content Strategy

Ann Rockley, Pamela Kostur, Steve Manning

**Copyright © 2003 Ann Rockley**

FIRST PRINTING: October, 2003

All rights reserved. No part of this book may be reproduced or transmitted in any form or by any means, electronic or mechanical, including photocopying, recording, or by any information storage and retrieval system, without written permission from the publisher, except for the inclusion of brief quotations in a review.

International Standard Book Number: 0-7357-1306-5

Library of Congress Catalog Card Number: 2002102635

8

Printed in the United States of America

## Trademarks

All terms mentioned in this book that are known to be trademarks or service marks have been appropriately capitalized. New Riders Publishing cannot attest to the accuracy of this information. Use of a term in this book should not be regarded as affecting the validity of any trademark or service mark.

## Warning and Disclaimer

This book is designed to provide information about *Managing Enterprise Content: A Unified Content Strategy*. Every effort has been made to make this book as complete and as accurate as possible, but no warranty of fitness is implied.

The information is provided on an as-is basis. The authors and New Riders Publishing shall have neither liability nor responsibility to any person or entity with respect to any loss or damages arising from the information contained in this book or from the use of the discs or programs that may accompany it.

**Publisher**
David Dwyer

**Associate Publisher**
Stephanie Wall

**Production Manager**
Gina Kanouse

**Managing Editor**
Kristy Knoop

**Acquisitions Editors**
Linda Anne Bump
Elise Walter

**Development Editor**
Chris Zahn

**Product Marketing Manager**
Tammy Detrich

**Publicity Manager**
Susan Nixon

**Copy Editor**
Margo Catts

**Indexer**
Cheryl Lenser

**Manufacturing Coordinator**
Jim Conway

**Book Designer**
Louisa Adair

**Cover Designer**
Brainstorm Design, Inc.

**Composition**
Jeff Bredensteiner

❖

*To all our clients, conference attendees, and students who kept saying, "When are you going to write that book?" And to all our family, friends, and staff who patiently listened when we repeatedly said "After the book is finished we'll…"*

❖

# Table of Contents

# About the Author

**Ann Rockley** is President of The Rockley Group, Inc. Ann Rockley has an international reputation in the field of e-content, content management, and e-learning. Ann is doing ground-breaking work in the field of information design for content reuse and enterprise content management. Ann regularly speaks at dozens of conferences (including STC Annual Conference, InfoProducer Conference, Documation, Forum, Hypertext Conference, SingleSource conference, medical writer conferences, and library conferences) around the world on the topic of e-content, content management, and single sourcing. Rockley is President of Content Management Professionals, a member organization that fosters the sharing of content management information, practices, and strategies. Rockely is a Fellow of the Society for Technical Communication and has a Master of Information Science from the University of Toronto. She teaches Enterprise Content Management at the University of Toronto.

# About the Contributing Authors

**Pamela Kostur** is a senior consultant with The Rockley Group; her expertise is in information analysis, information modeling, and structured writing to support a unified content strategy, as well as in developing e-learning solutions. Pamela has been working in the documentation field for over 16 years and regularly speaks at conferences (STC, IPCC, Documentation and Training) on topics including iterative usability, miscommunication, structured writing, building and managing intranets, creating usable online documentation, designing e-learning, and developing unified content strategies. Before joining The Rockley Group, Pamela was the Communication Manager for SaskTel Mobility in Regina, Saskatchewan, Canada. She is a senior member of the Society for Technical Communication, a member of the Professional Communication Society (a member society of the IEEE), and sits on the Advisory Committee for the University of Toronto's Advanced Certificate in Information Design program.

**Steve Manning** is a senior consultant with The Rockley Group and has over 13 years experience in the documentation field. He is a skilled developer of online documentation (WinHelp, HTML Help, web sites, XML, and Lotus Notes) and has created single-source production methodologies that use key online tools. Steve has extensive experience in project management and has managed a number of multiple-media, single-source projects. He also has extensive experience in the design and development of paper-based technical documentation. Before joining the Rockley Group, Steve was the Manager of Documentation for PROMIS Systems (now PRI Automation). While there, he managed a group of technical writers and course developers responsible for the creation of all documentation and training materials for new products. Steve is a frequent speaker at conferences (AUGI, WinWriters, STC) and teaches Introduction to XML at the University of Toronto.

**The Rockley Group, Inc.** is one of North America's leading providers of enterprise content management methodologies. They have helped organizations develop content reuse and unified content strategies across departments, divisions, and the enterprise. Working with customers in the life sciences (such as, Medtronic, IDX Systems and Centre of Forensic Sciences), financial services (Citibank, Bank of Canada, Deloitte & Touche, Norwest Services), and high technology (Alcatel, Cisco, Compaq, HP, Intel, Nortel) industries, The Rockley Group has developed content reuse solutions to reduce the cost and effort of complex information creation and management.

# About the Technical Reviewers

These reviewers contributed their considerable hands-on expertise to the entire development process for *Managing Enterprise Content: A Unified Content Strategy*. As the book was being written, these dedicated professionals reviewed all the material for technical content, organization, and flow. Their feedback was critical to ensuring that *Managing Enterprise Content: A Unified Content Strategy* fits our reader's need for the highest-quality technical information.

**Seth Maislin** is an Information Architecture and Indexing Consultant, specializing in the construction of usable web-based and knowledge hierarchies.

He is an adjunct professor at Bentley College; an instructor at Middlesex Community College; an IA and Indexing Trainer at nSight, Inc.; and the former integration manager at Terra Lycos. His company is Focus Information Services.

He provides information architecture, navigation, usability, indexing, content analysis, and other consulting services, presents regularly at conferences, and indexes books and web documents. Seth has written several articles for professional print and online periodicals; many are republished here.

Seth serves as elected director of the American Society of Indexers and participates in many of its technology subgroups. He is also Webmaster for STC's Indexing Special Interest Group. Past projects include indexing America Online, building content directories for Lycos.com and its partners, cataloguing clip art for Mattel, and indexing Microsoft's official product web sites.

**Scott Abel** is a Web Content Strategist and Technical Writing Consultant for Nims Associates, Inc. Scott helps clients move from document to content management, create usable Internet, intranet, and extranet sites, online help systems, and software documentation.

# Acknowledgments

A lot of people helped to make this book a reality. We would like to thank them for all their help.

We would like to start by thanking Scott Abel, who put us in touch with New Riders Publishing, then stayed on to act as a technical editor.

We would like to thank our reviewers Brenda Parr, Kelly McCurry, Tim Wilkes, and Charles Cantrell who put in much time and effort to review our early drafts, give pointed advice on how they could be improved, often—in fact, usually—under very tight deadlines. We worked with each of our reviewers on some aspect of a unified content strategy and it's through their experience in all aspects of the task and their ongoing role in the "trenches" that they were able to provide invaluable feedback. Brenda Parr was one of our clients who kept saying, "When are you going to write that book?," so when the book was becoming a reality she was the first person we called to ask for help with the review. Kelly McCurry and Tim Wilkes, after working toward unified content in their corporate jobs, went on to form Scratchcat Communication Consulting, a company specializing in documentation and online content solutions. Charles Cantrell, who was very involved in his company's DTD design, helped to review the design section from the implementation perspective.

We would like to thank our technical editors Scott Abel and Seth Maislin. Scott continually pressed us to identify why people should be reading this section and how it would affect them, and Seth pressed us to ensure that every detail was clear and complete.

We would like to thank Charles Cooper, a multi-talented senior consultant in The Rockley Group, for creating all the illustrations for the book.

Finally, this wouldn't have been possible without the team from New Riders Publishing. We would like to thank Linda Bump (Senior Acquisitions Editor) who believed in the book and worked hard to have it approved, even though it didn't exactly fit in the current offering. We'd also like to thank Chris Zahn (Development Editor) who guided us through the book publishing process and nudged us about deadlines.

## Ann Rockley

I would like to thank my family and friends who rolled their eyes when I kept saying "After the book…" but continued to wait patiently for that day.

I'd also like to thank Gord Graham who gave me a lot of advice on getting a book published. I would like to thank Strategic Coach, a program for entrepreneurs that I have been involved in for many years that has helped me to consistently focus on goals and identify my organization's unique methodology. I would also like to thank Angela Sutcliffe, my business coach, who helps to coach me on issues relating to the business, but also kept me on track with my major focus during this time—the book. I'd like to thank Laurel Simmons, who supplied ongoing support throughout.

And last, but not least, I would like to thank my co-authors, Pamela Kostur and Steve Manning. The Rockley Group works on most projects as a team, with team members focusing on their own areas of expertise, and supporting everyone wherever it is needed. The book was no different. We worked on the book collaboratively, making it a complete and comprehensive whole, sharing our insights and knowledge and feedback.

# Tell Us What You Think

As the reader of this book, you are the most important critic and commentator. We value your opinion and want to know what we're doing right, what we could do better, what areas you'd like to see us publish in, and any other words of wisdom you're willing to pass our way.

When you contact us, please be sure to include this book's title and author as well as your name and email address. We will carefully review your comments and share them with the author and editors who worked on the book.

**Email:**     errata@newriders.com

# Introduction

Content management has become a hot topic
as organizations have struggled to manage
their content. Web content has received the
most press and is the focus of most books on
the subject. However, the management of
enterprise content—content that spans many
different areas within an organization, created
by multiple authors, and distributed in many
different media (for example, paper, web, and
wireless)—has received little attention.
Enterprise content management is the focus of
this book. This focus is a result of the many
years we've spent helping our clients to manage their content in a unified way, designing
strategies to ensure their content is consistent
and accurate wherever it appears and flows
along a uniform continuum, from the first
information customers see, through the sales
process, to the support materials you provide
them with as part of your ongoing
commitment.

# Who should read this book

This book was written with a number of audiences in mind. It is designed to assist content managers who are responsible for creating and managing large volumes of content in many different media for many types of content users. Content managers will learn what they need to know about enterprise content management, and what is involved in developing a unified content strategy.

This book is also designed for information architects who are responsible for designing Internet or intranet sites, content management systems, publications systems, learning materials, and supporting multiple media. Information architects will receive practical advice on designing the architecture to support a unified content strategy.

This book is also designed for authors, specifically, anyone responsible for creating enterprise content such as brochures, newsletters, data sheets, product catalogs, proposals, reports, help desk/customer support materials, regulatory documents, user documentation, support documentation, service documentation, and training materials. Authors will receive practical advice on structured writing, writing for multiple media, and collaborative authoring.

The following section, "How this book is organized," identifies how each of these audiences will benefit from this book.

# How this book is organized

This book is divided into six sections. Each part focuses on a particular aspect of managing your enterprise content with a unified content strategy. Although you do not have to read this book in chronological order, it is designed to follow the unified content strategy life cycle.

## Part I: The basis of a unified content strategy (Chapters 1–3)

This section provides an understanding of a unified content strategy, where an organization's content comes from, the issues of creating and managing that content, and the fundamental concepts of reuse. This section also provides guidelines for identifying a return on investment for a unified content strategy. This is an important section for all readers to provide a basis of understanding for the rest of the book. Chapters 1 and 2 are targeted toward all audiences; Chapter 3 is more applicable to content managers.

## Part II: Performing a substantive audit: Determining business requirements (Chapters 4–7)

This section provides guidelines on how to analyze your organizational needs, analyze your content, determine your content life cycle, and build a vision of your unified content strategy. Knowing where to start, understanding the current situation and your needs, and building a vision for the future is important to the success of your project. Although all audiences will benefit from the chapters in Part II—specifically in understanding the content life cycle and auditing the content in your organization—Chapters 4 to 7 are targeted primarily toward content managers who will be responsible for envisioning and documenting the new unified content life cycle.

## Part III: Design (Chapters 8–12)

This section focuses on the design phase of a unified content strategy. Effective design is key to the success of authoring, managing, and delivering content. This section takes you through the concepts of information modeling, metadata design, workflow design, and the design of dynamic documents. The chapters in Part III form an essential core of the book and are targeted to all audiences. Parts I and III are critical to your understanding of what a unified content strategy is and how to design your information architecture to support it.

## Part IV: Tools and technologies (chapters 13–18)

Managing enterprise content through a unified content strategy is dependent on having the right tools in place for authoring, management, and delivery of content. This section helps you understand how to evaluate tools and the functionality of the key technologies (authoring, content management, workflow, and delivery). It also provides guidelines for evaluating these tools and accordingly, is targeted primarily toward content managers, who will be responsible for selecting the tools to support a unified content strategy.

## Part V: Moving to a unified content strategy (Chapters 19–22)

This section focuses on ways in which you can help your organization to adopt a unified content strategy. The section begins with a discussion of collaborative authoring—a new yet sometimes difficult process to adopt—then moves into the discussion of how to separate content from format so that authors can write content once and still ensure it is readable and effective in multiple media. Often, one of the more complex issues to deal with is the issue of change. This section focuses on change management and helps to identify potential pitfalls. Finally, this section helps you to move forward with a transition plan. Chapters 19 and 20 are applicable to all audiences, but Chapters 21 and 22, in their focus on management issues, are most applicable to content managers.

## Part VI: Resources (Glossary, Bibliography, Appendixes A-E, Index)

The book includes a glossary of content management terms and definitions, as well as a bibliography of the works consulted in the writing of this book.

The appendixes at the end of this book provide supplementary material, such as check-lists for implementing a unified content strategy and selecting appropriate tools. They also provide a vendor list, an explanation of content relationships, and further suggestions to help you write for multiple media. Content managers will benefit most from the checklists and vendor list, whereas authors and information architects will benefit most from suggestions on writing for multiple media and understanding content relationships.

## At what level is this book written?

This book is written with the assumption that readers have never worked with content management, structured content, or XML. It is designed to ensure that all the concepts are clear no matter what your existing knowledge level is.

## What you should take away

This book will assist you in creating, managing, and delivering your content. It will help you to define your requirements and build your vision, design your content architecture, pick the right tools, and overcome the hurdles of managing enterprise content. We hope that it will help you to see the broad spectrum of enterprise content, the requirements for effectively creating, managing, and delivering content, and the value of developing a unified content strategy for your organization.

# Conventions

This book follows a few typographical conventions:

- Program text, functions, variables, and other "computer language" are set in a fixed-pitch font—for example, `<html>`.

# Part I

# The basis of a unified content strategy

A unified content strategy helps you to get a handle on all the content—the intellectual capital—in your organization. A unified content strategy means integrating your processes from content creation to content management and delivery, ensuring that information is created, managed, and delivered consistently, in the way that users need it, without duplicating your efforts. The chapters in Part I explain the basis of a unified content strategy, starting from a discussion of content and where it all comes from, to assessing the return on your investment if you decide to move ahead with a unified content strategy.

Within your organization, you most likely create tremendous volumes of content to support your products, services, and business processes. Getting content out to the right people at the right time and in the right format is critical to your success. Not only is there a tremendous amount of content to get out, you may also publish it in number of different formats and for many different media (for example, paper, the Web, and wireless devices such as PDAs and cell phones). Chapter 1, "Content: The lifeblood of an organization," introduces the concept of unifying content within an organization, including the causes and effects of the "content silo trap" and the components of a unified content strategy.

Following the discussion of content, we introduce you to the fundamental concepts of reuse. Content reuse is key to a successful unified content strategy; through content reuse, you can make sure that everywhere the same or similar information appears, it is consistent and that you're not having to reproduce it each time you need it. Chapter 2, "Fundamental concepts of reuse," defines content reuse and how it benefits a unified content strategy. It explores how other industries have employed reuse for decades to improve their processes and quality of their products and describes the many ways content can be reused (for example, systematic, opportunistic) along with the pros and cons of each method.

Chapter 3, "Assessing return on investment for a unified content strategy," rounds out Part I by showing you how to calculate your potential return on investment (ROI). ROI is the anticipated savings after subtracting the cost of implementing a unified content strategy. Using a fictitious company as an example, this chapter focuses on where organizations incur costs, how to identify and measure those costs, how to identify and measure savings, and how to identify and calculate return on investment of implementing a unified content strategy.

Once you understand the basis of a unified content strategy, you can move ahead with such things as performing a content audit, building information models, and implementing new authoring and workflow processes. But first, what is content? Read on…

# Chapter 1

## Content: The lifeblood of an organization

Organizations create tremendous volumes of content to support their products, services, and business processes. Getting content out to the right people at the right time and in the right format is critical to an organization's success. Not only is there a tremendous amount of content to get out, it may also be published in a number of different formats and for many different media (such as paper, the Web, and wireless devices, such as PDAs and cell phones).

This chapter introduces the concept of unifying content within an organization, including the causes and effects of the "Content Silo Trap™" and the components of a unified content strategy.

## Content: Where does it all come from?

A typical organization has multiple content creators who design, create, manage, and distribute information. Virtually every department within an organization touches content in some way. For example, marketing and public affairs departments produce information targeted to customers and potential customers, as well as for the general public and the press. They create such things as newsletters, brochures, product information sheets, proposals, press releases, speeches, presentations, and annual reports. These "information products" may be published on paper, but often reside on the company's Internet site, as well as on the intranet for internal consumption. Content may also be delivered through portals.

Likewise, HR departments produce many materials that are published to different media (web, paper, portals) for different audiences. HR departments create information such as employee training materials and orientation programs (web-based or classroom-led, self-paced or guided), corporate policies and procedures, employee newsletters, and job openings and descriptions.

Technical publications is another area where much internal and external information is created, managed, and stored. Technical publications departments typically work on the information that accompanies products, including user guides, online help, reference documents, development guides, and application guides. They also create much of the internal documentation that supports products, such as specifications and reference materials for the company's front-line support staff. In many organizations, technical publications departments, along with HR, have been influential in making internal information available online via the company intranet.

Product/service development departments conceive of and build the products or services an organization produces. They design the computer programs, the medical devices, the coffee machines, the handheld devices. In their capacity as developers, they produce functional specifications, design documents, and quality assurance test plans.

Customer service departments respond to requests for information and assistance as rapidly as possible. To assist customer service representatives in responding to customer inquiries, they produce and maintain frequently asked question (FAQ) sites and problem-tracking databases.

Training publications and staff help customers embrace new products through practical customer-oriented instruction. They produce such information products as classroom or web-based course materials, application guides, and customer-specific courses.

Although these examples are not all-inclusive and not necessarily representative of how all organizations are structured, they serve to illustrate the many possible variations and iterations of content, churned into various information products, into a number of different media, for a number of different people. The number of iterations lend themselves to repetition (sometimes necessary, sometimes not) and to inconsistency. However, a unified content strategy brings together all content, so it is managed through a definitive source. Whoever needs information can find and access it through the definitive source, and wherever information is repeated, it is consistent rather than created "from scratch" each time. Naturally, one of the biggest challenges in implementing a unified content strategy is identifying and breaking down the "silos," which is where we'll begin.

## Understanding the Content Silo Trap

Too often, content is created by authors working in isolation from other authors within the organization. Walls are erected among content areas and even within content areas, which leads to content being created, and re-created, and re-created, often with changes or differences at each iteration. We call this the content silo trap (see Figure 1.1).

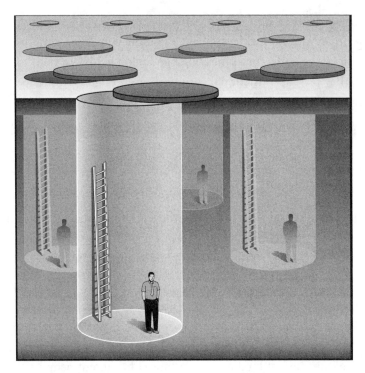

**Figure 1.1    The content silo trap.**

For example, a company develops a new product. A design document is created that explains the functionality and positioning of the product. Marketing rewrites that content for their product launch materials and all the supporting marketing materials such as brochures, press releases, and the web site. The material is written differently to accommodate each medium (such as web and paper). The training group works from the design document and works with the product development team to create an overview of the product and the functionality. Their content does not draw on any of the marketing materials because they are being developed simultaneously. Customer support works from the design document and with the product development team to create a product functionality overview. They also work on their own to create these materials. Three groups have essentially created the same content, often multiple times to accommodate paper and web requirements. However, every instance of the content is different because it has been created by different people with different requirements in mind. The reviewers have had to review it all multiple times. Now it needs to be translated into six languages. The cost of translation is very high because a minimum of six (two per department) variations of the content exist. Translation costs grow as last-minute changes need to be incorporated in multiple places. This organization spent a lot of time, money, and resources essentially creating, re-creating, and re-creating the same content. They were victims of the content silo trap.

## What causes content silos?

Most organizations do not set out to create silos; rather, silos are a result of organizational pressures and structure. Frequently, authors lack awareness of what others are doing elsewhere in the organization. They have a great deal "on their plate": always too much to do, rarely enough time to do it in, and never enough resources to do what needs to get done. There simply isn't enough time for them to find out what other groups are doing, especially when those other groups are just as busy focusing on their own activities.

All this struggling to get things done can result in isolation and a sometimes deliberate desire to "block out" other activities. Authors are often unaware how their behavior may impact others.

Further adding to the frustration of trying to get the job done is the inconsistent amount of information communicated throughout the organization. Whereas some employees do not get enough information, others get too much. Also, information is seldom prioritized for viewing; it merges into an overwhelming information flow, with little or no information being actually consumed.

Lack of awareness of other initiatives, shortage of time, and inconsistent amounts of information are leading contributors to silos within organizations. The content creation process itself is one that often occurs in isolation, leading to potential inconsistencies and extra work. Many authors believe that because content is displayed differently it must be created differently, and that because their audience is different, or the type of content they are creating is different, it must be created differently. Authors take great pride in the materials they create. They may have strong ideas about what is appropriate for their content areas, how that content should be organized, structured, and displayed, and how they believe it is different from other content being created in the organization. So, rather than relying on "outside" content, many authors prefer to handcraft their work.

In addition, when creating documents, authors often lack the tools or time to search out existing content, perceiving that it is faster to start from scratch than to spend the time figuring out whether content already exists. In a typical organization, content is stored in file systems that allow searching only by file name or file date. This makes it very difficult to search through multitudes of files on multiple servers; to find content, authors have to know exactly what they are looking for and where it is likely to be stored. If an organization does have a content or document management system, the content is seldom organized or classified with reuse in mind, so authors may have to search through volumes of incongruent content to identify the piece they want to reuse. When authors know their content very well, the difficulties in finding other authors' content make that content seem inaccessible by comparison.

Traditionally, information reuse opportunities have been difficult for organizations to identify. Members of each content creation group develop their own processes, and although interrelated processes typically occur for content review cycles, they do not occur for content creation cycles. Unless groups identify the commonality of their content, content creation processes remain isolated, making it difficult for content to be identified and reused across an organization.

## The effect of silos

Content silos can have detrimental effects on organizations, resulting in increased costs, reduced quality, and potentially ineffective materials. The effects of content silos are numerous and insidious, as illustrated in the following sections.

## *Poor communication*

When groups within an organization work in isolation, vital information is poorly communicated among all the areas that need it. Poor communication is evident when one group fails to inform another group that something has changed, that something exists, or that something has been discontinued. Poor communication can also occur within one group.

For example, a company's proposal authors, working to meet a tight deadline, might not have the most current information about a product offering. As a result, they include information about repositioned, repriced, and even discontinued products. In this company, as in many, the proposal authors don't have time to check with product development or engineering to find out whether something has changed each time they write a proposal. Instead, they assume that if the information in a recent proposal is correct, it is still correct. However, this is not always the case and presents conflicting messages to potential customers and can cost the organization money.

## Lack of sharing ("not invented here" syndrome)

Authors work on many different types of projects. They create content for different media (such as paper and the Web), for different customers (such as decision makers and end users), or for different contexts (such as support and training). Authors normally bring much experience and expertise to their work and use their knowledge to carefully craft content both for the users' needs and for the presentation format. Because of their deadline-driven environment, authors do not share their good ideas, lessons learned, and finished work with others working on similar projects, and they do not expect others to share with them. This can result in inconsistencies, mixed messages to the customer, and increased costs of development as each author "reinvents the wheel."

For example, a corporation is launching a new product that requires technical documentation and a variety of instructional materials. The technical communicators meet with the engineers and product marketing group to learn how the product works so they can create the user guide, the reference guide, and online help. The instructional design team also meets with the engineers and with product marketing personnel to gather the information they need to develop the training materials.

Both the technical communicators and the instructional designers document the same tasks, but they have documented them differently, resulting in confusion for customers. Additionally, they have consumed twice as much of the engineers' and product marketing groups' time.

## Reduced awareness of other initiatives

Within an organization, problems and resolutions are rarely restricted to just one area. Frequently, multiple groups within an organization experience the same problems, and to resolve them, each group often launches independent initiatives, likely duplicating another group's efforts. An initiative that one group is working on may benefit—or harm—another group, but because they are working in silos, they are not aware of the effects of their efforts outside their own departments.

If all the initiatives come to fruition, they may result in incompatible technology solutions, disparate process changes, and increased costs. In addition, one group may be forced to use a product or to implement a process that is inappropriate for their purposes, as in the following example.

In one organization, the web management group needs a content management system. They carefully specify their requirements, solicit proposals from vendors, and make a selection. The customer support area, which encompasses documentation, training, and front-line customer support, also needs a content management system. After careful research, they present their business case to management for the product they have decided to purchase. However, the web management group has already purchased its system, and is expecting it to be installed any day, so the customer support area is told to use the same system.

Although the selected web content management product meets the needs of the web team, it is neither flexible nor comprehensive enough to meet the needs of customer support. As a result, customer support has to make their requirements fit the solution, incur extensive costs to customize it to meet their needs, or settle for an ineffective partial solution.

## Lack of standardization and consistency

When content is created in multiple areas by multiple authors, it invariably differs, resulting in mixed, or even incorrect messages. This not only causes confusion, it can be potentially dangerous, as illustrated in the following example.

In this case, a company's product is potentially hazardous if used incorrectly. One group is responsible for publishing product information on the web site;

another group is responsible for writing the materials that accompany the product. Each group is careful to document the hazards and provide warnings on the potential dangers of using the product incorrectly. However, because the authors work in silos, the warnings are inconsistent in the level of detail provided. Unfortunately, a customer has experienced a problem using the product and has successfully sued the company based on the inconsistencies in the product warnings.

## Higher cost of content creation, management, and delivery

When content is created multiple times, by multiple people, and delivered in multiple ways, the costs to create and deliver it increase by the number of times the content is re-created or "massaged." Multiple versions of content also require that the content be managed and handled multiple times. Additionally, if content is translated, it must be translated each time it appears.

These costs are illustrated in the content silo trap example earlier in this chapter. See Chapter 3, "Assessing return on investment for a unified content strategy," for details about calculating actual costs.

## Content users suffer, too

It is not only organizations that suffer from content silos; content users suffer, too. When the same, similar, or related information exists in multiple places, it often differs in content and message. Users cannot tell which one is correct.

For example, a customer has just finished product training and is starting to use the product in the workplace. He gets stuck on one task he has forgotten how to do. Rather than looking it up in the material from the training he has just completed, he requests online help. The help is clear and understandable, but he thinks that it isn't telling him to do it in quite the same way he learned during the training, so he is uncomfortable about following the directions. Instead he takes the time to find it in the training material. This is a frustrating experience because the training material isn't indexed for quick access to information and he can't remember exactly which lesson covered this task. After an hour of digging he finds the information, and discovers that it really is different from the online help directions he was given. Which one is correct? Is one more current then the other? Not wanting to cause a problem, he calls customer support. The customer support representative verifies that the information is different between the training materials and the online documentation, and says she will get back to the customer as soon as possible with the correct information. The customer support representative gets back to the customer the next day with the correct information, which isn't exactly the same as either document; then she posts an FAQ to the web site explaining the correct steps. The customer wasted a tremendous amount of time determining the correct steps to take. The customer support representative wasted time tracking down and documenting the "correct answer." And the next customer that encounters this problem will now find *three* different ways to perform the task. Which one is correct?

## A unified content strategy

A unified content strategy can help your organization to avoid the content silo trap, reducing the costs of creating, managing, and distributing content, and ensuring that content effectively supports your organizational and customer needs. A unified content strategy is a repeatable method of identifying all content requirements up front, creating consistently structured content for reuse, managing that content in a definitive source, and assembling content on demand to meet your customers' needs.

You start by analyzing your audiences, information, needs, processes, and technology. You examine such things as:

- Who needs and uses what information (what content needs to be created, for whom and by whom)
- How the information currently supports the users
- How the information is produced

After you have a thorough understanding of all the information needs within your organization and the processes you use to create it, you can determine how to start unifying it, first from the authoring perspective. In a unified environment, departments and authors need to work together as a team to create content "objects" that can be assembled in a number of different "information products," for a number of different delivery methods. Rather than write entire documents, authors create "elements" that are compiled into an information product, such as a press release or brochure. Some elements are the core—that is, the information that is reused across information products—whereas other elements are unique to a particular information product.

However, writing reusable information elements does not mean that authors no longer have ownership of their information or that they will lose control over the structure of the final output. Rather, it means that one author may be responsible for creating the core information (the elements that are reused) whereas others are responsible for identifying how their information set differs from the core and creating the additional elements. Or it may mean that a number of authors work on different aspects of the core and work together to ensure that all the information is integrated.

When authors create elements in this way, they must work to defined standards for content creation and display to ensure that when elements are compiled into one information product, they are written and structured consistently. For example, a product description should follow the same model each time it is written so that it can be easily incorporated into a brochure, the Web, an e-catalog, in an introduction to a manual or training materials, and in a presentation. Every time that product description is presented in a specific medium, such as the Web, it is displayed in the same way for that medium. However, rather than fuss over the format, authors use style sheets to automatically convert the product description to the proper format, depending on its medium. This does not mean that creativity is stifled; rather it means that creativity is used where it has the most value—in creating effective content. Even though a product description is standardized, authors employ creativity in optimally explaining the benefits of the product or its key applications. The sometimes tedious process of content creation is facilitated by standardization and the creative process is unleashed to write really good content, or to customize it for specific customer needs.

Just as a unified authoring process and standardized models are required, appropriate technology is required to enable the unified content strategy. Too often technology is perceived as the solution, but technology on its own is not a solution. To support a unified content strategy, technology must be based on business needs; it must facilitate the authoring process, making it easy for authors to create standard content, store it, automatically reuse existing content, and facilitate customization where appropriate. Technology should also automatically route content through the review and publishing cycle, enabling automatic publishing without hands-on intervention. Technology must provide automation wherever possible in the content life cycle process to eliminate the burden on authors. For example, authors should not have to know that a piece of reusable content exists, then go out and search for it; rather, the system should automatically provide authors with the reusable piece when they begin to write. A definitive source for content ensures that authors are reusing the most current, applicable piece of approved content. No longer do authors have to spend time searching for content and ensuring that content is the most accurate.

## Unified content benefits

A unified content strategy is a coherent content strategy. Organizations can rely on content being the same wherever it appears, providing both internal and external customers with a consistent message, brand, and accuracy. No longer do organizations have to worry about contradicting themselves with differing information; where duplication occurs, the same content is used. Additional benefits include:

- **Faster time to market**

  Faster time to market is achieved through shorter and simpler content creation and maintenance cycles. Authors spend less time repeatedly authoring content because they reuse existing content wherever possible, supplementing it with new or modified content where appropriate. Reviewers also spend less time reviewing content because they have to review only the content that is new or changed; existing content has already been reviewed and has received sign-off.

- **Better use of resources**

  In a unified content strategy, resources are optimized because the repetitive processes of creation and maintenance are reduced. Because they are required to do less repetitive work, everyone involved in the content creation process can do more value-added work or respond to new requirements.

- **Reduced costs**

  In a unified content strategy, the costs of creating and managing content are reduced. Less work is required to get a product to market, not only decreasing internal costs, but potentially increasing revenue. Content is modified or corrected only once, reducing maintenance costs. Translation costs are reduced because reusable content is translated only once; derivatives of that content are eliminated or reduced.

- **Improved quality and usability of content**

  A unified content strategy helps to improve the quality of content. Content is clearly modeled for consistent structure, increasing its readability and usability. Most importantly, content is accurate and consistent wherever it appears. Issues of inaccurate content, inconsistent content, or missing content are reduced or eliminated.

- **Increased opportunity to innovate**

  A unified content strategy can make it easier to focus on innovation. The time normally spent on creating, managing, and distributing content is reduced, which leaves more time for innovation. Time, budget, and resources to focus on innovation can improve the quality of your content and help you to differentiate your product in the marketplace.

- **Improved workplace satisfaction**

  A unified content strategy results in an effective content life cycle. An effective content life cycle results in greater satisfaction from authors because they can focus on effectively creating content and reduce or eliminate mechanical tasks such as repetitive updates and formatting; reviewers gain satisfaction through a reduced review workload and assurance that changes have been correctly incorporated; the organization gains greater satisfaction through an integrated, consistent, and accurate content across all aspects of content.

- **Increased customer satisfaction**

  A unified content strategy increases customer satisfaction through consistent, accurate materials of all types. Customers receive an integrated message that ensures they have the right information, at the right time, and in the right format.

## Components of a unified content strategy

Implementing a unified content strategy means thinking about creating, managing, and storing content in a new way. A unified content strategy consists of three components:

- Content management system
- Reusable content
- Unified processes

These components, along with implementation strategies, are discussed in further detail throughout the book.

### Content management system

A unified content strategy requires a robust content management solution that manages content in a definitive source. Most content management systems provide traditional document management functionality, such as secure access to content (check-in/check-out), revision control, reporting, powerful search and retrieval mechanisms, and metadata. However, content management is not just about technology; it is about the nature of your business and content, people, processes, and tools.

Authors need content management to assist them in authoring. Specifically, they need help to find and distribute or publish content, and to ensure that the content they are distributing is accurate and appropriate. Organizations need content management to support the business needs, their product or service, and their corporate processes. Customers need content management to ensure that they get the right content at the right time, at the right level of detail, and in the right format.

A content management solution starts with analysis of your needs (customer, authoring, processes, cultural, technological), definition of your strategy, implementation support (information models, metadata, templates, and stylesheets), workflow (automated processes that support your content processes), and content delivery (dynamic content and multiple media delivery).

### Reusable content

Content reuse means writing content once and reusing it many times. Traditional documents are written in files that consist of sections. Reusable content is written as objects or elements, not documents. Documents are therefore made up of content objects that can be mixed and matched to meet specific information needs. For example, a product description (paragraph) could be used in a brochure, on the Web, in a parts catalog, in product support documentation, or even on a package.

Reusable content is broken down into the smallest reusable object (section, paragraph, sentence). When information is broken down to this level it is easy to select an element to reuse or repurpose it. However, even though content elements are reused, copying and pasting is eliminated. Instead, elements are stored in the database or content management system and are referenced (pointed to) for inclusion in a virtual document. In this way, the element can appear in multiple places, but reside in only one.

### Unified processes

A unified content strategy also involves people and unified (collaborative) processes. The unified processes must break down the silo walls to create a collaborative environment in which authors share in the development of content to create a single definitive source of information. The ultimate goal in defining unified processes is to ensure that all departments are aware of what content exists, all authors can reuse existing content automatically, and all processes are repeatable and transparent, regardless of which department and which authors are following them.

## Where does a unified content strategy fit?

A unified content strategy fits everywhere content is used, created, stored, and managed throughout an organization. In fact, if your organization is like most, there are already a number of initiatives underway to address problems related to content creation and management. Many companies focus on web content management, but other initiatives include product support and training materials. However, as the content silo trap illustrates, creating content in isolation—and addressing content problems in isolation—solves only the immediate problem. It does not address content creation and use in a unified way, and hence, may compound problems. As the name implies, a unified content strategy fits everywhere in your organization. Some areas where a unified content strategy may be integrated into your organization are described in the following list:

- **Customer data**

  Many organizations have begun to focus on customer relationship management to more effectively manage and support their customers. A unified content strategy ensures that every piece of content or information that reaches your customers reflects your initiatives accurately and consistently. It also ensures that information you receive from interaction with your customers is reflected back into the definitive content source, for reuse by others, including customers (dynamic/personalized content), and to help enhance his/her relationship with you.

- **Web site and e-commerce portal**

  Your web site also represents key information for your organization. A unified content strategy not only ensures that your web content is effectively managed, but also that the content "feeding" the web site—or that is fed by the site—is managed. Plus, it helps to ensure that your message and branding are consistent across your entire content set, on the Web or off.

  The e-commerce portion of a web site provides your customers with an alternative and potentially more effective way to purchase your product. A unified content strategy ensures that all your customer purchase strategies are consistent and accurate and that they portray the same level of customer excellence your customers demand.

- **Product support and training materials**

  Product support materials form a continuum proceeding from marketing materials through training, product support, troubleshooting, and problem solving. Your customers also perceive this information as a continuum; they don't care, and shouldn't have to care, which department initiates and manages the information. A unified content strategy ensures that your product support and training materials provide the continuum your customers expect, and like the information on your web site, reflect your branding accurately and consistently.

- **Policies and procedures**

  Internal policies and procedures ensure that all tasks performed within your organization are performed accurately and uniformly and that all staff have consistent information, targeted toward their needs. It's also critical that staff can access the most current information, whenever and wherever they need it. A unified content strategy ensures that policies and procedures can be instantly and dynamically adapted to reflect changing roles and responsibilities so your organization can adapt to change as required.

- **Proposals**

  Proposals help an organization acquire business or make sales, so it is imperative that your corporate branding, positioning, industry experience, pricing, and product or service details are correct. A unified content strategy ensures that content is consistent wherever it is used, and that when content changes, any new proposals reflect these changes.

- **Regulatory reports**

  Industries that are regulated produce large volumes of content to clearly detail their product or processes for regulatory approval. Frequently content is common across many of these reports. A unified content strategy ensures that reused content is consistent and accurate wherever it appears. The content management component of the strategy ensures that there is a clear and verifiable audit trail and that content is reviewed and an electronic signature applied to verify approval and sign-off.

## Scope of a unified content strategy

This chapter has described many opportunities for managing enterprise content through a unified content strategy. Your unified content strategy can encompass the content created by a department, across departments, across an organizational group or division, or across the whole enterprise. You may choose to start in one area and then expand to other areas, or remain in the one area alone. You need to determine what makes the most sense for your organization, now and into the future. The remainder of the book helps you to identify your organizational needs, the processes for creating a unified content strategy, and the technology for supporting it. Chapter 22, "Transition plan" helps you to identify how you can transition to a unified content strategy in phases.

---

## Summary

Content is created in every area of your organization. However, content is often created in "silos," with areas working in isolation from each other, and even authors within an area working in isolation from other authors. This isolation leads to increased costs, reduced quality, and inconsistency of content. Working in content silos is known as the Content Silo Trap™.

A unified content strategy can help your organization avoid the content silo trap, reduce the costs of creating, managing, and distributing content, and ensure your content effectively supports your organizational and customer needs. A unified content strategy is a repeatable method of identifying all content requirements up front, creating consistently structured content for reuse, managing that content in a definitive source, and assembling content on demand to meet your customers' needs.

A unified content strategy results in:

- Faster time to market
- Better use of resources
- Reduced costs
- Increased quality and consistency

A unified content strategy consists of:

- A content management system to manage your content in a definitive source
- Reusable content objects that enable you to write content once and use it many times
- Unified processes that encourage people to work collaboratively, which results in processes that are repeatable and transparent, regardless of department or author

A unified content strategy fits everywhere in your organization, such as customer relationship management, the web site, e-commerce, product training and support, corporate policies and procedures, proposals, and regulatory content.

Only a unified content strategy can ensure that your organization is addressing all the problems of content in a coherent unified manner. Your customers will benefit from a unified strategy and your employees will, too. The entire organization will benefit from a unified content strategy because it brings value to the organization as a whole.

# C h a p t e r   2

## Fundamental concepts of reuse

Content reuse is fundamental to a successful unified content strategy. This chapter defines content reuse and the benefits of its use. It explores how other industries have employed reuse for decades to improve their processes and the quality of their products. Content can be reused in many ways. The choice of the different methods and options for reuse are dependent upon your organization's needs and technology. This chapter details the pros and cons of using each method and the associated options, and it provides the concepts that underlie the remainder of the book.

## What is content reuse?

Content reuse is the practice of using existing content components to develop new "documents." Although the majority of reusable content is text-based, any content can be reused (such as graphics, charts, media). Text-based materials are the easiest to reuse. You can reuse sections, paragraphs, sentences, or even words. It is easier to reuse graphics, charts, and media in their entirety than it is to use portions of them, but new standards such as Scalable Vector Graphics (SVG), a new Internet graphics standard, make it possible to create reusable media. For example, in the past if you wanted to reuse a graphic but change the callouts (for example, translated versions of the callouts were required) you either had to re-create the graphic and callouts or use one tool to create the graphic and another to layer the callouts. Now, the XML aspect of SVG makes it possible to layer all the components of a web graphic, thereby facilitating reuse.

Most organizations already reuse content, though they copy and paste it. This works well until the content—and everywhere it appears—has to be updated. Then it can be time consuming to find every place the content has been copied and reused and change it. Not only is this time consuming, but some occurrences may be missed, resulting in inconsistencies and inaccuracies. In addition, over time, inconsistencies tend to layer themselves, until original inconsistencies become buried and you end up with two completely different content sources.

Reuse, as discussed throughout this book, is the process of "linking" to an element of reusable content. The reusable content is displayed in the document in which you are working, but it does not actually reside in the document. Your organization may have already practiced this kind of reuse with graphics in Microsoft Word (Insert>Picture>From File>Insert and Link). When the reusable element is updated, it is updated wherever it occurs. This saves a lot of time and money in maintenance (change once, automatically change many).

## Why reuse content?

Today's businesses are overwhelmed with the need to create more content, more quickly, customized for more customers and for more media than ever before. Combine this with the issues of decreasing resources, time, and budgets, and you have a stressful situation for organizations and their content creators.

Reusing content can provide a dramatic improvement in the way content is created in an organization. Improvements include increased quality and consistency and long-term reduced time and costs for development and maintenance. In addition, reuse provides support for rapid reconfiguration of your content to meet changing needs, facilitates content inventory, and makes it easier to assess content needs. Reusing content provides the following advantages:

- **Increased consistency**

  When content is written once and reused many times, it ensures that the content is consistent wherever it is used. This consistency leads to higher-quality content.

  Content written for reuse is structured content. Structured content is content that is similarly structured for similar types of information. Structured content leads to a more consistent writing style.

- **Reduced development and maintenance costs**

  Development costs are reduced because the amount of content a content creator has to create is reduced. Rather than writing all new content, or taking the time to find and copy content to be reused, reusable content is either rapidly available through improved management facilities (such as, metadata and content management) or is automatically made available to the author (systematic reuse). In addition, your content is better organized and processes are more efficient, reducing costs further.

  When content is changed, content is automatically changed everywhere it is reused. Your organization does not have to determine every place that content exists, either in its original form or in a modified form; it is automatically tracked by the content management system for rapid selection and update.

- **Rapid reconfiguration**

  Reusable content is modular content (small self-contained components that can be used in combination with other components). In today's rapidly changing world, products and customer requirements are constantly changing. Modular reusable content makes it easy for organizations to rapidly reconfigure their content to meet changing needs. You can easily change the order of modules, include new modules, exclude existing modules, identify whether something is missing (and what it might be), and use modules to build entirely new information products to meet new needs.

- **Translation**

  The cost of translation can be significantly reduced through reuse. Although translation memory systems have assisted organizations to reduce costs through pattern matching, reuse further reduces the cost. Each time content is sent for translation, it is run through the memory translation tool to identify content strings (text) that already have been translated. When content is reused, any content that has been reused and already translated can be automatically inserted into the version to be translated. This means that the previously translated content is skipped and the time to identify content that must be translated is reduced. Alternatively, if your content management system does not support the automatic insertion of previously translated content, you can ensure that the translator receives only the elements that require translation.

  You can also rapidly reconfigure translated content and even deliver brand new information products from existing elements that have already been translated, without ever having to send the content to translation and pay additional costs!

  The less easily measured benefits of consistent structure, consistent terminology, and standardized writing guidelines that reuse requires also reduce the costs of translation.

  Finally, often a large cost in translation is in reformatting content. Frequently content must be converted from the original source format to RTF (Rich Text Format) before it can be translated  into the target format (for example, Help, FrameMaker, HTML). When it is converted it loses much of its formatting. When content is separated from format, it is easy to automatically reformat content, regardless of language (see Chapter 20, "Separating content from format").

## The historical foundation for reuse

The concept of reuse is not new. Many industries have turned to reuse to reduce costs, increase productivity, and standardize their processes. The manufacturing and computer software industries have been using reuse strategies for years, and the technical communication industry developed content reuse strategies in the early 1990s.

## Manufacturing

Reuse has been employed in the manufacturing industry for decades. Manufacturing companies do not create new versions of the components of their product each time they manufacture the larger product. For example, cars differ in design, but rarely in structure. A significant portion of the car will be composed of the same parts that are included in other models (such as the chassis, for example) and even in models developed by different car manufacturers (such as axles, tires, and spark plugs).

## Software industry

Likewise, the concept of reuse was introduced in the software industry more than 30 years ago, but it has gained widespread acceptance in the last decade. Prior to adopting reuse strategies, the software industry created software in much the same way content is created today, with programmers creating their own code and sometimes copying and pasting existing code. However, as the concept of software reuse became accepted, organizations moved to software code that was modular and specifically designed to be reused.

## Technical publications

Pushed by the need to develop multiple versions of the same information, in multiple languages, in multiple media, on tight deadlines, the technical communication industry developed content reuse strategies in the early 1990s[1].

The technical communication industry refers to the concept of reusing content as *single sourcing*. Single sourcing implies that there is a single source for content; content is written once, stored in a single source location, and reused many times. As the technical communication industry started learning more about how to reuse content in different ways, single sourcing has moved through the following phases[2]:

---

1 Some organizations used Standard Generalized Markup Language (SGML) to reuse content in the 1980s but SGML-based reuse was not widespread.

2 Rockley, Ann. "Designing Effective Single Source Materials," Proceedings of the Society for Technical Communication, Annual Conference, 2001, Orlando, FL.

- **Phase 1—Identical content, multiple media**

  Identical content was made available in multiple media (such as paper, Help, and HTML). Little attempt was made to differentiate the content or the presentation of the information to accommodate for the differences in media and usage. If the materials were modified to fit the media or address the fact that online information is used differently than paper-based information, the materials became quite different and were not single sourced (updates had to be made to two sources).

  As writers became concerned about the effectiveness of identical content used in multiple media, they moved to Phase 2.

- **Phase 2—Static customized content**

  This type of single source material is customized to meet the needs of the user, the type of materials to be developed, and the media. The author deliberately "builds" the customized output from the single source to meet the specific user needs or output. Authors select from elements to create customized content (such as for different users or products). This results in customized information that is static (cannot be changed without the author's intervention).

  Although content is customized, it does not mean that the content is rewritten for each usage. Rather, sub-elements (for example, greater or lesser detail, or illustrations of screens in the paper document but not in the online document) are used where appropriate.

  This form of single sourcing produced much more effective and usable materials, but was also time consuming.

- **Phase 3—Dynamic customized content**

  Dynamic content does not exist in or as a document; it is information that is assembled only when it is requested. It exists as a series of information objects that are assembled in response to the user's requests or requirements. Users identify required content, or a user profile automatically identifies that user's requirements and delivers customized content.

  This type of reuse does not rely on the author to build the document, but does rely on effective information models that can predict how to provide the appropriate information at the right time.

  For more information about this type of reuse, see Chapter 10, "Designing dynamic content."

## Web content management

Those responsible for the creation of web content embraced the concept of reuse in the late 90s. As it became more and more difficult to maintain sites, develop consistent material, and deliver current content, "web masters" began to adopt content reuse. Initially, reuse extended only to banners and other visual and navigational components, but it has now extended to common content reuse where appropriate. A portal is a good example of dynamic content reuse.

## Learning materials

The educational and business learning industries have also begun to adopt reuse models. In 1997, Advanced Distributed Learning began working on a reference model that defines reusable learning content. This model is known as SCORM (Shareable Content Object Reference Model). This is a model for sharing learning objects. Organizations are beginning to adopt the principles of writing reusable learning objects (RLOs) and learning tools vendors are making their products SCORM-compliant.

## Media

The news media are using content reuse. Reporters write content once and elements of that original source are published to different media in a variety of formats and languages. Content from one story may appear in a multitude of media (in a newspaper, on a web site, on web sites of others who purchase content services, in PDAs and cell phones, on portal pages, radio broadcast scripts, marquee signs, electronic billboards, and in various languages).

# Reuse methods

There are two methods for reuse: opportunistic reuse (an author makes a conscious decision to reuse content) and systematic reuse (planned reuse where content is automatically inserted). Within each method of reuse are three options: locked reuse (reused content cannot be changed), derivative reuse (reused content can be changed) and nested reuse (multiple versions of the content are contained within the same element). This section details the methods and options for reuse.

## Opportunistic reuse

Opportunistic reuse occurs when the author makes a conscious decision to find an element, retrieve it, and reuse it. Opportunistic reuse requires that the author be aware of the opportunities for reuse and be motivated to search for and retrieve reusable content. Opportunistic reuse is the most common form of reuse. Opportunistic reuse does not rely on specific technology; it can be done without a content management system, although a CMS is advisable.

Any content can be used in an opportunistic reuse situation. In some ways, opportunistic reuse is a replacement for the "copy and paste" that many organizations use. However, opportunistic reuse is not copy and paste because reused content does not actually include the content in the "document"; it is actually a "pointer" to the source content.

Many organizations use opportunistic reuse when they need to rapidly reconfigure their information products to meet new product or customer requirements. One organization found that they could even create new translated documents by using existing reusable elements without having to have any new content translated (that is, they could use existing translated elements in a new configuration).

Opportunistic reuse provides authors with the greatest flexibility because it provides them with the choice to reuse content and to determine which reusable content is appropriate. However, opportunistic reuse results in the lowest incidence of reuse because it puts the burden on the authors to want to reuse content, to know that potential reusable content exists, and to go and find the content they want to reuse. If there is a lack of motivation, or a lack of awareness that a suitable reusable element exists or might exist, or if it is difficult for authors to find the appropriate element, reuse may not occur. In addition, authors may reuse content inappropriately; there are no safeguards to prevent this.

To increase the effectiveness of opportunistic reuse, organizations can optimize retrievability, provide guidelines, and ensure that authors are effectively trained. Retrievability can be optimized through the use of content management systems, effective categorization of content, and rich metadata. Reuse guidelines include models to help authors identify where content should be reused (see Chapter 8, "Information modeling"). Training ensures that authors are trained to use the models and the content management system and to follow guidelines for reuse. Organizational incentives can provide motivation for authors to reuse content.

## Systematic reuse

Systematic reuse is automatic reuse. Specific content is identified as reusable in a specific location. Then the content management system automatically inserts (auto-populates) the reusable content in the appropriate locations in the document. The author does not have to determine whether the reusable content exists or search for and retrieve it. Systematic reuse ensures that content is reused and reduces the burden on the author to know that reusable content exists, to find the reusable content, and to insert it appropriately.

Systematic reuse is dependent upon detailed information models, reuse maps (identification of where content is reused in your information set), and support for dynamic delivery of content through your content management system. This means that systematic reuse is planned for in advance, in the modeling and system configuration stage. Authors do not determine reuse; the system determines reuse.

The content management system uses your information models to identify where content can be reused. If a content element exists and matches the author's specific content requirements, the reusable elements are automatically inserted into appropriate spots in the document (that is, the document is pre-populated with content).

Systematic reuse is the most costly to implement because it requires the most planning for reuse, the creation of detailed models and reuse maps, and appropriate technology (for example, a dynamic content engine), but it provides the greatest return on investment. Return on investment is achieved through guaranteed reuse (reuse is automatic and not dependent on author motivation and knowledge of existing content).

Authors can perceive systematic reuse as being overly restrictive (that is, it does not provide flexibility and opportunities to be creative). This perception can be reduced if authors are provided with the opportunity to modify reusable content where appropriate (derivative reuse) and to choose not to use reusable elements when they are not appropriate in the given instance. However, care should be taken to ensure the effectiveness of systematic reuse is not diminished through increased flexibility. You need to ensure that content that *must* be included cannot be removed, that content that should not be changed is not editable, and that authors are educated on the value of systematic reuse.

Use systematic reuse when your content is very structured and you can explicitly identify where content is to be reused, and where you want to ensure that specific content is reused.

Examples of systematic reuse can include corporate standard information such as trademarks, copyrights, license information, and warranties. However, systematic reuse can be used wherever an organization wants to ensure that content is reused (for example, in product descriptions, warnings, cautions, notes, definitions, company profiles, and disclaimers).

## Example: Systematic reuse

A consulting company that does process re-engineering creates a series of reports (analysis, recommendations, implementation). To assist consultants in the report writing process the company has implemented systematic reuse. Analysis reports identify the issues observed within the organization. The consultant summarizes the issues at the beginning of each section. The summaries are reused in the Executive Summary unchanged (locked). The issues are reused (locked) in the recommendations report and each issue is addressed by a recommendation. The recommendations are summarized at the beginning of each section and are reused (derivative) in the Executive Summary. In this way, after consultants write the content, they don't have to worry about copying and pasting content into the other portions of the report or the next report; the content is automatically reused appropriately (see Figure 2.1). In addition, the author can choose to change the reused content to ensure it fits the current situation (for example, in the Executive Summary of the recommendations).

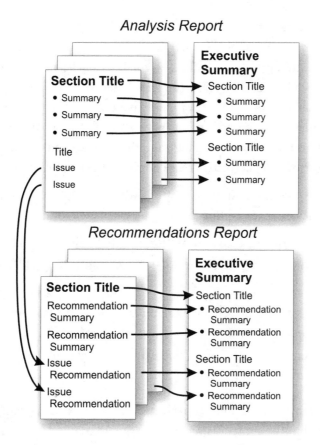

**Figure 2.1    Systematic reuse.**

## Locked reuse

Locked reuse is where a reusable element is reused unchanged. Only an author with appropriate permissions may change the content of the element. This ensures that key content is reused identically. You can systematically reuse or opportunistically reuse a locked element.

Types of content that are commonly locked include legal information, cautionary information, standard statements of disclaimer, company descriptions, product positioning, or branding information. Any content that you do not want changed by others can be locked.

Use locked reuse when you want to ensure content is not changed when it is reused.

**Derivative reuse**

When an author edits a reusable content element, the resulting element then becomes a derivative, or a "child" of the original "parent" element. An element that is systematically reused or opportunistically reused and is not locked can become a derivative element. A derivative element continues to be related to the original, such that if the original (parent) changes, the author of the derivative (child) element is notified of the change and the change can be incorporated or not as desired. Providing derivative reuse increases the flexibility of reuse.

Derivative reuse is common in organizations where key content should be retained, but such changes as the following may be made to the content:

- Tense (for example, in content used over time in different reports)
- Spelling (for example, American English versus British English)
- Order of the content
- Emphasis (for example, changing the focus of benefits from one set of features to another to address different regional needs)
- Use (for example, a brochure which would be very marketing oriented and a user guide which would be more product usage oriented)

Translated content is an example of derivative reuse (the original language element is reused, but the content is replaced by the translated content); however, the relationship is maintained to ensure that whenever the source element is changed, the translated element is identified as requiring change. In the case of translation, the entire content of the element is changed; however, in the majority of cases of derivative reuse, only a few words are changed or sentences are added or deleted. For more on content relationships see Appendix E, "Content relationships."

## Example: Usability reports

A company is planning to conduct a usability test of its new Internet site. They create a proposal for management to indicate the types of users they will select, then they conduct the test and write the summary report. They derivatively reuse content from the proposal in the summary report. Compare the pieces of the two reports (Table 2.1) to see how the content changes derivatively.

**Table 2.1    Example of derivative reuse**

| Usability test proposal report selecting test subjects | Usability summary report selected test subjects |
| --- | --- |
| The following criteria for selection **will be** used to ensure we **get** appropriate test subjects from all our key customer areas including: | The following criteria for selection **were** used to ensure we **got** appropriate test subjects from all our key customer areas including: |
| • Commercial customers<br>• General public customers<br>• Decision-makers | • Commercial customers<br>• General public customers<br>• Decision-makers |
| The selected test subjects **should meet** the following criteria: | The selected test subjects **met** the following criteria: |
| • English as a first language<br>• Uses the Internet at least twice a week<br>• Uses Product ABC<br>• Has previously used our Help Desk for assistance | • English as a first language<br>• Uses the Internet at least twice a week<br>• Uses Product ABC<br>• Has previously used our Help Desk for assistance |
| Each participant **will be** asked to complete a pre-test questionnaire (see Appendix A "Checklist for implementing a Unified Content Strategy") **to** enable us to assess prior knowledge and experience. | Each participant **was** asked to complete a pre-test questionnaire (see Appendix A) **that enabled** us to assess prior knowledge and experience. |

## Nested reuse

Nested reuse is content that has a number of reusable elements contained within a single element. The sum of all the elements creates an element, and subsets of the element can be used in alternate information products. Nested reuse does not involve building from small reusable elements; rather it involves an element that contains all the reusable sub-elements.

Nested reusable information enables authors to create content for all the outputs at the same time, thereby providing context and frequently speeding up the content authoring process. When content is nested, all the relevant content is available at a glance.

Nested reuse can be used any time when greater or lesser detail of content is required for one information product or another, or when it makes it easier for the author to create all the necessary content on a topic/subject in one place.

Use nested reuse when you want to retain the context for alternate content or when content is a subset of other content.

## Example: Product description

A company produces a product called the B-Brother. They reuse a product description (see Table 2.2) in three different information products: a brochure, an operations guide, and an e-commerce site.

**Table 2.2    Comparison of product description content**

| Brochure | Operations guide | E-commerce site |
| --- | --- | --- |
| The B-Brother model 1984 is a programmable device that connects directly to consumers' televisions to track the channels they flip to, what programs they record, and what commercials they skip. The information is instantly transmitted to the cable or satellite provider. | The B-Brother connects directly to consumers' televisions. It can be programmed to track what channels they flip to, what programs they record, and what commercials they skip. The information is transmitted to the cable or satellite provider. | The B-Brother model 1984 is a device that connects directly to consumers' televisions to track their television watching habits. |

As you can see by reading the three examples, the content is different, sometimes only slightly different, but still different. It doesn't need to be different. First the authors unify the content as shown in Figure 2.2 to create one product statement that encapsulates what the company is trying to say about the product.

> The B-Brother model 1984 is a device that connects directly
> to a consumer's television to track their television
> watching habits. It can be programmed to track the channels
> they flip to, what programs they record and what commercials
> they skip. The information is instantly transmitted to the
> cable or satellite provider.

**Figure 2.2   Unified product description.**

Then the content is identified, as shown in Figure 2.3, to indicate which components are appropriate for each information product.

> <The B-Brother model 1984 is a device that connects directly
> to a consumer's television to track their television
> watching habits.> *[Brochure, Operations Guide, E-Commerce]*
> <It can be programmed to track the channels they flip to,
> what programs they record and what commercials they skip.
> The information is instantly transmitted to the cable or
> satellite provider.> *[Brochure, Operations Guide]*

**Figure 2.3   Product description marked to indicate information product reuse.**

The product description includes a short description of the product (the first sentence) that can be used in all three information products. The second and third sentence can be used in the brochure and the operations guide, which require more content. This is illustrated in Table 2.3.

**Table 2.3   Product description reuse**

| Brochure | Operations Guide | E-commerce product description |
| --- | --- | --- |
| The B-Brother model 1984 is a device that connects directly to consumers' televisions to track their television watching habits. | The B-Brother model 1984 is a device that connects directly to consumers' televisions to track their television watching habits. | The B-Brother model 1984 is a device that connects directly to consumers' televisions to track their television watching habits. |
| It can be programmed to track what channels they flip to, what programs they record, and what commercials they skip. The information is instantly transmitted to the cable or satellite provider. | It can be programmed to track what  channels they flip to, what programs they record, and what commercials they skip. The information is instantly transmitted to the cable or satellite provider. | |

## *Example: Procedure*

A company has developed training, user documentation, and help for its time tracking system. The content needed to be updated and they have decided to redesign the common procedural information as a nested procedure. Figure 2.4 illustrates an original procedure that is common across training materials, user documentation, and Help.

| | Creating a time tracking entry | Creating a time tracking entry | Creating a time tracking entry |
|---|---|---|---|
| | **Objective:** The objective of this lesson is to create a time entry for a project. | 1. Open TimeTracker.<br>2. From the File menu select New. | 1. Open TimeTracker. |
| | 1. Open TimeTracker. | | 2. Select New. |
| | 2. Select New from the File menu. | | 3. Select the project to apply the time to. |
| **Select:** Intranet Redesign | 3. Select a project. | 3. Select the project to apply time to. Click the drop-down list to display the available projects. | 4. Select the task. |
| | 4. Click the project drop-down list to display available projects. | | 5. Enter a description of the work done. |
| **Select:** Meeting | 5. Select the task. | 4. Select the task. Click the drop-down list to display the list of tasks. | 6. Change the date if required. |
| | 6. Click the Task drop-down list to display the list of tasks. | | 7. Enter the time spent on the task to the nearest 15 minutes. |
| **Enter:** Identified the stakeholders for the redesign project. | 7. Enter a description of the work done in the Description box.<br><br>Make the description as descriptive as possible to help management better understand the work completed. If you had any problems accomplishing the task, record the problems here. | 5. Enter a description of the work done. Make the description as descriptive as possible to help management better understand the work completed. If you had any problems accomplishing the task, record the problems here. | 8. Save the entry.<br><br>**Related Topics**<br>· **Verifying time entries**<br>· **Submitting your timesheets**<br>· **Creating reports** |
| | | 6. The date defaults to today's date. Change the date if required. | |
| Change the date to yesterday's date. | 8. The date defaults to today's date. | 7. Enter the time spent on the task to the nearest 15 minutes. | |
| **Enter:** 1:30:00 | 9. Enter the time spent on the task to the nearest 15 minutes. | 8. Save the entry. | |
| | 10. Save the entry. | | |

**Figure 2.4   Original procedure content.**

Table 2.4 shows how the procedure was unified with nested reuse to create one procedure that could be used to produce each of the information products. All the content for the procedure is contained in one place. The content for the Help is nested within the content for the user guide, which in turn is nested in the training materials.

### Table 2.4   Unified procedure content

| Content | Information product | | |
|---|---|---|---|
| | **Training** | **User document-ation** | **Help** |
| **Creating a time tracking entry** | ✓ | ✓ | ✓ |
| **Objective:** The objective of this lesson is to create a time entry for a project. | ✓ | | |

| Content | Information product | | |
|---|---|---|---|
| | **Training** | **User document-ation** | **Help** |
| 1. Open TimeTracker. | ✓ | ✓ | ✓ |
| 2. Select New from the File menu. | ✓ | ✓ | ✓ |
| **Select:** Intranet Redesign | ✓ | | |
| 3. Select the project to apply the time to. | ✓ | ✓ | ✓ |
| Click the drop-down list to display the available projects. | ✓ | ✓ | |
| 4. Select the task. | ✓ | ✓ | ✓ |
| Click the drop-down list to display the list of tasks. | ✓ | ✓ | |
| **Select:** Meeting | ✓ | | |
| 5. Enter a description of the work done in the Description box. | ✓ | ✓ | ✓ |
| Make the description as descriptive as possible to help management better understand the work completed. If you had any problems accomplishing the task, record the problems here. | ✓ | ✓ | |
| **Enter:** Identify the stakeholders for the redesign project. | ✓ | | |
| 6. Enter a date. The date defaults to today's date. | ✓ | ✓ | ✓ |
| Change the date to yesterday's date. | ✓ | | |
| 7. Enter the time spent on the task to the nearest 15 minutes. | ✓ | ✓ | ✓ |
| **Enter:** 1:30:00 | ✓ | | |
| 8. Save the entry. | ✓ | ✓ | ✓ |
| **Related topics** | | | ✓ |
| • Verifying time entries. | | | ✓ |
| • Submitting your timesheets. | | | ✓ |
| • Creating reports. | | | ✓ |

Notice that the formatting that was visible in the training materials (exercise content in the left column) or Help (hypertext links) is not shown in this nested example. Formatting is applied when the content is published in the relevant information product, not during the authoring stage (see Figure 2.5).

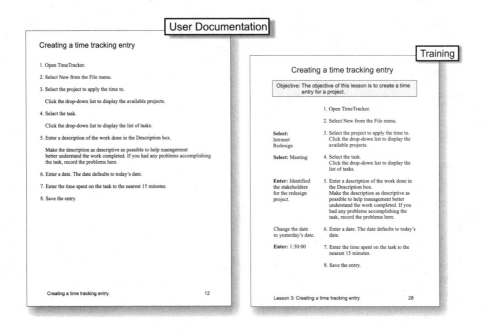

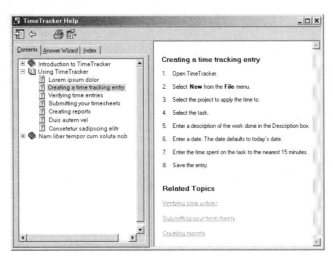

**Figure 2.5    Formatted published version of the nested procedure.**

The nested procedure enables an organization to create all the necessary content at the same time and publish the content as desired to the appropriate information product. Creating all the content in context makes it easier to write it and to ensure consistency.

## When doesn't reuse make sense?

While you should try to reuse as much content as possible, there are times when reuse is inappropriate. Not every piece of content is reusable, nor should content be reused when it is inappropriate in the context in which it is being reused.

Sentence fragments and individual words may not be appropriate for reuse. The smaller you break down your content elements for reuse, the more complex it is to reuse and manage the content. If individual words are the only component of information that changes, consider using variables, which can have a different value depending upon the instance. Variables are much easier to manage than individual word-size elements. If sentence fragments can be reused, consider creating the reusable element at the sentence level and creating a derivative element by changing the portion of the sentence that is not appropriate for reuse.

To ensure that an element is reusable in many instances, you may contemplate writing very generic elements. The generic reusable element may serve the reuse requirement, but may compromise the usability and comprehensibility of the content. Never compromise the quality of the content to reuse it. Consider not reusing the content, or using derivative reuse so the content can be adapted to meet the needs of the specific reuse instance.

There may be times when you need to create unique "one-off" content or ad-hoc content to meet a specific need where existing content is not appropriate for reuse.

As you perform your analysis and build your models, consider the value of the reuse. Reuse content where appropriate and effective and always ensure that the reuse will not compromise the quality and usability of your materials or make the reusable content very difficult to create, find, and manage.

## Summary

Reuse is not a new concept. Many industries have been using reuse to improve quality and consistency and realize reduced development time and maintenance costs.

Most organizations use multiple types of reuse. Each of the types of reuse may be appropriate in different instances and with different types of content. Your models identify what type of reuse is appropriate (see Chapter 8).

- Opportunistic reuse is when the author makes a conscious decision to find an element, retrieve it, and reuse it. Use opportunistic reuse when you do not have the technology to support systematic reuse, or when your content or corporate culture warrants the use of flexible reuse and choice.

- Systematic reuse is automatic reuse. Use systematic reuse when your content is very structured and you can explicitly identify where content is to be reused, and where you want to ensure that certain content is reused.

- Locked reuse is reusable content that cannot be changed except by the original author. Use locked reuse when you want to ensure content is not changed.

- Derivative reuse is content that is not reused identically; the content is changed. Use derivative reuse when you want to retain the relationships between pieces of information, but some of the content can be changed.

- Nested reuse involves content that has a number of reusable elements contained within a single element. The sum of all the elements creates one element, and subsets of the element can be used to create alternate information products. Use nested reuse when you want to retain the context for alternate content or when content is a subset of other content.

# Chapter 3

## Assessing return on investment for a unified content strategy

Many organizations have realized return on investment through the implementation of a unified content strategy. Return on investment (ROI) is the anticipated savings to be realized after subtracting the cost of implementing a unified content strategy. The savings are future savings and are used to determine whether implementing a unified content strategy is appropriate for your organization. ROI can and should be calculated on an ongoing basis after implementation to verify predictions and identify additional areas of improvement.

Using a fictitious company as an example, this chapter focuses on where organizations incur costs, how to identify and measure those costs, how to identify and measure savings, and how to identify and calculate return on investment of implementing a unified content strategy. Note that the example and the costs are for illustration purposes only; they may not be entirely representative of your situation. Also, the costs for tools and technology are average costs at the time of publication. For current costs refer to the accompanying website.

# Addressing the goals

Implementing a new technology and set of processes such as a unified content strategy should be undertaken only if it supports your overall business goals and objectives. See Chapter 4, "Where does it really hurt?" for information about identifying your organizational goals and objectives. Unless you can clearly state how the unified content strategy will help your organization reduce time-to-market, reduce costs, increase productivity, or meet whatever specific goals you have defined, you cannot effectively justify it.

## Identifying the goals

Rockhead Inc., a fictitious company, is a small, medical devices company. Multiple areas within the company (Regulatory Submissions, Marketing, Patient and Physician Support, and Labeling) are looking at using a unified content strategy to improve the way they produce, manage, and deliver content. An analysis of their goals includes:

- **Shorten time-to-market.**

  Like any medical devices company, getting a product approved by the regulatory bodies faster means greater market share. In addition, Rockhead is planning a new suite of products based on a currently popular product that will roll out over an 18-month period. The suite of products will have multiple potential configurations, but Rockhead won't know until the last minute which configuration will get approved. Immediately upon approval, they have to be able to assemble the appropriate labeling, marketing, and patient and physician support information so they can start marketing and shipping.

Rockhead Inc. has two goals in this area:

- Reduce the time to complete a submission by two months.
- Be able to assemble all appropriate marketing, labeling, and patient and physician support information within one week after approval.

- **Reduce the cost of product content development.**

The cost of developing content has been increasing significantly over the last few years. More product is being developed, which means more content must be created, but the cost of content development is increasing faster than product development and manufacturing development. Something needs to be done to reduce these costs. Rockhead's goal in this area is to reduce the cost of product content development by at least 25%.

- **Improve the accuracy and quality of content.**

Accurate content is critical to patient safety and product efficacy. Using current processes and technology, Rockhead has had difficulty ensuring that content is consistent and accurate everywhere it appears. In the past year, inconsistent information resulted in a successful lawsuit by a patient. This must be avoided at all cost. To achieve accuracy and quality of content, Rockhead must first bring its departments together. Rockhead's departments are a classic example of The Content Silo Trap; each department works individually creating and re-creating content, and reviewers repetitively review the same content, yet they cannot verify that they have seen and verified all appropriate content.

Rockhead has two goals in this area:

- Integrate the content development, maintenance, and delivery processes associated with marketing, patient and physician support information, and labeling.
- Ensure content is consistent and accurate everywhere it appears.

- **Reduce manufacturing defects.**

Rockhead manufacturers products that require adherence to close tolerances to ensure they function properly. In recent months, quality assurance (QA) has identified that settings are frequently out of specification. Product that does not pass QA cannot be shipped. Rockhead's goal in this area is to reduce defects to less than .01%

## Qualifying the goals

After you have identified the goals you need to ensure that they can be addressed by a unified content strategy. For example, using the goals Rockhead identified in the previous section, Rockhead qualifies their goals:

- **Reduce the time to complete a submission by two months.**

  A unified content strategy can reduce development and delivery time. Reusing content can reduce the development time by the percentage of reused content. If opportunistic reuse is employed, the percentage of reduction may be less than that of systematic reuse because opportunistic reuse requires more authoring time. Regulatory Submissions feels that at least 25% of the content can be reused across the various reports and among common product submissions. Content reuse can be one factor in assisting Regulatory Submissions in meeting its two-month goal, but it is not the only factor that influences the time to complete a submission. Regulatory Submissions needs to determine what other factors will help them to achieve this goal.

- **Be able to assemble all appropriate marketing, labeling, and patient and physician support information within one week after approval.**

  A unified content strategy can achieve this goal if content is created in reusable elements, the content is complete, and Rockhead pre-defines the elements that must be assembled to create the different configurations of content. Either the content management system can dynamically assemble the appropriate content, or the final documents can be manually assembled from available elements.

- **Reduce the cost of product content development by at least 25%.**

  Rockhead has identified that there is at least a 35% potential for reuse based on the common content and safety regulations among its products. Common content can be reused across the product suites. Common safety regulations (for example, warnings, cautions) can be reduced throughout the entire product line.

- **Integrate the content development, maintenance, and delivery processes associated with marketing, patient and physician support information, and labeling.**

Although this goal depends on the potential for reuse with all the content created in the individual departments, collaboration among departments also plays a key role in achieving this goal. Collaboration among teams or departments is a key component of a unified content strategy. However, successful collaboration depends on the ability of people to work together. Bringing widespread collaboration into the organization is more complex than integrating new tools; collaboration involves people who may resist change. For more information on achieving this goal see Chapter 19, "Collaborative authoring: Breaking down the silos" and Chapter 21, "Managing change." This goal can be achieved with a unified content strategy, but attention must be paid to the issues of change management to ensure its success.

- **Ensure content is consistent and accurate everywhere it appears.**

   The accuracy of the content depends on the quality of the reviews. The quality of the reviews depends on the qualifications of the reviewers. As part of the unified content strategy, Rockhead will have to ensure reviewers are qualified and that appropriate guidelines and safeguards are put in place to ensure accuracy. After content is reviewed and identified as accurate, a unified content strategy that uses a content management system can ensure that content reused in multiple places is consistent.

- **Reduce defects to less than .01%.**

   This is an important goal for Rockhead; however, it is not a goal that can be addressed by a unified content strategy. It must be addressed with another improvement initiative. This goal will not be used in the unified content strategy ROI.

## Quantifying the goals

After you have established your goals and identified that they can be addressed with a unified content strategy, you need to quantify them. Before you can quantify your goals you need to know what it costs you now—either in time or money—to perform the tasks that you believe will be improved by a unified content strategy. If you haven't collected these types of metrics before, see the sidebar "Identifying metrics" for some suggestions. For example, using the goals Rockhead identified in the preceding section, Rockhead now quantifies their goals:

- **Reduce the time to complete a submission by two months.**

  Rockhead has identified that they potentially lose $250,000/day for every day their product is delayed getting to market. First, Rockhead needs to determine what impact the content reuse will have on the time required to create a submission. Rockhead knows that a submission takes three content creators seven years to complete. In a typical development project, which lasts a year or slightly more, the expected calculation would be to multiple the opportunity for reuse (25%) by the length of time it takes to complete the task. However, a lot more than content creation happens in those seven years, so the calculation is not that straightforward. Content creation is estimated at 20% of the whole process, therefore Rockhead uses 20% of 25%, or 5%. The submission process requires three people at an average salary of $75,000 (some are more than this, others less).

  Table 3.1 illustrates the calculations.

**Table 3.1   Calculating savings for submissions**

| Metrics | Calculation | Interim value | Potential savings |
|---|---|---|---|
| **Development cost** | | | |
| Average salary[1] ($75,000) | | $75,000.00 | |
| Number of months saved | 12×7×.05 | 4.2 months | |
| Cost savings | (75,000/12)×4.2×3 | $78,750.00 | **$78,750.00** |
| **Lost Opportunity Cost** | | | |
| Number of business days in a month (see calculation) | 4.3 weeks[2]×5 business days/week[3] | 21.5 | |
| Number of days (4.2 months) | 21.5×4.2 | 90.3 days | |
| Opportunity cost per day ($250,000) | 90.3×$250,000 | $22,575,000.00 | **$22,575,000.00** |

---

1 Salary here is calculated as simple salary alone. However, some companies use salary plus benefits.

2 Standard figure for number of weeks in a month (52 weeks/12).

3 This example assumes that cost is calculated Monday to Friday (traditional business days). Use the full week if appropriate to your business.

- **Be able to assemble all appropriate marketing, labeling, and patient and physician support information within one week after approval.**

This goal is a little harder for Rockhead to quantify. They have never developed a product before where they did not know the final configuration. In this case they have to create a "guesstimate" for how much this will cost. They guesstimate that if they had the content already complete, then had to pull it together for the specific configuration using their current processes and tools, it would take six people six weeks. The current process requires that they find all the relevant content, copy and paste it into the appropriate documents, and have it reviewed and signed off. In a unified content strategy, they guesstimate that it will take one week. This figure is based on the assumption that content will be created in elements, information product models will be designed that define the elements of content based on configuration, and systematic reuse will be used to automatically "populate" the information products with the appropriate configuration elements. Review and sign-off still have to occur.

Table 3.2 illustrates the calculations.

**Table 3.2    Calculating savings for rapidly configurable content**

| Metrics | Calculation | Interim value | Potential savings |
|---|---|---|---|
| **Development cost** | | | |
| Average salary ($75,000) | | | $75,000.00 |
| Average salary per week | 75,000/52 | $1,442.31 | |
| Number of weeks (5 weeks[4]) | 1442.31×5 | $7,211.55 | |
| Number of people (6 people) | 7,211.55×6 | $43,269.30 | **$43,269.30** |
| **Lost Opportunity Cost** | | | |
| Number of days (5 business days per week) | 5×5 | 25 | |
| Opportunity cost per day ($250,000) | 25×$250,000 | $6,250,000.00 | **$6,250,000.00** |

---

4 Development using the current method is estimated to take 6 weeks; however, development is estimated to take 1 week with the new method, so the difference is 5 weeks.

- **Reduce the cost of product content development by at least 25%.**

  Rockhead has identified that there are potential cost savings of 35% within a department. This is based on 35% commonality between products and standard safety regulations.

  The following figures are used to calculate costs:

  - Total time to create content (1 year)
  - Subject matter expert time requirements (15%)
  - Reviewer time requirements (25%)
  - Translation into six languages

  Table 3.3 illustrates the calculations.

**Table 3.3    Calculating savings for product and safety content reuse**

| Metrics | Calculation | Interim value | Potential savings |
|---|---|---|---|
| **Development cost[5] by department** | | | |
| Marketing ($1,200,000) | | $1,200,000.00 | |
| Patient and Physician Support Information ($750,000) | | $750,000.00 | |
| Labeling ($350,000) | | $350,000.00 | |
| Total | 1,200,000 + 750,000 + 350,000 | $2,300,000.00 | |
| Subject Matter Experts | 2,300,000×.15 | $345,000.00 | |
| Reviewers | 2,300,000×.25 | $575,000.00 | |
| Translation ($1,900,000) | | $1,900,000.00 | |
| Total | 345,000 + 575,000 + 1,900,000 | $2,820,000.00 | |
| Total costs | 2,300,000 + 2,820,000 | $5,120,000.00 | |
| Potential savings | $5,120,000×.35 | $1,792,000.00 | **$1,792,000.00** |

---

5 Cost of resources only, not production costs.

- **Integrate the content development, maintenance, and delivery processes associated with Marketing, Patient and Physician support information, and Labeling.**

  The costs and savings associated with this goal are dependent on reuse. Rockhead estimates that if they integrate these departments, 30% of all the content they create can be reused across the information products that each department creates (for example, cross department). Rockhead assumes that they will undertake this process in addition to the cross-product reuse, so savings are calculated based on reduced content development costs.

  Table 3.4 illustrates the calculations.

**Table 3.4    Calculating savings for integration of content across departments**

| Metrics | Calculation | Interim value | Potential savings |
|---|---|---|---|
| Costs after product content reuse savings | $5,120,000–$1,792,000 | $3,328,000.00 | |
| Potential savings | $3,328,000×.35 | $998,400.00 | **$998,400.00** |

- **Ensure content is consistent and accurate everywhere it appears.**

  The cost of this goal can be calculated in two ways: first, based on the time it takes to ensure that content is accurate using the current processes and technology, and second, based on not paying out on a lawsuit.

  Rockhead calculates the cost of ensuring content is consistent and accurate everywhere it appears, based on a recent activity in which they had to change the occurrence of one warning in their information set to accommodate new safety guidelines. Two people took one month to scrutinize every document, identify where the warning occurred, and change it. Although ensuring that content is consistent wherever it appears should be a continuous activity, Rockhead uses the cost of the specific incident, assuming that if this cost was doubled it would approximate the cost of doing this activity on an ongoing basis.

Table 3.5 illustrates the calculations.

**Table 3.5    Calculating savings for content accuracy**

| Metrics | Calculation | Interim value | Potential savings |
|---|---|---|---|
| Costs | (75,000/12)×2 | $12,500.00 | |
| Potential savings | 12,500×2 | $25,000.00 | **$25,000.00** |

In addition, the amount awarded in the lawsuit was $10,000,000, not including the cost of the lawyers or the cost to prepare the case. Therefore Rockhead could avoid a minimum cost of $10,000,000 in the future if they ensure content is always consistent and accurate.

## Identifying metrics

It is not unusual for organizations not to know what it costs them to perform a task. General metrics may be available (for example, it takes two years to produce a new product), but you may not have specific costs for how much it costs to create a user guide, a brochure, or any other information product.

### Why gather metrics?

Not knowing your "real" costs can perpetuate ineffective processes and make it difficult to determine the effectiveness of change. Not gathering metrics makes it impossible to calculate a return on investment. Gathering metrics results in the following:

- Improved performance
- Improved estimates for future projects
- Identification of measurable activities
- Identification of best and worst practices
- Improved project costs
- "Proof" of effective processes

### Developing a baseline

A baseline (current state measurement) provides a starting point for your metrics. Before you can measure difference and effectiveness, you need a starting number. The starting number can be representative of where you are today (for example, number of documents created) or it can be estimated based on a quick evaluation of task information (duration, cost, effort, quality, value delivered, customer satisfaction). To gather this information,

- Identify your tasks.

  Start by identifying the tasks that you believe will be affected by a unified content strategy. Common tasks include content creation, searching for content, review, and publication preparation.

- Measure the duration of a task.

  Determine how much time it takes (duration) to complete the task. You need to measure the task multiple times to ensure you get a representative average duration. Have multiple employees perform the task a number of times. Remember that in a realistic scenario the tasks are unlikely to be performed in isolation. Time the tasks in isolation and time the tasks as a component of the entire task sequence. Average the findings.

  This may be hard to do with long tasks. Start timing tasks as soon as you determine there is a possibility of going ahead with a unified content strategy so that as you analyze all your requirements, you can also be developing your metrics:

  If you don't have time to measure all your tasks, identify some representative tasks that can be accomplished in a reasonable period of time (for example, less than a day or over a period of a few weeks) and measure the time of these tasks. Extrapolate these findings to your tasks as a whole.

- Calculate the cost of a task.

  The cost of a task is based on the time it takes to perform the task and the task's value. The task's value is usually the cost of that portion of the employee's salary. It could also include the value of the revenue or profit generation and the impact on customer satisfaction; however, these may be harder to measure.

### Ongoing metrics

After you collect metrics, continue to collect them well into the project, and preferably on an ongoing basis. Collect ongoing metrics to ensure that you are actually meeting or exceeding your expectations. To calculate ongoing metrics:

- Compare your current metrics to the baseline.

- Determine whether they have changed.

- Determine by how much have they changed.

- Identify any mitigating factors.

- Identify further adjustments to continue to improve your metrics.

Take these measurements at regular intervals such as after the pilot, three months after implementation, six months later, one year later.

You know you have been successful if you have been able to affect next year's budget by:

- Reducing costs

- Increasing the amount of work you can effectively accomplish

- Improving the quality of your materials

# Calculating investment costs

Now you need to identify what the investment costs of implementing a unified content strategy will be. Investment costs are incurred in three areas:

- Technology
- Training and consulting
- Lost productivity

## Technology

Technology costs include the cost of hardware and software. Part IV, "Tools and technologies," identifies four types of tools you may require: authoring, content management, workflow, and delivery.

Rockhead has decided to move to XML.

## *Authoring*

None of Rockhead's current authoring tools are XML-compliant, so they have to buy new tools. The current authoring areas that will be adopting a unified content strategy are using different authoring tools.

- **Regulatory Submissions**

  Regulatory Submissions is currently using a traditional authoring tool. They have decided to use an XML editor for internal staff and an XML-aware editor for external contractors/consultants (see Chapter 15, "Authoring tools").

- **Marketing**

  Marketing currently uses a traditional authoring tool, then moves the content into either a page layout program for layout and publication, or into an HTML tool. They do not want to move away from their traditional authoring tool, so they decide to purchase the same XML-aware tool as Regulatory Submissions.

- **Patient and physician information**

  The department creating patient and physician information is using a desktop publishing tool designed for technical documentation. Their current version is not XML-compliant, but the latest release is, so they decide to upgrade.

- **Labeling**

  Labeling is also using a traditional authoring tool. They decide to use the same XML-aware tool as the other departments.

  The potential costs of these tools are shown in Table 3.6. Note that these costs are for the software only, not for training. Training costs are included in table 3.7.

**Table 3.6    Calculating costs for authoring tools**

| Metrics | Calculation | Interim value | Cost |
|---|---|---|---|
| Regulatory Submissions (10 internal people and 3 external contractors) | $(10 \times \$700[6]/\text{seat}) + (3 \times \$500[7]/\text{seat})$ | $8,500.00 | |
| Marketing (16 people) | $16 \times \$500/\text{seat}$ | $8,000.00 | |
| Patient and Physician Support (10 people) | $10 \times \$200[8]/\text{seat}$ | $2,000.00 | |
| Labeling (3 people) | $3 \times \$500/\text{seat}$ | $1,500.00 | |
| **Total** | 8,500 + 8,000 + 2,000 + 1,500 | $20,000.00 | **$20,000.00** |

## Content management system

Rockhead does not have a content management system, but unlike authoring tools, all the groups will use the same content management system. Costs for a content management system are usually based on a combination of server costs plus seats. For the purposes of this calculation, we've used a round figure that includes both server and seats. Content management systems can typically range in cost from $100,000 to $250,000. Some large implementations may run into the millions. Rockhead is not a large company and their needs are relatively small (small number of users). Although they could use the lowest value for their estimate, we've estimated a conservative $200,000, which should also ensure that sufficient funds allocated.

---

6 XML editor approximate cost.

7 XML-aware tool approximate cost.

8 Upgrade approximate cost.

## Workflow

Workflow is a component of all the systems Rockhead is looking at, so there is no additional cost here.

If you are purchasing a separate workflow tool, consider using an average cost of $250,000. Separate workflow tools tend to be enterprise tools and as such are usually as expensive as a content management system.

## Delivery

Some content management systems include delivery to multiple media; however, XML-based content management systems require an additional delivery tool. Rockhead needs to deliver content in PDF and HTML. They can estimate a cost of approximately $25,000 for a delivery tool capable of converting XML to these formats.

If you are considering a dynamic delivery tool with multi-channel delivery, consider using an average cost of $100,000.

### Training and consulting

No implementation should occur without adequate training for all staff. Training should always be part of your investment costs.

Your organization may be able to implement the unified content strategy on your own without help from consultants for information modeling, DTD development or modification, software installation and configuration, and change management. However, most organizations use some level of consulting either from the tools' vendors or from other consultants in information design and management and change management. Costs for consulting can vary depending upon how much assistance you require. Rockhead has decided to optimize its investment in training and consulting by:

- Taking all the available training (user, installation and configuration, modeling, and DTD).
- Asking for consulting to facilitate the process of information analysis and modeling for one department's set of content, creation of the first DTD, and complete installation and configuration.
- Retaining the consultants for "as needed" assistance as they complete the project on their own.

In this way they have help as they get started, but then complete the process themselves. They feel this will optimize their funds and resources and help them develop internal knowledge and expertise of their own.

The approximate costs of the training and consulting are shown in Table 3.7.

**Table 3.7   Calculating costs of training and consulting**

| Metrics | Calculation | Interim value | Cost |
|---|---|---|---|
| Training | | $35,000.00 | |
| Facilitated analysis and modeling | | $50,000.00 | |
| DTD | | $25,000.00 | |
| Installation and configuration | | $50,000.00 | |
| Change management | | $75,000.00 | |
| **Total costs** | 35,000 + 50,000 + 25,000 + 50,000 + 75,000 | $235,000.00 | **$235,000.00** |

## Lost productivity

Even if you use consultants to help you implement your unified content strategy, there will be periods of lost productivity with your staff. Apart from their regular duties, your staff need to assist in:

- Analysis
- Design
- Modeling
- Configuration
- Testing
- Product acceptance
- Training
- Change management

Rockhead has decided to allocate the following resources to the project:

- 1 full-time project manager for 6 months
- 2 people from Regulatory Submissions for 6 months at 35% time
- 2 people from Marketing for 6 months at 35% time
- 2 people from Patient and Physician Support for 6 months at 35% time
- 1 person from labeling for 3 months at 25% time
- 2 people from Information Technology for 6 months at 35% time

Using personnel in this manner will get them up and running in one area only; then they will implement in the remaining two areas over the next two months. After the first implementation, Rockhead will allocate the following resources:

- 1 full-time Project Manager for 2 months
- 1 person from Regulatory Submissions for 2 months at 50% time
- 1 person from Marketing for 2 months at 50% time
- 1 person from Patient and Physician Support for 6 months at 50% time
- 1 person from Labeling for 1 month at 50% time
- 2 people from Information Technology for 2 months full time

Rockhead can calculate these costs two ways. It can calculate the costs of the individual salaries for the specified duration; it can also look at what it will cost the company to use contractors to fill in the gaps left by these people.

Table 3.8 illustrates the salaried costs, and Table 3.9 illustrates the contractor costs. Your organization needs to determine which calculation makes the most sense. Some organizations just use the additional costs (for example, the contractor cost) because this is a new cost, whereas the salaries have to be paid regardless of what the staff work on.

**Table 3.8   Calculating salaried costs**

| Metrics | Calculation | Interim value | Cost |
|---|---|---|---|
| **First implementation** | | | |
| Project Manager | 100,000.00/2 | $50,000.00 | |
| Regulator Submissions | 2×(75,000.00/2)×.35 | $26,250.00 | |
| Marketing | 2×(75,000.00/2)×.35 | $26,250.00 | |
| Patient and Physician Support | 2×(75,000.00/2)×.35 | $26,250.00 | |
| Labeling | (75,000.00/4)×.25 | $4687.50.00 | |
| Information Technology | 2×(75,000.00/2)×.35 | $26,250.00 | |
| Total cost | 50,000.00 + (26,250.00×4) + 4687.50 | $159,687.50 | **$159,687.50** |
| **Full implementation** | | | |
| Project Manager | (100,000.00/12)×2 | $16,666.67 | |
| Regulator Submissions | (75,000.00/12×2)×.5 | $6250.00 | |
| Marketing | (75,000.00/12×2)×.5 | $6250.00 | |
| Patient and Physician Information | (75,000.00/12×2)×.5 | $6250.00 | |
| Labeling | (75,000.00/12)×.5 | $3125.00 | |
| Information Technology | 2×(75,000.00/12×2) | $25,000.00 | |
| Total cost | 16,666.67 + (6,250.00×3) + 3,125 + 25,000.00 | $63,541.67 | **$63,541.67** |
| Project resource cost | 159,687.50 + 63,541.67 | $223,229.17 | **$223,229.17** |

Rockhead assumes that one contractor is required in each of Regulatory Submission, Marketing, and Patient and Physician Support. The contractor in Patient and Physician Information is shared with Labeling. A contractor is required to assist in Information Technology, but no contractor is used to replace the Project Manager. The cost of a contractor is assumed to be $8,000 per month.

**Table 3.9    Calculating contractor costs**

| Metrics | Calculation | Interim value | Cost |
|---|---|---|---|
| Contractors (3 for 8 months) | 4×8×8,000 | $256,000.00 | **$256,000.00** |

# Calculating return on investment

Now that you have calculated all the potential savings and costs, you can calculate your return on investment. Return on investment is calculated as savings minus costs. Table 3.10 illustrates the calculations for return on investment.

**Table 3.10    Calculating return on investment**

| Metrics | Potential development savings | Opportunity cost/savings |
|---|---|---|
| **Benefits** | | |
| Reduce the time to complete a submission by 2 months | $78,750.00 | $22,575,000.00 |
| Configure product documentation in one week | $43,269.00 | $6,250,000.00 |
| Cross-product and safety content reuse | $1,792,000.00 | |
| Cross-department content reuse | $998,400.00 | |
| Content accuracy | $25,000.00 | $10,000,000.00 |
| **Sub-total** | **$2,937,419.00** | **$38,825,000.00** |
| **Costs** | | |
| Authoring tools | ($20,000.00) | ($20,000.00) |
| Content management system | ($200,000.00) | ($200,000.00) |
| Workflow | n/a | n/a |
| Delivery | ($25,000.00) | ($25,000.00) |
| Training and consulting | ($235,000.00) | ($235,000.00) |
| Lost productivity | ($223,229.17) | ($223,229.17) |
| Contractor costs | ($256,000.00) | ($256,000.00) |
| **Sub-total** | **($959,229.17)** | **($959,229.17)** |
| **Total savings** | **$1,978,189.83** | **$37,865,770.83** |

The opportunity cost/savings holds the greatest potential if a unified content strategy is implemented. However, some organizations are reluctant to use just the opportunity cost to justify a new process and system implementation; they would rather use budget reductions or expenditure reductions. Rockhead Inc.'s development cost figures show a number of opportunities for reducing costs. Reusing content within one department alone would cover the costs of the unified content strategy. To increase the savings further, Rockhead could choose not to bring in contractors and just have existing staff fill in the gaps until the project is done, a common practice in many organizations. Alternately, fewer consultants could be used, but that might increase the lost productivity costs.

Frequently the costs of purchasing new tools are of great concern to an organization, but the "people costs" (for example, productivity, training, consulting) are higher. Care should be taken to look at all potential costs and savings to determine whether the savings outweigh the costs.

Some organizations may find the figures daunting even after identifying a positive return on investment. When that occurs it is important to look at the costs to determine whether they can be spread out over time or incurred in phases. Refer to Chapter 22, "Transition plan" for ideas on how to implement a unified content strategy in the most cost-effective way for your organization. It is also important to educate your organization on what things "really" cost so that the investment costs and opportunities can be put into perspective.

## Summary

Return on investment (ROI) is the anticipated savings after subtracting the cost of implementing a unified content strategy. The savings are future savings and are used to determine whether implementing a unified content strategy is appropriate for your organization. ROI can and should be calculated on an ongoing basis after implementation to verify predictions and identify additional areas of improvement.

The implementation of a unified content strategy should be undertaken only if it supports your organization's business goals and objectives. To determine whether it does, follow these steps:

1. Identify your organizational goals.

2. Qualify the goals to ensure that a unified content strategy can address them.

3. Quantify the goals to determine what these goals are worth to the organization (current costs and potential savings).

4. Calculate your cost of investment. Investment costs are incurred through the acquisition of new technology, addition of training and consulting, and lost productivity when staff are moved from their current tasks to the new project.

5. Calculate the return on investment by subtracting your anticipated investment costs from your potential savings.

6. Determine whether it is worthwhile for your organization to implement a unified content strategy.

# Part II

# Performing a substantive audit: Determining business requirements

In Part I, we discussed content as the lifeblood of your organization and explored the fundamental concepts of content reuse. Everyone in your organization uses content, often by accessing it on the company intranet. Depending on the type of business you're in, you also provide content to your customers in the form of brochures, press releases, user guides, web sites, newsletters, and more. But before content makes its way to either your employees, your stakeholders, or your customers, many different hands touch it—they write it, they review it, they revise it, they approve it, they publish it, and they store it. Many different people working on information can result in disparities, as well as duplicate efforts. By unifying information, you can enhance its usability and consistency and save your company considerable time and money.

However, unified content requires unified processes. You need to figure out what's going on with your content, how it's being used, as well as the processes to create, publish, and store it. We call this the substantive audit. There are two components of a substantive audit: analysis and recommendations. During the analysis, you examine audiences, information, needs, processes, and technology. You analyze who needs and uses what information, how that information currently supports them, and how it is produced. You also analyze the technology that supports the content life cycle processes in your organization. Following the analysis, you can formulate a new, unified content life cycle, and potentially, write it in a recommendations report that outlines how you will proceed. Part II guides you through the phases of the substantive audit.

When implementing a unified content strategy, it's good to start "where it really hurts." In Chapter 4, "Where does it really hurt?," you'll learn ways to identify the dangers, opportunities and strengths, as well as the goals you want to achieve in order to move ahead with a unified content strategy.

Chapter 5, "Analyzing the content life cycle," provides examples of typical issues an organization faces and the implications of those issues for a unified content strategy. Some of these issues may be relevant to your organization, but your organization may have entirely different issues that will need to be resolved before you move ahead.

During a content audit you analyze materials, looking for similar and identical information, as well as for information that is currently distinct but could be similar or identical. Once you see how your information is being used and reused, you can make decisions about how you might unify it. In Chapter 6, "Performing a content audit," you'll learn what a content audit is and how to perform one; it also provides examples of content audit findings.

Chapter 7, "Envisioning the unified content life cycle," rounds out Part II with two examples of unified content life cycles: a larger-scale one for an entire enterprise, as well as a smaller-scale one for a department within an enterprise.

# Chapter 4

## Where does it really hurt?

Every organization, and every department within an organization, faces challenges in successfully meeting goals. To build an effective unified content strategy you need to understand your organization's goals and needs. When implementing a unified content strategy, it's good to start "where it really hurts"—wherever there are significant content management and authoring issues.

Start in areas with the most "pain"—where processes, tools, and technology are failing or inadequate, and where your organization is seeing the most negative results and hearing about it from customers or management. This will help you to realize a higher return on investment; it will also show other areas in the organization how a more effective, unified authoring and publishing methodology can help them, getting your unified content strategy project off to a good start. Change typically occurs when the "pain" of existing authoring and publishing processes becomes too great, when tools no longer meet authoring needs, or when organizations are held back from both meeting ongoing requirements and taking advantage of new opportunities. Deadlines are missed, content is inconsistent, content is missing…and customers complain.

To discover where your organization is hurting the most, you need to understand the dangers and challenges facing your organization, the opportunities that can be realized if change occurs successfully, and the strengths your organization can build on to implement these changes. In most organizations, individual departments know the specific pain they are feeling; users may be frustrated by their inability to find relevant content, by duplicating their efforts, by tight deadlines. However, talking to both the management and individual members of other groups is also beneficial in identifying where it hurts across the organization—where the focus of your unified content strategy should be. Management has a broad-picture perspective on issues and can assist in determining the key issues and goals that must be addressed. And a mix of management and user feedback will paint a more realistic picture of the organization's issues.

This chapter discusses ways to identify the organizational dangers, opportunities, and strengths, as well as the goals you want to achieve to move ahead with a unified content strategy. This identification process helps you to position a unified content strategy in the context of the bigger organizational issues and goals, ensuring that you are addressing the real issues of the organization and better positioning yourself to differentiate your product or service to meet ongoing customer needs. This identification process also helps you to identify some strategies for helping your organization to achieve its goals.

# Identifying the dangers, opportunities, and strengths[1]

In a competitive business environment and sometimes difficult economy, every organization faces dangers, such as lost customers, lost sales, and subsequently, lost revenue. Yet even in difficult and challenging times, organizations can pursue many opportunities and build on their strengths. In fact, challenging times are often the best times to improve processes. However, before charging ahead, you need to first determine the dangers. Then you can address them by identifying opportunities and strengths.

## Dangers

At some point, every organization faces danger. This is especially true in a competitive environment in which it is difficult, if not impossible, for organizations to maintain their desired competitive position. After all, someone else is always coming up with a newer and better solution and customers' needs are always changing. From a business perspective, potential or perceived danger reflects the fear of losing something—the fear of losing competitive position, the fear of not meeting desired revenues, the fear of missed opportunities, and so on. Your organization's dangers can be enterprise-wide or related to a specific department. The first step in overcoming dangers is to identify them: danger can be a positive impetus to effect change. After you know what dangers you face, you can define strategies to overcome them.

To help you identify the dangers specific to your organization, ask key people to identify the three top dangers the organization faces, or will face if you don't meet your goals.

## *Common dangers*

The dangers facing your organization can be many and varied. These are a few of the common dangers and the ways in which a unified content strategy can help to address them:

---

1 The concept of dangers, opportunities, and strengths is adapted from "The D.O.S. Conversation," a concept and trademark of The Strategic Coach Inc. All rights reserved. http://www.strategiccoach.com

- **The economy**

  Business goes through repeated cycles of boom, slowdown, and even bust. As the economy enters a slowdown, revenues decrease. Decreasing revenues lead to tight budgets and reduced resources.

  A unified content strategy leads to reduced costs for content development and maintenance (see Chapter 3, "Assessing return on investment for a unified content strategy"). This can help to reduce the pressure on budgets as well as to reduce the resources necessary to maintain the current workload.

- **Missing the market window**

  The constant fear of losing market share is common. New products and services are being developed and marketed at an ever-increasing rate. Much cost and effort goes into building a new product or service, and if another company makes it to market first, you may lose your development cost and possibly market share.

  If your product is content, your ability to get content out faster and in a form that is relevant to customers' needs is key. A unified content strategy can reduce the time it takes you to create content. Plus, it gives you a definite market advantage if you can deliver customized content, designed to more effectively provide your customers with the information they need, when they need it.

  Alternatively, if content supports your products and services, a unified content strategy can assist you in making the content available as soon as, if not before, the product or service is available.

- **Legal liability**

  If your organization produces a product or provides a service that involves safety risks, the danger of legal liability is very real. Sometimes a lawsuit can revolve around missing information, unclear information, or contradictory information. You may also face legal liability through false representation of your product, misleading information, or incorrect information.

  If specific information must be included with a product (certain warnings, for example), a unified content strategy can ensure that information appears everywhere and every time it is supposed to appear. In addition, it can ensure that content is identical every time it is reused, eliminating contradictory information. Finally, if a change is made to the content, a unified content strategy can ensure that information is changed wherever it, or a derivative of the content, appears.

## Opportunities

Even when there are a multitude of dangers, opportunity exists. In fact, opportunity often arises from danger. However, when there are few dangers, there are even greater opportunities available: opportunities that you can pursue without feeling pressured by the need to address dangers, opportunities you can pursue solely with the prospect of success.

With many opportunities available, it's important to focus on key ones. To identify where your best chances for improvement lie, ask key people in your organization to identify the top three opportunities that they hope to take advantage of.

## Common opportunities

Frequently the opportunities an organization identifies are the corollary of the dangers (for example, missing the market window becomes faster time-to-market). The following list includes a few of the common opportunities and the ways in which a unified content strategy can help to support these opportunities.

- **Faster time-to-market**

  Bringing a product or service to market faster than your competition can result in increased revenues and market share.

  A unified content strategy enables an organization to create all the supporting content faster, more accurately, and more efficiently, thereby reducing the content creation and delivery cycle and subsequently, getting the product or service delivered faster.

- **New/improved product or service**

  New or improved products or services can help to retain existing customers and attract new ones.

A unified content strategy can help you use existing content for new or improved products in two ways. If your strategy includes modular reusable content, you can rapidly modify existing modules to reflect changes. If your strategy specifies content reuse across all supporting information products (for example, in a brochure, web site, supporting documentation, or training guide), you write content once and use it wherever it is required. This can greatly reduce the time required to create and deliver content.

- **Improved customer support**

  Customer relationship management involves tracking and acting upon everything you need to know about your customers: their buying history, budget, timeline, areas of interest, and future requirements. It also involves ensuring that customers have exactly the right information at exactly the right time and in exactly the right form.

  Combining detailed customer profiles along with a unified content strategy can help you build and maintain an even better relationship with your customer. A unified content strategy that specifies modular reusable content enables you to deliver the right modules to the right customer at the right time and in the right format. Rather than getting bombarded with information, customers receive only what is relevant to them. Customization can occur right down to the medium in which customers want information delivered to them. Customers are happier because they've gotten exactly what they needed, which results in cost savings to the organization because retaining a customer is much more cost effective than acquiring a new one. In addition, you can ensure that your branding and your message to customers are clear and consistent regardless of what information they receive.

## Strengths

Every organization has its strengths. Recognizing and building on your strengths is important because strengths allow you to realize your opportunities. Sometimes in difficult times it is easy to overlook your strengths and focus on the negatives. Focusing on your strengths provides a positive focus for moving forward. Ask the key people in your organization to identify what they feel are the organization's greatest strengths and why.

## Common strengths

These are a few of the common strengths and the ways in which a unified content strategy can help to support them:

- **The people**

  The people in your organization can be a source of strength. Often they are well-educated, eager to learn, and hard working. Good people are often the catalysts for change.

  A unified content strategy brings with it change in the form of new and better ways of creating, managing, and distributing content. People who are open to change will benefit from changed processes. People will also help you to make the changes happen.

- **Market recognition/customer loyalty**

  Your organization's market recognition indicates that customers have valued what you have provided them with in the past. Customers will continue to value you if you continue to produce products and services that meet, or better yet, exceed their needs. Retaining customers is cheaper than obtaining new ones.

  Customers are quick to respond to new and better products and services. Although the unified content strategy remains behind the scenes of your organization and hence is transparent to customers, they will respond positively to the more effective content they receive and will be more likely to remain loyal.

- **Innovation**

  Organizations that innovate internally to improve the way they do business and provide innovative products and services to their customers continue to retain their customers.

  A unified content strategy is an innovation in the way an organization creates, manages, and delivers content. In addition, creating modular content enables an organization to rapidly reconfigure their products and even more rapidly reconfigure their content to match the new product and service offerings.

# Identifying the goals

All organizations have many goals, often reflected in corporate and department strategic plans. Naturally, goals are based on the opportunities organizations have available to them. Although not all corporate goals can be addressed with a unified content strategy, you need to identify which ones can be. Your goals may be the same as your opportunities; however, they should be more tangible and measurable.

Determine goals by examining strategic plans, and by asking key people what their specific goals are for the coming year. It is important to have long-term goals, as well. You can also ask about two-year, three-year, or even five-year goals. In fact, many organizations have five-year strategic plans, broken down into what they hope to accomplish each year.

## Common goals

These are a few of the common goals related to content and the ways in which a unified content strategy can help to support them:

- **Reduce cycle time.**

  Content takes time to develop. The time it takes to create content can significantly influence your ability to get the product out the door, whether your content is part of the product or service, or it is the product itself. Often content creation and sign-off approval lags behind product completion. Delays can be significant at times.

  Writing content once and reusing it many times reduces the amount of original content that must be created. This in turn reduces the amount of time required to create and approve content. Review times can be reduced because only new or revised content is reviewed and approved. The further addition of appropriate authoring and content management technologies coupled with appropriate business process improvements can reduce the cycle time even further.

- **Create flexible content that can easily be reused to create information products for multiple products and multiple media.**

The ability to reconfigure content rapidly is both an opportunity and a necessity for many companies. As products change rapidly, so must the content. With a goal such as this, it is worthwhile to measure the time and resources required to reconfigure content in your current environment, then qualify the word "easily" with an exact measure of time.

Modular reusable content can make it easier to build a definitive information source. From the source, authors can retrieve and opportunistically or systematically reuse content for multiple products.

- **Reduce the cost of translation.**

Translation is often a large and growing expense within an organization, so the goal of reducing translation costs is a common one.

A unified content strategy reduces translation costs because less original content is translated. Improved standards for the creation of content make content more consistent, thereby increasing the probability of translation memory matches and reducing the requirement for new translation.

- **Make content more accessible.**

Making content accessible to people with disabilities is an important aspect of content. It has even been mandated in the "Americans with Disabilities Act." But making content accessible can be costly because it requires multiple media to deliver content.

Some accessibility costs can be reduced with a unified content strategy. Separating content from format makes it possible for content to be displayed automatically in a format appropriate to the disability (for example, in a different font size).

# Identifying the challenges

Along with goals come challenges, whether they are challenges of money, time, technology, or people. It's important to identify challenges before forging ahead with change, so that you can address them successfully during implementation. The best way to determine what the challenges are is to ask key people what they perceive as the challenges that may impact your ability to meet the goals.

These are some of the common challenges and their impact on your unified content strategy:

- Time and money

  There is never enough time to get your regular daily tasks completed, never mind new tasks. In addition to lack of time, there are usually insufficient funds to do both daily and new work.

  In the long term, a unified content strategy will increase the time available (fewer people can do more) and decrease costs (fewer people means lower costs; lower translation, accessibility, and customer support costs further decrease total costs). However, these savings are not realized until after implementation. To realize savings, you need to allocate some time and money up front. You can optimize the time and money you invest by starting small with a proof-of-concept, a pilot, and a small rollout.

  See Chapter 22, "Transition plan," for more information about addressing this challenge.

- Resistance to change

  People become comfortable in their approach to their tasks, even if they are aware that their processes are ineffective or more difficult than they need to be. Change brings with it the unknown, and the fear of the unknown can be even stronger than the pain of continuing to work in the same way.

  Resistance to change is a real challenge in a unified content strategy. A unified content strategy brings with it many new changes that are unavoidable, but opposition can be reduced through ongoing communication, participation, and strong management support for the changes.

  See Chapter 21, "Managing change," for more information on addressing this challenge.

- Maintaining existing deliverables

  When an organization introduces new processes or technology, there is a period of time required to implement these changes. The time required to implement the change can impact an organization's ability to meet current deliverables. In addition, the resources required to effect the change are usually also the same resources required to complete the deliverables.

The most effective way to address this challenge is to create a strategic planning and implementation team to devote attention to the new strategy and implementation. This is the team that will conduct the analysis of your content and processes, then develop the plans to move ahead with a unified content strategy, both in processes and tools. If possible, you can supplement this team with consultants, and supplement the deliverables team that handles the day-to-day work with subcontractors.

See Chapter 22 for more information about addressing this challenge.

- **Lack of support from management**

  You may not receive the support you require to move forward with a unified content strategy; you may lack budget or management "buy-in" for the concept. Management is cautious when expending money, and unlikely to provide the support you require unless you build a solid business case and show tangible ROI. Take the time to establish the credentials for a unified content strategy so you have the necessary support right from the beginning of the project.

  See Chapter 3 for more information about addressing this challenge.

## Where a unified content strategy won't help

A unified content strategy will not be a solution to all the dangers you identify (such as employee turnover, for example). Its focus is on helping to solve the problems your organization is experiencing in the areas of content creation, management, delivery, and communication with your internal and external customers. A unified content strategy is just one piece of your overall corporate strategy to address your dangers, realize your opportunities, and build on your strengths, not the whole solution. As you gather your information, ensure that you and the rest of the organization understand what a unified content strategy will help you to do and what it won't.

## Moving toward a unified content strategy: A case study

"I can't find the information I need, even though I know it's probably there." Sound familiar? Between 1997 and 1998, this complaint was heard from some of Intel's (previously Dialogic Corporation's) customers. The TIPs (Technical Information Products) group decided to do something about it. As a global OEM (Original Equipment Manufacturer) provider of telecommunications equipment, Dialogic makes money when its customers deploy their product in volume (products are not sold directly to end users; rather, they are integrated into other companies' products). Their greatest danger lies in delaying their customers' time to market. However, the difficulty customers were having finding information was becoming increasingly problematic, and was causing delays.

To begin with, customers expected different outputs—HTML, PDF, .hlp, paper—on more platforms, covering a wider array of products, than ever before. They wanted "how-to" information, not simply product-centric reference information and the TIPs group had to accommodate customers' increasing needs for information. However, after 15 years of additions and revisions, the information had little discernable architecture. Problems grew more difficult to fix. With no central organizational control until late 1998, writers routinely created their own styles (as many as 150) to "supplement" the 125 official styles. As a result, publishing was a long, slow nightmare. Not only did TIPs have difficulty in meeting customers' current needs for information, they were in danger of not meeting customers' new needs. A new approach to creating and publishing information was essential.

TIPs' main goal was to improve customer satisfaction. Their secondary goal was to improve the way they developed content to improve customer satisfaction, as well as the authoring and publishing process. To their credit, TIPs had a strong team of writers, editors, and team leaders willing to pitch in and make positive change; plus, management supported their endeavours.

### What we did and why

Initially TIPs set out to find the perfect tool to solve the problem. However, after testing a number of tools they discovered that tools were not the solution. Giving in to the notion that new tools can transform poorly structured content was a significant danger. Trying a few new SGML/XML-based tools quickly dispelled this naïveté: Conversion of poorly-structured content was impossible.

Although XML tools were very attractive, the conversion process and the learning curve were daunting, given the state of the content. Instead, TIPs chose to stay with more traditional authoring tools, but develop structured modular content that would significantly improve the quality of the content and make it possible to meet customers' needs more effectively. The modular content architecture opened up numerous publishing options, most notably via XML. Most important, customers can recognize the information they're looking for with confidence because there's consistent structure throughout the information set. The new modular content design supports multiple outputs, multiple audiences, and reuse of information for solution-level documentation. TIPs is currently revising about 10,000 pages of content.

**Challenges**

What TIPS found is that the biggest challenges are organizational. Developing a unified information strategy means taking away some individual control. It requires strong senior management leadership, support, and vision. It also requires the organization to be functionally aligned: everybody needs to work towards a common goal.

Making time to design and implement a new content architecture given the relentless demands of ongoing product development poses another challenge. It's easy to lose focus and question what you're doing when you have deadlines to meet. There's also the challenge of maintaining two publishing systems while transitioning from old to new. Depending on the state of the content, the transition can take years.

**Benefits**

However, in spite of the challenges, the TIPs group is currently in the implementation and trial phase of its transition to the new publishing system. Anticipated benefits include:

- Greater customer satisfaction with the information available

- Reuse of content in solution guides

- A path to greater customization

Secondary benefits include a more unified organization with a clearer picture of where content management and delivery are headed. TIPs is now trying to understand customer needs and translate them into changes to the content architecture systematically, rather than haphazardly. This outcome holds the most promise of all.

**Lessons learned**

Start with the content.

- Examine the content critically to determine whether or not it's structured and consistent.

- Identify the kinds of tasks or uses customers have for products and organize your information around them.

- Bring in expert advice.

    This increases credibility.

    It helps you maintain your workload.

    You probably don't really know how to do it all yourself, even if you think you do.

Don't bite off more than you can chew

- Phase the approach.

    Do not expect perfection, seamless integration, or any foolish notion of how there'll be no tweaking required.

**Summary**

Although the transition from desktop publishing to unified content management is difficult, it promises to increase operational efficiency and customer satisfaction in the long term.

**Biography**

Sal Manetta was Director of Technical Information Products at Dialogic and is now an Engineering Manager at Intel. Over the last 20 years, he has held several positions in the technical communications field, including writer, editor, and manager. He has also taught technical writing in the Master's Degree program at Drexel University and has served on the Board of Directors for the Technical Communications Program at Michigan Tech.

# Summary

To successfully move ahead with a unified content strategy, you need to determine where content management and authoring issues are really causing pain in the organization. You do this by determining the dangers and challenges facing your organization, the opportunities that can be realized if change occurs successfully, the strengths your organization can build upon to implement these changes, the goals of the organization, and the challenges you may face while implementing a unified content strategy.

Ask the following questions to gather your information for analyzing your organization:

- What are the three top dangers your organization is facing, or will face if you don't meet your goals or make changes in the organization?
- What are the top three opportunities the organization hopes to take advantage of?
- What are your organization's greatest strengths?
- What are your organization's goals for the next year?
- What are the challenges your organization will have to overcome to meet these goals?

# Chapter 5

## Analyzing the content life cycle

Within your organization, content is developed in many different ways, by many different people, and by many different departments. Development may follow a predefined process or it may not, and if there is an established process, it may differ from department to department. To implement a unified content strategy, you need unified processes so that everyone involved in developing, storing, and publishing content does it the same way, or at minimum is able to interact effectively and share content. To understand where you need to focus your efforts, though, you need to examine your content life cycle and any issues associated with it.

This chapter provides examples of typical issues an organization faces in the content life cycle and the implications of those issues for a unified content strategy. Some of these issues may be relevant to your organization, but your organization may have entirely different issues that will need to be resolved before you move ahead. Issues include anything that may impede your ability to implement a unified content strategy, such as processes that aren't working as well as they could be, gaps in processes, or technology that isn't meeting your needs.

## Your task

The phases in your content life cycle need to be identified and detailed to help you identify areas for improvement. Recognizing the issues will help you plan and define your unified content strategy. Where your organization currently has challenges, you need to improve the processes and technology to eliminate these issues. Where processes and technology are working well, you need to know whether they will continue to work effectively in the new strategy, and if so, incorporate them. Identifying the issues helps you to determine the scope and required functionality of your unified content strategy, define the tools selection criteria, and define which processes you must redesign or create.

Implementing a new system and methodology can be a costly and time-consuming undertaking. You want to do it right. This means taking a hard look at your processes. Finding problems now means that you will implement a better solution. Identifying problems should not be viewed or approached negatively; rather it should be viewed as an opportunity to positively change the way you do business.

Although your organization has identified the need to improve the way it creates and manages content, some people may become uncomfortable when you start examining issues. Assure management and staff that identifying issues is important, that finding issues now will enable you to address, correct, or prevent any problems from continuing in the new processes and technology. After all, no process is without its problems. Processes that worked well in the past can become problematic as the company and its requirements continue to change and grow. Make sure to identify what works well so you can retain successes.

Be aware that interviewees may answer questions the way they think the interviewer wants them to, rather than being truthful in their feedback. Review effective interviewing and data collection techniques before beginning this process.

Some of these content management topics may be foreign or new to the people you interview. Be prepared to help educate them so that you can better understand their needs.

## Identifying your content life cycle

Content moves through various phases of development, such as creation, review, management, and delivery. These phases are collectively known as the *content life cycle.*

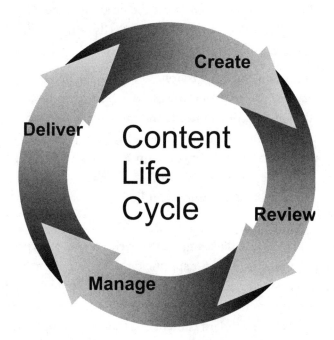

**Figure 5.1    Content life cycle.**

Although your organization may have different phases—or call them by different names—these four are the most common. To identify the content life cycle in your organization, look at how content is developed for one area or across the enterprise. Is it the same across all content creation areas, or does it vary from area to area? How effective is the content life cycle in each area?

This section poses questions about your content life cycle and its effectiveness. To answer these questions, you will need to interview all the players (everyone involved in the content life cycle). Sample interview questions are included farther on in this chapter.

## Content creation

The content creation phase can include planning, design, authoring, and revision. Each of these processes is described in the following sections.

## Planning

Planning is the first stage in content creation and usually includes activities such as analysis and decision-making, frequently not controlled by a content management system. Planning involves identifying the need for content and determining what content will most effectively meet the needs of the business and the content users.

In a typical organization, planning is done at a departmental or authoring-group level. How is planning done in your organization? Is there a project manager who identifies the specific content needs and then assigns individual groups to deliver them? Or, as is often the case, is a new product or service planned, then each content area determines what to develop, develops a schedule, then goes away and develops the appropriate content? If you have no centralized coordination of content now, this will become a requirement as you move toward a unified content strategy.

Part of the planning stage is determining the need for specific types of content. How do you determine the need for specific types of content in your organization? Is each project standardized with certain types of content already defined? Or do you revisit your content user (for example, customer) needs before determining what to develop? Standard content creation is good because it ensures that a repeatable process and quality of content is created; however, it can also allow content-related problems to perpetuate if the standards are not revisited on a regular basis to ensure that they continue to meet authors' and users' needs. If you don't already do so, include a review of known problems, customer complaints, and of course new requirements necessitated by the new product or service. You should assess your customer requirements annually, or every two years at a minimum, to ensure that you continue to meet customer needs.

Identify the tasks performed as part of your current planning process. Who are the people responsible for each segment in the task? Is there only one person or many? Determine whether tasks are effective or not. You want to retain what works and you want to change what doesn't.

## Design

There are typically two aspects to design: visual design and content and structural design.

Visual design applies to the physical appearance of the published materials, such as marketing materials and customer support materials. Does your organization have standardized visual templates for the presentation of material? Are there any controls on the visual design (that is, can anyone make a change at any time)? How frequently is the design of your content reviewed?

Typically, in our experience, content and structural design happen infrequently or not at all. Customer support materials are most likely to be consciously designed with a focus on required content and structure, whereas marketing materials may be focused on fitting content into the visual design. Web materials may have some consistency from author to author, or their structure may depend upon the content author. Consistent content and structural design are an important component of a unified content strategy.

Identify the tasks performed as part of your design stage. Who are the people responsible for each segment in the task? Is there only one person or many? Determine whether tasks are effective or not. What are the standards you employ? How widely are the standards accepted?

## Authoring and revision

Authoring involves creating new content or revising existing content. (Content can include text, graphics, and/or media.) Content is typically reviewed before it is published to ensure completeness and accuracy. After content is reviewed it is revised to incorporate reviewer changes.

What is involved in your authoring process? Which areas in the company author or revise content? How does each area create content? Are there any similarities among the ways in which content is created in each content area, or does each area have its own process? Who, within each area, creates content? Is that their sole job (for example, if they are a writers/illustrators/instructional designers), or is this just a portion of their job (for example, if they are business analysts)?

## Review

Content is usually reviewed before it is delivered to users. The review process can involve one or many reviewers, in addition to multiple reviews as content is refined before final approval. Approval usually happens when content is considered accurate, complete, and ready for delivery.

Identify the tasks performed as part of your review phase. Who are the people responsible for each stage of the review process? Is there only one person or are there many? Do reviewers feel the review process is effective or not?

## Content management

Content is managed in many ways within an organization. Some groups, like the Internet/intranet content team, may use a web content management tool. Others may use revision control software, originally designed to manage software code, but frequently applied to content. Some content groups may use document management software, and still others may have manual control systems in which content is stored on a central server and authors follow rules for modifying and adding content. Yet others may manually control content with paper copies and traditional file cabinets.

The following are some of the common management processes.

## *Version control*

Version control ensures that each time content is saved, it is *versioned*. Software management tools can automate version control, but otherwise, it must be manually enforced.

Does your organization version content? Is it tracked only in relation to a product version, or is it tracked each time the content is saved? How stringent is your tracking of versions (for example, do you meet regulatory guidelines)? Do you version whole documents or can you version the content within a document (for example, the paragraphs)?

## Authoring access control

In organizations where no management software is in place, pretty much anyone can open and modify a file. In a controlled environment, only the author or another designated person (such as an editor) can modify content. In some cases, some content is not even viewable outside a specific controlled group of authors and reviewers. Reports can be used to help managers identify who is working with content, how they work with it, and whether they are following policies and procedures.

Do you control access to your content? If you do, how effective is the control? If you don't, does this cause problems? Do these problems indicate you should control content?

### Publication and delivery

During the delivery phase, content is provided to users through a variety of methods, such as multiple media publication of content. Few companies just create content in one medium. The most common delivery medium is the Web, but paper and PDF are also important. In addition to paper and the Web, some companies produce content for wireless devices, such as telephones and PDAs, and distribute content on CDs. Although many companies publish to many different media, publication is rarely automated unless a content management system is in place. Instead, there are separate processes for each medium to which content is published.

How many media does your organization publish to? How easy or difficult is the publication process? What are the issues? Is the same or similar content published in multiple media? If so, is the content reworked for each medium?

# Identifying the players and issues

The previous sections pose many questions that you should ask as you analyze your content life cycle. To answer these questions, you interview all the players (everyone involved in the content life cycle). This section provides sample interview questions.

Developing content not only involves many different phases; it also involves many players with differing skills participating in many steps over an extended period of time. Each player may bring to the table different insights into the issues related to the content life cycle, so it's important to interview them to learn their different perspectives.

Typical players include:

- Content users (internal and external)
- Content authors
- Visual designers
- Reviewers
- Publication staff (web/paper)
- Information technology staff

## Content users

Before restructuring the content for effective reuse and delivery to content users, you need to determine how well your current content is meeting their needs. Simply improving the way you produce content will not help users use it.

Your content is used by many different users, both internal and external. Internal users are those within your organization who use content to assist them in doing their jobs, making decisions, and supporting the customer. External users are those outside your organization (such as customers and stakeholders) who use content to get information about your company, such as what products and services you provide, how to use your products or services, and how to contact you. You may not be able to interview your customers directly, but you can interview people in your organization who do have contact with your customers, such as those who work in marketing or customer support.

User interviews are critical to help you understand how the intended audiences use and access your content, and to determine what changes should be made to accommodate them. User interviews can help you to realize how similar groups of people need similar types of information and whether the content they use contains it. User interviews can also tell you in which format users prefer to receive information. If users are currently receiving paper user guides, but prefer to receive information on your web site, you can design web-based static, customized, or dynamic information for them. Alternatively, you may find that they prefer to receive content in paper form.

## Sample internal audience questions

Interview questions for an internal audience might include some of the following:

- What is your job or role?
- What challenges do you face in getting your job done?
- What information do you use to help you in your job?
- Has the content been designed to help you meet the challenges of your job, that is, can you find and access the correct information, when you need it? If so, what is it about the content that helps you?
- What types of information do you look for in a document? How does that information help you to do your job better?
- How much information is useful? What do you consider too much information? What is too little?
- When do you use content?
- What do you like best about the content you use? What do you like least? Why?
- How would you prefer to receive information?

## Sample external audience questions

Interview questions for an external audience might include some of the following:

- What products do you use?
- Do you refer to the user documentation? If so, what do you look up most frequently? If not, why not?
- Do you ever use the web site? Could you find what you were looking for on it? If so, was it useful? If you weren't able to find it, what was missing?
- Do you prefer to call customer support or do you prefer to look up the information yourself? If you prefer customer support, what types of questions do you ask them?
- What do you like best about the information you receive or have access to? What do you like least?
- How would you prefer to receive information?
- What suggestions can you make to improve the content?

## Common issues for content users

Interviews with content users often bring to light common issues:

- **Too much detail/too little detail**

  The depth and breadth of your content may not be meeting your users' needs. Sometimes there is too much content for users to wade through to find what they need. At other times the content may be too cursory to enable users to accomplish their tasks, or it may not be there at all.

  This issue may be a result of content not being designed to meet your customers' needs. Or it may be a result of users having different requirements. Consider providing more customized content that more accurately reflects their needs. A unified content strategy lets you easily configure different content for different customers. In addition, you could provide dynamic (personalized) content to customers to provide the level of content they require at any specific time.

- **Unable to find content**

  It's quite common for users to have trouble finding content, especially when they are accessing it from a web site. The content may exist, but users are unable to find it or there may be so much information on the site that they don't know where to look. Alternatively, if you provide paper-based content, it may lack an index or a clear and comprehensive table of contents.

  A unified content strategy may help to address this in a number of ways. Well-thought-out metadata combined with an appropriate search engine can assist users in correctly finding the content they require. A traditional index or table of contents can benefit from more rigorous writing standards. A unified content strategy that employs dynamic content will remove the responsibility for users to know what they need just to be able to find it. Dynamic content can provide them with content specific to their roles and their current requirements.

- **Difficult to understand**

  The content may not be written with the appropriate level of detail or language to meet the needs of users. That is, there may be too much or too little detail.

  A thorough understanding of user requirements can assist in addressing this issue as well as in designing customized content or dynamic content geared to users' level of understanding. In addition, clear writing standards can help to ensure that content is well written and easy to understand.

- **Lack of consistency**

  Sometimes different authors in the same group, different groups in the same department, different departments, and even different business units all write content differently.

  Detailed guidelines and standards may assist in helping authors become more consistent in their authoring, but you have to ensure that authors follow them. Structured writing and detailed models will more effectively help authors become consistent in their writing.

## Content authors

Asking questions related to the authoring processes is critical if you are going to uncover issues related to the writing and management of content—issues that may hinder the usefulness of the documents, their timeliness, and their overlap with other documents. For example, do authors have access to the subject matter experts and the information they need? If authors are also subject matter experts, how does this affect their jobs? Do authors have the necessary tools? Are time frames realistic? Where do authors get the information they need?

Translation is often a component of the authoring process and should be analyzed as well. Translation involves translating content and modifying it to meet local language and cultural requirements. Questions related to translation are important in understanding how content is provided to translation services, how effective the translation process is, and the issues involved in translating content in a timely and cost-effective manner.

Looking at global requirements is also very important. If you distribute content globally, global locations may have similar or very different requirements and issues.

### *Sample author questions*

Questions to be posed to authors might include the following:

- What are your current content creation processes? Which processes are effective? Which processes are ineffective? Why are these processes effective or ineffective?

- Who do you work with during the content creation process? How effective are these relationships?

- How do you collect information to write your content? How well does this work?

- Do you usually know about other initiatives in the organization and how they may affect what you are working on?

- How do you currently handle sign off/review?

- Do other departments ever see the documents you produce? Do you see theirs?

- What do you do to control documents? Version control? Access control?

- How do you handle authors working on sections that may be published simultaneously for different documents? (In other words, how do you ensure that content is the same when it needs to be and different when it needs to be?)

- How are documents created (for example, are there stylesheets or templates)?

- What tools do you use? How well do the tools support your authoring tasks?

- What works well in the current processes?

- What are the problems or frustrations you face in creating content?

- What features would you like to see in an authoring, content management, or publishing tool?

## Common issues for content authors

Based on your interviews with content authors, you may discover some of the following issues, common to many organizations:

- **Different authoring tools that don't interact well**

  Content can be created with many different tools, but sharing information among these tools is often difficult. Ensuring a similar look in content created with different tools is also difficult.

  A unified content strategy that provides standard templates, consistent style names, common metadata, and standard writing practices—in conjunction with a good conversion tool—can make it easier to exchange content among tools.

- **Inability to find information**

  Authors may find it difficult to find information to create content because it is stored on multiple servers in multiple tools. To make matters worse, it may not be indexed or tracked for easy access. Authors may remember creating content, but may not remember what the file was called or where it was stored, particularly if a long period of time has elapsed since the content was created.

A unified content strategy ensures that content is stored in a single repository or can be shared across repositories. Robust metadata attached to all content makes it easier to find. Systematic reuse can make content available to authors automatically so they don't have to go looking for it.

- **Ongoing change to content**

  Content may continue to change right up until product is shipped or content is published. Constant changes make it difficult for authors to keep up and determine all the appropriate locations where content should be modified. As a result, sometimes content that should change is missed.

  Ongoing change can be a result of your organization's development processes. A more rigorous change management process could assist in reducing the number of last-minute changes. In addition, a content management system can assist in making it easier to make changes. A content management system manages the relationships between information. If information is reused, a "where used" report can quickly identify all locations of reuse. Alternatively, when the source element is updated, all the locations in which it is reused can be automatically updated. Finally, if derivative content is reused, authors of the derivative content can be automatically informed of the change so they can incorporate the change in their element.

- **Lack of support for the authoring process**

  Sometimes the authoring process is made more difficult than it should be. Subject matter experts may not provide the information the author requires, or management may not support the author in getting the appropriate support from subject matter experts, reviewers or access to appropriate technology.

  Such a lack may be a result of not understanding how important authoring is and what the authoring process requires. Ongoing education of all interested parties may help to alleviate this problem.

- **Hard-to-reuse content**

  Authors may want to reuse content, but either they can't find it, or if they do find it, the content does not readily integrate with their documents (different styles are used, or existing styles are modified from the norm so layout may not work).

In a unified content strategy, where content is created separate from format, the content can easily be reused (no formatting is embedded that may cause problems in reuse). Common templates, style names, and metadata can assist in the sharing of content.

- **Decreasing document lifespan**

  In many organizations, content used to have a lifespan (that is, time before it needed to be changed) of about six months to a year; now, it may only exist unchanged for a few months or even a few weeks. The speed at which content must be created, modified, or completely reconfigured is increasing, making authoring very stressful. Authors often have difficulty keeping up with the pace and still ensuring quality.

  A unified content strategy can't lengthen the lifespan of a document, but it can make it easier to create content and change content rapidly to meet new needs. Modular reusable elements of content can make it easier to rapidly reconfigure content. Changing content in one place and having it automatically change in many places can make maintenance much easier. In addition, structured writing, standardized processes, and better interaction among tools can make it easier to create new content.

## Sample translation questions

Translation questions might include:

- What are the current localization processes? Which processes are effective? Which processes are ineffective? Why are these processes effective or ineffective?

- What do you do to control documents? Version control? Access control? Distribution control?

- What tools do you use? How well do the tools support your localization tasks?

- Do you have written standards and guidelines for authors to prepare content for translation?

- What are the problems or frustrations you face in translating content?

## Common translation issues

Translation questions often uncover the following issues:

- **Ongoing change to content**

  Changes continue to occur to the content after it has been sent for translation. Ongoing changes are problematic because translation staff may have to start over from the beginning each time new content is received. Also, a change in one piece of content may affect the translation of another piece of content. This makes it difficult to complete the translation in a timely manner.

  In the past, translation staff may have received "whole" documents to translate when the source language documentation was complete. Modular content that is complete and signed off can be translated when it is ready, not at the end of the cycle. In addition, like the source language content, translated content that is changed in one location and reused in another can be automatically changed wherever it occurs. Improved change management processes can also assist in reducing last-minute changes.

- **Lack of standardized English**

  Many authors do not use standardized English, resulting in fewer "matches" with translation memory tools. Memory tools look for patterns and match common words and phrases. When a match is found based on previously translated content, the translation content is used in the current document. When different terms or phrases are used, matches cannot be made.

  A unified content strategy provides writing standards for authors. These standards can assist in making content more consistent. If you localize content, standardized English can be integrated into your unified content authoring guidelines.

- **Lack of reviewers**

  In many organizations, there are insufficient reviewers to verify the translated content. Finding reviewers who are knowledgeable about the content and fluent in the language and culture is often difficult.

  A unified content strategy cannot assist in finding more people to review translated content; however, if there is less content to review (content that has already been translated and reused is already reviewed), fewer reviewers are needed to meet the review requirements.

- **Incompatible formats**

  Most translation memory tools were designed to work with Microsoft RTF. Some translation memory tools accept XML or SGML files or other formats, but some do not. A document format that is not readable by the memory translation tool must be converted to a compatible format; after translation, it must be converted back and reformatted appropriately. Each time content is converted, formatting is lost and must be reapplied when converted back to the source.

  A unified content strategy that separates format from content removes the issues of reformatting.

## Sample global author questions

Global author questions might include:

- What are the current content creation and management processes? Which processes are effective? Which processes are ineffective? Why are these processes effective or ineffective?

- Do you share content with other offices? If so, how well does that work?

- Do you create original content? What original content do you create and why do you create it?

- Do you use the same tools as other content authors? If so, how well does that work? If not, why not?

- Do you have special requirements for authoring, content management, or publishing issues that you would like to see addressed?

- What features would you like to see in an authoring, content management, or publishing tool?

## Common global author issues

Questions for global authors often uncover the following issues:

- **Slow software**

  If global authors are using the same content management system and actually accessing the same physical location as other authors, their method of connection to the server can make it very slow to respond.

A web-enabled content management system may help to improve the speed.

- **Multi-language requirements**

Global authors often have multi-language requirements, so the software they use must be able to handle a variety of languages. Some tools do this well; others do not.

Any selected tools must be able to support the requirements of multiple languages.

- **Reworking of the original materials**

Even though global authors receive existing content, it is often not in the same order as their customers require, or the emphasis on certain content is wrong. Sometimes they need to completely rewrite the content.

If content is modular, it makes it easier for someone to reorganize it to meet different customer needs. If content must be reworked, the relationship between derivative content will be maintained so that changes to the original can be identified in the derivative.

- **Different processes**

Global authors may have different business processes than expected. Cultural, legal, and other factors may account for their needs being different.

Although this is not directly a content management system issue, it is important to note their processes and why they are different. It can become an issue if their specific needs are ignored.

## Reviewers

The review and approval process is a phase in the content life cycle that can be a roadblock or an enabler for the delivery of content. There can be many different types of reviewers, such as subject matter experts, managers, quality assurance or customer support personnel, compliance/standards groups, or lawyers. Each reviewer looks for different things in the content and may have different issues. To cover all the bases, make sure you interview representative reviewers from each type.

## Sample reviewer questions

Questions to pose to reviewers might include the following:

- What is the current review processes? Which processes are effective? Which processes are ineffective? Which processes do you want that you currently don't have?
- What kinds of information do you look for when reviewing content?
- What standards are the materials expected to meet?
- How do you communicate your requirements to authors?
- What are the major issues that you identify?
- What improvements would you recommend for the review process?

## Common review issues

Issues common to the review process include the following:

- **Changes continuing to occur after review and sign-off**

  When changes continue to occur after review and sign-off, the content must be reviewed repeatedly. Alternatively, content may not receive a final review before release or publication, which may result in undetected errors.

  Unified content can make the review process more efficient. Content that has changed needs to be reviewed only once, and approved content is reflected in all resulting occurrences of the content. A more rigorous change management process may assist in reducing last-minute changes.

- **The review task not being recognized as part of the job**

  Effective reviews are critical to ensure accuracy and consistency, yet the review task is not always recognized as a valid task and no time is allocated to it. This may result in overwork for reviewers, cursory reviews as reviewers try to evaluate content as quickly as possible, or delayed reviews.

  Content management tools frequently incorporate workflow. Workflow tools automate the movement of content throughout the content life cycle. Identifying a step for review in the workflow and the person responsible for specific content review formalizes the review responsibility. Workflow can also identify the time required for the content to be in review. This can assist in formalizing the review role and the importance of review to the successful creation and management of content. In addition, the amount of time required to review content can be reduced because content that is reused and has been reviewed does not have to be reviewed again. This can give reviewers more time to review only new and modified content, thereby increasing the quality of their reviews.

- **Repetitive reviews**

  Reviewers often feel they review content they have already seen in another document, resulting in frustration over spending time reviewing content again. Also, reviewers may change already reviewed content, causing inconsistencies.

  This problem is easily addressed with a unified content strategy. Only new or changed content is given to reviewers, resulting in less content to review. If the reviewers feel it is necessary to review new or changed content in the context of the whole document to ensure that it is still applicable, any changes they identify in reviewed content can be managed through change control. When reviewers become aware of the impact of changing content that is reused in many places, they are less likely to request change.

- **Inability to verify change**

  Often reviewers cannot compare different versions of the content (for example, the original content versus the changed content), and so they are unable to verify that changes have been made. Alternatively, reviewers may go to a lot of effort to ensure that they can verify change, increasing the time required for reviewing content.

  A content management system can enable reviewers to look at the previous version, the commented version, and the revised version to verify change.

- **Confusion about decision-making processes**

  If there is a difference of opinion between the author and the reviewer, it may be unclear who has the final "say."

  Clear guidelines and processes may help to clarify who has the final authority on a difference of opinion on content. You may have authority fall in each area depending upon the issue (such as, spelling, style, grammar could be within the author's authority, whereas accuracy of the content could up to the reviewer).

## Publication and delivery

In many organizations, authors are responsible for publishing their own content. Other organizations have publications staff whose sole task is to publish content to paper or the Web. Publications staff may accept content from multiple authors and format the content appropriately for the specified media. In yet other organizations, writers may work with subject matter experts to publish content.

## *Sample publications questions*

Publications questions might include the following:

- What are the current publication processes? Which processes are effective? Which processes are ineffective? Why are these processes effective or ineffective?

- What do you do to control documents? Version control? Access control? Distribution control?

- How are documents created (for example, are there stylesheets or templates)?

- What tools do you use? How well do the tools support your publications tasks?

- What are the problems or frustrations you face in publishing content?

- What features would you like to see in an authoring, content management, or publishing tool?

## *Common publication issues*

Several publications issues might present themselves:

- **Media that require reformatting**

    If content appears in multiple media, each designated output requires that the content be reformatted. This can be time consuming.

    Reformatting for multiple media is required because traditional content creation embeds the content's format (look and feel) in the authored content. A unified content strategy separates content from format. The use of templates, standards, consistent tags, and stylesheets makes it easy to take content and repurpose it in any media.

- **Translation**

  If content is converted into another format for translation, it must be reformatted when it is converted back. This can also be time consuming.

  Again, this is the issue of format being tied to content. When content is separated from format, this is no longer an issue.

- **Authors who don't always provide what is required**

  Authors don't always provide all the information that is required to create the specific output (for example, a web page) and if they do, it is not in a form that can be easily formatted.

  A unified content strategy provides authors with templates, structure frameworks (for example, DTD), and guidelines. Templates and structured frameworks prompt authors for required content. In some cases, authors cannot save unless they have included all the necessary content. This helps to ensure that the correct information is provided.

## Information technology

The Information Technology group plays an important role in selecting, managing, and deploying technology throughout the organization. To uncover technology issues, ask all interview subjects what tools they use and how effective they are. Questions about tools are included with the sample questions for each type of interview.

In addition, ask IT personnel the following:

- Is there a standard for databases? If so, what is it and why is it a standard? What is the process for changing an existing standard where appropriate or adopting a second alternative standard?
- Are there any specific product requirements (for example, Microsoft versus UNIX server)?
- Are there issues such as firewalls for remote users?
- What is the process for adopting new technology? How effective is this process?
- What is the relationship between IT and the "business"? How effective is this relationship?

## *Common IT issues*

The following list describes some issues that are common to the IT processes:

- Business units failing to include IT in their decision-making process

  Sometimes business units research and acquire new technology without IT's participation. This may result in non-standard or unsupportable technology.

  Standard purchasing practices may need to ensure that products are not purchased without the support of IT, and IT may need to educate others in the value of working with IT.

- Philosophical differences between business units and IT

  Sometimes the relationship between business units and IT can be strained with misperceptions on both sides. IT may need to work more closely with the business units to better understand their needs and to help them work within corporate constraints, and business units need to work with IT to ensure that IT understands the business needs so IT personnel can more effectively support them.

# Summary

The various phases in your content life cycle need to be identified and detailed to help you identify areas for improvement. Recognizing the issues will help you to plan and define your unified content strategy. For example, where your organization currently has "issues", you need to improve the processes and technology to eliminate these problems. Where processes and technology are working well, you want to incorporate them into the new systems and processes where appropriate. Identifying all the issues involved will help you to determine the scope and functionality of your unified content strategy, define the criteria for selection of appropriate tools, and define the processes that must be redesigned or created.

# Chapter 6

## Performing a content audit

At the heart of a unified content strategy is content. Before you can model your content—and, subsequently, unify it—you need to gain an intimate understanding of its nature and structure. During a content audit, you look at your organization's content analytically and critically, so that you can identify opportunities for reuse and the type of reuse. (Types of reuse are discussed in Chapter 2, "Fundamental concepts of reuse".)

You look for similar and identical information, as well as for information that could be similar or identical, but is currently distinct. After you see how your information is being used and reused, you can make decisions about how you might unify it.

This chapter describes what a content audit is and how to perform one; it also provides examples of content audit findings.

## What is a content audit?

A content audit, like the name implies, is an accounting of the information in your organization. However, unlike the usual associations with the word "audit"—associations that strike fear into the hearts of many taxpayers—a content audit has positive results that enable your organization to save money if your findings are implemented. The purpose of a content audit is to analyze how content is used, reused, and delivered to its various audiences. You need to understand how information—as well as the processes to create it—can be unified, eliminating the "cut and paste" method many authors employ in their attempt to unify content wherever possible.

In most traditional authoring environments, if authors want to reuse information they must:

- Look at other content in the organization to determine which information they want to reuse.
- Find the information in another document or section, or even on another server in another area of the company.
- Cut and paste the information from one section of the document to another section, or from one document to another document.
- Rewrite or reformat the reused information to fit the new context.

An attempt to unify content in this manner results in multiple (potentially inconsistent) instances of the same piece of information in the document or across documents. These instances are not linked or referenced to one another physically within the authoring or publishing tool. If the information needs to be updated, authors must first locate all instances of reuse, then update each instance separately. This can be an extremely time-consuming process, and introduces much opportunity for error and inconsistency. The content audit is intended to illustrate where there are opportunities to unify content throughout your organization; it provides the basis for your reuse strategy and modeling decisions.

# What's involved in doing a content audit?

To get started on a content audit within your organization, you need to first identify your scope, then select representative materials within that scope. The larger the scope, the more work is involved, but the greater the return on investment. For more information on calculating return on investment, refer to Chapter 3, "Assessing return on investment for a unified content strategy."

## Identifying scope of the audit

You don't have to start big; doing a content audit within one area of an organization can realize significant returns and show members of the organization in other areas how, by including their content, the organization can realize even greater returns. A technical publications group often starts an audit by looking at the content they produce to streamline their procedures and help themselves meet deadlines. During the audit, they realize that the product descriptions in the manuals are similar to the product descriptions the marketing department includes in both their printed brochures and on the external web site. As a result, the two groups get together to decide how to unify the product descriptions so both groups can use them consistently. Although the scope of your audit determines your unified content strategy, even if you start small, you can expand your decisions later on. Be aware, however, that starting small can lead you to make technology choices that may not meet your future needs. If you do start small, select tools that can expand to meet your future needs. Refer to Chapter 13, "Evaluating tools."

## Selecting representative materials

Once you've determined the scope of the audit, you need to select representative materials. Select as much content as you can, representing all the different departments included in your scope, not just the content that you create. For example, you could look at samples in the following categories: collateral (including brochures, web site, product packaging, point-of-sale materials, newsletters), press releases, technical specifications, internal support staff materials (often published on the company intranet), user manuals, quick reference cards, as well as any learning materials associated with the product.

When you're selecting materials, remember that the content audit is a comparative exercise, which means you need to compare like information. Select all the content (for example, the brochure, web site content, user guide, online help, training materials) produced for a single product or service, as well as the content produced for other similar products/services. So, you could select all the content produced for a television and compare it to see how content is used or reused. Is the product description consistent in the brochure, the user guide, and on the web site? Then, you would examine the content for other similar products, such as VCRs, DVD players, or different makes of televisions, looking for similarities and differences. Is the warranty information the same for all products? What about definitions? How similar are troubleshooting procedures for the different television sets?

## Analyzing the content

Once you have gathered together a representative sample of materials, you're ready to start "digging" into it. This is the fun part and usually involves spreading large amounts of information all over your office, walking around with a highlighter and a stack of sticky notes, highlighting your findings, and taking notes as you go. It's fun because it doesn't involve "doing" anything beyond really examining your content closely to see what it contains and how it's put together. Analyzing materials in this way is a discovery process about your content, something most organizations don't have the opportunity to do in their day-to-day work. You're not making any decisions at this point; instead, you're seeing what you have and making observations about it.

Analyzing content occurs at two levels: at the "top" level of your representative samples, followed by a more detailed examination of the content.

## Top-level analysis

A top-level analysis involves scanning various information products to find common pieces of information (for example, product descriptions, introductory information, procedures, disclaimers, topics, headings within, documents). If you have large documents that include tables of contents, you can compare the tables of contents to find similarities in chapter or section names. Such similarities in labels and headings often indicate similar or identical content within and across a documentation set. Start by spreading your information products out in front of you (or opening them all up on your computer desktop) and highlighting areas that look like they might contain similar information. When you're finished, compile your results into a table. It should look something like the example shown in Table 6.1 later in the chapter. Your table should list content category and the information product where it appears. Use an "X" to indicate that content appears in an information product. Leave the table cell empty if an information product does not appear to contain that particular content. (Note that the table usually does not represent the entire scope of the content, but only representative portions where reuse is clearly identified.)

## In-depth analysis

During the in-depth analysis, you examine the repeated information you identified during the top-level analysis. Repeated information can be as simple as copyright notices and warranty information, and as complex as whole sections of detail, particularly for product suites. Once you've found instances of repeated information to scrutinize more closely, you can lay them out in a tabular format to see them all together, at a glance. (See the examples that follow.) As you look at instances of repeated information, identify whether the content is identical or similar. If it is similar (or almost identical), which parts differ? Do the parts that differ need to differ? Are there valid reasons for differences such as product or information uniqueness? If the parts differ and there is no valid reason for the difference, identify this content as something that should be standardized for reuse in the future.

# Content audit examples

The following examples show content audit findings for five fictional companies. Each example includes a top-level analysis showing potential content reuse, as well as a small in-depth analysis showing how the company could select a portion of the content for further analysis and interpret the findings.

- Example 1 is for a medical devices company that produces blood glucose monitoring meters. Because there are several versions of the meters, the company suspects there may be similarities or inconsistencies in the information products produced for each version.

- Example 2 is for a consumer electronics company that produces products such as televisions, VCRs, DVD players, and other television accessories. They produce a great deal of marketing information and are concerned about how their product branding carries over wherever the marketing information is used. They conduct an audit to see how their information is being used on various parts of their own site, as well as on the sites of their resellers.

- Example 3 shows the procedures that various bank personnel must follow to certify a check. In this case, different groups often perform similar tasks, and the bank wants to figure out who does what and where the content overlaps. This way, role-based information can be provided to each group, reusing identical components. Accordingly, their audit focuses on role-based dynamic content.

- Example 4 shows reuse in learning materials. A business college that teaches investment courses receives feedback from students, complaining that similar information in different courses (or even in the same course) is inconsistent. The college wants to build a database of "reusable learning objects" (RLOs), so that wherever information is repeated, it is the same. In their audit, the college looks for places where the same information is used (for example, places where the same topics are covered, but with a different depth or focus), so that it can ensure the information is consistent.

- Example 5 is from the pharmaceutical industry. This industry produces a great deal of information on drug products for different audiences. Example 5 compares the physician's product information sheet with the patient's, showing how much of the information can be reused systematically.

## Example 1: Medical devices

Example 1 shows how a medical devices company compares content across information products for blood glucose monitoring meters.

### Top-level analysis

Table 6.1 represents the top-level analysis of their materials.

**Table 6.1    Comparing information products for blood glucose monitoring devices**

| Content | Information product | | | | | | | |
|---|---|---|---|---|---|---|---|---|
|  | Owner's guide | Quick reference card | Quick start guide | Press release | Web site | Brochure | Product package | Label (package insert) |
| Company logo | X | X | X | X | X | X | X | X |
| Contact information | X | X | X | X | X | X | X | X |
| Important (read the owner's guide before…) | X | X | X |  | X |  | X | X |
| Product description | X |  |  | X | X | X | X |  |
| Setting up the meter | X | X |  |  |  |  |  | X |
| Testing the meter | X |  |  |  |  |  |  | X |
| Sampling the blood | X |  | X |  |  |  |  | X |
| Inserting the test strip | X | X | X |  |  |  |  | X |
| Interpreting the results | X | X |  |  |  |  |  | X |
| Caring for your meter | X |  |  |  |  |  |  |  |
| Solving problems | X | X |  |  |  |  |  |  |

**Interpreting the findings**

The top-level analysis shows areas that warrant closer examination. For example, the company logo and contact information are used in every information product and the product description is used in all but three. In addition, a number of topics related to the setup and use of the product are repeated throughout. This top-level analysis shows the findings for just one product: the blood glucose monitoring meter. Expanding the analysis to look at other products in the same family shows that up to 80% of the content could be reused. Looking even further to other related product lines, shows additional commonality in conceptual information about the company and its products.

## In-Depth Analysis

The results of the top-level analysis are used to drive the in-depth analysis. In this case, the top-level analysis shows similar information in the setup and use of the product as shown in Table 6.2.

**Table 6.2    Analyzing content further**

| Owner's guide | Quick reference card | Quick start card |
| --- | --- | --- |
| **Step 1** | **Step 1** | **Step 1** |
| Insert the test strip. Make sure the contact bars go in end first and facing up. The meter will turn on automatically. - - - appears briefly on the display.<br><br>*Note*: The bars must be all the way into the meter to avoid an inaccurate result. | Insert the test strip. After inserted, meter turns on automatically. | Insert a test strip to turn on the meter. |
| **Step 2** | **Step 2** | **Step 2** |
| Apply the blood sample… | Apply the sample… | - - - appears on the screen. |
| | | **Step 3** |
| | | Apply the blood sample… |

### Interpreting the findings

There are subtle differences in the first two samples (Owner's guide and Quick reference card), but the third sample (Quick start card) has a different second step. Are the differences necessary or will they confuse users? Quick reference Cards provide concise information so the shorter steps are appropriate. The same holds true for the Quick start guide; however, the second step isn't really a step. The differences in the steps should be reconsidered.

## Conclusion

Although this example shows just a small portion of content, it illustrates the seemingly insignificant, yet critical, variations that can occur in content. In this case, the content would benefit from a unified strategy to ensure that each time the same information appears, it is consistent. The core steps that apply to all information products would remain the same; if some steps require supplementary information (for example, information based on user analysis), it can be "nested" within the core. (See Chapter 2 for types of reuse.) Regardless of how the core steps are supplemented, they remain consistent.

### Example 2: Consumer electronics

The following example is for a consumer electronics company that produces products such as televisions, VCRs, DVD players, and other television accessories. Their marketing information appears in many places: on the Web, in brochures, in product sheets, in manuals, and so on. Accordingly, the company is concerned about how their branding carries over wherever the marketing information is used. They conduct an audit to see how their information is being used on various parts of their own site (specifically, the e-catalog and e-commerce parts), as well as on their resellers' sites.

## Top-level analysis

Table 6.3 represents the top-level analysis of the materials for a single product: a television monitor.

**Table 6.3    Comparing information products for a television monitor**

| Content | Information product | | |
| --- | --- | --- | --- |
| | E-catalog | E-commerce | Third-party sites |
| Overview | X | X | X |
| Features | X | X | X |
| Price | X | X | X |

**Interpreting the findings**

At first glance, the e-catalog, the e-commerce content, and the third-party sites appear to contain very similar content. Closer inspection of the content, discovered during in-depth analysis, shows variations.

## In-depth analysis

The content in the overview of each information product appears similar, but closer examination, as documented in Table 6.4, reveals differences.

**Table 6.4    Analyzing the Overviews**

| E-catalog | E-commerce | Third-party sites |
| --- | --- | --- |
| XXX Television 15-inch XXX picture tube | XXX Television 15-inch XXX picture tube | Most third-party sites matched the E-commerce site, and a few matched the product catalog. |
| 3-line digital comb filter | 3-line digital comb filter | |
| Black and silver metallic cabinet | 3 colors available (Blue, Grey, White) | |
| Sleep timer (15/30/45/60/90) | 2 video inputs (1 at side) | |
| Front and rear audio/video inputs | Remote control/ sleep timer | |

Table 6.5 shows additional inconsistencies in the features information.

**Table 6.5    Analyzing the features**

| E-catalog | E-commerce | Third-party sites[1] |
|---|---|---|
| **Video features** | 3 Line Digital Comb Filter | 3-Line Digital comb filter |
| Digital Comb Filter: 3 Line | | |
| | Auto White Balance | Headphone output |
| Auto White Balance | Enhanced Audio Power (3 Watts) | Auto Channel Programming |
| Tilt Correction | Side Speaker | Multi-language display |
| Audio features | Auto Mute | |
| Audio Power: 3w | Auto Channel Programming | Favorite channel |
| Auto Mute | | V-chip parental control |
| **Convenience** | Favorite Channel (5 Channels) | Clock Timer (15/30/45/60/90) |
| Auto Channel Programming | V-Chip Parental Control | Front and rear audio/video inputs |
| Front Menu Control | Sleep Timer (15/30/45/60/90) | |
| Channel Label | Clock/Timer (2 event) | |
| Favorite Channel (5 Channels) | | |
| V-Chip Parental Control | | |
| Clock Timer (2 events) | | |
| Sleep (15/30/45/60/90) | | |

---

1 One example site only

**Interpreting the findings**

The overviews say much the same thing, yet there are subtle differences in each sample. Because the differences in content potentially dilute the branding of the product, the company must determine how they want to position the product. What are the most important aspects of the product they should present? Once they know the answer to this question, they can position the product consistently, regardless of where the information appears.

There are further variations in the content about features—content produced by the company and not by a third party. Note the differences between the e-product catalog and the e-commerce content that are shown in Table 6.6.

**Table 6.6    Analyzing further inconsistencies**

|         | E-product catalog | | E-commerce |
|---------|-------------------|-----|------------|
| Compare | Digital Comb Filter: 3 Line | vs. | 3-Line Digital Comb Filter |
| Compare | Audio Power: 3w | vs. | Enhanced Audio Power (3 Watts) |

Both examples say the same thing, so readers are getting the same information. However, the inconsistencies indicate that different people created this content, possibly two or even three people, if you count members of the product team who originally wrote the specification. This means that the work has been done at least three times at three times the cost of one person doing it. If any of these specifications change, the content must be found and changed in three places, which not only increases costs, but introduces the possibility of error. Additionally, if this content is translated to other languages it must be translated each time it appears, increasing the translation costs significantly.

Furthermore, although you cannot directly control what another company does with your information, it is beneficial to provide electronic content to everyone who needs it. That way, third parties can ensure they have consistent and up-to-date information in their materials; after all, even though consumers often buy the product from a third party, the quality of the information reflects on the supplier—in this case, the consumer electronics company. Providing electronic content also helps third parties to reduce their costs, so they may be happier to promote your product.

## Conclusion

The preceding analysis is of a small piece of content, but it points out a number of inconsistencies. Further content analysis shows that the differences are common across all the information products. In addition to identifying branding issues, the results of this audit show that the increasing number of content variations can result in significant costs to the organization.

## Example 3: Banking institution

A banking institution has thousands of policies and procedures that branch staff use to conduct their business. Sometimes only one staff member performs a task; sometimes multiple staff members perform the same task or portions of the task. The bank wants to figure out who does what and where the content overlaps, so they can provide dynamic role-based content to each group, reusing identical components. Their top-level analysis shows opportunities for reuse in many procedures, so they chose one to examine more closely—the procedure to certify a check.

## In-depth analysis

Three different groups can perform the task to certify a check (the side counter person, the teller, and the supervisor). Their procedures are shown in Table 6.7.

**Table 6.7　Comparing procedures to certify a check**

| Side counter | Teller | Supervisor |
|---|---|---|
| **Purpose:** To provide a certified check to customers in less than five minutes. | **Purpose:** To provide a certified check to customers in less than five minutes. | **Purpose:** To provide a certified check to customers in less than five minutes. |
| Where possible, this process should be perceived as simple and fast for the customer. | | Where possible, this process should be perceived as simple and fast for the customer. |
| 1. Ask for personal identification to ensure the identity of the customer. | 1. Check the customer's personal identification to verify identity. | |

*continues* ▶

**Table 6.7    Continued**

| Side counter | Teller | Supervisor |
|---|---|---|
| Use SystemXYZ to determine that there are sufficient funds in the account and that no future dated transactions are pending. | Use SystemXYZ to determine that there are sufficient funds in the account and that no future dated transactions are pending. | |
| 2. Verify the customer has sufficient funds in the account. | 2. Check the balance of the customer's account to verify he has sufficient funds. | |
| 3. Use certified check form CQ123 and complete the following:<br><br>&bull; Receiver<br>&bull; Customer<br>&bull; Customer account<br>&bull; Check amount | 3. Use certified check form CQ123 and complete the following:<br><br>&bull; Receiver<br>&bull; Customer<br>&bull; Customer account<br>&bull; Check amount | |
| 4. Use the check embosser to impress the amount onto the form. | 4. Emboss the amount of the check with the check embosser. | |
| 5. If the amount is over $1000, have your supervisor verify the transaction. | 5. If the amount is over $1000, have your supervisor verify the transaction. | |
| | | When a certified check is brought to you for verification it is important to verify all the details to avoid fraud.<br><br>1. Verify the identity of the customer and the certified check details. |
| 6. Withdraw the funds from the account. | 6. Withdraw the funds from the account. | |
| 7. Provide the customer with the certified check and a copy of the transaction. | 7. Provide the customer with the certified check and a copy of the transaction. | |

### Interpreting the findings

The procedures for the side counter person and the teller are very similar; steps 1, 2, and 4 are worded slightly differently, and steps 3, 5, 6, and 7 are identical. Steps 1, 2, and 4 could easily be made identical, making the entire procedure the same for both the side counter and teller. The procedure for the supervisor is quite different, but the title and purpose are the same.

## Conclusion

Because of their similarities, the procedures could be unified to a single procedure for the teller and the side counter person. The procedure for the supervisor could reuse content from this unified procedure. Analysis of other bank procedures reveals similar patterns. Based on their audit findings, the bank can be confident in creating dynamic content, specific to roles.

### Example 4: Learning materials

A business college teaches classes in investment strategies, targeted to both practitioners seeking further education or accreditation in financial planning, as well as people who just want more information about their own investment planning. After receiving a number of student feedback forms complaining about inconsistencies in the content, the college decided to conduct an audit of their materials, in an attempt to unify common information. The college wants to build a database of "reusable learning objects" so that wherever information is repeated, it is the same. Their audit focuses on looking for places where the same information is used so that they can ensure it is consistent.

## Top-level analysis

A top-level analysis of four courses shows that much content is repeated in a number of different course textbooks:

**Table 6.8   Comparing course content**

| Content | Found in |
|---|---|
| Income Tax Planning | Course 1  ch. 7 |
|  | Course 2  entire course |
|  | Course 3  ch. 4 |
|  | Course 4  ch. 5 |

*continues* ▶

**Table 6.8    Continued**

| Content | Found in |
| --- | --- |
| Investment Strategies | Course 1  ch. 10 |
| | Course 2  ch. 6 |
| | Course 3  ch. 8 |
| | Course 4  entire course |
| Retirement Planning | Course 1  entire course |
| | Course 2  ch. 3 |
| | Course 3  ch. 2 |
| | Course 4  ch. 7 |
| Wills and Estates | Course 1  ch. 13 |
| | Course 2  ch. 8 |
| | Course 3  entire course |
| | Course 4  ch. 8 |

**Interpreting the findings**

The top-level analysis indicates that there is much repetition of certain subject areas throughout the different courses, and although the focus and the level of detail may be different from course to course, content should be examined more closely to determine whether there are inconsistencies, and to see whether there are similarities that could potentially be unified.

## In-depth analysis

A more in-depth analysis of the topics on investment strategies shows similarities in the overviews of Course 2, which touches on investment strategies, and Course 4, whose entire focus is investing. Table 6.9 outlines the similarities.

**Table 6.9    Analyzing Course Content Further**

| Course 2 topics | Course 4 topics |
| --- | --- |
| The investment planning process | An overview of investment planning |
| Taxable and non-taxable investments | High risk versus low risk investments |
| When to invest for optimum tax benefits | Investing to reduce taxes |
| Tax on investment income | How much to invest and when |
| | Sources of investment income |

Note that many of the topics covered in Course 2 are similar to the topics in Course 4—similar enough that they should be compared to see whether they are inconsistent, where they differ, where they should differ, and where they are alike.

### Interpreting the findings

Closer examination of each topic shows that much of the content in "investing to reduce taxes" and "taxable and non-taxable investments" is similar. This is also the case for "how much to invest and when" and "when to invest for optimum tax benefits." The information on the investment planning, though, is inconsistent.

## Conclusion

The findings in both the top-level and in-depth analyses show numerous opportunities for the college to reuse content as well as correct inconsistencies. Correcting discrepancies is critical in learning materials; students learn information one way, then when they encounter an inconsistency in a future course (or sometimes even the same course), they have to either figure out which version is correct or deal with conflicting information. This is especially critical in an e-learning environment where the materials themselves become the instructor; students often don't have another source to help them figure out what's wrong, or even to discover that something might be wrong. Some students may not notice inconsistencies, and may learn incorrect information.

After discrepancies are corrected, information can be chunked into RLOs and reused in whichever course is appropriate. If more detail is required to teach the same topic in a more advanced course or to accommodate different learning objectives, information can be added to the RLO, each level of detail comprising another RLO. Wherever the "core" RLO is used, however, it is consistent.

### Example 5: Pharmaceutical product label

The pharmaceutical industry produces masses of information on new drug products for different audiences: product information sheets for regulatory agencies (such as the U.S. Food and Drug Administration) and doctors, and pamphlets, brochures, and information inserts for patients. Doctors use the product information sheets, also known as labels, to learn the uses for the drug and how to prescribe and administer the treatments. The information includes indications (conditions that the drug will alleviate), dosages, warnings, and so on. In addition, there are different information sheets for patients. These are the pamphlets, brochures, and information inserts you find in the drug packaging when you purchase the product.

## Top-level analysis

A comparison between the table of contents for a physician's product information sheet and a patient's information insert for an asthma medication shows numerous similarities. Figure 6.1 shows the tables of contents for both samples and the content relationship between the two.

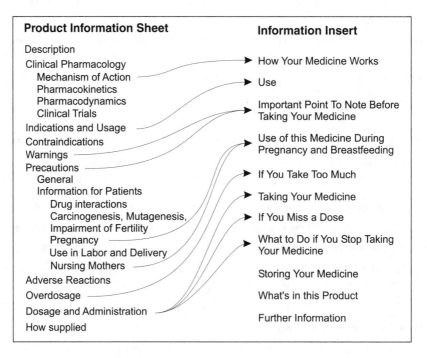

**Figure 6.1   A comparison of product and patient information.**

### Interpreting the findings

The headings provided for physician and patient are obviously different, but all the content in the patient's information sheet appears in the physician's information sheet as well, indicating that much of the information can be reused. The difference is primarily in the organization of content. In addition, although the content is the same, the language in the patient information sheet has been simplified to increase readability.

## Conclusion

This example clearly indicates there are a number of opportunities for paragraph reuse. A unified content strategy would enable the content to be systematically reused in alternate structures. Once the content appears in alternate structures, authors can create derivative versions of the original to increase readability for the patient version. Reusing content in this manner ensures it is the same and accurate in all locations; also, if the source content changes, the derivative content authors are notified of the change so they can maintain consistency and accuracy in their derivative versions.

# Building a reuse map

While you are analyzing your content, it's a good idea to build a reuse map. A reuse map identifies which elements of your content are reusable, where they are reusable, and whether they should be reused identically or derivatively. The person responsible for setting up your content management system will use the map to set up the reuse logic. For now, the reuse map serves to keep track of potential reuse and it will be refined further when you create your information models (see Chapter 8, "Information modeling"). The map uses the symbols shown in Table 6.10 to indicate the types of reuse.

**Table 6.10   Reuse symbols**

| Reuse | Symbol |
| --- | --- |
| Identical | I |
| Derivative | D |
| Source[2] | S |

2 Note that "Source" is somewhat arbitrary. In an audit, it is simply the first document to which you compare other documents. Later, when you create content, it is the first instance of the content. Your processes may define which content should be created first and therefore define your source.

For example, the reuse map for the medical devices example would look like the one shown in Table 6.11.

**Table 6.11    Reuse map for blood glucose monitoring devices**

| Content | Owner's guide | Quick reference card | Quick start | Press release guide | Web site | Brochure | Product package | Label (package insert) |
|---|---|---|---|---|---|---|---|---|
| Company logo | I | I | I | I | I | I | I | I | |
| Contact information | I | I | I | I | I | I | I | I | |
| Important (read the owner's guide before…) | I | I | I | | I | | | I | I |
| Product description | D | | | D | I | S | D | |
| Setting up the meter | S | D | | | | | | D |
| Testing the meter | S | | | | | | | D |
| Sampling the blood | S | | D | | | | | D |
| Inserting the test strip | S | D | D | | | | | D |
| Interpreting the results | S | D | | | | | | D |
| Caring for your meter | S | | | | | | | |
| Solving problems | S | D | | | D | | | |

## Identifying opportunities for reuse

As shown in the previous examples, a content audit can help you determine how to reuse content across a number of different information products. Where content is different, does it have to be different? Can information that is similar be made identical? Are there reasons for it being similar as opposed to identical (product name, for example)? Should content in one media be identical to most of the content in another media (for example, on paper versus on the Web)? How will your information products be used and are there valid reasons to distinguish them from each other (for example, to accommodate differences in users and their needs)? These are the types of questions that you need to answer as you develop an intimate understanding of the content in your information products.

# What comes after the audit?

Once you've done a thorough, critical analysis of your content and drawn up a reuse map, do the following:

- Summarize your findings in an analysis report, which contains your observations about the content and what you learned about your current content life cycle. (See Chapter 5, "Analyzing the content life cycle.") You use the analysis report to confirm your findings with other members of your team (whose content you may have analyzed during the audit). You also present it to others in your organization whose support you will need to move ahead with your unified content strategy.

- Document your recommendations and your plan for a unified content strategy. Include information on the new content life cycle, because it will be supported by a unified content strategy. (See Chapter 7, "Envisioning the unified content life cycle.") Again, present your report to others in your organization whose support or approval you will need as you move forward with a unified content strategy. For example, you may need to request additional funds—beyond your established budget—for some of the research and design.

### Addressing usability issues

Beyond unifying content and identifying reuse, a thorough content audit can also identify usability issues, such as where information is found, what it is called, and even whether an information product contains a certain type of information that other similar information products do. As users become experienced with your information products, they expect information to be presented in a certain way. When their expectations are not met, they become frustrated and often abandon the information completely.

Typical usability issues that are discovered during a content audit include:

- Inconsistent structure

  Similar types of information are often structured differently from document to document, and even within the same document. Procedures may be in numbered steps, bulleted lists, step/action tables, or step/action/result tables. Certain types of information are best presented in a certain way and the content—combined with users' needs—should always dictate the structure. Once the structure is defined, that same structure should be used consistently. So, if you determine that based on your type of content, a step/action/result table is the best way to present procedures, then that structure should be used consistently, not only enabling reuse, but enhancing usability. Similar structures also help users to scan information to find the content they need quickly; they learn to recognize it based on its structure. When structure varies, users lose this ability.

- Inconsistent types or amounts of information contained in similar elements

  When inconsistent amounts of information are contained in similar elements, users lose their ability to know what to expect. The following samples show different amounts of information provided in a definition of Marsala on a web site about cooking. In a recipe for Chicken Marsala, a link to a definition of Marsala reads:

  *Imported from Sicily and made from local grapes, Marsala is Italy's most famous fortified wine. It has a rich, smoky flavor that can range from sweet to dry. Sweet Marsala is used as a dessert wine, as well as to flavor desserts such as zabaglione. Dry marsala makes an excellent aperitif. There are also special marsala blends with added ingredients such as cream, eggs, and almonds.*

  A definition of Marsala in the wine dictionary on the same site reads:

  *Marsala wines come in various styles—secco (dry), semisecco (semisweet), and dolce (sweet). Dry Marsalas are best served as aperitifs, whereas many of the semisweet and sweet styles are best as dessert wines. The official terms of ambra (amber), oro (gold), and rubino (ruby) are optional additional descriptions for any of the Marsala wine's quality levels. Ambra and oro describe Marsala wines made from white grapes. The addition of cotto is not allowed in the ambra versions. Ambra wines darken as they age, turning from the paler yellowish hues, to gold, to amber. The term "rubino" describes Marsala wines made from red grapes. Cremevo is a wine made from 80% Marsala and other flavorings such as coffee or egg and was once called Marsala Speciali.*

  Although the additional details may be useful in the dictionary, they are not necessary in the recipe. Furthermore, readers may be confused by finding two different definitions for the same item. Layering the definition to include a shorter version in the recipe, but a longer one in the dictionary (building on the shorter version), would make the definition more usable and reusable.

Additional usability issues that often turn up in a content audit include:

- Inconsistent terminology

- Excessive information

- Ineffective labeling

- Content that is incongruent with its stated purpose

As you analyze your content, look for issues that may decrease its usability and develop usability criteria that are reflected in the information model. The information model will identify how information must be structured and what each information product must contain, so information products will become consistent and hence, usable. Writing guidelines contained in the model will also help you to ensure content is written in a way that best suits users' needs, as determined in user interviews as well as in iterative usability assessments.

## Summary

Doing a thorough content audit is critical to implementing a reuse strategy because it tells you how content is currently being used, how it could be reused, and what needs to be done to create effective unified content.

- Establish the scope of the audit, remembering to look beyond one document set. Look at content across media and across content areas to see the potential for reuse.

- Select representative samples of your content, based on the scope of your project.

- Examine a document's TOCs and top-level structure for structural or heading similarities so you can determine where to look further.

- Look at selected samples closely, making observations about how information is used and how it could be reused. Decide whether differences are necessary, what information should be unique, and what information must be consistent.

- Draw up a reuse map that illustrates potential reuse of information elements, as well as the type of reuse.

# Chapter 7

# Envisioning your unified content life cycle

As described in the previous chapters, to prepare for a unified content strategy you first need to identify organizational goals and issues, examine your current content life cycle, and analyze your existing and published content to determine potential reuse. Armed with your findings, you can envision a new content life cycle that provides the basis for a unified content strategy, as well as the basis for selecting tools.

Your new content life cycle describes the processes as you would like to see them implemented and the ways in which both tools and processes will help you to address any issues you have identified.

Ideally, you should create your unified content life cycle before you begin the content design process and certainly before you select your tools. Too often organizations design content and select tools before they have figured out how processes and tools will support the new content life cycle. Premature content design and tool selection may result in processes and technology that do not meet your needs or that too quickly become obsolete.

Designing your unified content life cycle can be difficult unless you understand what is involved in the design process and the different options the tools offer. This chapter describes some of the common issues uncovered during the initial analyses of issues and content and identifies where those issues should be addressed in a new content life cycle. It also shows two sample unified content life cycles—one for an entire enterprise and one for a department—and points out the differences between the two. Consider reading Part III, "Design," and Part IV, "Tools and technologies," in conjunction with this chapter. They will help you to understand all the possibilities and issues associated with a unified content life cycle and assist you in understanding the examples included in this chapter.

## Addressing issues

Your new content life cycle should address challenges in your organization issues that you identified during your analyses of processes and content. Table 7.1 shows some common issues (see Chapter 5, "Analyzing the content life cycle") their requirements in a unified content strategy, and the process in the unified content life cycle phase where the issue should be addressed. Issues are grouped into categories, such as issues related to content use, content authoring, localization, and so on.

**Table 7.1     Identifying how issues can be addressed**

| Issue | Requirements | Phase and process |
|---|---|---|
| **Content use** | | |
| Too much detail/ too little detail | Re-evaluate requirements and rewrite materials accordingly. | Create (Authoring) |
| | Provide customized content (specific to content user needs). | |
| | Provide dynamic content (specific to content user needs). | |
| Difficult to understand | Re-evaluate requirements and rewrite materials accordingly. | |
| | Provide customized content (specific to content user needs). | |
| | Provide dynamic content (specific to content user needs). | |
| Content users are unable to find content | Categorize content in multiple ways for multiple access points. | Create (Authoring) |
| | Add metadata to all content (aids in retrieval). | |
| **Content authoring** | | |
| Different authoring tools don't interact well | Consider XML as the authoring language (excellent exchange language). | Create (Authoring) |

*continues* ▶

**Table 7.1    Continued**

| Issue | Requirements | Phase and process |
|---|---|---|
| Hard-to-reuse content | Ensure all authoring tools use enterprise-wide standard templates, style tags, and metadata (facilitates content interchange). | Create (Authoring) |
| Authors are unable to find information | Store content in a single repository or ensure all content can be shared among multiple repositories (simplifies access). | Manage (Workflow)<br><br>Create (Authoring) |
| | Consider systematic reuse (system finds the content for the author). | |
| | Develop better organizational schemes and categorization for internal information storage. | |
| Ongoing change to content is difficult to manage | Implement change management processes (regulates how and when change can occur). | Manage (Workflow) |
| | Implement workflow (standardizes processes for where change can occur). | |
| | Ensure the CMS can track all versions of content and their associated relationships (facilitates change to multiple elements). | |
| Lifespan of a document is decreasing | Create content in modules (facilitates fast updates). | Create (Authoring) |

| Issue | Requirements | Phase and process |
|---|---|---|
| | Create a document structure that can be modified easily (facilitates recon-figuration). | |
| **Translation** | | |
| Ongoing changes to content | Implement change management processes (regulates how and when change can occur). | Create (Localization) |
| | Provide only changed elements to the translator (focuses change). | |
| Use of English is inconsistent | Use standardized English (simplifies content). | Create (Planning) |
| Insufficient reviewers | Quantity: Route only changed/new content to reviewers (fewer can do more). | Manage (Workflow) |
| | Quality: Route specific content to specific reviewers, based on internal appropriateness guidelines. | |
| Incompatible formats | Consider XML as the authoring language (excellent exchange language). | Create (Authoring) |
| | Ensure all authoring tools use enterprise-standard templates, style tags, and metadata (facilitates conversion). | |

*continues* ▶

**Table 7.1    Continued**

| Issue | Requirements | Phase and process |
|---|---|---|
| **Global requirements** | | |
| Software access is very slow for authors in other countries | Ensure the CMS is Internet accessible (speeds up access). | Manage (Workflow) |
| | If you are using XML, ensure you are using an XML-native content management system (speeds up access). | |
| Multi-language requirements | Ensure the CMS can support multiple languages (display content in appropriate language and provide a language-specific interface). | Create (Authoring)<br><br>Manage (Workflow) |
| Authors often have to rework the original materials (for example, to reflect different cultural or safety requirements) | Ensure authoring templates reflect global requirements | Create (Design)<br><br>Manage (Workflow) |
| | Ensure the CMS supports tracking of content relationships (enables derivative reuse). | |
| | Use systematic reuse to automatically replace content (for example, replace "NTSC" with "PAL" or replace "December 30 with "30 December"). | |
| **Review** | | |
| Changes continue to occur after review and sign-off | Implement change management (regulates how and when change can occur). | Manage (Workflow) |

| Issue | Requirements | Phase and process |
|---|---|---|
| The review task is not recognized as part of the job | Implement workflow (explicitly identifies review as a task). | Manage (Workflow) |
| Redundant reviews | Implement change management processes (regulates how and when change can occur). | Manage (Workflow) |
| | Route only changed/new content to reviewers (ensures approved content is not re-reviewed, thereby reducing workload). | |
| Inability to verify change | Provide the ability to look at multiple versions of content and "redlined" content (facilitates comparison of content). | Review |
| **Publication and delivery** | | |
| Content must be reformatted for different media or locales | Consider using XML as the authoring language (facilitates publishing to multiple media). | Create (Authoring) |
| | Ensure all authoring tools use enterprise-standard templates, style tags, and metadata (facilitates conversion). | |
| Content must be reformatted for different locales | Consider using XML as the authoring language (facilitates conversion). | Create (Authoring) |
| | Ensure all authoring tools use enterprise-standard templates, style tags, and metadata (facilitates conversion). | |

*continues* ▶

**Table 7.1    Continued**

| Issue | Requirements | Phase and process |
|---|---|---|
| Authors don't always provide what's needed | Ensure authors only use authoring templates or standardized stylesheets to create content (provides authoring guidance).<br><br>Consider providing a style guide to assist authors in determining what they should provide (provides authoring guidance). | Create (Authoring) |

## Sample unified content life cycles

A unified content strategy can be implemented in a number of ways, depending on the needs of the organization. No two organizations have the same needs, the same budget, the same goals, or the same culture. Further, companies change over time. Everything you have discovered about your company, your goals, and your issues is used to design a unified content strategy that will work for you.

This section describes two sample unified content life cycles, representing how two different companies address their particular issues. One sample illustrates the content life cycle for an enterprise, whereas the other example illustrates the life cycle for a department. Each sample includes a description of how the company decided to address certain issues, followed by an explanation of the differences. Note, however, that there is no reason why the department could not have made the same decisions as the enterprise or vice versa; these examples are just illustrative of two different sets of decisions.

## Background

Envigor creates fitness products. They have discovered that they can reuse content across many content creation areas (such as marketing, sales, documentation, and training) and across many media (such as paper, web, and wireless). They have been experiencing problems with consistency that have resulted in numerous customer calls and one lawsuit. Their customers have many different requirements and the current information frustrates them because it doesn't always address their needs.

Envigor has chosen to move to XML, which will give them a lot of control over their content and help to ensure consistency. They have also decided to implement a content management system that will provide standard content management functionality (access control, version control workflow and check-in, check-out). To address the issues of content consistency, they plan to implement systematic reuse so that content is consistent wherever it is used and appears wherever it should appear. To support customers' requirements for customized content, Envigor plans to offer dynamic content through a portal. They've also decided to implement workflow to move content through the life cycle efficiently.

CreateSoft has many different software product suites, and consequently, a great deal of supporting product information. In their analysis, they discover an opportunity to reuse content within a set of supporting product information and among products in a product suite. They have had some customer complaints about the quality of the materials, but their major issue is keeping up with the ever-increasing number of products and the rapid changes that must be implemented when products are reconfigured. In the past, authors have occasionally been the cause of a delayed shipment of product because the supporting materials weren't ready on time, even with the authors working overtime to keep up with the workload. In addition, the cost of translation has been growing astronomically and they must bring the costs down.

Recognizing that they have a tight budget, CreateSoft has decided to stay with their current desktop publishing tools, which they are pretty happy with, but add a content management system to help them manage and distribute their content better. This means that they will retain much of what they already have, but augment their processes with the addition of a content management system.

## Comparing the life cycles

Tables 7.2–7.5 illustrate how Envigor and CreateSoft envision their unified content life cycles. Each table represents one of the major phases. The companies' visions are provided side by side in the tables to enable a comparison between the different functionalities, and the differences are explained.

## *Create*

The content creation phase consists of planning, design, authoring, and revision. Because Envigor is implementing an XML-based solution, the content creation process is supported by models, a DTD, and authoring templates and stylesheets. For CreateSoft, it is supported by models and stylesheets. The content creation processes for each company are described in Table 7.2, with an explanation of the differences.

**Table 7.2    Create**

| Envigor | CreateSoft | Understanding the differences |
|---|---|---|
| **Planning** A project manager will be assigned to manage all aspects of a new product release. The project manager will be responsible for identifying the information products required. An inter-departmental team will define the content requirements for each information product, including what content is to be created, what content is to be reused, and who is responsible for creating the source content. The inter-departmental team will base these decisions on what content will most effectively meet the needs of the business and the content users. | A senior writer will be assigned the role of team leader for a product document suite. Authors will be assigned to the team leader, with each author responsible for a particular aspect of the product suite. Authors will be responsible for creating content for multiple information products and multiple media delivery. The senior writer will define the content requirements for each information product, including what content is to be created, what content is to be reused, | Envigor is integrating the content creation process across a number of existing departments. This requires an inter-departmental team to redefine processes, roles, and deliverables. CreateSoft is implementing content management within an existing department. This requires a knowledgeable individual within the department; a senior writer to redefine processes, roles, and deliverables. |

| Envigor | CreateSoft | Understanding the differences |
|---|---|---|
| | and who is responsible for creating the source content. The senior writer will base these decisions on what content will most effectively meet the needs of the business and the content users. | |
| **Design** Design includes models, DTD, authoring templates, visual design, and stylesheets. | Design includes models and revision of the existing stylesheets to support the models. | Envigor has to design the models, authoring templates, the DTD, and stylesheets. They have chosen to modify the existing visual design. CreateSoft has to design their models, but they already have existing stylesheets and visual design. |
| **Modeling** An information architect (see Chapter 21, "Managing change") will be responsible for creating the information models. | A senior writer will take on the role of an information architect and will be responsible for creating the information models. The information architect will work with the stylesheet designer to ensure that the stylesheets reflect the models. | Both companies must model their content. Envigor has decided to create a new position for an information architect to assist in the information modeling process, whereas CreateSoft has decided to have one of their senior writers take on the role of the information architect. |

*continues* ▶

**Table 7.2   Continued**

| Envigor | CreateSoft | Understanding the differences |
|---------|------------|-------------------------------|
| | | CreateSoft is keeping its traditional authoring tools, which use stylesheets. The stylesheets must be modified to reflect the models. |
| **DTD** | | |
| An information technologist will develop the DTD based on the information models. | Not applicable. | XML requires a DTD. Envigor is using XML, so their models must be implemented in a DTD. |
| **Authoring templates** | | |
| Authoring templates support the information product models and the authoring requirements. An authoring template is a predefined set of tags that matches the information model for a specific information product as well as the DTD, but provides more guidance than a standard DTD structure.<br><br>A dynamic authoring template will also be provided that allows authors to select from a number of optional elements to create a configurable template. | Not applicable in this scenario. See "Visual Design and Stylesheets," in this table. | Envigor has decided to provide authoring templates to provide a guided interface for authoring. Note, however, that authoring templates are not required with XML, but they are nice to have.<br><br>CreateSoft has decided not to provide authoring templates because they are not easily supported with traditional authoring tools. |

| Envigor | CreateSoft | Understanding the differences |
| --- | --- | --- |
| Because Envigor is using systematic reuse, the template will be automatically populated with existing reusable content. | | |
| The template will provide authors with the basic structural elements for the model to which they are writing, as well as instructions about how to use the template and how to write the content effectively. | | |
| Authoring templates will be controlled (locked) so that authors cannot make changes to them. Changes to templates will follow the same process for change control as will content. | | |

### Visual design and style sheets

| | | |
| --- | --- | --- |
| A layout specialist will be responsible for creating the visual design to support each information product model. | The models will change how content is created, but not how content is displayed, so the visual design will remain unchanged at this time. | Envigor is revisiting its visual design, whereas CreateSoft is not. Envigor is adopting new authoring tools, so stylesheets must be created to support the visual design and models. |

*continues* ▶

**Table 7.2    Continued**

| Envigor | CreateSoft | Understanding the differences |
|---------|------------|-------------------------------|
| An information technologist will convert the visual design to a stylesheet. Stylesheets automatically format the content created in the authoring templates for any designated media. Stylesheets will be created for each designated media. | The existing stylesheets will be modified to reflect the new models. | CreateSoft is continuing to use its traditional authoring tools with existing stylesheets. However, the stylesheets must be modified to match the models. |

**Content authoring**

| Envigor | CreateSoft | Understanding the differences |
|---------|------------|-------------------------------|
| Authoring involves creating new content or reusing existing content. The authoring process is supported through systematic reuse, a clear reuse strategy, and authoring templates. | Authoring involves creating new content or reusing existing content. The authoring process is supported through opportunistic reuse, a clear reuse strategy, and a style guide. | Both companies provide a clear reuse strategy to assist authors in creating effective content. Envigor has chosen to use systematic reuse to help ensure consistency and to support authors in the content creation process. Guidelines for authors will be included in the authoring templates. CreateSoft has chosen to use opportunistic reuse because authors are very familiar with the content and the opportunities for reuse. Guidelines will be included in a style guide. |

| Envigor | CreateSoft | Understanding the differences |
|---------|------------|------------------------------|

**Create new content/reuse content**

Before beginning to create content, authors will select an authoring template and identify the subject of the content (for example, a specific product). The content management system will search for existing information elements that are valid for the template and the subject. It then pre-populates (systematic reuse) appropriate content.

Authors can either keep the automatically populated content or they can choose to remove it (unless the content is identified as mandatory). If authors keep the reusable content, they can retain it untouched or modify it to create derivative content (unless the reusable content element is locked). Reusable content that is mandatory or locked can be modified only by its owner or a supervisor.

Authors can also use the search tool contained within the content management system and retrieve appropriate

Authors select the appropriate stylesheet based on the guidelines in the style guide. They will use the reuse maps also contained in the style guide to determine whether reusable text should already exist for the materials they are creating.

If reusable content exists, authors will use the search tool contained within the content management system to search and retrieve appropriate elements (opportunistic reuse). They can search using text or phrases contained in the reusable element (full text search) and use metadata to narrow the search to specifically the type of information they are looking for (for example, a product description or a procedure).

Authors will be educated on the structure and

Envigor has selected XML (structured authoring tools) and authoring templates, whereas CreateSoft is using traditional authoring tools and a style guide.

Envigor has selected systematic reuse.

Systematic reuse is planned reuse; authors do not need to know an element exists and then search to find it.

CreateSoft has selected opportunistic reuse. Opportunistic reuse requires authors to know an element exists and find and retrieve the appropriate element.

*continues* ▶

**Table 7.2    Continued**

| Envigor | CreateSoft | Understanding the differences |
|---|---|---|
| elements (opportunistic reuse). They can search using text or phrases contained in the reusable element (full text search) and use metadata to narrow the search to specifically the type of information they are looking for (for example, a product description or a procedure).<br><br>Authors are then responsible for completing all the components of the template that are incomplete. If no reusable text exists, the content they create will become the first occurrence of content that can be reused in other templates. | organization of content in the content management system to make it easier for them to effectively search for content.<br><br>After the reusable content has been retrieved, authors link it to their document. Authors are then responsible for completing all the components that are incomplete. If no reusable text exists, the content they create will become the first occurrence of content that can then be reused in other documents where appropriate. Using the style guide for guidance, they will create content based on the models. | |

| Envigor | CreateSoft | Understanding the differences |
|---|---|---|

**Add metadata**

Wherever possible, metadata will be automatically applied to the content based on the authoring template and DTD, relieving the authors of having to manually add it. Metadata applied to a higher level of a document (for example, a section or chapter) will be automatically applied to (inherited by) all the sub-elements. As much metadata as possible will be added automatically, based on the context of the element, the template, and the subject of the content.

Authors will apply some metadata, such as information about the status of the content (for example, whether it is ready for review), as well as metadata that the CMS cannot determine automatically.

To apply metadata to an element, authors will select from a list of predefined values for each type of metadata. These values are defined during the design phase. There will be some

Wherever possible, metadata will be automatically applied to the content when it is checked into the content management system, based on the stylesheet structure map, relieving the authors of having to manually add metadata. Metadata applied to a higher level of a document (for example, a section or chapter) will be automatically applied to (inherited by) all the sub-elements. As much metadata as possible will be added automatically based on the context of the element, the template, and the subject of the content.

Authors will apply some metadata, such as information about the status of the content (for example, with it is ready for review), as well as metadata that the CMS cannot

Envigor is using an XML-based system, so metadata can be added at the authoring stage.

CreateSoft is using a traditional authoring environment integrated with a CMS, so metadata is added as the content is checked in.

*continues* ▶

**Table 7.2   Continued**

| Envigor | CreateSoft | Understanding the differences |
|---|---|---|
| metadata fields that allow authors to enter their own metadata; however, the information architect will define the majority of metadata in advance. | determine automatically. <br><br> To apply metadata to an element, authors will select from a list of predefined values for each type of metadata. These values are defined during the design phase. There will be some metadata fields that allow authors to enter their own metadata; however, the information architect will define the majority of metadata in advance. | |
| **Supporting authors** <br> The new system and associated processes will assist authors in effectively creating and managing content. <br><br> Using the authoring template, authors are prompted to fill in the content as the structure specifies. The authoring template provides writing guidelines that show how an element should be written or structured. | The new system and associated processes will assist authors in effectively creating and managing content. <br><br> A style guide provides authors with detailed guidance about how to write to the models and which templates to select. A reuse map indicates common areas of reuse to | Envigor has chosen to use systematic reuse to help ensure consistency and to support authors in the content creation process. Guidelines will be included in the authoring templates. <br><br> CreateSoft has chosen to use opportunistic reuse because authors are very familiar with the content and the opportunities for reuse. Because they are not |

| Envigor | CreateSoft | Understanding the differences |
|---|---|---|
| If authors require flexibility, alternate elements can be provided to select from. However, after an element is selected, authors will still be prompted through the process of creating consistent structured content for that element. | assist authors in determining whether reusable content already exists. The models are documented in the style guide. The style guide provides guidance about how to follow the model and about which style tags to use to write to the model. | using XML and authoring templates, guidelines will be included in a style guide. |

**Translation**

| | | |
|---|---|---|
| The content management system will be integrated directly with the memory translation tool. Existing translated content will be automatically inserted (systematic reuse) into the document, making it clear that content does not have to be retranslated. The entire document will be supplied to translators as a PDF file, so they can see the components to be translated in the context of the whole. However, only the elements requiring translation will be sent to the translator. | To assist in translation, redlining (text is marked with change bars to indicate what has changed) will be used to indicate where content has been changed since the last translation. | The combination of systematic reuse and an integrated memory translation tool make it possible for Envigor to automatically update or populate documents to be translated with existing translated content (for example, reusable content that has already been translated). CreateSoft has not chosen to integrate the memory translation tool in the content management system. They will use redlining to assist in change identification. |

*continues* ▶

**Table 7.2    Continued**

| Envigor | CreateSoft | Understanding the differences |
|---|---|---|
| When the source language content receives final approval, the component will be automatically routed to the translator for translation. After content has been translated, any changes to the source language content will automatically generate a workflow identifier to identify that this content must be retranslated. | | |

**Revise/edit content**

| | | |
|---|---|---|
| Authors can revise or edit the content they own at any time while content is in draft mode. However, after content has been approved it cannot be edited without management permission. Editors can edit only the content they have permission to access, and reviewers cannot directly edit content, only add comments to content. | | Both companies have chosen to implement the same revision and editing process. |

| Envigor | CreateSoft | Understanding the differences |
|---|---|---|
| To reduce the number of reviews necessary for approval, continuous editing or revision of content is not encouraged after it moves into the review/approval phase. Same as Envigor | | |

## Review

The review phase consists of reviewing and approving content. Envigor has chosen to use workflow to support the review process. CreateSoft has chosen not to implement workflow in the first phase of their unified content strategy. The review processes for each company are described in Table 7.3, with an explanation of the differences.

**Table 7.3   Review**

| Envigor | CreateSoft | Understanding the differences |
|---|---|---|
| **Review** | | |
| Content can be reviewed and/or edited as soon as authors consider it ready for review. Through workflow, reviewers will be notified that content is ready for review. Reviewers can annotate the content with comments. Reviewers can compare the new or revised element against previous versions of the element. By comparing versions, | Authors can send a complete document or any portion of the document for review. Reviewers can annotate the PDF version of the content. Reviewers can compare the new or revised element against previous versions of the element. By comparing versions, reviewers will be able to ensure the changes they | Workflow enables Envigor to automatically route the content to reviewers when it is ready for review. CreateSoft authors manually route content to reviewers and identify breakdowns in the process (for example, reviewers on vacation or insufficient review resources). |

*continues* ▶

**Table 7.3    Continued**

| Envigor | CreateSoft | Understanding the differences |
|---|---|---|
| reviewers will be able to ensure the changes they requested have been included and that review comments have been integrated properly. | requested have been included and that review comments have been integrated properly. | |
| If a reviewer is unavailable, or insufficient reviewers are available to complete all reviews, the workflow system will route content to an alternate reviewer or notify content authors that review resources are unavailable at this time and the schedule may be adversely affected. | When review is complete, authors will update the content based on compiled review comments. | |
| When review is complete, authors will update the content based on compiled review comments. Authors will send the content in PDF format to the reviewer when it is ready for review. | | |

**Approval**

| Envigor | CreateSoft | Understanding the differences |
|---|---|---|
| After all comments have been received and merged into the source content, authors use metadata to indicate content that is ready for final approval. | After all comments have been received and merged into the source content, authors use metadata to indicate content that is ready for final approval. | Whereas Envigor has chosen to implement workflow to automatically route content to reviewers when approval is required, CreateSoft is maintaining their existing process to have authors route content manually. |
| Through workflow, reviewers identified as having permission to | | |

**Table 7.3    Review**

| Envigor | CreateSoft | Understanding the differences |
|---|---|---|
| approve content will be notified that content is ready for approval.<br><br>Reviewers will review the content and indicate whether it has final approval by selecting the final approval metadata.<br><br>After it has final approval, content requiring translation will be automatically routed to translation.<br><br>Approved content will trigger automatic publishing (see "Delivery"). | Reviewers with permission to approve content will review the content and indicate whether it has final approval by selecting the final approval metadata. | |

## Manage

Standard content management functionality consists of version control, access control, and check-in/check-out. Envigor will additionally support content authorization because they plan to provide dynamic content. They have also chosen to support this phase using workflow. Further details are presented in Table 7.4.

**Table 7.4    Manage**

| Envigor | CreateSoft | Understanding the differences |
|---|---|---|
| **Version control** | | |
| Each time content is saved a new version will be created. There will be two levels of versioning: draft version and full version. Content will remain in draft version | Same as Envigor. | Version control functionality is standard in most content management systems, therefore this process is identical for both companies. |

*continues* ▶

**Table 7.4    Continued**

| Envigor | CreateSoft | Understanding the differences |
|---|---|---|
| until approved, then it will be fully versioned. | | |
| To ensure all content remains within the system, working on draft content outside the CMS will be strictly discouraged. However, it will not be prevented because authors working off site will have to work outside the CMS. | | |
| Through version control, authors will be able to view previous versions of the content or revert to an earlier version if necessary. | | |
| Authors and reviewers can see the complete detailed history for each item. The history will indicate who made the change (automatic), when the change was made (automatic), and the reason for the change (authors will complete this information). | | |

| Envigor | CreateSoft | Understanding the differences |
|---|---|---|
| **Access control** | | |
| Content will be controlled, meaning no one will be able to create, view, or modify content without the appropriate permissions. Different users of the CMS will have different permissions. | Same as Envigor. | Access control functionality is standard in most content management systems, so it is identical for both companies. Envigor has also chosen to control their authoring templates in the same way that they control content. |

The system administrator will define access control. After access control is applied to a document, the same access control will be inherited (automatically applied) to all the components that comprise the document. If content is reused in multiple locations, the most restricted level of access will be applied to the element unless it is standard content such as a logo, disclaimer, and so on.

To ensure consistency across the organization, authoring templates will be controlled in the same way that content is controlled. The authoring templates cannot be changed except by the template owner or a supervisor.

*continues* ▶

**Table 7.4    Continued**

| Envigor | CreateSoft | Understanding the differences |
|---|---|---|
| **Check-in content** At any point in the content creation process, authors will be able to check the content in to the content management system. If the content is ready for review or approval, authors will add the appropriate metadata and reviewers will be automatically notified that it is available for review. | At any point in the content creation process, authors will be able to check the content in to the content management system. If the content is ready for review or approval, authors will add the appropriate metadata. | Workflow enables Envigor to automatically notify reviewers when content is ready for review or approval; CreateSoft manually routes content to reviewers. |
| After the content is checked in, it will be automatically stored in the correct location in the content management system. | After the content is checked in, it will be automatically stored in the correct location in the content management system. | |
| **Content authorization** Content authorization identifies the access rights for the dynamic content. Employees and customers will be assigned roles, each role with an associated profile that identifies appropriate content for the system to display. The CMS will compare the access rights of the content to the user's profile to determine whether the user has authorization to view the content. | Not applicable. | Envigor requires content authorization to support dynamic content. |

| Envigor | CreateSoft | Understanding the differences |
|---|---|---|
| Users will not be prevented from seeing other content unless the content has a restricted access. | | |
| **Workflow** | | |
| Workflow is used throughout the content life cycle to control and route content automatically. Actions will automatically occur at each phase (for example, identifying a piece of content as "ready for review" will cause the workflow to automatically route the content to the review list for review).<br><br>Workflow will be created by the system administrator. | Not applicable. | Envigor will use workflow to support the unified content life cycle. |

## Delivery

Content delivery consists of publishing. Envigor manages the content delivery process from the content management tool. Its content delivery process is supported through automated publishing, requested publishing, dynamic content assembly, and multiple media publishing. CreateSoft continues to manage the content delivery process from the authoring tool. Its content delivery process is supported through requested publishing and multiple media publishing. Table 7.5 describes the delivery processes for both Envigor and CreateSoft, as well as the differences between them.

**Table 7.5    Deliver**

| Envigor | CreateSoft | Understanding the differences |
|---|---|---|
| **Automated publishing** | | |
| Automated publishing requires no human intervention. Content that the workflow has identified as ready to publish (for example, it has received final approval) will be automatically published to the required media. | Not applicable. | Envigor has chosen to manage delivery from the content management system. A CMS can support automated publishing. |
| **Dynamic content assembly** | | |
| Content will be dynamically assembled for users based on their profiles. | Not applicable. | Envigor has chosen to provide dynamic content to its users. |
| **Requested publishing** | | |
| Authors will be able to request publishing at any time to any media if they have permission to publish the content. | Authors will select the appropriate media stylesheet, then publish to a designated media. | Envigor authors can choose to selectively publish as desired, in addition to automated publishing or dynamic content assembly, whereas CreateSoft authors always choose what to publish, when to publish it, and in what media. |
| **Multiple media publishing** | | |
| Stylesheets control the look and feel of the content. Information products are automatically assigned an appropriate publishing medium (for example, a | Authors will continue to publish to multiple media as they currently do. Authors will create paper from the authoring tool and | Envigor can automatically publish to multiple media, depending upon the stylesheets that have been identified for an information product. |

**Table 7.5    Deliver**

| Envigor | CreateSoft | Understanding the differences |
|---|---|---|
| brochure may be designated as paper, PDF, and HTML). When an information product is published, the appropriate stylesheet will be automatically selected for use. | will use a variety of conversion tools for HTML. Conversion will require some hand manipulation to refine the output of the conversion. <br><br> Style sheets control the content's look and feel. | CreateSoft authors are responsible for using conversion tools to create HTML output. |

## Summary

Envigor's content life cycle describes how they will implement a unified content strategy across the enterprise. Their decision to move to XML for consistent structure, systematic reuse to help ensure consistency, and dynamic content to meet customers' unique needs means that they confront a larger task to move toward a unified content strategy. It will require more design work, more extensive processes, and the implementation of more technology. However, long term, the return on investment (ROI) could be larger because more content is being controlled.

CreateSoft's content life cycle operates on a smaller scale, but it identifies a manageable unified content strategy that will result in an improved ROI. It relies more on authors to ensure success than Envigor's content life cycle does. CreateSoft's choice to remain with existing authoring tools reduces the learning curve for authors, and their choice of opportunistic reuse will work effectively because these authors are very familiar with the content. This unified content life cycle can serve as a solid solution or could provide a good starting point for growth into greater functionality in the future.

Your unified content life cycle, just like Envigor's and CreateSoft's, should address your organizational goals and requirements. Your vision for your unified content life cycle will form the basis for designing your content and process, as well as for selecting tools. As you formulate your content life cycle, remember to

- Identify how the issues can be addressed.
- Create a unified content life cycle that envisions how your company will support each phase (create, review, manage, deliver) and address your issues and needs.

# Part III

# Design

Good design is essential to the success of your unified content strategy. Once you've analyzed your information (through a thorough content audit) and analyzed your content life cycle, you're ready to begin designing how your information will be structured to support reuse, how it will be tagged, and how it will be produced. The five chapters in this part discuss various aspects of design, from information modeling to implementing your design decisions.

Chapter 8, "Information modeling" begins the discussion with the first—and probably the most critical—phase of design. Once you have identified opportunities to reuse content in your organization, you need to model the content you plan to reuse. Models formalize the structure of your content in guidelines, templates, and structured frameworks such as DTDs or schemas. Through information modeling, you identify and document the framework upon which your reuse strategy is based. Just as architectural blueprints define how houses are built, information models design how your information products are built.

In addition to information models, you also need some way of classifying and identifying all of the information or elements so that they can be retrieved and combined in meaningful ways for authors and for users. Metadata allows you to describe elements in terms of their behavior, processes, rules, and structure. Chapter 9, "Designing metadata" describes what metadata is as well as its role in a unified content strategy, both in terms of categorizing documents and in defining content elements. While metadata has been a buzzword in the information technology and data warehousing fields for some time, it has recently emerged as an important concept for enterprise content management solutions. After all, information is only effective if users can get to it in a way that's useful for them.

Chapter 10, "Designing dynamic content" takes design further by offering strategies for personalizing content. Within any organization, and certainly on the Internet, there is so much content being created and being delivered that users can't find what they want and authors can't find what they need. Adding metadata can help to further categorize content, but it can only do so much. Users must still know that particular content exists to be able to find it or reuse it. Dynamic content can help by providing users with the right content, at the right time, and in the right format. But, designing dynamic content is a lot of work; this chapter also describes when dynamic content makes sense.

As you design how information products will be built and how information will be categorized and delivered to users, you also need to design your internal processes for making sure all tasks are completed in the right order, such as adding metadata before content is published. Workflow, in the context of a unified content strategy, defines how people and tasks interact to create, update, manage, and deliver content. Workflow moves content from task to task, ensuring that the business rules specific to your organization are followed, for example, making sure that sign off occurs at the appropriate levels. Chapter 11, "Designing workflow" describes the concepts of workflow and its benefits, and takes you through the basics of designing workflow to support your unified content life cycle.

Finally, Chapter 12, "Implementing your design" rounds out Part III with suggestions for implementing your unified content solution. It discusses factors that affect implementation, as well as some of the options available, such as implementing your design in XML, or using authoring forms or structured templates with traditional authoring tools. It also discusses where metadata is stored, managed, and maintained. While this chapter does not provide technical "how-to" information, it guides you through some of the technical issues so you'll have a better understanding of how to map your design to a software or process solution.

# Chapter 8

## Information modeling

Once you have identified opportunities to reuse content in your organization, you need to "model" the content you plan to reuse. Models formalize the structure of your content in guidelines, templates, and structured frameworks, such as DTDs or schemas. Through information modeling, you identify and document the framework upon which your reuse strategy is based.

Chapter 1 "Content: The lifeblood of an organization," established that content is the life blood of an organization, and that content is created and used by many independent and often disparate areas of an organization. Walls are erected between content areas and even within content areas, which leads to content being created, and re-created, and re-created, often with permutations at each iteration. However, for content to be truly unified, it must follow a consistent approach in writing style and structure, and it must be stored so that whoever needs it can find it, access it, reuse or repurpose it, and deliver it (often dynamically) to everyone who needs it when and where it's needed. The information model is your blueprint for the effective writing, structuring, and delivery of reusable content. As such, it's important to start with strong analysis of your information and audiences to make sure the model reflects all potential uses and users of your content.

This chapter discusses the basics of information architecture, as well as structure, in relation to information models. It describes granularity, information product and element models, and components of information models, including examples. At the end of the chapter there is a discussion on buying versus building information models.

## Understanding information architecture

When you build a house, the builder doesn't simply show up at the building site and start pouring the foundation and erecting the walls without having a building plan that shows how the house will be constructed and out of what materials. This is the architectural blueprint; it defines how many rooms are in the house, their dimensions, the building materials, and so on. It also defines which parts of the house should adhere to a standard, such as the width of doorways and the thickness of the insulation.

Likewise, software developers follow specifications when designing new software, and each developer or programmer who works on the project designs according to the specification.

Architecture also applies to information. Information architecture is the blueprint that defines how content will be organized and structured to make up the various "information products" in your organization. (An information product is any output consisting of content, such as user guides, catalogs, documents,

brochures, press releases, annual reports, intranets, web sites, or technical specifications.) An effective information architecture helps people (both internal and
external to your organization) find, manage, and continue to add to the existing
information consistently, following defined rules for structure and semantics.

Information modeling is critical in a unified content strategy because it provides
the blueprint upon which your information products are based. In a unified
content strategy you break content down into objects, and rather than write
documents, you write objects that are stored in your repository (often a database). Elements are then compiled into information products from that repository. The power of a unified strategy lies in effectively reusing content
elements—whether they're paragraphs, procedures, or sentences—over and over
again, reducing costs and increasing productivity. Information models identify
all the required elements and illustrate how to structure and reuse them. The
goal of information modeling is a complete specification outlining how content
is used—and reused—throughout your organization.

### Benefits of information architecture

When you build information models that consider information requirements
across an entire organization, you look beyond your own department to determine how other areas can use your information and how you can use theirs. An
effective information model serves to identify all the knowledge within an organization, and to capture and reuse it effectively. The information modeling
process forces you to consider all information requirements (either for a specific
project or within an entire organization) and to assess what information is available to fulfill those requirements. In a unified content strategy, the information
model becomes the "catalog" of all the information products, and it outlines the
necessary information elements for each, based on thorough analysis of your
audiences and their information needs.

## Modeling based on analysis

Information modeling is a critical task in your unified content strategy and it
can seem daunting. However, after you have done thorough information, audience, and process analyses, the modeling is the next logical step in implementing
your findings.

Information modeling takes place after the analysis and recommendations are completed and signed off (see Chapter 6, "Performing a content audit"). Through your analysis, you develop an understanding of the types of information within your organization, who uses what information, and in what context. Most important, your analysis also helps you to see how information can be reused to support its various uses.

For example, you may have discovered that you have product descriptions published in 20 different places and written by 10 different people in 5 different groups (and translated into 7 different languages) within your organization. You may also have discovered that many product descriptions are inconsistent in meaning, contain different types of information (some contain costs, some do not), and are structured/written differently, so that users have trouble identifying them as product descriptions. In addition, each time authors update a description, they do it in isolation, so the other uses of that description are not updated concurrently and are thus inconsistent.

During information modeling, you form a strategy for unifying the product descriptions so that wherever they appear, they are consistent, contain the same types of information, and are structured and written the same. However, you must have completed the analysis and identified key areas to unify to make valuable modeling decisions, and to know which inconsistencies are valid and which are not. It's also important to model what you want the structure of your information products to be, not what their structures currently are. This is your opportunity to make improvements in how your information products are structured, to improve their consistency and usability.

### Understanding structure

Models reflect the structure of information products, so it's necessary to understand exactly what structure is. Information products such as product descriptions, press releases, letters, catalogs, and so on have a recognizable structure that is repeated every time the information product is created. For example, a letter has a repeatable structure, as shown in Figure 8.1.

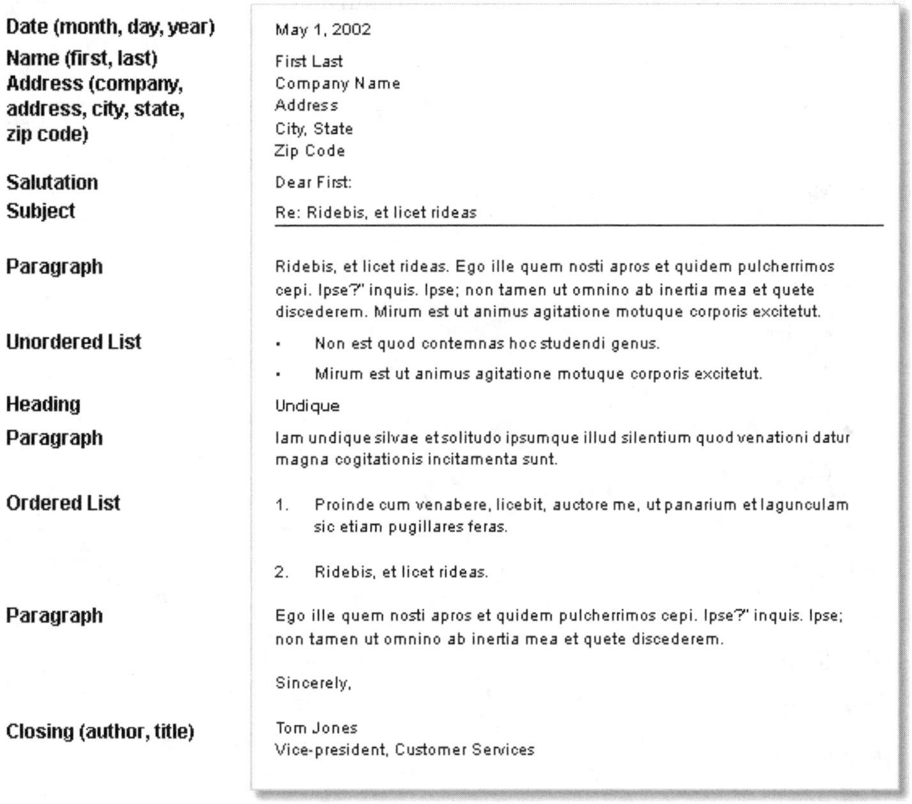

| | |
|---|---|
| **Date (month, day, year)** | May 1, 2002 |
| **Name (first, last)** **Address (company, address, city, state, zip code)** | First Last Company Name Address City, State Zip Code |
| **Salutation** | Dear First: |
| **Subject** | Re: Ridebis, et licet rideas |
| **Paragraph** | Ridebis, et licet rideas. Ego ille quem nosti apros et quidem pulcherrimos cepi. Ipse?" inquis. Ipse; non tamen ut omnino ab inertia mea et quete discederem. Mirum est ut animus agitatione motuque corporis excitetut. |
| **Unordered List** | • Non est quod contemnas hoc studendi genus. • Mirum est ut animus agitatione motuque corporis excitetut. |
| **Heading** | Undique |
| **Paragraph** | Iam undique silvae et solitudo ipsumque illud silentium quod venationi datur magna cogitationis incitamenta sunt. |
| **Ordered List** | 1. Proinde cum venabere, licebit, auctore me, ut panarium et lagunculam sic etiam pugillares feras. 2. Ridebis, et licet rideas. |
| **Paragraph** | Ego ille quem nosti apros et quidem pulcherrimos cepi. Ipse?" inquis. Ipse; non tamen ut omnino ab inertia mea et quete discederem. Sincerely, |
| **Closing (author, title)** | Tom Jones Vice-president, Customer Services |

**Figure 8.1    The structure of a letter.**

Note that the letter has the following structural elements:

- Date
- Address
- Salutation
- Subject
- Body
- Closing

Notice that these elements can be broken down further:

- Date
  - Month
  - Day
  - Year
- Address
  - Name
    - First
    - Last
  - Street Address
  - City
  - State
  - Zip Code
- Salutation
  - Dear
  - First name
- Subject
  - Re:
  - Topic
- Body
- Closing
  - Author
  - Title

However, it is much harder to break down the body of the letter because it is less structured. Authors can choose to structure the body of the letter in a number of ways depending upon their styles, the nature of the content, and the impact they want to have. The body of the letter can be broken down into only very generic elements that can be used in any order:

- Body
  - Paragraphs
  - Ordered lists
  - Unordered lists
  - Heading

## Why is structure important?

Structure is critical because it unifies the content, regardless of who is writing it. If the model is supported by a DTD (Document Type Definition), the DTD allows authors to create documents only according to the structure defined in the DTD. If the model is not supported by a DTD, authors may select from style tags or complete areas within a form, or they can enter text into a template that tells them what content must appear in the document. Authors rely on the model itself for the hierarchy.

The degree to which you break down the structure of your content depends upon the granularity of your material and your desire for consistency.

# Understanding granularity

An information model reflects all the components that make up each information product; the level of detail in the model depends on the granularity. Granularity determines the smallest piece of information that is reusable. To identify granularity, you determine the smallest possible piece of content you plan to reuse. Although granularity must be reflected in the information model, the level of granularity can change throughout your content. In one instance you may reuse large sections of information unchanged; in others, you may reuse content at the sentence or even the word level.

You may have different levels of granularity for authoring, for reuse, and for delivery. You may want to break content down to a very granular level for authors so that they can see exactly what to include as they write, but you can reuse content at whatever level of granularity is appropriate for your reuse strategy. See Chapter 12, "Implementing your design," for more information about granularity.

However, care should be exercised when determining the level of granularity. The more granular the content, the greater the complexity of modeling, authoring, and managing the content. Yet if the content is not granular enough, you compromise your ability to easily reuse information. After a reuse strategy is implemented, it may be difficult to increase the level of granularity later on. Weigh the benefits and reasons for very granular content before modeling and implementing it. You also need to consider that the meaning of a granule may change if it's used out of context. If an element relies on surrounding information to make its meaning clear, the surrounding information may need to be included as part of the element. You may find it necessary to model very granular information at first, then before implementing it, review the model in the context of how information will actually be authored. Note, for example, that granularity at the word level is not recommended. It's extremely difficult to model and maintain and can impede the writing process. In cases where word variations are required to make content reusable (for example, product name or version), you can use metadata to define variables that are inserted as required.

Keep in mind, too, that regardless of the level of granularity, authors still write complete documents, not elements. If your granularity is at the sentence level, authors don't write a number of disparate sentences that are stored in a database to be compiled into documents. Rather, authors write documents, assigning the required granularity to elements (as defined by the information model) as they write. The main difference for authors is in following the assigned structure and in assigning or selecting metadata. The granularity defines how the completed document is broken down, tagged, and stored for reuse; it doesn't define the authoring process. Chapter 12 provides more information on implementing your model.

## Information product and element models

After you've determined granularity, you're ready to start building the model. There are two levels of modeling required: modeling at the information product level and modeling at the information element level. Modeling at the information product level is like determining the framework of a house; modeling at the information element level is like determining everything that goes into the house—the rooms as well as all the elements within the rooms.

When you design a house, you specify what all the components (for example, rooms) are as well as what the structure of each room is. You also ensure that repeated components, such as doorways, are structured consistently. The "product" model for a house specifies which rooms comprise the house. The "element" model tells you how each room is constructed and which elements are reused from room to room. Architects and builders follow the model to ensure the house is built according to specifications, and that wherever an element is reused, it is reused consistently and not redesigned from scratch.

## Mandatory and optional elements

Models also indicate which elements are mandatory and which are optional. For example, some elements are standard in a kitchen and others are optional. However, the contents of a kitchen would never be the same as the contents of a bathroom or a bedroom. A kitchen model might include

- Windows
- Sink
- Butcher's block island (optional)
- Cabinets
- Countertop
- Door

And, the elements for the bedroom might include:

- Closet
- Windows
- En suite bathroom (optional)
- Door

For the purposes of this analogy, you can consider the door and window elements as reusable elements that are the same regardless of where they are used.

## Information product models

Just as you specify which rooms a house has and which elements each room contains, when you model an information product (such as a press release, a training manual, user guide, or brochure), you specify what its components are, as well as what the structure for each component is. The product model defines the content's elements, attributes and metadata, as well as the relationship among elements. Authors follow the model to create and compile information products consistently.

The information product model also provides information on what type of information should be included in a particular information product. For example, an information product model for a press release may include the following elements:

- Subject
- Date
- Contact
- Body
- Web site address

## Element models

In addition to product models, you need to create element models. An element model breaks the information product model down even further, describing the components that are assembled to create the information product. For example, the body element of the press release might include:

- Corporate description (short)
- Announcement
- Product description
- Features
- Benefits
- Quote
- Availability
- Corporate description (longer)

## Elements as containers

Building on the house analogy, you can think of each information element as a "container." The house is a container element for each room, and each room is a container element for all the components that make up each room. In this way, there can be containers within containers.

The same applies to information. Elements are containers of information, for example, Date = Month + Day + Year and may contain additional containers, for example, Contact = (First Name + Last Name) + (Area Code + Local Number). An information product model is a container for its elements and each element may also be a container for subelements.

Figure 8.2 shows which elements are complete on their own and which are containers for other elements, using the press release information product model as an example.

| | A | B |
|---|---|---|
| 1 | | |
| 2 | | |
| 3 | **Semantic** | **Element type** |
| 4 | Subject | Element |
| 5 | Date | Container |
| 6 | Month | Element |
| 7 | Day | Element |
| 8 | Year | Element |
| 9 | Contact | Container |
| 10 | Name | Container |
| 11 | First | Element |
| 12 | Last | Element |
| 13 | Contact Phone | Element |
| 14 | Contact Email | Element |
| 15 | Body | Container |
| 16 | Corporate Desc Short | Element |
| 17 | Announcement | Container |
| 18 | Paragraphs | Element |
| 19 | Ordered lists | Element |
| 20 | Unordered lists | Element |
| 21 | Product Desc. Short | Element |
| 22 | Features | Element |
| 23 | Benefits | Element |
| 24 | Quote | Element |
| 25 | Availability | Element |
| 26 | Corp. Desc. | Container |
| 27 | Corp. Desc. Short | Element |
| 28 | Corp. Desc. Med. | Element |
| 29 | Web site address | Element |

**Figure 8.2   Press release elements.**

# Components of models

An information model comprises a number of components, which describe the semantic information, the base information, the metadata, the architectural information, and the production information for each element.

## Semantic information

Semantic information uses semantic tags to describe what goes into each element, that is, tags that have a specific meaning. The press release information product model (shown previously) identifies semantically what goes in the press release. Instead of referring to the structure generically, it uses semantic tags to describe the structure. For example, the element <Website address> explicitly identifies that the content to be included within this element is the web site address. The opposite of a semantic tag is a generic tag (for example, <para>). If you use a generic tag such as <para> for the web site address or the product features, it is not clear what content is to be included in the paragraph.

Semantic information is extremely valuable in guiding authors as they create content. Semantic information explicitly defines the structure of the information. However, you may not want to use semantic tags when you implement your model. You may choose to use metadata instead because using a semantic tag may limit your ability to reuse content. The semantic tag <Features> may contain information required in another information product, but in the other information product, the information has a different semantic structure. Thus, the reuse is not identifiable from the semantic tag. See Chapter 12, for more information about semantic tags and metadata.

## Base information

Base information describes the common naming of each element within a container and uses generic tags or "base elements." Base elements guide information technologists as they implement the models (see Chapter 21, "Managing change"). Base elements help them to understand what underlying structure your elements should include. They also indicate what generic tag your elements should use if you choose not to use semantic tags. If you are using a traditional authoring tool, base elements guide authors in selecting the correct tag for the

model. Figure 8.3 shows semantic tags and their corresponding base elements
for the press release model. You would typically only have one column of base
elements. For the purpose of this example, base elements are shown for XML,
Microsoft Word, and Adobe FrameMaker to provide multiple examples of base
elements.

| | A | C | D | E |
|---|---|---|---|---|
| 1 | | **Base element** | | |
| 2 | | **XML** | **Word** | **FrameMaker** |
| 3 | **Semantic** | | | |
| 4 | Subject | title | Heading 1 | Heading1 |
| 5 | Date | Container | | |
| 6 | Month | PCDATA | Normal | Body |
| 7 | Day | PCDATA | Normal | Body |
| 8 | Year | PCDATA | Normal | Body |
| 9 | Contact | Container | | |
| 10 | Name | Container | | |
| 11 | First | PCDATA | Normal | Body |
| 12 | Last | PCDATA | Normal | Body |
| 13 | Contact Phone | para | Normal | Body |
| 14 | Contact Email | para | Normal | Body |
| 15 | Body | Container | | |
| 16 | Corporate Desc Short | para | Normal | Body |
| 17 | Announcement | Container | | |
| 18 | Paragraphs | para | Normal | Body |
| 19 | Ordered lists | ordered list | list | Numbered |
| 20 | Unordered lists | unordered list | numbered list | Bulleted |
| 21 | Product Desc. Short | para | Normal | Body |
| 22 | Features | | | |
| 23 | Benefits | unordered list | | |
| 24 | Quote | para | Normal | Body |
| 25 | Availability | para | Normal | Body |
| 26 | Corp. Desc | Container | | |
| 27 | Corp. Desc Short | para | Normal | Body |
| 28 | Corp. Desc. Med. | para | Normal | Body |
| 29 | Web site address | link | link | Link |

**Figure 8.3    Semantic elements and base elements for the press release.**

## Metadata

Within your model, you also need to indicate what metadata applies to which elements. Metadata provides data about data, or information about your information. While semantic tags help to direct the authoring of the text and the reuse, metadata provides search criteria, similar to index entries. Metadata is required to uniquely identify content so that authors can find it, reuse it, and move it. Depending on the authoring tool, some metadata can be automatically applied to the elements that require them (as defined by the model), whereas some are selected by authors as they create content. Again, depending on the authoring tool, authors are shown the available metadata for the particular element they are authoring. The element is then stored with its associated metadata, so if people are looking for everything written for a particular audience, for a particular product, for a particular version, or by a particular author, they can find it in the database, then reuse it if necessary.

Refer to Chapter 9, "Defining metadata," for a further discussion of metadata and its role in a unified content strategy.

## Architectural information

Architectural information provides details on the type of reuse (for example, systematic), guidelines for how you want the content formalized in your DTD or templates (for example, use semantic tags or not), where content is reused, and how it is reused (for example, Locked [L] or Derivative [D]). Figure 8.4 illustrates the architectural information for the press release.

| | A | F | G | H | I | J | K |
|---|---|---|---|---|---|---|---|
| 1 | | | | Architectural | | | |
| 2 | | Reuse | Guideline | | Reuse Map | | |
| 3 | Semantic | | | Product Sheet | Brochure | Web Site | E-catalog |
| 4 | Subject | | Semantic | | | | |
| 5 | Date | | Semantic | | | | |
| 6 | Month | | Semantic | | | | |
| 7 | Day | | Semantic | | | | |
| 8 | Year | | Semantic | | | | |
| 9 | Contact | | Semantic | | | D | D |
| 10 | Name | | Semantic | | | D | D |
| 11 | First | | Semantic | | | D | D |
| 12 | Last | | Semantic | | | D | D |
| 13 | Contact Phone | | Semantic | | | D | D |
| 14 | Contact Email | | Semantic | | | D | D |
| 15 | Body | | Semantic | | | D | |
| 16 | Corporate Desc Shor | Systematic | Semantic | L | L | L | |
| 17 | Announcement | | | | | D | |
| 18 | Paragraphs | | | | | D | |
| 19 | Ordered lists | | | | | D | |
| 20 | Unordered lists | | | | | D | |
| 21 | Product Desc. Short | Systematic | Semantic | L | L | L | L |
| 22 | Features | | | L | L | L | L |
| 23 | Benefits | | | L | L | L | L |
| 24 | Quote | | | | | L | |
| 25 | Availability | Systematic | Semantic | | | | |
| 26 | Corp. Desc. | Systematic | Semantic | L | L | L | |
| 27 | Corp. Desc. Short | Systematic | Semantic | L | L | L | |
| 28 | Corp. Desc. Med. | Systematic | Semantic | L | L | L | |
| 29 | Web site address | Systematic | Semantic | L | L | | |

**Figure 8.4   Architectural information for the press release.**

## Production information

Further adding to the model, production information guides the information technologist in creating the stylesheets or templates. Figure 8.5 shows production information added to the press release model.

| | A | L |
|---|---|---|
| 1 | | **Production** |
| 2 | | |
| 3 | **Semantic** | |
| 4 | Subject | |
| 5 | Date | |
| 6 | Month | |
| 7 | Day | |
| 8 | Year | |
| 9 | Contact | |
| 10 | Name | |
| 11 | First | |
| 12 | Last | |
| 13 | Contact Phone | |
| 14 | Contact Email | |
| 15 | Body | |
| 16 | Corporate Desc Shor | |
| 17 | Announcement | |
| 18 | Paragraphs | |
| 19 | Ordered lists | |
| 20 | Unordered lists | |
| 21 | Product Desc. Short | |
| 22 | Features | |
| 23 | Benefits | |
| 24 | Quote | This should display in italics on paper, but in quotes online. |
| 25 | Availability | |
| 26 | Corp. Desc. | |
| 27 | Corp. Desc. Short | |
| 28 | Corp. Desc. Med. | |
| 29 | Web site address | |

Figure 8.5  Production information for the press release.

## The complete model

Figures 8.2 through 8.5 show you various parts of the model, hiding certain columns to focus on the components relevant to the point being illustrated. Figure 8.6 shows the complete model.

| | | Base element | | | | | Architectural | | | | Production |
|---|---|---|---|---|---|---|---|---|---|---|---|
| | | XML | Word | FrameMaker | Reuse | Guideline | | Reuse Map | | | |
| Semantic | Element type | | | | | | Product Sheet | Brochure | Web Site | E-catalog | |
| Subject | Element | title | Heading 1 | Heading1 | | Semantic | | | | | |
| Date | Container | Container | | | | Semantic | | | | | |
| Month | Element | PCDATA | Normal | Body | | Semantic | | | | | |
| Day | Element | PCDATA | Normal | Body | | Semantic | | | | | |
| Year | Element | PCDATA | Normal | Body | | Semantic | | | | | |
| Contact | Container | Container | | | | Semantic | | | D | D | |
| Name | Container | Container | | | | Semantic | | | D | D | |
| First | Element | PCDATA | Normal | Body | | Semantic | | | D | D | |
| Last | Element | PCDATA | Normal | Body | | Semantic | | | D | D | |
| Contact Phone | Element | para | Normal | Body | | Semantic | | | D | D | |
| Contact Email | Element | para | Normal | Body | | Semantic | | | D | D | |
| Body | Container | Container | | | | Semantic | | | D | | |
| Corporate Desc Short | Element | para | Normal | Body | Systematic | Semantic | L | L | L | | |
| Announcement | Container | Container | | | | | | | D | | |
| Paragraphs | Element | para | Normal | Body | | | | | D | | |
| Ordered lists | Element | ordered list | list | Numbered | | | | | D | | |
| Unordered lists | Element | unordered li: | numbered list | Bulleted | | | | | D | | |
| Product Desc. Short | Element | para | Normal | Body | Systematic | Semantic | L | L | L | L | |
| Features | Element | | | | | | L | L | L | L | |
| Benefits | Element | unordered list | | | | | L | L | L | L | |
| Quote | Element | para | Normal | Body | | | | | L | | This should display in italics on paper, but in quotes online. |
| Availability | Element | para | Normal | Body | Systematic | Semantic | | | | | |
| Corp. Desc. | Container | Container | | | Systematic | Semantic | L | L | L | | |
| Corp. Desc. Short | Element | para | Normal | Body | Systematic | Semantic | L | L | L | | |
| Corp. Desc. Med. | Element | para | Normal | Body | Systematic | Semantic | L | L | L | | |
| Web site address | Element | link | link | Link | Systematic | Semantic | L | L | | | |

**Figure 8.6   Complete press release model.**

# How are models used?

Once models are developed, they need to be implemented throughout your organization, so that all authors and reviewers can use them as they create, edit, and review content. Authors use information models to determine what information goes in which information product, as well as how to structure each element. Referring to the information model, they can determine, for example, that an information product requires an overview, and then they can determine the structure of the overview and get hints or rules (writing notes) about how to write certain components. Depending on the type of reuse (that is, opportunistic, systematic, derivative, locked, or nested), authors may select elements from the content management system based on what the model tells them they have to include. Or systematic reuse may automatically populate a document with some elements, guide authors on how to write or structure the other elements, and show them in what order elements appear.

Content reviewers use information models to review authors' drafts. Reviewers compare drafts against the information model to ensure that they contain all the necessary elements. They also review the models to ensure that they contain all the necessary elements for each information product.

Information technologists use models to guide them in creating authoring templates or DTDs, implementing the content management system, and developing delivery stylesheets.

### Single sourcing remodeled: A case study

OCLC Online Computer Library Center is a nonprofit membership organization serving more than 41,000 libraries in 82 countries and territories. We employ content reuse techniques for the help and documentation for the OCLC FirstSearch service, which provides access to more than more than 70 reference databases. Through FirstSearch, library patrons can use more than 3,500 full-text journals or more than 47 million citations contained in WorldCat, the world's largest bibliographic database.

Reuse of text became very important to us in the Documentation department when we started to work on version 5 of the FirstSearch service in 2000. This new release would provide three levels of searching as well as translation of the interface, help, and all documentation into French and Spanish. The challenge was to achieve consistency among the three searching levels and the 70 databases. Some information could be repeated as many as 210 times (3 levels × the 70 databases). In addition, many text strings from the two system interfaces (user and administrative) were repeated in the help files, so having a way to access that information for help rather than copying and pasting it as it changed would save us time and labor and reduce errors.

### In the beginning

To address these needs, we started out by using technology to address the problem. We started authoring in FrameMaker+SGML with SGML templates. With the help of an SGML consultant, we developed a method of using "mother" documents that contained the standardized, repeatable text and references to "chunk documents" that contained the content variations (from the three searching levels and 70 databases). The variable content was included in a definition document that represented all the possible values of the variable data. We used a Perl script to create chunk files to contain the content variations that the mother document then called. We also used embedded references to system entities (text strings from the FirstSearch interface screens) to avoid copying, pasting, and maintaining this content multiple times.

### A focus on models

We accomplished the project goals and had developed considerable experience and expertise with structured authoring and text reuse, but the overall publishing process was laborious and not sustainable. There had to be a better way! It was time to focus on the content again and determine whether we could improve the authoring process.

With the help of a consultant, we compared and examined multiple versions of FirstSearch documentation, training materials, help, marketing materials, database specifications, and knowledgebase. Looking at content across sources enabled us to identify that content was reused much more broadly than we had expected, clearly identifying that we could reduce rework by starting with the content where it was first created and reusing it elsewhere. Most importantly, we were able to clearly identify how the content could be modeled to make the authoring process less painful for our writers and to improve authoring efficiencies.

Start early with information modeling for future projects. To avoid rework effort and missed opportunities for the efficiency that content reuse brings, you should begin with a thorough analysis of the information users need and model the content to support the authoring process. The tools should be configured to support the models and the author-ing process. They are not a solution in themselves.

**The result**

The benefits of analyzing our content resulted in a better understanding of how content is reused in the department and across other areas of the corporation, which resulted in less rework. Information models enabled us to create a faster, less costly method for implementing changes and support for the authoring process.

**Deborah A. Hysell**
**Biography**

Debbie Hysell has over 20 years of experience in technical communications, as a writer, editor, and manager. For the past 8 years, she has been manager of the OCLC Documentation Department and a staff of 20. Debbie has a BA and MA in English. She has presented papers at STC regional conferences, the 1999 First International Workshop on Internationalisation of Products and Systems, and at several ACM SIGDOC (Association for Computing Machinery's Special Interest Group on Documentation) conferences. She is a member of ACM, STC (Society for Technical Communication), and Toastmasters International.

**Information models: Buy versus build**

This chapter started by comparing information models to architectural plans.

Imagine that you want to build your dream home. Where do you start? Would you call a contractor in and have him start slapping boards together? You'd probably start with an architect and have a set of plans developed. Or, perhaps you'd buy a set of plans. Architectural magazines advertise plans for all kinds of houses—ranch, Victorian, Cape Cod, and thousands of permutations just waiting for a builder to put them together.

Just as you can buy a set of plans for your house, you can also buy information models, or use models that others have developed and have made available to anyone wanting to use them. These models are defined as SGML/XML DTDs. But, you should consider them only a starting point for your own information model. Very few of the models have an enter-prise-wide scope; most were developed as specific solutions to information use and reuse. For example, there are models available in the public domain for training materials, soft-ware guides, financial reports, and legislative reports, ad infinitum. There are also models for different industries, such as software, telecommunications, aerospace, pharmaceutical, and so on.

For an organization looking to exchange information with other organizations, the models can be a great enabler for open communication. In some circumstances, the models become a *requirement* for doing business (as in military, government, and aerospace) and thus, a *standard* for that industry.

However, most of the standards are developed by committees of companies, or initially by an individual or individual company, and maintained by a committee. As a result, many of the available models take on a consensus view of what the information model should look like and what the information elements should be called. This can conflict with your own *specific* needs for information or labeling and as such, they are not complete solutions by themselves.

With the increasing popularity of XML, models are being published every day. Many are solutions to very specific information needs, such as financial publishing, for example. Some have a broader focus and can be applied to many different problems. There are many models available for you to use; three are discussed here.

You can find more information on published models at the World Wide Web Consortium (W3C) web site, `http://www.w3.org/`.

## DocBook

DocBook is a very popular information model for software documentation. It was originally created over 10 years ago as an SGML markup language (the forerunner of XML) for sharing and ultimately authoring technical manuals for UNIX computer systems. Eventually, its development was taken over by a Technical Committee (TC) of the Organization for the Advancement of Structured Information Standards (OASIS).

The standard has undergone multiple revisions since its initial version, with contributions from a wide variety of users. As a result, it's a very robust model, which can accommodate pretty much any model of system software guide that you can imagine. However, with over 300 individual elements, it is very complex and can be difficult to use. To mitigate that, the DocBook developers have designed the model and DTD to facilitate the use of a customization layer. This layer is built on top of DocBook to simplify the models authors actually use.

If you're looking for a stable software documentation model, look at DocBook; it's a mature, tested model. It has been used and tuned over a long period of time and over varied applications. As a result, it has built-in models to cover most, if not all, typical software documentation applications. It is complete! You could implement DocBook "straight out of the box."

An additional advantage is that over time, as people have implemented DocBook, they have built tools and stylesheets for the application. These tools and stylesheets are also available—some commercially, some public domain—for you to use.

But if you're looking for a simple model, DocBook probably won't be your solution. It is a very complex model and although you can simplify it for your users, it takes considerable effort to learn and understand. Additional effort is required to build a customization layer to filter out the complexity.

If your focus is a model for multiple outputs, you might find DocBook's book focus to be an additional disadvantage. Its structures and even tag nomenclatures map to the book metaphor for publishing. It needs to be customized to filter out that focus for authors who are writing output-independent materials.

## DITA

The Darwin Information Typing Architecture (DITA) is an XML-based, end-to-end architecture for authoring, producing, and delivering technical information. The architecture and resulting DTD were developed by a team from IBM, Lotus, and Tivoli. Their goal was to create an architecture that would truly support information interchange and reuse. The team's view was that other universal DTDs failed because corporate information is tightly tied to corporate culture and jargon, which the DTDs could not accommodate. The result is an architecture that defines four layers:

- Delivery context—The processing and delivery context

- Typed topic structures—The formal content structure

- Common structures—Metadata and table structures that can be shared with any topic

- Shared Structures—Content models for structures that can be used in all documentation

In other words, DITA is not really a directly implementable model; instead, it defines how to construct your model. The DITA DTD defines only base models and its developers expect that you will create your own topic types to meet your own information needs.

A real advantage to DITA it is that it has been designed with reuse in mind. From day one, the DITA team has considered that the information modeled in a DITA architecture could be delivered on paper, on the web, to PDAs, or to any other form. The topic model is the core of DITA, unlike the book model that is the core of DocBook. Topic models map very well to online information and can also be easily adapted for book or print-based information.

On the other hand, DITA is just a starting point. You must create your own topic types; you cannot just implement DITA. The base content model does not provide enough detail for you to properly model any complex information. However, this disadvantage can also be an advantage in that you can use DITA's structure and add your own customized topics to reflect your specific information requirements.

DITA is a powerful model. But because it is a relatively new model, there are few implementations from which to learn and adapt. And there currently are no tools or stylesheets available to build upon.

## SCORM

SCORM (Shareable Content Object Reference Model) is an XML-based method for representing course structures. SCORM enables the reuse of web-based learning content across multiple environments and products. It is an initiative that is gaining recognition as organizations strive to improve their learning materials and move to XML. For the average course developer, the SCORM standard is difficult to understand. It is positioned as a single-sourcing initiative, but its focus is not on the creation of learning material. Rather, it focuses on distributing packaged learning objects for reuse. As such, it is not a model for learning content; it is a model for content delivery and has been adopted by learning tool vendors to assist users in creating reusable content. For most users, SCORM is invisible.

SCORM is a set of specifications that describes

- How to create web-based learning content that can be delivered and tracked by learning management systems
- What a learning management system must do to properly deliver and track SCORM-compliant learning content.

The SCORM model is not intended to replace the instructional design models. It does not specify how tracking information is stored and what reports are generated, what pedagogical or training models should be used, or how learner information is assembled. Instead, it specifies that SCORM-compliant learning content is

- Delivered through a web browser

- Described by meta-data

- Organized as a collection or sequence

- Packaged in such a way that it can be imported by a compliant learning management system or into a repository used by such a system.

SCORM provides a model for the distribution of packaged learning objects for reuse; it is not a model for designing effective reusable learning objects. Selecting a SCORM-compliant tool will enable you to share your reusable learning objects, but you must still use sound pedagogical methods for designing learning models.

## Summary

Off-the-shelf models may be appropriate for your environment. If you plan to move to XML and want structured content, they can be the right solution for you. However, if you plan to extensively reuse content and if you have a content structure that is unique to your organization or information set, purchasable models may not be the appropriate way to go.

Before you begin your modeling phase, take a look at existing models to determine whether they will meet your needs, will meet your needs if customized, or at minimum will serve as an instructional tool to help you to determine how you can best model your information.

## Summary

Information modeling is one of the most critical phases of designing your reuse strategy. Information models specify how information is reused and how it must be written and structured to support reuse. Information models provide the framework that guides authors, reviewers, and architects in creating, reviewing, managing, and publishing content. A good information model also improves the usability of your information products; your analyses of information and audiences may turn up usability issues that your models can address.

The level of detail in your information model depends on the level of reuse you are trying to achieve. The more granular the reuse, the more detail you need in the model; each element of information must be defined. The level of detail in the model also depends on the level of guidance your authors need and how much control you want them to have over authoring. For example, if you write regulatory documents with strictly defined components, you should include more guidance in your model. Authors need to know exactly how each element of content is used and how it is structured.

Accordingly, the information model should include

- Which information products the model supports.
- Which elements (based on granularity) are used for which product; which information containers the information product must contain.
- The type of reuse or architecture that applies to the model, for example,
  - Opportunistic
  - Systematic
  - Derivative
  - Locked
  - Nested
- The semantic structure of each element, a tagging structure that uniquely identifies the element's content. Semantic tags are based on content (as opposed to format), helping authors to identify elements for reuse and to structure them consistently.

- The metatags that apply to each element.
- The base structure (common naming) of each element (for example, paragraph, unordered list, ordered list, title, and so on). The base structure identifies more clearly what kind of text the element comprises.
- Any production notes, such as instructions to information technologists to autopopulate an element with pre-defined data.

# Chapter 9

## Designing metadata

As you have no doubt noticed, more information is available than ever before—on the Web, your company intranet, in your content management repository, and elsewhere. This is both exciting and problematic, and extremely frustrating when you can't find what you're looking for.

What is missing is information about the information—that is, labeling, cataloging and descriptive information—that enables a computer to properly process and search the content elements. This information about information is known as *metadata*.

Although metadata has been a buzz word in the information technology and data warehousing business for some time, it has recently emerged as an important concept for those who are developing search and retrieval strategies for information in reference databases or on the Web, for authors of structured content, and for developers of enterprise content management and Web publishing solutions. With more complex authoring processes and information delivery requirements, you need some way of classifying and identifying all of the information or content "bits" so that they can be retrieved and combined in meaningful ways for users. Well-designed metadata can provide the classification and identification you need.

This chapter introduces the levels and types of metadata that will be appropriate to your unified content strategy. It also describes methods for defining metadata and suggests ways to ensure that your authors apply metadata consistently.

## What is metadata?

Traditionally, metadata has been defined as "data about data." Although this is true, metadata is actually much more. It is the encoded knowledge of your organization, described by David Marco as:

> ...all physical data (contained in software and other media) and knowledge (contained in employees and various media) from inside and outside an organization, including information about the physical data, technical and business processes, rules and constraints of the data, and structures of the data used by a corporation.[1]

This definition is significant because it includes the often-overlooked idea that metadata can be used to describe the data's behavior, processes, rules, and structure. Describing information in this way is important when developing a sound metadata strategy for content search and retrieval, reuse, and dynamic content delivery, because you can determine not only what the content is, but who uses it, how it will be used, how it will be delivered, and when.

---

1 Marco, David. *Building and Managing the Meta Data Repository: A Full Lifecycle Guide.* New York:, John Wiley & Sons, Inc., 2000, p.5.

In a unified content strategy, metadata enables content to be retrieved, tracked, and assembled automatically. Metadata enables

- Effective retrieval
- Systematic reuse
- Automatic routing based on workflow status
- Tracking of status
- Reporting

Properly defining and categorizing the types of metadata you want to use is extremely important to the success of your unified content strategy. Improperly identified metadata, or missed categories, can cause problems ranging from misfiled and therefore inaccessible content to more serious problems such as those encountered by the National Aeronautics and Space Administration's (NASA's) 1999 Mars Climate Orbiter mission, in which misidentified metadata resulted in the loss of the spacecraft, at a cost of $300 million![2]

## Benefits of metadata to a unified content strategy

Using metadata for retrieval and content management enables content to be retrieved, tracked, and assembled automatically, resulting in the following benefits:

- **Reduction of redundant content**

    If content is consistently labeled with metadata, authors can easily retrieve existing reusable content, and if multiple authors accidentally create the same piece of content, your content management system identifies that multiple versions of the same content exist. With systematic reuse, the system automatically populates a document with the appropriate reusable content. If the content is already in place when authors start to write, they are aware that they do not need to create it again.

---

2 Marco, David. *Building and Managing the Meta Data Repository: A Full Lifecycle Guide.* New York: John Wiley & Sons, Inc., 2000.

- **Improved workflow**

  When you tag content with metadata that identifies its status, workflow automatically manages that content. For example, an element marked with "ready for review" can be compiled automatically into an information product such as a brochure, after which the brochure is automatically routed for review and approval.

- **Reduced costs**

  There are many ways in which metadata can help to reduce costs in a unified content strategy. For example, content is reusable only if it can be correctly identified with metadata and retrieved. If content exists and can be easily retrieved, the work required to create it again is eliminated. Metadata can also be used to automatically identify source elements that have changed. Triggering a translation process for the element saves the author or translator time and energy identifying the content to be translated. Additionally, if a reusable element is already translated, the metadata can facilitate the automatic population everywhere the source element is reused to ensure that the element is not translated again.

# Types of metadata

Unified content requires two types of metadata: categorization and element. Users tend to retrieve information based on categorization metadata, whereas authors tend to retrieve information based on element metadata.

## Categorization metadata

For years, libraries have used metadata to catalog and categorize documents. Originally they used card catalogs to provide information about the books stored in the library. The card catalog provided such information as title, author, publication date, subject, and a brief description (abstract) of what was contained within the document. In today's world, the items on the card would be referred to as metadata. Without the card catalog and the Dewey Decimal system it would have been impossible to find content in a library. Without metadata it is nearly impossible to find content online (for example on the Internet, a company intranet, or a content management systems).

The increasing use of portals has encouraged organizations to make the portal the central location for access to organizational content. However, as each new piece of content is added, users' ability to find content decreases. Corporate information needs to be just as accessible as library content, which means organizing content in a logical structure, categorizing it, and using the categories to add metadata to the information. Metadata is like the old card catalog, presenting information to users in context, and enabling them to quickly find relevant information. Metadata hierarchies or metadata taxonomies are used to organize the content.

Both metadata hierarchies and metadata taxonomies are similar in appearance: They are represented as tree structures, but are different in design and usage. A hierarchy provides the content user with an understanding of how content is organized. Content may be organized under multiple categories to provide the content user with multiple ways to find the information. For example, in an index (which is a hierarchy), information on Boston may be found under Cities or under Massachusetts. This provides the content user with multiple ways to find the information.

However, in a taxonomy, content may be categorized in only one place, not in multiple places. In the case of Boston, the taxonomy designer decided it can only be classified under Massachusetts.

Content users use hierarchies to retrieve content because hierarchies give them multiple "paths" to the same information, but taxonomies are used by authors to ensure that content is categorized in only one way, not in multiple ways. Categorizing content in multiple ways makes it difficult to retrieve.

Categorizing content can be a difficult and time-consuming process. Frequently it involves a manual approach, with people finding, reviewing, and categorizing content. Often it is the job of a corporate librarian or information architect to manually identify and tag content appropriately. Corporate content can be any content the corporation creates, receives, or wants to make available to its employees, customers, or suppliers. This body of content is much broader than the content we refer to in this book; it encompasses email, reports, correspondence, strategic analysis, and much more. The volume of this content grows at a tremendous pace, making it difficult for organizations to maintain if they do it all manually. Vendors are starting to provide tools that can assist your organization in categorizing your content and automatically adding metadata (see the sidebar "Categorization metadata standards."); however, these tools will not assist you in the task of creating element metadata.

Some industries have created industry-specific taxonomies, sometimes known as *vertical taxonomies*. Vertical taxonomies have been developed to help save organizations from the task of having to create everything themselves (thereby creating inconsistent taxonomies from company to company), and to facilitate the sharing of content. For example, bookstores use a taxonomy that helps them shelve books so that readers can more easily locate their desired subject matter: nonfiction, reference, travel reference, European travel and so on. Vertical taxonomies have been created for such areas as IT, healthcare, telecommunications, HR, financial, legal, e-learning, sales and marketing, and geography, and more are being created daily.

In the absence of a vertical taxonomy, industries are creating standards for the format, structure, and syntax of metadata to enable different organizations and even different departments within an organization to share metadata. For more information on metadata standards see the sidebar "Categorization metadata standards."

If you have a lot of content to categorize, check to see whether a vertical taxonomy already exists for your industry, and check with vendors to see whether they can support your information set. Categorization metadata is a large, sometimes costly, and intensive ongoing task. If you don't have to do this task on your own, don't try to. If you do decide to tackle the job, consider including corporate librarians or information architects on the team.

To begin the process of creating categorization metadata you need to understand your users. Understanding your users helps you to define the ways in which they will retrieve information. Ask the following questions:

- **Who is going to retrieve the content?**

  For example, customers will want to retrieve product information, marketing will want to retrieve reports, product information, and industry materials, and employees will want to retrieve policies and procedures.

- **What tasks are they trying to accomplish with the content?**

  For example, are they trying to complete a task or make a decision? You need to categorize content for tasks in areas such as procedures, while policies may be categorized separately.

- **What terms will they use when retrieving the content?**

  Anticipating the terms that people will use is always difficult. Everyone uses different terms and thinks about information in different ways. You will never be able to ensure that content will be accessible under everyone's terms, but understanding how people will refer to content helps you to determine your taxonomy. After you develop a taxonomy you can educate your users to use the available terms.

Now you need to categorize your content and create a taxonomy. This involves:

- **Grouping or clustering related content**

  As you start to categorize your content, you need to start grouping like or similar content together. These groups create categories, which are then refined by individual items in the category. For example:

  - Company benefits
    - Benefit policies
    - Benefit forms
    - Benefit frequently asked questions

  Which can be simplified to:

  - Company benefits
    - Policies
    - Forms
    - Frequently asked questions

- **Developing your taxonomy**

  As you group content, categorize it, and define the terms to be used to identify your content, you are automatically creating your taxonomy. Each term in your taxonomy becomes metadata.

- **Testing your taxonomy to ensure that it is appropriate and comprehensive.**
  You need to ensure that the metadata you have created is appropriate and usable by your audience. Before even using the metadata electronically, categorize some sample content and ask users to perform a usability test to ensure your taxonomy is appropriate.

**Categorization metadata standards**

One of the most valuable components of a unified content strategy is the ability to reuse content. As long as you are using one system, sharing content among users of the system is relatively easy. However, many organizations have multiple systems because they have existing legacy systems, or because one system is unable to meet all the organization's needs. Sharing content across multiple systems can be more problematic. The effective use of metadata requires common conventions for defining the semantics (meaning) of metadata. Typically, each system carries its own metadata with its own semantics and its own structure, and there are no matches or very few matches across the systems. In addition, if content is stored in multiple locations that use multiple metadata structures, the task of categorization metadata is even more difficult. Information retrieval becomes very complex because users need to learn multiple methods for retrieving content. To address this problem, standards for the structure and semantics of metadata and for sharing metadata are being created.

Dublin Core

The Dublin Core Metadata Initiative is an organization promoting the widespread adoption of interoperable metadata standards. The Dublin Core Metadata Element Set defines 15 elements of semantic metadata (Contributor, Coverage, Creator, Date, Description, Format, Identifier, Language, Publisher, Relation, Rights, Source, Subject, Title, and Type).

Dublin Core metadata has been designed to make it simple to understand and use. Dublin Core can be used to create metadata that can be used across a number of knowledge domains, including corporate content. Dublin Core is also extensible to allow for site-specific or application-specific metadata, which means that you can customize it. Dublin Core is now RDF-compliant (see the following).

RDF

The Resource Description Framework (RDF) was developed by the World Wide Web Consortium (W3C). Unlike Dublin Core, RDF is a framework for describing and interchanging metadata; it does not actually define metadata. RDF is an application of XML that imposes a specific structure to ensure consistent encoding and exchange of standardized metadata. By using XML, RDF imposes a structure that explicitly defines semantics, ensuring consistent encoding, exchange, and machine-readable processing of standardized metadata.

RDF provides a model for describing resources (content). Resources have properties (attributes or characteristics). A resource is an object that can be uniquely defined by a Uniform Resource Identifier (URI). RDF allows descriptions of web resources (any object with a URL as its address) to be made available in machine-readable form.

RDF helps to solve the problem industries have faced in exchanging metadata and its associated content among different systems. It does not define the metadata; rather, it enables organizations to define the metadata they need for their applications, yet still share that metadata with other RDF-compliant metadata applications.

Other standards such as Dublin Core and XMP have adopted RDF as the underlying structure for their standard.

### XMP

eXtensible Metadata Platform (XMP) is a metadata framework (way of labeling content) created by Adobe. XMP provides a method for combining metadata from "documents" and all its associated elements. The metadata for each element is preserved within the container document.

XMP can also be used to facilitate workflow. The labels of different types of content (for example, photograph versus text) can assist in appropriately directing content through workflow or to databases. Developers of workflow tools, particularly those designed to support the publishing process, are seriously looking at XMP as a potential metadata standard in their products.

XMP has been built on existing RDF standards. Adobe has made XMP public and extensible and has distributed it to developers of content creation applications, content management systems, database publishing systems, web-integrated production systems, and document repositories.

### Crosswalks

The best way to share content is through a consistent content structure and through consistent metadata. RDF enables organizations to exchange metadata; however, the success of RDF requires that all the developers of the metadata for the multiple systems use RDF. If the systems pre-date the creation of RDF, or if RDF was not used, you may need to map one metadata schema to another metadata schema. The mapping of metadata is achieved through the use of "crosswalks," which are essentially tables that map one metadata value to another.

For example, say you have a knowledge management (KM) system in your company, a customer relationship management (CRM) system, and now a content management system. A simple example of the differences in the three systems is in how a "document" is named. The CRM system refers to the name of a document such as a brochure with the metadata tag "Title." The KM system calls it "Subject," and the CMS uses a combination of "Information product" and "Title." The CMS introduces further complexity because it uses "Title" in multiple ways, because a title can exist at many levels in an XML document (for example, document title, section title, and subsection title are all considered titles, but are clarified by their location in the document hierarchy). Table 9.1 illustrates a sample crosswalk:

**Table 9.1    Sample crosswalk**

| CRM | KM | CM |
|-----|-----|-----|
| Title | Subject | Information Product Title[3] |

However, mapping metadata from one system to another may not be so straightforward. Some common problems include

- Two or more elements in one system may be represented by a single element in another system.

- There may be no comparable element in the other system.

These and other problems may make it difficult to retrieve and share content. If you do plan to set up a crosswalk, be sure to clearly identify the rules of conversion and track the decisions that were made.

You can also consider using crosswalks when your metadata terms change. For example, a product may have had a specific name for a year, but is renamed in a new product offering. You don't want to have to try to retrieve both the old product name (particularly when new people start and don't even know the old product name) and the new product name. Instead, you can use a crosswalk to map the old product name to the new product name.

Tools

There are a number of tools that provide automated categorization of content and application of metadata.

## Element metadata

Element metadata identifies your content at the element level, based on the elements defined in your information model (see Chapter 8, "Information modeling"). Authors use element metadata to help them manage content throughout the authoring process. There are three main types of element metadata:

- Reuse metadata
- Retrieval metadata
- Tracking metadata

---

3 Where the title is drawn from the highest level of title in the document hierarchy.

This section explains these three types of metadata.

## Metadata for reuse

Metadata for reuse identifies the components of content that can be reused in multiple areas. For example, if an overview already exists for the ABC product, you can use metadata like "content type = overview, product = ABC" to help you find the correct content to reuse.

Before even beginning to write, authors can search the content management system by metadata for reusable content. Alternatively, the content management system can automatically search for appropriate reusable content (based on models and metadata) and deliver it (systematic reuse) to authors. In both cases, metadata is very important to correctly identify the elements of content.

To determine what metadata you need to enable reuse, you need to determine the business result you are trying to achieve and build your metadata backward to achieve that result. Think about the following:

- **Where is content going to be reused?**

    Across product? Across information product? If you answered yes to any of these then you need to create metadata to identify each reuse. For example:

    - Product, such as:

        - ABC

        - EFG

        - HIJ

    - Information product, such as:

        - Brochure

        - Web

        - Help

        - User guide

    Note that metadata such as information product can be derived from the template type.

- **What type of content is it?**

    You also need to know the element content type for which the content is valid. Your metadata might include

- Content type, for example:
  - Overview
  - Caution
  - Warning
  - Troubleshooting
  - Example

Note that metadata such as content type can be derived from your model or semantic tags.

- **What else do you need to know about the content to ensure that the correct piece of content is reused?**

For example, you might also need to know to which version of the product the content applies:

- Version, for example:
  - 1
  - 2
  - 2.5

Furthermore, you may need to know the region or location where the product is being sold or used, so that you can identify content such as safety regulations, language, and configuration. In this case, your metadata might include

- Region, for example:
  - United States
  - Canada
  - South America
  - Europe
  - Language, for example:
  - English
  - Spanish
  - French
  - Italian
  - German

Finally, you may need to know the audience so that appropriate content is provided for each audience.

- Audience, for example:
  - Consumer
  - Decision maker
  - Technical support

## Metadata for retrieval

Metadata for retrieval is used to help authors retrieve content and may include much or all of the metadata used for reuse. However, metadata for retrieval is more extensive then metadata for reuse, providing additional information about an element that facilitates retrieval. Think about what other information would help you retrieve content more effectively. For example, your retrieval metadata might include

- **Title/Subject**

  This type of metadata can be entered by the author, or the system can use the title that appears in the content to create this metadata.

- **Author**

  The system usually automatically generates this type of metadata, based on the author information.

- **Date (creation, completion, modification)**

  The system usually automatically generates this metadata as it is checked into the content management system.

- **Keywords**

  This metadata can be entered by the author; however, it is preferable to provide the author with a list of keywords from which to choose. This way keywords will be used consistently (see the section "Creating a controlled vocabulary," later in this chapter).

- **Security level (who can view the content)**

  This type of metadata is usually applied by the author from a selected list of options.

As you do with metadata for reuse, you identify your metadata for retrieval by determining the business result you are trying to achieve and building your metadata backward to achieve that result. Think about the following issues:

- **Who is going to retrieve your content?**

  You will probably have two levels of users interested in retrieving your content: authors and users. Understanding your users' information requirements helps you to determine what kind of metadata they will use for retrieval. Authors will want to retrieve content at many levels of granularity (individual elements, sections, and whole information products). They will need metadata that enables them to identify the desired content at any level of granularity. Users probably don't want to retrieve granular content; instead, they want to retrieve whole "documents" and will need categorization metadata such as date, author, and subject, in addition to retrieval metadata.

- **In what form do they want to retrieve it?**

  Authors probably want to retrieve content in a format that is appropriate for a particular authoring tool, whereas users want to retrieve content in the form in which the content was designed to be displayed (for example, PDF, HTML, or Windows Help). For authors, the metadata needs to define the source format and the desired format (for example, XML may be the source format, but Word is the desired format) so that the system can convert content appropriately. For users, the metadata needs to define the appropriate format for the content (for example, PDF or HTML) so the system can either retrieve the content in this format or, if it needs to be converted, convert to the appropriate format.

- **What permissions should users have for retrieving content?**

  Typically the permission to create, edit, or modify content is restricted. Authors and users may have restrictions on what content they are allowed to see or even to know exists. Each element, container, and information product needs to have appropriate security permissions expressed through metadata.

- **How are they going to specifically identify the desired content?**

  People articulate their desire for specific content in different ways, using different terms. You need to analyze the terms your authors and users will use, then determine what metadata the content should carry to enable a match between the search and the content. You may want to consider adding keywords to metadata to facilitate this retrieval; however, to ensure consistency, consider using a controlled list of keywords rather than author-created keywords.

## Metadata for tracking (status)

Metadata for tracking is particularly useful when you are implementing workflow as part of your unified content strategy. By assigning status metadata to each content element, you can determine which elements are active. You can also control what can to be done to an element and who can do it. Generally, status changes based on the metadata are controlled through workflow automation, not by end users. Sometimes an author will identify a status change such as "ready for review" because the system cannot automate this type of information. Status metadata can include such tracking items as:

- Draft (under development by the author)
- Ready for review
- Reviewed
- Approved
- Final
- Submitted
- Published
- Archived

Again, like your other metadata, you identify tracking metadata by determining the business result you are trying to achieve, and then build your metadata backward to achieve that result. Design your metadata for tracking after you have designed your workflow (see Chapter 11, "Designing workflow"). This enables you to identify what metadata needs to be applied to the content at each stage of workflow to enable the workflow system to manage it. For example, the metadata for the Review and Approval Workflow shown in Figure 11.3 could look like the following:

- **Content status**

  Indicates status of the content. Before it can be reviewed it must have the appropriate metadata attached to identify that it is ready for review. For example, the metadata could include:

  - Draft
  - Ready for review
  - In review
  - Final
  - In approval
  - Approved

  When the content is ready for review, authors apply the "Ready for review" metadata. When the content includes the feedback from review and is ready for final approval, authors apply the "final" metadata. When the final approval reviewers approve the content, they apply the "Approved" metadata.

  The system needs to identify the status of the content at any point in time. When the content has been passed to review, its status is automatically changed to "In review" and later, when it is passed onto final approval, the status is changed to "In approval."

- **Review status**

  Indicates the status of the review content. A reviewer can either accept the content without changes or reject the content by asking for changes and returning it to the author. For example, the review status metadata could include:

  - Accept
  - Reject

  If the metadata is "Accept," the system moves the content to the final approval stage, but if the metadata is "Reject," the content is routed back to the author for changes.

After you have designed your metadata to support your workflow, you need to identify other metadata that can help you to track your content. For example:

- Who created the content (author)?
- When was it created/modified (date)?
- Who modified the content (editor)?

- Who reviewed/approved the content (reviewer/approver)?
- How long did it take to create/modify/review (time)?
- Where has it been reused (information product, product)?
- Has it been translated (content status)?

Most content management systems automatically create some of this metadata (for example, author, date), whereas other metadata may already be defined in retrieval metadata and reuse metadata, but you should go through this exercise to make sure that you have identified all the possible metadata you require for tracking and reports.

## Creating a controlled vocabulary

Metadata needs to be consistent to facilitate reuse, retrieval, and tracking. This requires a controlled vocabulary. A controlled vocabulary reconciles all the various possible words that can be used to identify content and to differentiate among all the possible meanings that can be attached to certain words. Using an unlimited or uncontrolled set of metadata terms leads to additional work for authors (they have to figure out the metadata each time they apply it) and reduces the percentage of content that can be effectively retrieved (different terms means either using multiple terms to search or missing some content because retrievers are unaware of alternate terms). If authors can create their own metadata tags, there is a high probability they will create different metadata.

To create a controlled vocabulary:

1. Identify your metadata categories (for example, Content type, Product).
2. Identify the terms that make up that metadata category.

   For example:
   - Content status
   - Draft
   - Ready for review
   - In review
   - Final
   - In approval
   - Approved

In this example, "content status" is the metadata category and the controlled terms are "Draft," "Ready for review," and so on.

Uncontrolled metadata terms should be the exception to the rule. If possible, do not provide any metadata that can be defined by the author. If that is not possible, monitor the uncontrolled metadata terms to see whether patterns are emerging that could then be used to create a controlled vocabulary.

## Ensuring metadata gets used

Metadata can be very valuable and useful; however, it is only valuable if it gets used. Wherever possible, automate the application of metadata. Leaving the application of metadata up to authors adds yet another burden to the authoring process and leads to inconsistency. Some authors diligently apply the correct metadata, some apply some of it correctly and some of it incorrectly, and some don't apply it at all. Unless it is applied appropriately all the time, your metadata could become useless.

Wherever possible, have the system apply the metadata. This can include automatic:

- Categorization metadata based on the content
- Metadata based on the template and model
- Inheritance of metadata based on the parent (for example, if a container element is given a restricted security, all the elements within the container automatically have the same security metadata applied to them)
- Metadata based on position in the workflow

If it is necessary for authors to add metadata, make it possible for them to add the metadata as they are authoring so that they don't have to wait until the content is checked into the content management system. For example, if a step varies based on role, let them add the role metadata as soon as they finish writing the step. If it has to wait until the content is checked into the content management system, the system either has to prompt them to add the metadata for every single element (a very tedious process), or it may be up to the author to remember to add the metadata in all the relevant places (a recipe for missed metadata).

# Summary

Metadata is critical to the success of your unified content strategy. It is more than just data about data; it is the encoded knowledge of your organization. Metadata can be used to describe the behavior, processes, rules, and structure or data, as well as to add descriptive information.

There are two types of metadata:

- Categorization metadata

  Categorization metadata categorizes your documents. Categorization metadata is usually used by content users to retrieve content.

- Element metadata

  Element metadata identifies your content at the element level. Element metadata is used by authors to retrieve elements of content. There are three kinds of element metadata:

  - Metadata for reuse is used to identify the components of content that can be reused in multiple areas.

  - Metadata for retrieval is used to retrieve content. It may consist of metadata for reuse as well as additional retrieval metadata.

  - Metadata for tracking (status) is used to identify the status of your content in a workflow system.

To define your metadata, start by identifying the business result you want to achieve with your metadata and work backward to identify what metadata will achieve that result.

Use a controlled vocabulary for your metadata to ensure that metadata is named and applied consistently.

If you need to share metadata across systems consider using RDF (a W3C framework for describing interchangeable metadata) to design your metadata. If RDF has not been used to create your metadata, consider using a crosswalk (a table to map metadata from one structure to another) to provide a metadata interchange.

Automate as much of the application of metadata as possible to ensure that metadata gets used and to enable authors to add metadata in the authoring tool rather than as they check the content back into the content management system.

# Chapter 10

## Designing dynamic content

Dynamic content is assembled to match users' and customers' requirements, automatically providing them with information when they need it and in the form they need it. However, dynamic content is not just for customers; dynamic content is also used to provide authors with documents that are "pre-populated" with appropriate reusable content upon request (systematic reuse).

Content can be assembled dynamically to accommodate:

- **Personalization**
  Content is assembled to meet users' specific needs, providing them with exactly what they are looking for, when they are looking for it, and in the format they are looking for.

- **Systematic reuse**
  Content is assembled based on author requirements and business rules, reducing the need for authors to search out appropriate reusable information.

- **Collaborative learning**
  Content is assembled based on specific objectives or learner requirements, customizing the learning experience for the learner.

## Why dynamic content?

As Chapter 1, "Content: The lifeblood of an organization," points out, content is integral to the continued existence of your organization and is critical to your customers as well. Without the right information, external and internal customers cannot make appropriate decisions. However, there is so much content being created and being delivered that users can't find what they want and authors can't find what they need. According to a study done by Berkeley[1], "The world produces between 1 and 2 exabytes (1 billion gigabytes) of unique information per year, which is roughly 250 megabytes for every man, woman, and child on earth." Although those figures represent content in many different formats (for example paper, web, video, CD/DVD), as well as both structured and unstructured content, the amount of information that users have to search through to find what they need is often overwhelming.

Organizations need to do as much as they can to help users find the information they require. It's all there, but the trick is to find it and determine what is relevant. Content categorization systems such as tables of contents, human- and librarian-built indexes, and automatically generated web site maps for web materials help users find what they need, but these navigational aids mean that a user needs to already know what they need to know to be able to find it. Finding the

---

1  "How Much Information", 2000. Retrieved from http://www.sims.berkeley.edu/how-much-info on April 24, 2002.

right information can be a difficult process for users. The addition of metadata can help to further categorize content to aid in content retrieval, but as with TOCs and indexes, again users need to know the appropriate metadata to be able to find the information they need. Standard search mechanisms require that users explicitly know what they need to know to be able to find it. That means that if they don't know particular content exists or if they use different terms than are used in the content, they may never find it, or they may also unknowingly find the wrong content.

Another inherent problem in finding the correct information is knowing what content is relevant. Although users may be able to retrieve information that appears to meet their needs, they must look at it to determine whether it's appropriate. This can be a time-consuming process and they may incorrectly determine that the information is appropriate to their needs.

Dynamic content can help to solve these problems by providing users with the right content at the right time and in the right format. Dynamic content minimizes the amount of searching and relevance testing users must do to find the information they need.

Note that dynamic content is not a replacement for well-designed web sites with clearly-structured content or intelligent navigational systems; it is simply one more tool that helps your organization to make content accessible to your users.

## When does dynamic content make sense?

Dynamic content delivery can be a very powerful feature of your content offering, enhancing both user and author experiences. However, dynamic content is a lot of work to design and maintain. Dynamic content requires more in-depth audience analysis, increased metadata, the creation and maintenance of business rules, and additional technology to support delivery. You need to consider the pros and cons of delivering dynamic content to see whether the benefits outweigh the costs.

In addition, dynamic content delivery can slow down the access to your system. The time required to identify the user profile, trigger the business rules, and retrieve and deliver the content can put a strain on your system. Significant volumes of processing reduce performance. To mitigate this issue you can pre-build content based on known configurations. This removes the assembly component of the process, leaving user profile matching and the search and retrieval processes. Pre-built dynamic content is customized to meet users' needs, but because it is built in advance, the time required to assemble and deliver the content is reduced, lessening the strain on the system. In many cases, pre-built content is sufficient. Dynamic content that is built "on-the-fly" may still be required, but the system requirements may be minimized with a combination of pre-built and "on-the-fly" content. Alternatively, dynamic content performance can be improved by the use of an XML-native content management system.

## Examples of dynamic content

Throughout this chapter, three fictional companies are used as examples to illustrate the process of designing dynamic content.

### Example 1: Universal Reach, Inc.

A multi-national corporation (Universal Reach, Inc.) has selected a new Health Maintenance Organization (HMO) for its American employees. Employees need to understand the new plan and its options so that they can choose the correct plan for their needs. The last time the organization made major changes to their benefits, they had to create large volumes of print materials, resulting in endless calls to the Human Resources (HR) department asking for help in explaining the options. HR spent weeks verifying employee options and helping employees correct incorrectly completed forms. This time the organization has decided to provide customized content to their employees through the intranet and supply customized forms to ensure that employees complete the correct form. Their goal is to increase employee understanding of the new program, reduce errors, and reduce the amount of time HR spends providing support. There is only one area of differentiation for employees in addition to their personal information. There are three levels of coverage available (80%, 90%, 100%). Most staff get 80% coverage, management gets 90% coverage, and senior management gets full coverage. However, anyone can choose to purchase increased coverage if desired.

## Example 2: Investors Guide, Inc.

An investment services corporation (Investors Guide, Inc.) sells a series of mutual funds. The funds are designed for a variety of investors who want to select investments based on their level of risk, level of environmental and social consciousness, and which industry sectors to invest in, but investors don't want to pick all the individual stocks themselves. Investors have been slow to re-invest in the stock market after the effects of the "dot com" meltdown and subsequent recession. The corporation has decided to run a campaign to encourage their investors to once again invest in the stock market. They have 27,000 investors, who can choose any combination of 25 different funds. They plan to start with a customized direct mailing, then point investors to the web site for more information. They also plan to send a series of emails.

## Example 3: IPlan, Inc.

A software vendor (IPlan, Inc.) sells large ERP (enterprise resource planning) systems. The software integrates all aspects of a business, including planning, manufacturing, sales, and marketing. The software is modular so that customers can purchase the modules that are appropriate for their organization.

However, customers can go further in their software customization. Fields can be changed to reflect individual corporate terminology, deleted if they are inappropriate, and added if necessary. Screens can be deleted if they are inappropriate or added if necessary.

This level of customization has pleased customers because they can now make the software uniquely their own, but it has also been frustrating because they still get the same generic documentation. This has meant that customers have had to either create all new documentation or create supplementary documentation that is confusing to users (they don't know when to look at the generic information and when to look at the company-specific information).

The software vendor has decided to take on the challenge of enabling their customers to easily customize their documentation. The software vendor already delivers the software application to link with a database, so they plan to deliver the content in the database as well. They plan to provide forms so customers can change, add, or delete content that is then saved into the database along with the vendor-generated content.

# Supporting dynamic content

To deliver dynamic content, your content management system needs to match content user requirements with appropriate content in the repository, then assemble that content and deliver it to users. To support dynamic content you need to:

- Identify your user needs.
- Design metadata and user profiles.
- Identify dynamic elements in models.
- Define business rules for the assembly of dynamic content.

### Identifying user needs

The focus of dynamic content is to deliver the right content to the right user at the right time and in the right format. To do this you need to clearly understand what your users' needs, when they need it, and in what form they need it.

In Chapter 5, "Analyzing the content life cycle," you interviewed users to get an understanding of how they use your content and what issues they may have in using it. However, to determine user requirements for dynamic content, you will have to understand their needs in more depth. You need answers to the following questions:

- Can you group your users into categories? How many categories? What defines each category?
- What content do which users use and when?
- Is the content for one user group different from another user group? How is it different? Where and at what level does it differ (document, section, paragraph)?

- Is content for one product different from another? How is it different? Where and at what level does it differ (document, section, paragraph)?

- What content do users *need* to know? What content is *nice* to know?

- At what level of detail do users want to see content? Do they always want to see it at the same level of detail or do they want to be able to switch from very detailed to a top-level overview?

- What are their interests in your content?

- What are their goals in using your content?

- Do users need to access the same content more than once?

## Personas

Consider creating a persona for each of your user types. A persona is a profile of a typical user. It is created based on a series of interviews with actual users. The persona is not impersonal like a standard user description or a stereotype; you write a persona as though you are describing a real person. The persona has a name, a history, and a set of goals. Personas help designers and others within your organization understand for whom they are designing the dynamic content. When designers satisfy the persona's goals, they also meet the needs of users with similar goals. It is easier to design when you have real people with real goals in mind. The persona makes the design exercise real and applicable rather than abstract.

For example:

> Jane Smith is 35 years old, married, with two children. She is a cautious investor, thoroughly investigating the companies in which she invests.

The concept of using a persona to help software developers more effectively design to meet user needs was popularized by Alan Cooper in his book *The Inmates are Running the Asylum: Why High Tech Products drive Us Crazy and How to Restore the Sanity* (Sams, 1999). Since then, personas have been used to create marketing campaigns, software, and web sites. It makes a lot of sense to use personas to create effective content, as well.

To create a persona, follow these steps:

1. Determine how many personas you require to effectively address your user base.
2. Give each persona a name and a picture.[2]
3. Describe the persona. Include as much detail as possible (likes, dislikes, needs, desires, personality type).
4. Define each persona's goals. Design decisions are based on goals, so take great care in preparing the goals.

For example, the investment services corporation has identified 13 different investor personas. Using these personas, the company has planned the following outputs:

- Direct mailer
- Colorful envelope with a photograph on the back and a phrase that the investor can immediately relate to
- Three to four single-fold inserts that have a photograph on the front and open to a short educational piece and a list of representative funds
- Prominent display of the number to call and the web site address
- Web site
- Personalized welcome screen
- Personalized home page (direct links to fund descriptions and status)
- Annual report customized to the investor's funds
- Matching content to direct mailer
- Links to more related information
- Customer support
- Overview of the campaign
- Sample direct mails
- Persona description
- Dynamic link to the investor's customized web site and mailer material
- Details of all the product offerings

---

2  You can take pictures from a magazine, if desired, but make sure they typify your personas (age, sex, profession, and so on).

Figure 10.1 illustrates a persona for a family investor who invests in the investment services corporation funds.

**Figure 10.1    Family investor persona.**

Kristin and Alan—Dual-income family, 2 kids, a house and a cottage. Kristin and Alan have been married for 20 years. They have one child heading to college next year and one child in middle school. They both have good jobs and have been promoted in the last year. Although their income is increasing, they are also experiencing rising costs with two mortgages and upcoming college fees. They have two credit cards in common and Kristin has an additional department store card.

Both are comfortable using the Internet to research products prior to making purchases and do this regularly from home. Kristin and Alan discuss all their investment decisions together before making a final decision.   Goals:

- Pay down debt faster
- Increase cash flow
- Save sufficient funds for their child's college of choice
- Pay off the mortgages before retirement

This persona lets the designers design an appropriate campaign to meet their needs. A categorization scheme is set up that enables the designer to match the profile to the appropriate content. In the case of Kristin and Alan, the designers provide the following:

- Mailer
- Colorful envelope with a photograph on the back of a couple sitting at a computer on a desk that has a number of items on it like the stock page, books about investment, and so on, and the phrase "Investing for the future, but not at the expense of today."
- Inserts
  - Overview of investor services.
  - Educational piece on balancing risk for long term investment with reasonable payments.
  - Two balanced risk funds that have slightly more risk than those currently held by the investor, but with some prospect of rapid growth.
- Prominent display of the number to call and the web site address
- Web site
  - Personalized welcome screen.
  - Personalized home page (direct links to their fund descriptions and status).
  - Annual report customized to their funds.
  - Matching content to mailer.
  - Links to more related information.

Personas can assist you in designing effective dynamic content.

## Designing metadata and user profiles

The content management system uses metadata to identify content that is appropriate for a particular user. The users' needs are defined in their user profiles, which are developed based on the metadata. To define your metadata you need to define which information differentiates users so you can match the appropriate content to their needs.

User profiles are tied to a user login. When users log in, their login identifies them to the system, which then activates their profile. The user profile can be used to configure content, so that when users log in to the site they see only the information that is relevant to them, or to provide them with appropriate options for viewing content.

Table 10.1 shows some of the metadata for Universal Reach. (Note that the metadata values are samples only; the lists are incomplete.)

**Table 10.1    Universal Reach metadata**

| Metadata | Value |
| --- | --- |
| Role | Senior Management |
| | Management |
| | Executive Assistant |
| | Engineer |
| | Programmer |
| Location | Brazil |
| | Canada |
| | England |
| | France |
| | Germany |
| | Hong Kong |
| | Singapore |
| | United States |
| Language | English |
| | French |
| | German |
| | Spanish |
| Security permissions | None |
| | Level 2 |
| | Level 4 |

Similarly, Table 10.2 shows some of the metadata for Investors Guide, Inc.

**Table 10.2    Investors Guide metadata**

| Metadata | Value |
|---|---|
| Name | This metadata does not have a fixed vocabulary (taxonomy); it is given the value of the person's name. |
| Investor profile | Family<br>Young and single<br>Double income, no kids<br>Empty nester<br>Reaching retirement |
| Fund | Fund 1<br>Fund 2<br>Fund 3 |
| Goals | Long-term growth<br>High-tech stocks<br>Biotechnology |

Metadata isn't necessary for the software vendor because the content to be displayed is not dependent upon metadata. Instead, it is dependent upon the values that have been assigned to the customer configuration. After these values have been set, the content does not change.

## Matching metadata to the user profile

After you have established metadata, you can match it to each user profile. The user profile then becomes the known information (metadata) for that particular user. Table 10.3 illustrates the user profile for Kristin and Alan.

**Table 10.3   Kristin and Alan's user profile**

| Profile | Value |
| --- | --- |
| Name | Kristin Jordan<br>Alan Becker |
| Investor profile | Family |
| Fund | Fund 1<br>Fund 4<br>Fund 7<br>Fund 9 |
| Goals | Long-term growth |

Table 10.4 illustrates a portion of a user profile for an employee from Universal Reach.

**Table 10.4   Sample Universal Reach employee profile**

| Profile | Value |
| --- | --- |
| Name | Christine Farmer |
| Role | Engineer |
| Location | United States |
| Language | English |
| Security permissions | Level 2 |

As before, IPlan's situation is different from the other two companies. In this case the user is the customer, not the individual employees of the customer. However, as Table 10.5 illustrates, the user profile is very similar.

**Table 10.5   IPlan customer profile**

| Profile | Value |
| --- | --- |
| Name | Acadian, Inc. |
| Modules | HR<br>Accounting |
| Customization | Table of the customizations the customer made to each module |

## *Dynamic user profiles*

Good user profiles are not static; they are dynamic (can be updated to reflect more detailed user information and changes in current user information), just like the content. You can start by identifying what you know about users, but their profiles should change depending upon their actions. Additional user profile information is identified through

- **User selection**

  Users can identify the type of information they want to view. They do this by selecting options on a web-based form. For example:

  - **Universal Reach Inc.**—The default dental coverage for all employees except management is 80%. Employees can select the dental upgrade option to bring their coverage to 100% at their own cost. Their user profiles are then updated to reflect this selection and the intranet customizes their standard employee forms to include full coverage and associated cost.

  - **Investors Guide Inc.**—If an investor selects "Biotech" to learn more about opportunities for investment in the Biotech industry, the user profile is updated so the investor receives emails about new Biotech opportunities as they become available.

  - **IPlan Inc.**—Each time IPlan customizes the software, the changes are added to the customization table in the user profile. Imagine, for example, that the customer changes the field named Social Security Number to Social Insurance Number. Now, if employees ask for help on how to complete the field, they are provided with content that explains that they must include the nine-digit code without hyphens.

- **Personalization**

  User profiles contain known or explicit information. With personalization, the software "learns" about users by observing what they do and predicting their requirements. In the case of the three fictional companies, Universal

Reach and IPlan decide not to use personalization. Universal Reach feels that they know their employees' content requirements very well and can explicitly define them by using a customer profile. IPlan does not provide personalization because usage of their product requires the delivery of specific content; it does not lend itself to personalization.

On the other hand, Investor's Guide decides to use personalization to determine investors' interests based on the content they browse on the site. If an investor whose profile indicates he is adverse to risks looks at stocks that get high returns, but are considered riskier, it may indicate that the investor is willing to incorporate a little more risk into the portfolio. The system would then recommend a different fund, which has a higher risk than the investor currently has selected, while still providing some less risky stocks as well. The system would also deliver educational materials to help the investor understand the value of risk.

The additional information identified through user selection or personalization is added to the user profile. The next time the user logs on, the content is refined by the modified profile.

## Identifying dynamic elements in models

Chapter 8, "Information modeling," described how to design your content models and in particular how to identify the elements of reusable content. When content is being dynamically assembled it relies on detailed information models to ensure that the correct content is assembled in the correct order and in the correct context.

Figure 10.2 illustrates the components of the HMO content to be displayed based on role. In this case, the dynamic content is based on sections, rather than elements within a section. This means that the information product model identifies which content should be displayed based on role.

| | A | B |
|---|---|---|
| 1 | | Role |
| 2 | Overview | All |
| 3 | Introduction | All |
| 4 | Policy | All |
| 5 | Procedure | All |
| 6 | Coverage | All |
| 7 | Basic | All |
| 8 | Extended | Management |
| 9 | | Purchased |
| 10 | | Senior Management |
| 11 | Full | Purchased |
| 12 | | Senior Management |
| 13 | Limitations | All |
| 14 | Accidental Injury | All |
| 15 | Braces | All |
| 16 | Making a claim | All |
| 17 | Enrollment Form | All |
| 18 | Basic | All |
| 19 | Extended | Management |
| 20 | | Purchased |
| 21 | | Senior Management |
| 22 | Full | Purchased |
| 23 | | Senior Management |

**Figure 10.2    Universal Reach information product model.**

Much of the content for investors is also dynamic at the section level. For example, all content related to a fund is displayed if an investor has purchased that fund. Other content, such as proposed funds and educational materials, is based on user interest and investor profile.

The content for IPlan's customers is dynamic at a much more granular level—content can change at the field level, which can be a word or phrase within a sentence. Figure 10.3 illustrates a standard employee information screen. A Canadian company, Acadian, Inc., has purchased the software and needs to change Social Security Number to Social Insurance Number, State to Province, and Zip Code to Postal Code. These changes in turn impact the associated content (everywhere these fields were referred to is changed in the dynamic content).

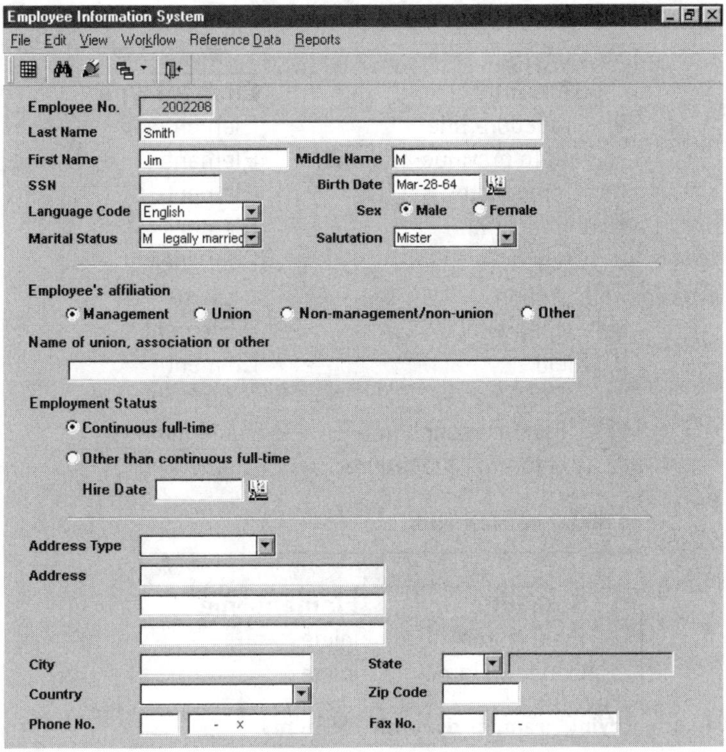

**Figure 10.3    Employee information screen.**

Typically, when you create an information model, your elements are block elements (elements that exist on their own as a paragraph); however, the model for the software vendor's dynamic content also needs inline elements (elements that exist within a line such as a sentence). The inline elements let you use a variable or attribute to dynamically change their values in the content. In this case, the two inline elements are Field Name and Window Name. Figure 10.4 illustrates the information model (10.4a) and the inline elements (10.4b). The inline elements are common elements in that can be used in any other model.

**10.4a Semantic model**

| | A | B |
|---|---|---|
| 1 | **Semantic** | **Element type** |
| 2 | Procedure title | Element |
| 3 | Xref to previous procedure | Element |
| 4 | Prerequisites | Element |
| 5 | Introduction | Element |
| 6 | Step | Container |
| 7 | Action | Element |
| 8 | Step explanation | Element |
| 9 | Field | Element |
| 10 | Field Name | Element |
| 11 | Field Description | Element |
| 12 | Xref to next procedure | Element |

**10.4b Inline elements**

| | A | B |
|---|---|---|
| 1 | **Semantic** | **Element type** |
| 2 | Field Name | Inline |
| 3 | Window Name | Inline |

**Figure 10.4   Identifying granular dynamic elements.**

## Designing dynamic content business rules

In addition to user profiles and information models, a dynamic content system requires retrieval rules. These rules are often referred to as *business rules* and your content management system needs them to control when content is displayed, what content is displayed, and under what circumstances. You need to base your business rules on many aspects of the content user, such as the following:

- Specific knowledge requirements
- Related knowledge requirements
- Permissions to view certain content

Rules typically operate by an "if-then" process. If something is true, then specific content is displayed. Figure 10.5 illustrates the business rules for an employee of Universal Reach.

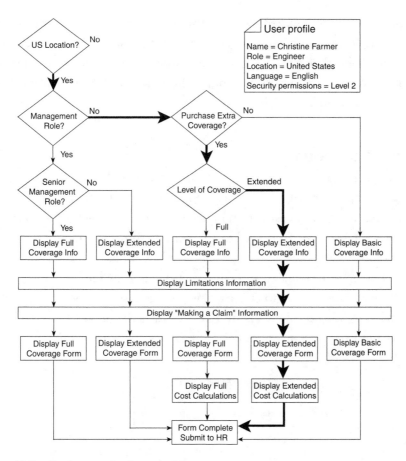

**Figure 10.5   Business rules for employee.**

The business rules for the investor are similar to those of the employee. Content is displayed based on the values of user profiles and through user selections. However, Investors Guide has selected to use personalization. This means that an additional component of the content management system tracks what the investor looks at, compares this activity to other similar investors, and determines what suggestions to make or additional information to display. For example, two funds have been suggested to the investor. One component of one of the new funds is biotechnology stocks. If the investor looks at a number of additional components on biotechnology, the system displays another fund that has a greater percentage of biotechnology stocks. The business rule might look like this:

if biotechnology article equal to or greater than 3, display suggest fund #23

Business rules are not required for the software vendor's content. Dynamic content happens when customers make changes to their systems; the changes are reflected in a table that maps the new information to the appropriate content. After this customization occurs, the content becomes static until additional system changes are made.

## Systematic reuse

Dynamic content is also used to help authors, providing them with documents that are pre-populated with reusable content. Systematic reuse employs exactly the same technology and design techniques as dynamic content or personalization for customers, except it is used to dynamically compile content for an author to edit. Systematic reuse uses a combination of business rules and user selection to determine which information is automatically reused. For example, a marketing author is about to create a new press release for a new expanded version of an existing product. Figure 10.6 illustrates the press release model first introduced in Chapter 8. Everything identified as systematic is automatically inserted.

| | A | F |
|---|---|---|
| 1 | | |
| 2 | | Reuse |
| 3 | **Semantic** | |
| 4 | Subject | |
| 5 | Date | |
| 6 | Month | |
| 7 | Day | |
| 8 | Year | |
| 9 | Contact | |
| 10 | Name | |
| 11 | First | |
| 12 | Last | |
| 13 | Contact Phone | |
| 14 | Contact Email | |
| 15 | Body | |
| 16 | Corporate Desc Short | Systematic |
| 17 | Announcement | |
| 18 | Paragraphs | |
| 19 | Ordered lists | |
| 20 | Unordered lists | |
| 21 | Product Desc. Short | Systematic |
| 22 | Features | |
| 23 | Benefits | |
| | Quote | |
| 24 | | |
| 25 | Availability | Systematic |
| 26 | Corp. Desc | Systematic |
| 27 | Corp. Desc Short | Systematic |
| 28 | Corp. Desc. Med. | Systematic |
| 29 | Website address | Systematic |

**Figure 10.6   Press release systematic reuse elements.**

Systematic reuse requires that you analyze your author's requirements and your policies on corporate content reuse. Think about how you can make authors' jobs easier by automatically making appropriate reusable content available as they begin to author, or by ensuring that corporate standard content is automatically reused. For more about systematic reuse see Chapter 2, "Fundamental concepts of reuse."

---

**Dynamic content: A case study**

Scotiabank is one of North America's leading financial institutions, and Canada's most international bank. We provide innovative financial products and services to individuals, small and medium-size businesses, corporations and governments across Canada and around the world.

**What we did and why**

We had 61,000 pages of policies and procedures information. Each procedure contained both policy and procedure information, and included all the steps for every employee who had to perform part of the procedure. This meant that users had to pick out the steps that applied to them, which was confusing not to mention time consuming.

In the first phase of the project we took key procedures and rewrote them as job aids. A job aid contains procedural content only and is written for a specific role, meaning employees no longer had to determine which portion of the procedure was applicable to them. Everything was applicable, because it was role specific. Employees responded very positively to the job aids and were eager to see all content rewritten this way.

Initially, job aids were written for paper with reusable content copied and pasted among the different versions of the procedure (such as, common content applicable to a number of different roles). During the second phase, we planned to move the job aids online. We were implementing a new version of the intranet, using a web content management system and a portal. This provided an excellent opportunity to take advantage of dynamic content to deliver roles-based job aids. Each employee was assigned a user profile that gave them appropriate access to content and applications. The user profile could also be used to determine customized delivery of job aid content.

However, before the job aids could be moved online, we needed an information model to identify how job aids should be structured for automated reuse and dynamic delivery. We created a job aid model and associated metadata. The model employed nested reuse, allowing authors to create one procedure with all the roles-based versions of the procedure contained within it. We identified that the granularity of reuse was at the step level because different steps applied to different roles. Our initial analysis identified that the procedure's "Aim" was based on role as well, but more detailed analysis showed that the Aim should be identical for all roles. Once we determined which information should be different and which should be the same, the model became the specification for the HTML form authors would use to input content, allowing authors to create content and apply metadata based on who performs the step in the procedure.

*continues* ▶

*continues*

---

**Benefits**

The old process of creating multiple paper versions of the job aid using a copy and paste process was very time consuming. Updating content was very difficult since all versions of the content had to be found and updated. Having all the content in one place makes it very simple to maintain.

Making content available to employees based on role makes it easy for them to get exactly the information they needed when they need it.

**Lessons learned**

Forms are not the best way to handle granular reusable content. Since our content varied at the step level, it was difficult to create a form that allowed authors to write individual steps, then add the metadata identifying which roles the steps apply to. The first version of the form was unusable by authors; it had to be redesigned.

In addition, as we began to plan for conversion we realized that in some cases an employee's actual title did not correspond to a unique role and sometimes multiple roles applied to the same job title. Some job aids had to be rethought before they could be moved online.

**Wendy Shrubsole**

**Biography**

Wendy Shrubsole is Assistant General Manager of the Business Process Delivery team at Scotiabank. She has a total of 22 years experience in the financial industry, 8 of these years with Scotiabank. Her department is responsible for researching new methodologies and technologies, establishing and maintaining user interface standards for Domestic Banking Applications, performing heuristic reviews and usability testing, developing and maintaining conceptual models for the field staff desktop application, and identifying and conducting proof-of-concept opportunities with developing technologies.

---

# Summary

Dynamic content enables your organization to give customers the content they need, when they need it, and in the format they need it. However, dynamic content doesn't just happen. It requires a lot of analysis and intelligent thinking to create user profiles, dynamic content models, business rules, and appropriate content.

Systematic reuse involves using the same dynamic content functionality to dynamically assemble content to meet the authors' needs rather than the users' needs. Analyze your authors' needs as thoroughly as you would your customers' needs to design effective systematic reuse.

Content user requirements are defined through:

- User profiles (known information about the user)
- User selection (additional information identified/requested by users)
- Personalization (learned information based on user actions)

To support dynamic content you need to:

- Identify your user needs.

  Conduct a thorough audience analysis and develop user personas (profile of a typical user), clearly identify who uses your content, how they use it, and what their ongoing content requirements are.

- Design metadata and user profiles.

  The content management system uses metadata to identify content that is appropriate for a particular content user. The requirements of the content are defined in the user profile; the metadata further ensures that content is retrieved appropriately. Use the metadata to create user profiles that explicitly identify the user requirements.

- Identify dynamic elements in models.

  Dynamic content relies on detailed information models to ensure that the correct content is assembled in the correct order and in the correct context.

- Define rules for the assembly of dynamic content.

  Rules determine what content is to be displayed, when it should be displayed, and under what circumstances.

# Chapter 11

## Designing workflow

Workflow, in the context of a unified
content strategy, defines how people
and tasks interact to create, update,
manage, and deliver content. Workflow moves content from task to task,
ensuring that the business rules specific to your organization are followed,
for example, that sign-off occurs at the
appropriate levels. This chapter
describes the concepts of workflow
and its benefits, and takes you through
the basics of designing workflow to
support your unified content life cycle.

Once you've determined what your workflow processes should be, you can select tools to support and automate them. Refer to Chapter 17, "Workflow systems," for information on tools that support workflow.

## What is workflow?

Workflow, as its name implies, is the way tasks flow through a cycle on their way to getting a job done. Workflow helps organizations perform tasks in an efficient and repeatable manner.

Workflow is a process that may or may not be automated. However, when numerous people and activities are involved in a process, human-controlled workflows can be problematic; steps can be missed, work forgotten or misplaced, and approvals omitted, all delaying the finished product. With automated workflow, organizations can create repeatable and verifiable processes to ensure that all stages of a project are completed in the proper order. But, before automating a workflow, you must first design and test it so that processes are consistent with your unified content life cycle. When designing workflow, you represent it diagrammatically, showing the various tasks involved in a project. Your workflow representation not only illustrates all the tasks and players, it also shows where your processes need to be simplified before they are automated. Just as you are improving the way you create and manage content, you are improving the processes involved through the content life cycle.

The following are the components of workflow:

- **Roles (players)**
  The people who do the tasks, identified by their role

- **Responsibilities (tasks)**
  The steps to complete a particular piece of work; everything that must get done within a process

- **Processes**
  The flow of tasks, as performed by the various players, showing the interactions and interdependencies among players

These components are described in more detail later in this chapter.

# Benefits of workflow

Chapter 8, "Information modeling," compares building information products to building a house. Houses are constructed based on their blueprints, and information products are constructed based on their information models. Once the blueprint is completed and sign-off has taken place, the builders follow processes to make sure all the construction tasks happen in the correct order. Some tasks are dependent on others, some are concurrent, and at some stages, the building inspectors, the architects, and the home owners review the completed work before construction of the next components can proceed. In the construction industry, despite the best blueprints, timing and planning are critical. The blueprint simply lays out the plan; the workflow ensures it gets done properly. Accordingly, workflow is tracked throughout construction to ensure that certain things occur:

- Materials are delivered in the order that they are used (for example, concrete before shingles, framing materials before windows).

- Other players (subtrades) come in when they're supposed to (for example, electricians can't do their part before the frame is up) and concurrent jobs are scheduled appropriately, so that time isn't wasted.

- Approvals are done at the right time (for example, inspection of the electrical work has to be done before the walls are up, obscuring the wiring).

Workflow in a unified content life cycle is similar to the workflow that builders follow. Despite the best information models, creating information products should progress in a logical, well-designed flow to ensure that tasks are completed in the proper order, by the correct people, and that approvals occur when they are supposed to. In the content management world, good workflow design ensures that:

- Departments that should be creating content—or that should at least know about it—aren't left out.

- Content and all other supporting elements—such as graphics—are created in the proper order (for example, content is written before graphics are drawn, ensuring the graphics support the content).

- Content is reviewed at the right time, by the right people, eliminating reviews and approvals that have to be redone if additional changes are made.

- Departments are notified when content is published (for example, customer service staff are notified when a new brochure is out in case they get phone calls about it).

- Efforts aren't duplicated and content is consistent (for example, different departments don't end up creating different versions of the same content).

- Work isn't held up at any given stage of the workflow.

- Content is stored in the right place after it's written, reviewed, approved, and delivered.

An effective workflow is really just the organized and managed application of common sense, as governed by the business rules of your organization.

### Improving and simplifying processes

Through workflow representation, you can see processes as they exist now, then depict them as you'd like them to be. Simplification should always be one of your goals when depicting your workflow. Otherwise, you may end up including tasks that don't need to be done in the first place, like sending information to a department as part of the approval or review process, when all they really need is notification that the information has been published. It's not only critical to depict everything that happens, but also what should happen. This is similar to information modeling, in which you don't model information products as they are currently structured, but rather, as they should be structured.

To improve or simplify a process, you analyze and change the tasks, then test the process to make sure the work will flow properly. Tasks may be eliminated or combined, the sequence and location where the task is performed may be changed, as can the person who performs the task. Benefits of such change include:

- **Greater efficiency**

   With well-designed workflow, the work is easier and can be done more quickly, and the tasks require fewer steps to complete. Tasks are handled concurrently wherever possible and "what ifs" are built into the processes, eliminating delays.

- **Better quality**

  Better quality results from focusing tasks more clearly. Tasks become more individualized; they are smaller and less complicated, taking less time to complete. With more focused tasks, authors can visualize the big picture without being pressured by it. Instead, they focus on their particular tasks as those tasks relate to the big picture.

- **Lower costs**

  When duplicate efforts are eliminated, costs are lower. When content is consistent, less effort is required to address inconsistencies, either from internal or external users.

# Depicting workflow

A good workflow system must be able to support your workflow design, but for your workflow system to work effectively, you must first design what you want it to do. You need to figure out how—given certain business situations—tasks such as authoring, editing, reviewing, approval, publishing, and distribution should flow throughout your organization and what should happen if, at any given stage, a task cannot be completed as dictated by the workflow.

Because workflow describes the "flow" of tasks, it is usually depicted diagrammatically in either a linear flowchart or a swimlane diagram.

## Flowcharts

Linear flowcharts depict a process from beginning to end, often using flowcharting symbols to indicate the types of tasks in the process. Flowcharting symbols illustrate such things as which task is a process, which task is a decision, which task is a predefined process, which task is a manual operation, and so on. Although flowcharting symbols can be useful in representing meaning visually, we recommend a simpler approach: boxes with clear task descriptions written in them. Flowcharts should be understandable to most people, with minimal training or effort. They should also be universal. Many people become frustrated trying to interpret what the many different flowcharting symbols mean and their frustration is compounded if there are no clear task descriptions accompanying the symbols.

## Swimlane diagrams

Swimlane diagrams show processes in "lanes" (like the in which lanes you swim laps) to depict tasks that occur concurrently, illustrating who does what, and when. Swimlane diagrams are known by many other names, among them process maps, business process maps, process responsibility diagrams, and LOV (line of visibility) charts. Like in a pool, where swimmers are expected to stay in their own lanes, players stay in their process lanes. However, with all the lanes shown, players can see how what they do depends on what others do and vice versa. In addition to using arrows to connect tasks linearly, you use arrows to connect the tasks in the various swimlanes. Figure 11.1 uses a swimlane diagram to illustrate the opportunistic reuse process. (Note that players are shown by their roles, followed by the names of their departments in parentheses.)

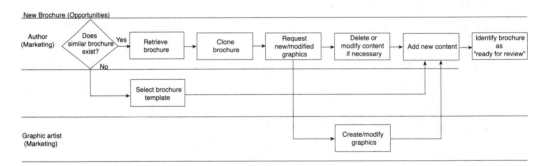

**Figure 11.1    Opportunistic reuse workflow.**

Figure 11.2 illustrates the systematic reuse process. Note the similarities and the dissimilarities between the systematic reuse process with the opportunistic reuse process.

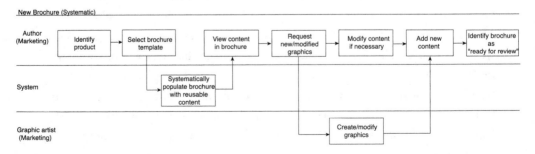

**Figure 11.2    Systematic reuse workflow.**

## Swimlane diagrams or flowcharts?

How should you depict your workflow? It really depends on what you want to depict. We like to use swimlane diagrams because they show the interdependencies of tasks. Linear flowcharts are useful if you want to show all the tasks within a process, with a view to simplifying them. This technique can be effective when you need buy-in from others in your organization. Linear flowcharts that detail every step, including hand-offs and wait-tasks, may end up being many feet long. Their size alone may convince others that the process should be simplified.

To design workflow as it will be supported by a workflow system, you may want to use a swimlane diagram. A swimlane diagram shows all roles and all tasks, as they relate to each other, which is critical in a unified content strategy. Also, people can highlight their particular role on a printout for quick reference. However, with that said, while depicting workflow, simplification should always be one of your goals regardless of what type of diagram you use. While drafting your swimlane diagrams, you may want to use flowcharts to illustrate where you can simplify tasks.

# Roles, responsibilities, and processes

Workflow consists of roles (the people or "players" who participate in the process), responsibilities (the tasks for which the players are responsible), and processes (the workflows that connect all the people and tasks together and define the path that each task must take).

## Roles (players)

Developing, managing, and delivering content involves many people with different skills, spanning many tasks over an extended period of time. Content comprises many elements: text, images (and potentially video and sound), layout and design, and so on. This multi-faceted nature of content introduces complexity into its development process. Many different departments create content in a number of different formats for a number of different audiences; once content is created and delivered, it must be stored so that it can be accessed later on.

## Who is a player?

Generally, a player is any person or group that handles the work between the initial event and the achievement of the process's results. A player can be anyone who fulfills a role within your organization, or a player can be an external customer or supplier. Information systems are also players. The role of a player may be very complex or as simple as being notified that a new product or new information is available. Regardless of the complexity—or simplicity—of each role, the workflow must accommodate all roles. If you leave out roles, you will not have an accurate depiction of all the project phases, which could unnecessarily delay your project.

Some common players are:

- **Authors**

  An author is anyone involved with creating content of any type (for example, text or graphics). Authors should have full permission to create, modify, and delete their own content, but not anyone else's. Authors can be broken down into as many types of authors as your organization has.

- **Reviewers**

  Reviewers check content for such things as accuracy, completeness, appropriateness. Reviewers are usually limited to making comments on the content without changing it.

- **Editors**

  Editors review and make changes to content; the scope of their changes depends on their role as either substantive or copy editors. Editors can also be reviewers, but unlike reviewers, their permissions allow them to modify the content.

- **Approvers**

  Approvers provide the final sign-off for content before it is "posted" or published. Approvers can also be reviewers, and although their permissions are similar to the reviewers' permissions, approvers have the final authority to determine whether the content is ready to go to the public.

The workflow doesn't tell the players how to do their part; it tells them that they have a part, what that part is, and when it must be done. The workflow must also allow for alternatives if players are not available when they are required.

## Depicting roles

In a swimlane diagram, the players are the swimmers actually doing the work (tasks) shown in the swimlanes. Your workflow must depict how all the different swimmers collaborate on the different aspects of your project in a tightly integrated manner, without swimming into other swimmers' lanes! In a swimlane diagram, each player is shown on the left side of the diagram, beside the lane which they belong in. Players are shown by their roles (for example, Information Architect), not by their individual names, along with the name of the department.

### Responsibilities (tasks)

One of the most common questions people ask when charting their workflows is, "What is a task; how do I know what to include?" A task is a particular series of actions that accomplish a particular goal. A good rule of thumb is if it must "get done," then it's a task and you need to show it. To determine all the tasks within a workflow, you need to talk to the various players about their responsibilities, keeping the discussion focused on the particular process, not all the activities of the players their department.

## Types of tasks

You can categorize tasks into three types:

- **Tasks that add value (work tasks)**
  When value is added to a task, the work is changed in some way. Content may be written, approved, revised, returned for correction, have metadata added to it, and so on. Work is being performed on a work item, including inspection or validation activities. This is also known as "work time" and it advances the progress of the workflow as a whole.

- **Tasks that move the work along (transport tasks)**
  A task that moves the work along does not change a work item (for example, content isn't written or edited); instead, it moves the work item from task to task in the workflow. People tend to exclude these tasks from their workflow, but transport tasks are critical to include because they illustrate important parts of the process, such as how a work item gets to the next person. Also, a transport task that moves information to a different location may take longer. In a transport task, include information on how the

work item is transported. For example, "route first draft by email to supervisor in head office," or "courier original artwork to ad agency," or "post to intranet."

- **Tasks that introduce a delay (wait tasks)**

  When a task introduces a delay, the subsequent task cannot proceed until the previous one is finished. A task that introduces a delay may not actually do anything to the work item; instead, it pauses the process temporarily. Most tasks introduce a delay simply by their nature; after all, it takes time for work to get done or transported. Sometimes when a delay is introduced, the next task may still be able to proceed. For example, while waiting for graphics, an author may still be able to complete a draft, then insert the graphics when they arrive. However, a delay-introducing task means that the next task has to wait for the previous one to be finished. An example of this is "wait for content from marketing before completing draft." While waiting, the author can do other work, but not work that moves this process along. It's important to include these types of delays because they give you a more accurate depiction of how long a process will take. A process may appear to take only 42 hours, but the delays may extend it up to 80 hours or more.

## Writing and depicting tasks

Regardless of the type of task, we recommend writing tasks consistently in a verb-noun format. Anyone who reads a workflow diagram should be able to understand it, so you should avoid cryptic descriptions such as "Form CP-13." A task is something that is performed, and accordingly, should be written as an action. Instead of writing "Form CP-13"—which is highly open to interpretation—you would write something like "Submit graphics request on Form CP-13." Optionally, you can include "how" information in your step, for example, "Sort graphics requests" could become "Sort graphics requests by due date," providing additional information on how the task should be completed. You can also use qualifiers to modify the noun, for example, "Sort graphics requests from marketing by their due date." The more descriptive you can make your task, the better. Tasks must never be open to interpretation. Although the task name must convey its result (for example, the result of "sort graphics request by due date" is that graphics requests are sorted by due date), do not write the task by focusing on the result, as in "Graphics requests are sorted." The task should focus on the verb, the action of performing the task. It is not necessary to include players in the task description because they are indicated in the swimlane diagram and all the tasks belonging to a particular player are put in that player's lane.

The system can have tasks as well. It can do such things as publish content to PDF, post content to the web site, or notify a reviewer that content is ready to review. These are tasks that are programmed by a system developer or integrator and to be included in workflow, they must available in your system. When you're setting up your workflow system, be sure that it can perform the tasks you're asking it to do (refer to Chapter 17).

In a swimlane diagram, tasks are shown in the swimlane of the player who does the task, with descriptive text depicting each task.

## Processes (flow)

A process has a start point and an end point between which various tasks are performed, usually by a number of different people located in different places, who are often using different equipment or systems. A process comprises the tasks and responsibilities, as performed by the various players, and the workflow must illustrate the entire process from beginning to end. So, where to start? First, you need to decide where your process begins, where it ends, then start charting everything that happens in between.

Processes may start outside the system, but automated workflow starts when the system can manage a task. For example, the process to create a web product page may start with a meeting to discuss the requirements for the page. But the meeting may occur long before the system takes the content and routes it. This is not to say that you might not capture the meeting in a set of minutes with action items. In fact, you can store the meeting minutes in the content management system, designating them as "content of record" for access by team members. When you are depicting workflow, you may also include such tasks as "determining project requirements" and "holding meetings." Even though they are not managed by the workflow system, it's a good idea to include such tasks; they form part of the entire process and may be overlooked if not described.

However, the automated workflow starts when work begins on the action items, such as when the specification is created or when the marketing writer begins to write. At whichever point the process must be managed automatically, workflow begins. If you include requirements tasks, or tasks that are not managed through the system in your swimlane diagrams, you should indicate where the automated workflow begins; the automated tasks form your requirements for selecting and configuring a workflow system.

It can also be difficult to determine the end of workflow. For example, a web product page is posted to the Web, but it is modified over time to remain current. You could include the updates in the initial creation workflow, but it probably makes sense to end the workflow when the page has been posted. Then you can create an additional workflow that handles the content when it needs to be updated, modified, or corrected.

In a sense, the entire workflow process is like a virtual assembly line on which the various players perform various tasks to support the unified content life cycle. For example, research and development develops a new version of a software package; marketing gets the word out to potential customers; subject matter experts review the existing documentation to determine which elements can be used as is and which should be revised; technical publications makes the necessary changes, and so on. After all the tasks on the assembly line are complete, the last task is to notify the originator, thus ending the process.

Your company may also have specific processes for different types of projects. For example, you may need to develop workflows to support the content life cycle for:

- New products or services
- Updates to existing products or services
- Discontinued products or services

You may also need to develop workflows for special situations, such as emergency notification of changes to your products. Depending on how complex they are, each of your workflows may also be broken down into various supporting workflows, but they must all relate to the common goal. That is, don't have separate workflows for the various tasks in individual departments. You need to see how departments coordinate their tasks for them to be truly unified. For example, in the construction industry, there are workflows for the framing, the electrical work, and the plumbing, but they all relate to the master plan and depend on each other. Likewise, in a unified content strategy there may be workflows for writing user documentation, for developing collateral and graphics, and for creating training materials. All the processes are part of an overall project and are dependent on each other.

## Business requirements often govern workflow

Processes are also usually governed by business requirements, specific to your organization. Business requirements include such things as:

- Budgets that dictate how much can be spent on any given task
- Hours of work in which tasks can be completed
- Union job descriptions (or other associations) that govern who can perform a certain task and under which conditions
- Physical location of the company that dictates where a task is performed (physical location can affect such things as handoffs and transport tasks, as well as translation and localization)
- Suppliers that your company does business with and their particular constraints

When determining your workflow, you need to consider the business rules specific to your environment.

## Depicting processes

Processes are shown in swimlane diagrams with specific start and end points, and with all lanes completed with all relevant tasks, including such things as handoffs and delays. Where a task is performed by two players at the same time, you can write the task in each lane, but draw a box around them both to show they are performed together. Use arrows to connect the flow of tasks and to show when they transfer to another role/lane. Figure 11.3 illustrates the parallel tasks of review with all the members of the review team.

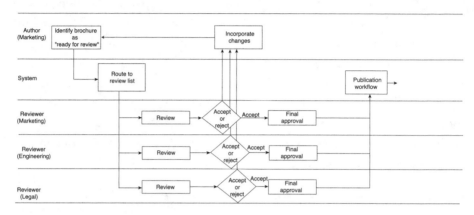

**Figure 11.3    Review and approval workflow.**

Remember that when designing workflow, it's important that you don't chart the processes as they currently exist in your organization, but instead, try to improve, or simplify, them. Accordingly, your first draft flowcharts may show processes in their current state, but your unified content life cycle workflows should show your processes as they will support your unified content strategy

## Designing effective workflow

The components of an effective workflow are players, their responsibilities (or tasks) and the processes they all follow. Designing an effective workflow involves analysis of players and their tasks, as well as identification of patterns and inter-actions, then a documenting of detailed tasks, followed by testing.

To design effective workflow, follow these steps, referring to your content life cycle:

1. Determine a starting point for your workflow. Usually a process starts with an incoming event, such as a new product being made ready for market, or a request to update existing documentation. A starting point can also be a crisis that you need to respond to. If you include tasks that are not part of the automated workflow, indicate where automated workflow begins.

2. Figure out a logical place for the workflow to end. This is typically when the incoming event that triggered the beginning has been handled satisfactorily. In a unified content life cycle, content must be stored in the repository for the event to be considered complete.

3. Identify all players from the beginning to the end of the workflow. Identify players by their roles rather than by their names. A task should be associated with a role to accommodate people moving in and out of jobs. If tasks are assigned to roles, regardless of where particular people move in your organization, the task stays with the role. If you assign tasks to people, you have to go into your workflow system and make changes every time the people change jobs.

4. Sketch the tasks. Start by identifying all the tasks that belong to each player, including when those tasks are waiting for something else to happen, or when they are handing off work to someone else. Remember to write tasks clearly so that everyone who looks at the flow knows exactly what the task is about. (You may omit notification in your first iteration, allowing you to focus more clearly on the tasks themselves. However, notification must be included before your workflow can be considered complete. See step 7.) Look for potential bottlenecks that may slow your workflow down, such as one player having too many tasks at a certain stage, while other players wait for those tasks to be done so they can contribute theirs. Can tasks be delegated to other roles? Can tasks be completed concurrently?

5. Identify interaction patterns among players and tasks. When are players working alone and when are they working with others? A critical component of workflow is in designing the interactions among players and their tasks. Who relies on whom or on what information? When there are numerous interactions, there may also be bottlenecks; look for potential bottlenecks that may slow your workflow down, such as information not being ready so one player is delayed in performing a task. Can you build in an alternative?

6. Allocate timeframes for tasks. In addition to selecting a start and end for the entire workflow, you should allocate start and end times for each task. When is each task complete and how much time should you allow from the time a task is assigned until it is completed? How much leeway should you build into the timeframe?

7. Identify notification patterns. Who needs to know what at any given stage of the workflow?

8. Identify approval patterns. Who is responsible for reviewing work items throughout the workflow? It's important to distinguish approval from notification. Sometimes a department only needs to know about what you're doing, but they don't necessarily have to approve it. Make sure all your approvals are valid.

9. Determine all the "what ifs" that may knock your workflow off its path. Try to think of everything that could happen to deter workflow. For example, what happens if an approver is away? Can work be routed to someone else for approval? What happens to other tasks if a deadline is missed? What if a tool breaks or if content is lost somewhere along the way?

10. After all roles are identified, tasks are sketched, and notification and approval patterns are identified, examine your workflow to see whether it can be simplified.

11. Repeat these steps for all the workflow processes you need to support your unified content life cycle, for example, workflow for new projects, workflow for different types of new products, or workflow for updates to existing content.

Now that your workflow is documented, you can focus on selecting a workflow system to support your design. It's important to design your workflow before selecting a workflow system because you need to make sure the system will do what you need it to do. For example, if notification is important to keep your workflow moving, you want to make sure that a workflow system sends notifications automatically. For more information on selecting a workflow system, refer to Chapter 17.

## Summary

A unified content strategy requires unified processes that are supported by well-designed workflow. A workflow representation shows how tasks are assigned to the appropriate players, how tasks and players interact, and how players interact. It also shows the dependencies within the workflow. A well-designed workflow saves time and reduces duplicate work and potential errors. To design an effective workflow, keep the following points in mind:

- Select start and end points.
- Determine everything that has to happen in between, assigning tasks to roles. Remember to accommodate business requirements specific to your organization.
- Identify all the interactions and dependencies, notifications and approvals.
- Figure in the "what ifs."
- Document your workflow in swimlane diagrams, showing players' roles in the appropriate swimlanes.
- Examine your documented workflow to simplify where possible.

After you've designed workflows to support your unified content life cycle, you're ready to find a workflow system to support them.

# Chapter 12

## Implementing your design

After you have your information model, metadata, and workflow decided, you need to determine how you are going to implement your unified content solution. This chapter discusses the options available. Note that it is not designed to provide technical "how-to" information; the design model (for information, metadata, and workflow) will not necessarily map directly to an off-the-shelf process or software solution.

# Factors affecting implementation

You can implement a unified content solution in an infinite number of ways; no single architecture or solution will suit all needs. Some of the factors that will affect your implementation include:

- **Budget**
  The budget for a unified content solution could cost from tens of thousands of dollars to millions of dollars, depending on the scope of your implementation. For example, a unified content solution for a single department requires a smaller budget than one for an enterprise.

- **Technical resources**
  A large corporation with a large IT department may be in a better position to investigate and invest in new, leading-edge technologies. Having technical resources available for your implementation will give you an advantage over a small department that may not have similar access. IT resources (internal or contracted) will be required for any customization or integration that you undertake in your implementation.

- **Technical ability of authors**
  The technical capabilities of your users will have a significant effect on your implementation. You should target your implementation to the computing skills and technology comfort level of your authors. You cannot implement a system that requires expert computing skills or a high level of comfort with technology if your authors do not have that skill or comfort level. The solution you implement must support your authors.

- **Diversity of users**
  If you are creating a unified content solution for an enterprise-wide group of content providers, you will need to address their range of abilities. This means that a "one size fits all" solution has a high risk of failure. You will probably need to develop a solution that presents different suites of tools to different authors.

- **Required outputs**
  The information you create must ultimately be delivered to users. How information is delivered will have a large impact on the technologies that you choose for your implementation. If you are confining outputs to HTML for web delivery and PDF for paper, you can build your solution around traditional desktop publishing tools. If you need to output to formats such as Wireless Markup Language (WML) for display on hand-held devices or text-enabled cell phones, then XML-based technology should probably be the backbone of your system.

The requirements for implementing any unified content solution depend on the needs that the solution must satisfy. However, there are common requirements that must be considered in any implementation. These requirements are listed in the following sections.

## Scalability

Any unified content solution you implement today must be able to support your business for some time into the future. An implementation could consume considerable resources, so it is best to plan ahead and ensure that the system will be able to handle the volumes of information or numbers of authors you anticipate having for as far into the future as you plan your business (that is, it should support your five-or ten-year business plan, depending on how far ahead you plan).

## Ease of use

One of the key requirements for any implementation is that it must be easy for users to use. "Ease of use" means different things depending on the technology. If you are using traditional desktop publishing technology, you may need to create custom scripts to add functionality. If you are using non-traditional tools (such as XML), you may need to customize the interface to remove functionality that you don't want the authors to access—or functionality that may be confusing. XML tools can also be customized to insert or add reusable text systematic reuse.

## Ease of finding information

Finding information is an extremely important requirement for any unified content implementation. The return (in improved efficiency, faster time to market, increased consistency, or financial savings) of a unified content strategy depends on the ability of authors to find the information they need. In some implementations, depending on the amount of reuse, authors may spend more time finding and assembling blocks of information into information products than they spend writing original content.

In a typical scenario, authors begin to write a piece of content. When they need certain reusable content elements, they search for them in the content management system (CMS). If they cannot easily find the information that they are looking for, they are sure to re-create it. Then you have multiple versions of the same information, reducing the effectiveness of the unified content solution.

This need to quickly and efficiently find information places importance on two different aspects of your system: the search capabilities of your CMS and the metadata that you apply to the chunks of information. If you choose to depend on the CMS for systematic reuse (reducing the need for authors to search for content), then metadata and detailed models are of even greater importance.

## Physical granularity

Chapter 8, "Information modeling," discusses granularity in the context of creating your information model. In that context, granularity refers to the size of the elements that you will reuse, and therefore the size of the building blocks. In implementing your design, you must again consider granularity, but against the functionality of your content management and delivery systems. In this context, granularity really refers to the physical chunk of information that you create and store in your CMS.

The granularity that you settle on depends to some degree on your CMS's capabilities. With document management systems, the physical chunk of information stored in the system had to match the structural granularity for reuse. That is, if you were reusing paragraphs, every paragraph that you wanted to reuse had to be saved in a separate physical file. With the increase of "structurally aware" content management systems, the physical chunk does not always have to match your reuse granularity. Some content management systems are capable of treating elements in your document as logically separate pieces.

The granularity that you manage in your CMS affects the efficiency of your unified content solution. So how granular should your information be? What is the optimum size for chunks of information? There is no single correct answer. However, there are risks if you make your information too granular or not granular enough. The proper level of granularity depends on the information and what you want to do with it, coupled with the capabilities of the CMS that you implement.

### The impact of making your content granular

When you are designing models for information products and elements, you need to identify all the unique information elements in your document. You also identify the elements that will be used or reused. Each element—unique and reusable—will have a unique name.

One approach to granularity would be to consider every element reusable, and therefore manage each element. This is certainly possible, but would probably be inefficient and ineffective. There are two issues:

- In breaking your information into small pieces, you create a large number of chunks that the CMS must manage, which places a strain on the system as well as on the network structures that provide access to the CMS. When authors retrieve a complete piece (book, section, and so on), the system must assemble and send all the small pieces that make up the complete piece.

- The greater the number of pieces that you manage in your CMS, the more difficult it is to find information. There are more pieces of information to choose from in searches.

### The impact of not making your content granular enough

The opposite approach to granularity is to set the physical file size of managed chunks to match the higher-level structures of the information, such as book, chapter, section, and report. Granularity at this level is very comfortable for authors because it mirrors what they are typically used to. However, it may impact your ability to reuse information from the CMS. If the chunks are too big, authors may not be able to separate the smaller pieces of information they need to reuse.

## Options for implementation

You can implement your models in many ways, depending on your authoring requirements, technology, and desired results, including those discussed in the following sections.

### Implementing your model in XML

XML is a very powerful technology for unified content strategies (see Chapter 14, "The role of XML"). It provides capabilities not available in traditional tools. An XML Document Type Definitions (DTD) provides a highly structured way to enforce your models. XML DTDs can be implemented in many ways: semantic, generic, a mixture of semantic elements and generic elements.

## What is a DTD?

A DTD is a formal definition of the XML elements that a specific type of document can include. The DTD defines the names of the elements, their relationship, and their frequency. For example, the DTD entry for a procedure can be defined as something like this:

- The procedure starts with a title.

- Following the title is an introduction.

- The introduction contains a paragraph, followed by 0 or more additional paragraphs, tables, lists, or images.

- After the introduction is a stem sentence.

- Following the stem sentence are instruction steps, and so on.

You can define your own DTD, use the DTD provided with XML editors, or use "industry-standard" DTDs freely available on the Web.

## Is a DTD required?

When considering implementing an XML solution, the first question people ask is "Do we need a DTD?" The answer, really, is yes.

XML itself does not require that files be associated with a DTD. XML files can be "well formed," which means that they follow the rules of syntax defined in the XML specification. However, for a unified content solution, particularly where reuse is involved, DTDs are mandatory.

The key to effective reuse is consistency. Common types of information should have a consistent structure, and reusable pieces of information should have a predictable structure. With a DTD, structural consistency is assured. You can quite clearly define the elements and the structure for all your information products and types. When you use a DTD, XML editing tools (both native XML and XML-aware editors) can check documents to ensure that all required elements are in place, in the correct order. The editors can also ensure that authors do not add elements or change element names.

Predictability is also a key requirement for formatting. You use external style sheets to format XML documents. These style sheets associate specific formatting commands with specific elements in the document. The association is by name. For example, if you have an element named "procedure" in your document, you need formatting instructions with the name "procedure" in your style sheet. If you cannot control the element names your authors use, you cannot ensure that each element has a style definition. Without the style definition, you have no control over the output.

Chapter 8, "Information modeling," describes the value of and how to develop information models. If you are implementing your model in XML, you must create a DTD to support that model, or you must provide some other mechanism to validate content.

### How many DTDs?

The number of DTDs that you create depends on personal choice and organization, more than on information volume or complexity, even for the largest implementation. For example, if you have content owned by different divisions or departments, and specific individuals in the departments will be responsible for maintaining the content models for their respective departments, you may want to create multiple DTDs, so that separate departments can work on their DTDs without conflict.

If you do create a single DTD, you should modularize your DTD to simplify maintenance. This involves grouping content models and elements in your DTD together by purpose or relationship. Some groupings include:

- Common block elements such as generic paragraphs, tables, lists, or graphics
- Common inline elements such as emphasis, links, or cross-references
- Book-level content models such as books, manuals, reports, or brochures
- Specific content models such as procedures, concepts, or policies

Also, with a single DTD, you must build your DTD to provide different views for different authors. In an enterprise-wide implementation you will have authors who provide specific subsets of your content. For example, business analysts may be limited to providing policy information for your corporation. Your DTD should be designed and built to give these authors a policy content model and nothing else. However, authors who are responsible for putting together an entire policy guide should have access to the content model for the an entire guide, including policy models.

### DTD or Schema?

DTDs have traditionally been the structural definition format for publication markup languages. Now, increased use of XML for business applications has lead to the development of an alternative to DTDs: XML Schemas. For business applications, DTDs are seen as limited. They define the elements of content, but give you no control over the content itself. The definition of an element is that it can contain other elements or text.

Schemas, like DTDs, are a formalized language for defining structure, but they introduce data typing to element definitions. For example, if you define an element representing a date, you can define that the content must be in a date format. The validating tools that support schemas can recognize the data types and will report when content does not conform to type.

The decision to use schemas depends on two factors:

- Do you need data typing?
- Does the tool you need support it?

Most publishing solutions work very well with DTDs. But if you need data typing, you need schemas. Or, if you have chosen a tool that does not support schemas, but still need to check content against data types, you need to build custom scripting to supplement standard validation against DTDs.

## Authoring forms

Authoring forms are HTML forms that can guide authors in entering structured content. Users enter content in a browser by entering content in the form fields. Authoring forms can be used in conjunction with XML and a DTD, as an alternative to a DTD, or as an interface to a CMS or database.

Typically forms-based authoring systems are implemented using functionality that is part of many CMSs. The CMS provides utilities to create HTML forms with individual fields to capture content model elements. The form is used to write only a controlled chunk of content, such as a concept, feature, policy, or procedure. You would not usually use a form to build a book.

Forms-based implementations have advantages over implementations that use full authoring tools:

- They enable collaborative authoring with remote access. Anyone with a browser and access to the Internet/extranet/intranet can author content in the forms.
- Forms hide the complexity of XML editing from the authors. Authors do not need to apply styles or tagging at all. Authors enter content into the fields provided in the form. When they post the form to the server, the server converts the field data in the appropriate tags or codes.

Forms-based systems also have their limitations:

- Forms require IT support (to build the forms and the mechanisms for managing the data from the forms).
- Forms are not effective for large information product models.
- Forms are very inflexible; you require coding support to change them.
- Forms do not support very granular reuse.

It can be difficult to implement granular reuse within paragraphs or even among paragraphs. For example, it may be difficult to identify individual steps in a procedure that are applicable to different roles. You need to separate each step as a field in the form, but that can be cumbersome.

## Structural templates (traditional authoring tools)

*Structural templates* are formatting templates that use structural names to represent the structural elements of documents. They are used in implementations where traditional word-processing or desktop publishing tools provide the authoring functionality. Structural templates use semantic names as style names.

Structural templates do not have the same power as DTDs or forms because the tools that use templates cannot control when the tags are used. For example, an XML editor can filter the list of elements that authors can apply so that the DTD is followed. If the DTD defines a series of tags (a title, followed by a introduction, followed by a procedure,…) the authoring software can ensure that the tags are included. Traditional tools have none of these controls. There is nothing to prevent authors from changing the structure, changing the tag names, or even creating new tags.

Structural templates can be very good for providing boilerplate information, or at least hints to common information.

## Semantic versus generic element or style names

When you develop your information model you should identify all the content elements in your information and give each a unique semantic name (a semantic component of the model—see Chapter 8). An important part of the modeling exercise is to understand every possible level of structure. Without a complete understanding of your content, you cannot really make informed decisions about the outputs you require and what information you can use.

The complete model is used to guide authors, so it should uniquely identify all the content elements. However, that does not mean that you create elements or style tags that match every element in your content. You do not need to—and probably should not—create a one-to-one mapping of elements in a model to elements or style tags. Some elements should ultimately be generic or common elements.

### Number of elements or tags

The number of elements or tags is a key issue on deciding whether to use semantic names to match every element in your information model. Too many elements or style tags can make authoring difficult.

For example, one of the key complaints about the DocBook DTD is that with over 400 elements it is too complicated for most authors. Think of having a huge drop-down list for style tags in a traditional authoring tool. Authors simply will not scroll through this list to select the appropriate style tag. Frequently, authors will use just a few style tags and will hand format the rest. This defeats the purpose of uniquely identifying content and your ability to automatically convert the content to multiple outputs in multiple information products.

## Identifying content

If you need to be able to do something with a piece of content such as find it easily, reuse it, or manipulate it, it should have a semantic identity. There are two ways to give semantic identity to an element of text:

- Give it a semantic element name or style tag.
- Use a generic element name or style tag, but add metadata that qualifies what the element is used for or represents.

For example, listing 12.1 shows an XML sample procedure that uses semantic names for all elements.

### Listing 12.1    Semantically tagged procedure

```
<procedure>
    <title>Logging On to AccSoft </title>
    <introduction>The first time you click on a component in AccSoft
        you are required to log on to the system before you can
        complete any tasks.</introduction>
    <stem>To log on to AccSoft:</stem>
    <procedure_steps>
        <step>Double-click the AccSoft application.
          <result>The system displays the AccSoft main window.</result>
        </step>
        <step>Select AP from the Explorer.
            <result>The system displays the login dialog.</result>
        </step>
        <step>Type your USERID into the Name field.</step>
        <step>Type your password into the Password field.
            <result>The system displays the customer dialog.</result>
        </step>
        <step>Select the customer to update.</step>
        <step>Click the OK button to log on to AccSoft.</step>
    </procedure_steps>
    <note>If you do not know your USERID or Password, consult
            your System Administrator.
    </note>
    <warning>This database contains personal
            information about our clients. If you are logged on,
            do not leave your terminal unattended at any time.
    </warning>
</procedure>
```

Listing 12.2 shows a sample procedure that uses generic names for some elements, but includes attributes (the XML way of identifying metadata) to give semantic identity to other elements.

**Listing 12.2     Combination of semantic and generic tagging with attributes**

```
<procedure>
    <title>Logging On to AccSoft </title>
    <para type="introduction">The first time you click on a
            component in AccSoft you are required to log on to the
            system before you can complete any tasks.</para>
    <para>To log on to AccSoft:</para>
    <procedure_steps>
        <step>Double-click the AccSoft application.
            <para>The system displays the AccSoft main window.</para>
        </step>
        <step>Select AP from the Explorer.
            <para>The system displays the login dialog.</para>
        </step>
        <step>Type your USERID into the Name field.</step>
        <step>Type your password into the Password field.
                <para>The system displays the customer dialog.</para>
        </step>
        <step>Select the customer to update.</step>
        <step>Click the OK button to log on to AccSoft.</step>
    </procedure_steps>
    <para type="note">If you do not know your USERID or Password,
            consult your System Administrator.</para>
    <para type="warning">This database contains personal
            information about our clients. If you are logged on,
            do not leave your terminal unattended at any time.</para>
</procedure>
```

If you compare the two examples you can see that Listing 12.2 uses five fewer element names than Listing 12.1. The introduction, stem, result, note, and warning have been replaced by generic paragraph elements as summarized in Table 12.1.

**Table 12.1   Generic paragraph elements**

| Semantic name | Generic name with attribute |
|---|---|
| `<introduction>` | `<para type="introduction">` |
| `<stem>` | `<para>` |
| `<result>` | `<para>` |
| `<note>` | `<para type="note">` |
| `<warning>` | `<para type="warning">` |

Identifying the lead-in stem sentence is important information for your authors and should be included in your model, but does not have to be implemented in your structure; a generic element is sufficient. The result element is replaced by a generic element with no attribute. The result is a part of the step and not likely to be reused separately from the step, so it does not need to be identified separately. The note and warning have been given generic element names (para) but have been modified with an attribute (metadata) that uniquely defines them. As you begin to model, you'll notice structures such as note, important, tip, caution, warning are often identical with the exception of the title and an icon. You can create a common model for these elements that is implemented as a generic element, then add metadata to differentiate them.

If you were using a traditional authoring tool to create this procedure you might make some different decisions. Table 12.2 illustrates the same procedure as it might be tagged in Microsoft Word or FrameMaker (unstructured version). Notice that a semantic style tag is used for the note and warning. In this case you might want the template to automatically insert the title (Note or Warning) and possibly an icon. These tools can do this only if you have defined a unique style tag.

**Table 12.2   Authoring in Word versus FrameMaker**

| Procedure | Microsoft Word | FrameMaker |
|---|---|---|
| Logging On to AccSoft | Heading 1 | Heading1 |
| The first time you click on a component in AccSoft you are required to log on to the system before you can complete any tasks. | Normal | Body |
| To log on to AccSoft: | Normal | Body |
| Double-click the AccSoft application. | Normal (numbers applied) | Numbered1 |
| The system displays the AccSoft main window. | Normal (indent applied) | Indented |
| Select AP from the Explorer. | Normal (numbers applied) | Numbered |
| The system displays the Login dialog. | Normal (indent applied) | Indented |
| Type your USERID into the Name field. | Normal (numbers applied) | Numbered |
| Type your password into the Password field. | Normal (numbers applied) | Numbered |
| The system displays the Customer dialog. | Normal (indent applied) | Indented |
| Select the customer to update. | Normal (numbers applied) | Numbered |
| Click the OK button to log on to AccSoft. | Normal (numbers applied) | Numbered |
| **Note:** If you do not know your USERID or Password, consult your System Administrator. | Note | Note |

| Procedure | Microsoft Word | FrameMaker |
|---|---|---|
| **Warning:** This database contains personal information about our clients. If you are logged on, do not leave your terminal unattended at any time. | Warning | Warning |

# Metadata

An effective metadata strategy is vital to a unified content implementation. Without effective metadata, authors cannot find information. If authors can't find it, they can't reuse it. Chapter 9, "Designing metadata," defines what metadata is and describes how to determine the required metadata for your information. During implementation, you need to be concerned about where the metadata is stored and how it is managed and maintained.

In implementation, metadata can be stored in different places, depending on the capabilities of your CMS and the data format you are using. A CMS usually enables you to define metadata when you check files into the database. Rather than store the metadata values in the datafile, the CMS stores metadata in tables in the underlying database. If you are managing binary data formats (usually the format created by traditional tools) this is your only option. Ideally, metadata should be stored in the data file it is describing, with the content that it identifies.

In XML, metadata can be stored in elements or in attributes. Most interfaces between XML authoring tools and the CMS include functionality to extract the metadata from the XML file when it is checked in and apply it to the metadata fields in the CMS interface. If this functionality is not available, it can be implemented as a customization. Where possible, the update should be bidirectional. For example, if the metadata is updated in the source file, the changes should be saved to the CMS metadata database when the file is checked in. If the metadata is updated in the CMS, it should automatically be updated in the source file.

For traditional authoring tools, metadata is stored in the CMS.

# Style sheets

Style sheets have different purposes, depending on the technology that you are using. When used with traditional authoring tools, style sheets control both the look of the document in the editor and the look of the document in the output. In XML, style sheets have a much broader capability.

## Style sheet purposes

Style sheets can have different purposes. You can have style sheets for specific outputs, which we will refer to as *output style sheets*. You can also have *display style sheets*, which are used to format content for display in authoring tools. For an enterprise solution, it is important to give authors control over their own display templates, whenever possible. This enables them to change the look of information in their authoring tool to make the tool most effective for them. However, authors should be educated to understand that the changes they make to their display of content will not be reflected in the output.

After the authoring is complete, the content management or publication engine uses the output templates to provide the format for the specified output. While authors should control their own display templates, output templates should remain "locked" to maintain their consistency and make them easier to manage.

## How many style sheets are needed?

The minimum number of style sheets you need is one for each format of output that you plan to create, for example, one for paper, one for online, and so on. In actual application, you probably need one for each output that you need to create.

## Capabilities of XSL style sheets

Style sheets created for XML have capabilities beyond the simple display of content. They have all the power of traditional style sheets and templates, but can also provide additional functionality, such as

- Sorting
- Supplying boiler plate text
- Hiding text
- Repeating or rearranging text

These functions can be extremely powerful in a unified content solution. The more manipulation or processing that you can do in a style sheet, the better. In solutions featuring traditional desktop publishing tools and formats, manipulating text usually requires you to create scripts in specialized languages (proprietary to the tool) or in common programming/scripting languages, such as VB or JavaScript. XSL style sheets are easily created, and they do not need to be compiled. The formatting engine or parser can apply them immediately to a document.

### Designing style sheets for output

Output style sheets can be used to configure and structure content for delivery. They can also filter the content for dynamic delivery. When you create style sheets, you should borrow from the best principles of reuse and the best principles of software development:

- Make your style sheets modular.
- Use your style sheet to generate as much text as possible.
- Use variables whenever possible.
- Use parameters whenever possible.

Note that not all authoring and publications tools will support all these principles. However, any time you can automate a task in a style sheet, eliminating a manual task for authors, you improve the consistency and predictability of your output.

## *Modular style sheets*

Style sheets should be designed and implemented as modular components. Modular style sheets create reusable styles and layer format for simpler maintenance. For example, the following style sheet components could each be maintained in separate style modules:

- Corporate look and feel—Fonts, colors, logos, and so on
- Page description—Page size, margins, headers, footers, and so on
- Inline elements—Emphasis, link, cross-references, and so on
- Block elements—Sections, subsections, paragraphs, lists, and tables

## Generated text

If you examine specific outputs, you are sure to see that often people treat certain information like content when it is really format. For example, headings for the following sections typically found in books and manuals are constant:

- Table of Contents
- List of Tables
- List of Figures
- Index
- Glossary
- Preface

These are not really content; they are navigation elements. No author should have to type the title "Table of Contents." This heading should be applied by the style sheet. Whenever possible, you should build your style sheets to provide these types of textual elements automatically. This will guarantee consistency across your information set because repetitive text is applied programmatically and is not subject to the author's typing skill.

Providing textual elements automatically can be done easily in XML with an XSL style sheet. In addition, many traditional authoring tools enable you to use paragraph numbering functions to provide the same text.

Style sheets can also generate all structural numbering in your document. Structural numbering includes chapter numbers, section numbers, appendix letters, and list numbers. You should avoid having to rely on authors to manually update these numbers.

Finally, whenever possible, you should use style sheets to generate the actual content of the table of contents, compile the index and glossary, and produce lists of tables and graphics. In traditional authoring tools, this functionality is in the tool, not the stylesheet.

## *Control of production style sheets*

The ideal situation for any unified content solution is to isolate production style sheets from authors; production style sheets should be maintained by an individual or group of individuals responsible for the style sheets (for example, an information technologist as described in Chapter 21, "Managing change"). The information technologist is responsible for making required changes and updates as content changes over time. Most authors do not have any access to the production style sheets. However, there may be times when you want to give authors options in presentation. For example, you may want to give authors an option of format (5×9 or 8.5×11) for paper output, or enable them to select from a variety of ways of displaying content, such as inline or in a sidebar or example.

# Summary

You can implement a unified content solution in a variety of ways:

- There are many factors that affect implementation, including
  - Scalability
  - Ease of use
  - Ease of finding information
- Selecting the correct level of physical granularity depends on many factors, including the complexity of reuse and the capabilities of your CMS.
- There are many options for implementing a unified CMS, including
  - Implementing your model in XML
  - Authoring forms
  - Structural templates (traditional authoring tools)
- If you implement in XML, a DTD or Schema is required.
- You should balance the use of semantic versus generic element or style names to ensure that you can find, reuse, and manipulate all required elements easily, without creating unworkable style sheets or DTDs.

- Metadata tends to be stored with information components in the CMS, but can also be stored in XML files.
- You should design style sheets very carefully to ensure that you
    - Use the maximum capabilities of the style sheets.
    - Make the style sheets modular for reuse.
    - Make the style sheets easy to maintain.

# Part IV

# Tools and technologies

Evaluating and selecting tools is a large part of implementing a unified content strategy. There are numerous tools available for every type of task your organization could possibly require assistance with. New tools are being announced regularly and existing vendors with a solid offering in one particular application are continuously upgrading and extending their tools to better meet market needs. In other cases, products are purchased by other vendors and integrated into their product offering and yet other tools are disappearing in the wake of tough economic times.

The number of tools available makes it very hard to know which one to select. Naturally, you want a tool that meets your specific needs, and you want it provided by a vendor with a solid reputation and financial standing. Finding such a tool is not an easy task. To start, it is important to understand that there is no perfect solution. There are pros and cons for every tool and supporting technology. What works well for one organization may not work well for another. Your best defense is to be armed with as much information as possible, to develop detailed evaluation criteria, and to test before you buy. Chapter 13, "Evaluating tools," provides you with an understanding of how to evaluate tools for selection.

One of the decisions you will have to make is whether you want to work with XML-based tools. Chapter 14, "The role of XML," describes XML and its origins and explains why XML is so valuable in a unified content strategy.

The unified content life cycle is dependent upon a variety of tools (authoring, content management, workflow and delivery). The remainder of Part IV focuses on these tools, what they do, and how you can use them to support your unified content strategy. Each chapter also includes vendor questions or considerations to help you figure out what you want the tools to do in your organization.

Before content can be managed, manipulated, or reused, it must be created. Authoring tools enable authors to create content. Chapter 15, "Authoring tools," helps you to understand the pros and cons of staying with traditional authoring tools or moving to XML or other structured authoring tools.

Content management is an integral component of a successful unified content strategy and selecting the right content management system can be a lengthy investigational process. Chapter 16, "Content management systems," provides you with an understanding of the different types of content management systems and their functionality.

Workflow systems are critical in a unified content strategy because they help to ensure that content flows through the content life cycle. Workflow systems make sure that everybody contributes their required content, that content is reviewed and approved at the necessary stages, and is delivered to its various outputs. Chapter 17, "Workflow systems," describes the functionality of workflow systems.

Content is created in authoring tools, managed in a content management system, processed through workflow then assembled, formatted, and delivered to users through a delivery system. Chapter 18, "Delivery systems," describes the capabilities of delivery systems.

As you work through the tools and technology chapters and formulate the directions you want to take with your unified content strategy, remember that tools alone are not the solution—tools enable solutions. Never pick the tools before determining your strategy. Always understand your issues and goals, develop your unified content strategy and vision, then pick the tools to support you in achieving this vision.

# Chapter 13

## Evaluating tools

Selecting appropriate software tools to support your unified content strategy can be a difficult and lengthy process. Your best defense for selecting tools is to be armed with as much information about them as possible. You need to develop detailed evaluation criteria and test before you buy. This chapter describes the process of evaluating tools, from identifying your needs to conducting a proof of concept.

## Identifying your needs

Begin your evaluation process by identifying your needs. Part II, "Performing a substantive audit: Determining business requirements" provides guidelines on how you can identify your organizational needs, and Chapter 7, "Envisioning your unified content life cycle," provides guidelines for creating a vision of the functionality of your unified content life cycle. After you've documented your vision, you can use it to identify your criteria for tools selection. For example, Table 13.1 illustrates how Company A's vision translates into their tools selection criteria. Note that although the task in Table 13.1 is to create new content, much of its associated criteria relate to the content management system.

**Table 13.1    Identifying tools criteria**

| Function: Create new content | Tool | Criteria: Must support |
|---|---|---|
| Before beginning to create content, reuse authors select an authoring template and identify the subject of the content (for example, a specific product). The content management system searches for existing information elements that are valid for the template and the subject. It then pre-populates (systematic reuse) the template with appropriate content. | CMS | Systematic |
| Authors can either keep the automatically populated content or choose to remove it (unless the content is identified as mandatory).If authors keep the reusable content, security they can retain it untouched or modify it to create derivative content when (unless the reusable content element exist is locked). Reusable content that is mandatory or locked can be modified by only its owner or a supervisor. | CMS | Derivative reuse<br><br>Locked reuse<br><br>Element level<br><br>Identifying derivatives |

| Function: Create new content | Tool | Criteria: Must support |
|---|---|---|
| Authors can use the search tool contained within the content management system and retrieve appropriate elements (opportunistic reuse). They can search using text or phrases contained in the reusable element (full text search), and use metadata to narrow searches to specifically the type of information they are looking for (for example, a product description or procedure). | CMS | Opportunistic reuse<br><br>Search using full text retrieval<br><br>Search based on metadata |

Use your criteria to develop a series of questions to ask the vendor. In addition to asking, "Does your product support X," ask "How does it support it?" Company A's sample search criteria could look something like Table 13.2.

Don't stop with just the criteria you derive from your vision; do some research about everything the tools can do. For example, the vision in Table 13.1 identifies both full-text searches and searches that use metadata among selection criteria. When evaluating tools, you may find other kinds of searching that are useful. How about searching based on the status of the element (such as all elements that are currently checked out, or all elements that are approved)? What about searching across other content formats? A CMS can store your content elements in one format, but may be able to store whole documents in formats such as PDF. Would that be useful? In finding out more about what the tools can do, you may identify functions that are useful to you that you hadn't thought of before.

**Table 13.2    Sample criteria**

| Criteria | Specifics (how) |
|---|---|
| What types of searching are supported? | Full text? |
| | Boolean? |
| | Natural language? |
| | Index? |
| | Keyword? |
| | Structural? |
| | Metadata? |
| | Standard CMS metadata such as check-in/check-out data; create, modify, obsolete? |
| | Can you search across output files (for example, web, PDF), as well as content? |

## General criteria

Develop general criteria for the product, as well as specific criteria. General criteria address functionality or support that all vendors should provide, regardless of the type of product they are selling. Don't forget to evaluate the company, as well as the product, to see how reliable they are. Some of the general criteria you should consider include the following:

- **Usability**

  How easy is the tool to learn, use, and master (become better than merely proficient)? Can new users be easily trained to use the system effectively? Can the interface be customized for increased usability or different functionality? If so, how easy is it to customize (can you do it or do you need a specialized programmer)?

- **Training**

  What training is provided? Are there different levels of training? Is it all classroom, or is there web-based training as well? What is the cost? Is on-site training provided? Who are the instructors? What are their qualifications?

- **Supporting documentation**

  What type of documentation is provided (user manual, reference manual, help, web)? How is it provided (CD, paper, web)? If vendors don't provide hard copy (manuals), can you buy them? Ask to see a copy (or sample) and evaluate its quality. How are updates to documentation provided?

- **Technical support**

  What type of technical support is provided (email, phone)? Is it included in the price of the product or is there a fee? If it is included, for how long? What is the guaranteed turn-around time on answers to questions?

- **Future upgrades/enhancements**

  How are future enhancements or upgrades handled? How many updates/enhancements are there per year? Are upgrades included in the price? If so, how many? How receptive is the vendor to your suggestions and requests for new features and bug fixes?

- **Implementation time**

  How long will it take to install and configure the tool? How long does it take the vendor to figure out what you need, design any customized components, and get the system up and running?

- **Cost**

  What is the total cost of the product? Are consulting services provided and what are their costs? Are training and technical support provided and what are the additional costs, if any? What other costs might you incur (for example, evaluation copy cost)?

  What is the total cost of ownership, including maintenance, lifetime support (life of product), upgrades, fixes, add-ons, documentation, and training?

- **Vendor viability**

  Will the vendor survive as the market evolves? Does the vendor have the talent and organization to be successful? How committed is the vendor? What is the company's strategic plan for the next three to five years? How consistent is the strategy of the vendor with your strategy? What is the vendor's product road map? How does the vendor plan to fulfill its customer service needs now and into the future? Who are the vendor's competitors? How dedicated is the vendor to this product, compared to its other products?

- **Partnerships**

  Who does the vendor partner with to provide an expanded solution?

- **References**

  Who are the vendor's customers? What types of projects have they done with other customers? (Get descriptions where possible.) Can they provide references? Are there external reviews, endorsements, articles, published comparisons?

## Weighting your criteria

Not all criteria should be valued equally in your final scoring; some issues will be more important than others, depending on your needs. Begin by sorting criteria into categories:

- **Must have**

  If the product does not meet "must have" criteria, it is not eligible for selection. However, it may receive a partial score if the tool provides a necessary functionality, but not necessarily to the level of functionality desired.

- **Should have**

  If a product does not meet "should have" criteria, it should not be eliminated immediately, but its ranking will be lower, which may eventually eliminate it.

- **Nice to have**

  "Nice to have" criteria are just that—nice to have. If a product does not meet "nice to have" criteria, its ranking is not significantly reduced. But products that meet more of your "nice to have" criteria will be ranked higher.

Next you need to give each category a weight. For example:

- Must have: 5
- Should have: 3
- Nice to have: 1

Each of the weights represents a range of scores. The scoring is used to identify how well the feature meets your need. For example, a "must have" score could be 3 out of a possible 5. This means that the tool has the desired feature, but it does not merit a full score for its functionality (for example, it may be very hard to use). Therefore, a 5 represents full functionality and a 1 represents minimal functionality. As you rank each criterion, score it against the total value of the criteria and record why it did not receive a full score. Table 13.3 illustrates how to record your scores, using searching as an example. In this example, searching is considered "must have," so its maximum ranking could be 5. The product doesn't receive full marks because it does not have the full functionality requested. However, the missing functionality is not critical, so it loses only one point. The stars make the ranking very easy to see at glance. You may want to create a simpler chart to provide an at-a-glance summary of the criteria ranking, and leave the detailed criteria and reason for the ranking score to an appendix in your report.

**Table 13.3   Ranking criteria**

| Criteria | Ranking | Reason |
| --- | --- | --- |
| What types of searching are supported?<br>Full text?<br>   Boolean?<br>   Natural language?<br>Index?<br>Keyword?<br>Structural?<br>Metadata?<br><br>Standard CMS metadata such as check-in/check-out data; create, modify, obsolete?<br><br>Can you search across output files (for example, web, PDF) as well as content? | ◆◆◆◆ | Can perform full text, keyword, structural, and metadata serching. Cannot search on the index or across output files. |

Group criteria according to their category—"must have," "should have," and "nice to have," in that order. If a product has a very low score or a zero on many of the "must have" criteria, it should be eliminated. You may find that if all the tools score low in the "must have" section that the products have not reached the maturity level you desire, or that you may have to do some customizing to make the product properly meet your needs. If all the products score reasonably well in this area, look at the total score and move on to the "should have" category. A poor score on any of the "should have" criteria should not eliminate the product, but an overall poor score in comparison to the other products should eliminate it or classify it as only a "maybe." The "nice to have" scores can be used as a tie breaker or to give a product an edge over a closely ranked product.

## Creating a list of potential vendors

There are hundreds of options for any type of tool, making it difficult to know where to start looking. Gather information from many sources to help you create a list of potential vendors. Some good sources include:

- **Conferences**

  Industry-related conferences, or conferences that focus on key topics such as content management, are a very good place to start. Many have exhibit areas full of vendors interested in selling you their products. Come armed with your criteria and questions and plan to spend a lot of time in the exhibit hall watching demonstrations and asking questions. Sometimes vendors have presentation sessions where you can get a better understanding of their products. Attending sessions where products are compared by objective speakers is also very valuable. Ask other conference attendees which products they use or are planning to use. If a vendor has a product that looks like it may meet your needs, have their representatives get back to you with more information and a customized demonstration at your site.

- **Web conferences or Webinars**

  Web conferences or Webinars are a great way to learn about products or subjects of interest. Many vendors give regular conferences. Sometimes they are specifically designed to demonstrate their product, but often they are on a related subject. They are a great way to get a lot of information for only the cost of your time (no travel costs).

- **Electronic mailing lists**

  Subscribe to electronic mailing lists about tools, your type of business, or the type of task you hope to accomplish. Although you can get flooded with a lot of irrelevant information, electronic mailing lists are an excellent place to ask about the products that others use.

- **Magazines**

  Magazines frequently review products on an annual or semiannual basis. Many also feature products in each issue.

- **Web sites and online discussion boards and newsgroups**

  There are web sites that list available products of a certain type. They rarely provide any comparative information, but they do provide a series of links to vendor sites.

# Narrowing down the list

After you've created a list of potential vendors, you need to narrow it down.

1. Request a demonstration. Give the vendor advance notice if you want something custom, and be prepared to send them your materials to work with. (A simple canned demo, though, is certainly an easy thing to request and should be considered first.)

   Invite the vendor to your site or request a web demonstration to provide an opportunity to specifically address your questions. If you don't plan to send out a request for proposal (RFP), use the demonstration to ask all your detailed questions. Allocate a minimum of two hours (potentially, three to four) depending on the complexity of the product and the level of detail in your criteria.

   Review your criteria in light of these demonstrations to determine whether you need to revise them before you create an RFP.

2. Send out an RFP that includes your detailed criteria.

   If you are purchasing a large product like a content management system, sending an RFP to potential vendors enables you to gather a lot of information and directly compare vendor responses. Give vendors as much information about your desired project as possible to enable them to respond to your needs. Have them sign a non-disclosure agreement, if appropriate, to ensure your information is kept confidential, but that enables you to provide them with the appropriate level of detail.

3. Evaluate the responses.

   Evaluate the responses to the RFP. Add weighting (values) to your criteria to help you determine an objective numeric ranking for each vendor. If you don't issue an RFP, use the custom demonstration to evaluate the product against your criteria.

4. Pick the vendors that most effectively meet your criteria.

   Add up the scores for all the vendors, eliminating those with low scores or glaring gaps in their functionality. Reduce the list to three vendors, reviewing the results with others in your organization who may have some insight into selecting tools.

5.  Ask for a *content-specific* demonstration.

    Ask each selected vendor to demonstrate their product, using some of your
    selected content. Ensure that the selected content is representative of the
    materials you eventually want to create/manage/deliver. If possible, have
    vendors incorporate your content into their tools while you watch. This
    enables you to see what it really takes to work with your content.
    If you see only the final results, you may not see some of a tool's
    complexities.

6.  Narrow your selection further.

    After the demonstration, narrow your selection to one or at most two
    vendors.

7.  Conduct a proof-of-concept.

    Before purchasing a product, you need to evaluate it thoroughly. Don't
    believe everything you read (vendor marketing materials), hear (demon-
    strations, presentations), or see (demonstrations). Use this information as a
    starting point, then conduct a proof-of-concept to make sure the tool can
    perform to your expectations. Proof-of-concept is described in more detail
    in the following section. Ask for an evaluation copy and try the product
    yourself.

8.  If the product performs well during the proof-of-concept, purchase it.

## Proof-of-concept

Before committing to purchasing a product, evaluate it through a proof-of-concept. If you have narrowed your selection to two tools, you may want to conduct
a face-off, where both tools are tested and the results are compared. The proof-
of-concept makes sure that the product meets your organization's needs and
provides the desired functionality. Some organizations have been positive that a
product would meet their needs, then during a proof-of-concept discovered
glaring problems that were not revealed during the initial evaluation. It is better
to determine the problems before you buy. A proof-of-concept can also point
out what changes or customization are required before you can implement the
product in your organization.

Set this up as a test situation with the software running on a test system (that is, not a live system you are currently using) to ensure that there are no incompatibilities with your current software. Most content management systems require a separate system after they are installed for full implementation.

A proof-of-concept involves testing the product in your organization in a small implementation. It is important to identify a series of tasks and outcomes to:

- Test what the product does
- Validate your assumptions about the product
- Test the product's capability to meet your specific needs

The tasks should be comprehensive enough to effectively test the product's functionality, but not so comprehensive that it results in a tremendous amount of work and cost for your organization.

To perform a proof-of-concept you must get vendor support. Vendor support includes:

- **Evaluation copy of the software**

  An evaluation copy is typically a time-limited but fully functional version of the software, or it may not be time limited, but have restricted functionality. It may be provided to your organization at a nominal fee or free of charge.

- **Consulting services**

  You probably do not have the resources or skills in-house to install and configure the software appropriately. These skills can be learned, but typically not in the timeframe of the proof-of-concept. Negotiate a reasonable consulting fee with the vendor to have them install and configure the software to meet your requirements. These requirements should be limited to the scope of the proof-of-concept only, not full configuration.

- **Training**

  Participants in the proof-of-concept will need training to understand how to use the product. If the vendor already has a scheduled training session planned close to your test date you may be able to negotiate low-cost or no-cost participation. Otherwise, you may need a session scheduled just for your needs. This will certainly entail a cost.

- **Technical support**

  Technical support to answer questions and troubleshoot problems will be required during the test period.

Do not let the vendor actually conduct the proof-of-concept. The vendor knows the product too well and can rapidly create work-arounds when there are problems. You want to see the product "warts and all" to ensure that it will meet your needs. Give yourself the resources to break the program, find its limitations, and make mistakes that require correcting so you can test the program's ability to handle changes and failure recovery.

You can conduct your proof-of-concept in two ways: as a functionality test or as a combined usability and functionality test. A functionality test usually involves a small team using sample materials to walk through test scenarios. This enables you to test the features to ensure they meet your functionality. A combined usability and functionality test involves representative users of the new system testing the materials in a simulated environment. A usability test is more complex because it involves training the participants. In addition, you have to design the test so that users with minimal training can effectively participate. A usability test is critical before you pilot the product, but may or may not be necessary before you purchase the product. However, if there are concerns about users accepting the product, a usability test that tests the key features of the system at the proof-of-concept stage may be appropriate.

Track the results of the proof-of-concept throughout the test period. If you are doing a usability test, collect results through questionnaires, observation, and participant questions. Create a method for tracking (discussed in the following section) both the test and the results. Use your original criteria list, but this time rank the functionality based on your test. Analyze the results and summarize your findings in a report. Decide whether the product is the most appropriate purchase for your requirements. If it is close but needs some customization, talk to the vendor to see what this will cost. If it isn't the correct product for your organization, evaluate another one.

# One size fits all?

The remaining chapters in Part IV "Tools and technologies" (Chapters 14-18) introduce the different types of software required to support your unified content strategy and the many different variations within each type of software (for example, web content management versus integrated document management). Your evaluation of the products is certain to reinforce the idea that there are many different options among which to choose. Many vendors have chosen to make "best-of-breed" products that meet a very specific requirement in your organization and do it very well. In isolation, best-of-breed products make a lot of sense because they meet your specific needs at that particular time. Unfortunately, best-of-breed products may reinforce silos (for example, web content functionality only, not enterprise content management), delegating certain tasks and deliverables into separate areas, each with its own best-of-breed tools specific to its tasks.

Some vendors create products that address many different needs within the organization (for example, enterprise content management) with the understanding that their product must serve many needs. Some critics argue that generalized products are mediocre in their effectiveness and performance (jack of all trades, master of none). However, some vendors have succeeded in developing effective broad-based solutions. Sometimes they succeed through the effective design of their product, but often they succeed through the acquisition of other products that complement each other to produce a tightly integrated suite.

Where possible, select a suite of tools that meets your enterprise content needs. If your organization decides to go with best-of-breed tools, the key to a successful unified content strategy lies in your ability to share content among the systems. To support these systems in sharing content, your content and consequently your tools should include the following:

- **Common information models (structures) and tagging**

  Common information models with common tag standards (for example, both systems refer to the first heading as "Heading 1," rather than "Heading 1" in one information model and "Title" in another model) make it possible for elements of content to be interpreted consistently, and they make it possible for content that has been created or maintained in one system to be reused transparently with content created or managed in another system.

- **Common metadata**

  Common metadata ensures that the meaning and classification of elements is the same among systems. Common metadata makes it possible to automatically retrieve, reuse, and track content regardless of the system (see Chapter 9, "Designing metadata").

- **Compatibility with other systems**

  The capability to integrate with other systems (for example, authoring, other content management) is important to ensure that content can be shared. If a tool has built-in compatibility with other systems or a provides the facility to integrate with other systems, the tool will be more effective in ensuring that content can be shared.

## Summary

Selecting the correct tool can be a difficult and lengthy process. However, arming yourself with as much information as possible, developing detailed criteria, and testing the product before you buy can help you make a successful selection.

Identify your criteria for selection.

1. Develop a weighting system for your criteria.
2. Develop a list of vendors to investigate.
3. Request a custom demonstration from vendors that interest you.
4. Send selected vendors an RFI or RFP that includes your detailed criteria and ask them to respond to your questions.
5. Evaluate the responses or compare the custom demonstration against your criteria.
6. Pick three vendors that most effectively meet your criteria (best ranking).
7. Ask vendors to use a sample of your content and create a content-specific demonstration for you.
8. Narrow your selection further to one or two vendors.
9. Conduct a proof-of-concept to test the required functionality and determine whether the product meets your needs.
10. Purchase the product if it performs well in the proof-of-concept.

# Chapter 14

## The role of XML

XML is fast becoming the new
Internet standard for information
exchange. For complex information
reuse, XML is the technology of
choice. In this chapter, we briefly
describe XML and its origins and
explain why XML is so valuable in a
unified content strategy.

# A brief history of XML

XML, eXtensible Markup Language, is advertised as many things, including the successor to HTML as the language of the Web. But unlike HTML, XML is not a specific markup language; it is a standard for defining your own markup language.

XML is not new; it is a recasting of an existing standard: Standard Generalized Markup Language (SGML). In its current iteration, the XML specification is at version 1.0. People sometimes interpret that to mean that the specification is immature and to expect big changes. They are waiting for a "stable" version of the standard. But this is misleading; XML is based on SGML, so it originates from an already stable background.

## First SGML

SGML is an International Standards Organization (ISO) standard for markup of text. It began life as a solution to a very common problem in large organizations: How do you take information created by different groups, using different software, and on different operating systems, and share it for use and reuse among those groups? In the 1970s, the answer to that question was, "You don't." Files created on one operating system (OS) could not be read on another OS. Applications could not read the formats of other applications. For that matter, files created on one version of an application could not always be read by later versions of the same application. Information was created and re-created as needed, but never reused.

This was the problem identified by Charles Goldfarb in 1969 when he was leading a project to integrate law office systems. He and his colleagues developed Generalized Markup Language (GML) as a mechanism for creating and sharing text. GML focused on the structure of a document, not the formatting, and was the first text processing language to view and formalize the hierarchical nature of information. It was also the first language to explicitly define the hierarchy of documents in a separate form. GML was implemented in mainframe-based text processing systems.

In 1978, the American National Standards Institute (ANSI) invited Goldfarb to participate on their Computer Languages for the Processing of Text committee. As a member of this committee, Goldfarb lead an effort to develop a text processing language based on GML. Over time, this was developed into ISO standard 8879—Standard Generalized Markup Language.

SGML, like GML, describes the logical structure of a document, its components, and their relationship to each other, not how the document should be formatted. A paragraph, for example might be marked with a "begin paragraph tag," `<para>`, and an "end paragraph tag," `</para>`, rather than with formatting instructions to leave a blank line and indent.

SGML gained wide use in industries such as aerospace and defense. It was also adopted in several branches of the government. SGML markup languages and applications provide authors with a tremendous amount of power and control over their documents. So why not stick with SGML?

Well, there are several reasons:

- SGML is very complex and is difficult to learn and apply.
- SGML tools have traditionally been very expensive.
- SGML has been primarily a technology for print publishing.

## Then HTML

The best known application of SGML is the language of the Web: HTML. It was created in the early 1990s by Tim Berners-Lee at CERN (the European Laboratory for Particle Physics) as a way for scientists to share information. With the popularity of the Web, HTML has become ubiquitous. So why not stick with HTML? HTML is limited, in a number of ways:

- HTML is a fixed tag set. You cannot add your own tags to HTML. It is a fixed language.
- HTML is designed for display. It is perfectly suited for rendering documents in your browser, but that's all. It is not effective for print or other formats.
- HTML is static. Its display is fixed, so providing information in different ways based on user requests is difficult. Dynamic HTML does allow some manipulation of display, but it requires some pretty complex scripting to do so. Scripting requires developers to create and maintain the scripts, which is expensive.
- HTML is not structural. It is primarily a linear presentation markup. With the exception of lists and tables, it doesn't contain any structural markup. Its focus on presentation makes it difficult, if not impossible, to process or manipulate chunks of HTML.

- HTML is not really a standard. The rush to capture market share has meant that tools for HTML, including browsers, frequently appeared on the market before HTML was complete and stable. As a result, the tools incorporate their designer's best guesses of what HTML would become. Browser vendors have created their own proprietary codes (flavors of HTML), which impedes standardization.

So although HTML has been a useful tool for displaying content on the Web, it has severe limitations. These limitations, at least in part, have spurred the development of XML.

# What is XML?

First, let's discuss what XML is not. XML is not a set of tags that you can apply to documents. XML is a specification that sets rules for the creation of tag sets that you can apply to documents. That's the *eXtensible* part. That's also the most confusing part to many people starting to learn XML. People coming from an HTML background automatically expect to see a list of tags they can apply to documents. XML does not define the tag names—you do.

## Design goals of XML

In 1998, the first version of the XML specification was released as a recommendation. For this first version, a design committee of the World Wide Web Consortium (W3C)—the people who develop and maintain XML—had very specific goals in mind, including the following:

- XML will be designed for use on the Internet, but shall support a wide variety of applications.

  First and foremost, XML was designed to be used on the Web. But the designers foresaw many uses for XML, including Web-based publishing and e-commerce.

- XML will be based on and compatible with SGML.

  SGML had over a dozen years to "iron out the bugs." It's a very solid, stable standard, just too complex for Web-based use. XML keeps the best of SGML and reduces the complexity.

- It will be easy to write programs that process XML documents.

  "Process" in this context can mean render, sort, parse, transform, assemble, and so on. Having easy-to-write programs means that there are far more tools available for processing XML than there ever were for SGML.

- XML documents will be easy to create, readable without specialized tools, and reasonably clear.

  As with SGML, XML documents are saved in ASCII format. You can open and edit them with any text editor or XML editing tool.

- The design of XML will be formal and concise.

  Unlike HTML, XML is a precise standard that sets out clear rules for the creation and application of tag sets. This has made it easier for tool vendors to create new tools for XML. Plus, the standard makes it easy to predict how XML documents will look and be structured.

Compared to HTML and SGML, XML is the best of both worlds. The best functionality of SGML has been extracted and the ease-of-use of HTML has been preserved.

## A look at XML

You can best understand XML if you work through a quick example. First look at a small procedure marked up in HTML (see Listing 14.1).

### Listing 14.1   Sample HTML document

```
<html>
   <body>
      <h2>Logging On to AccSoft </h2>
      <p >The first time you click on a component in AccSoft you are
required to log on to the system before you can complete any tasks.
      <paragraph>To log on to AccSoft:
      <ol>
         <li>Double-click the AccSoft application.
         <li>Select Accounts Payable from the Explorer. <
         <li>Type your USERID into the Name field.
         <li>Type your password into the Password field.
         <li>Select the customer to update.
         <li>Click the OK button to log on to AccSoft.
      </ol>
```

*continues* ▶

### Listing 14.1    Continued

```
    <paragraph>If you do not know your USERID or
        password, consult your System Administrator.
    </body>
</html>
```

This is simple HTML code and though plain, it works. Figure 14.1 shows what it looks like when displayed in a browser.

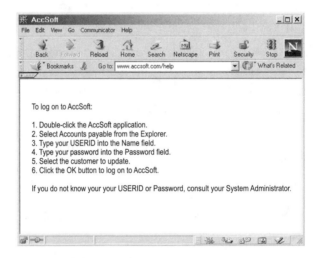

**Figure 14.1.    Simple procedure displayed in a browser.**

For pure display, HTML is very effective. The code is simple and the output is very workable. This HTML could be displayed in any browser.

HTML is a good example of a simple markup language:

- There are start tags and end tags. For example, the procedure title is surrounded by an <h2> start tag and end tag:

  ```
  <h2>Logging On to AccSoft </h2>
  ```

- The end tag is differentiated from the start tag by the forward slash (<h2> versus </h2>) so there's clear delineation of where the title begins and ends.

- The procedure file also shows nesting of the elements of the document. The <html> element contains a <body> element. The <body> element contains an <h2> element, followed by two <p> elements, followed by an <ol> element, followed by a <p> element. The <ol> element contains six <li> elements.

As the example illustrates, HTML can be pretty effective. The code is simple, the output is workable, and the tags delineate content elements and their nesting very clearly. The issue is that HTML is concerned solely with presentation. It does nothing to help you understand what the information *is*. To most observers, the content in the example is obviously a procedure. But we reach that conclusion through interpretation of the content, not through the HTML tags. What does an <h2> represent? It's interpreted as a title. What is an <ol>? You only know that it's an ordered list if you know HTML. Furthermore, there are three different occurrences of the <p> tags, representing different paragraphs. Are they different semantically? Not knowing this can be a problem when it comes time to process the document. There must be a way to distinguish among ambiguous tags.

Now let's look at an XML version of the same procedure. Listing 14.2 shows the same procedure marked up in XML.

**Listing 14.2    Sample XML file**

```xml
<?xml version="1.0"?>
<procedure>
 <title>Logging On to AccSoft </title>
 <paragraph>The first time you click on a component in AccSoft you are
 required to log on to the system before you can complete any tasks.
 </paragraph>
 <intro>To log on to AccSoft:</intro>
 <procedure_steps>
    <step>Double-click the AccSoft application.</step>
    <step>Select Accounts Payable from the Explorer.</step>
    <step>Type your USERID into the Name field.</step>
    <step>Type your password into the Password field.</step>
    <step product="extended">Select the customer to update.</step>
    <step>Click the OK button to log on to AccSoft.</step>
 </procedure_steps>
 <note>If you do not know your USERID or Password, consult your System
Administrator.
 </note>
</procedure>
```

The content of the two procedures is the same, but there are significant differences in the tagging. Tagging for XML is similar to HTML, with start and end tags enclosing content, but it has some very specific rules you need to follow:

- You must have closing tags for all elements.
- Tags must be nested, never overlapping.
- Tag names must match case.

In the XML file the tag names identify what they contain. There can be absolutely no doubt that this is a procedure because the first tag (`<procedure>`) says so. The title is obviously a title. The steps of the procedure are clearly identified. Also, there is only one generic paragraph (`<paragraph>`) in the XML file. In the XML file, paragraphs that were identified generically in the HTML sample are tagged as `<intro>` and `<note>`.

So where did the tags in the XML document come from? We made them up for this example. And that is one of the great advantages of XML; you define the tag names to suit the information that you are marking up. Instead of generic tags, you get semantic tags. Ideally, the names should come from the semantic model for your information, as described in Chapter 8, "Information modeling." Semantic names for model elements describe what goes in each element. The semantic names can therefore be used as the XML tag names and eliminate the need for users to interpret or guess at each tag's purpose.

There are benefits to defining your own tag names:

- **Tag names have meaning for you and your authors.**

  You don't have to guess about the meaning or purpose of a tag name. Tag names can be made specific (as specific or as precise as needed) so authors (and other content handlers) don't have to interpret how a tag should be or has been used.

- **Names can reflect the content.**

  The tag names can clearly identify what they contain. This is a procedure. That is a note.

- **Tag names have nothing to do with formatting.**

  Formatting can be defined later, when you know the exact purpose or purposes of the document. Nothing in the markup will limit the formats to which you can output.

- **You can have as many or as few tags as you need.**

  HTML has a fixed number of tags. You can't add any more and it's very difficult to prevent authors from using those you don't want them to use.

# Importance of **XML** to a unified content strategy

You can implement a unified content strategy without XML, using traditional authoring tools, but XML provides you with the ability to do a whole lot more. There are disadvantages to XML, notably that it is a new technology that brings issues in dealing with the learning curve, the complexity, and the implementation. However, the disadvantages are outweighed by the advantages. The characteristics of XML that best support reuse are:

- Structured content
- Separation of content and format
- Built-in metadata
- Database orientation
- XSL style sheets
- Personalization

These are described in more detail in the following sections.

## XML and structured content

Authors typically have a high-level understanding of the concept of structured content. For example, they understand that books have front matter, body chapters, and back matter. Authors may also recognize repeatable structures at a lower level. Chapters have titles, overviews, sections containing the "meat" of the chapter, and a summary. Some authors can even describe the structure in individual sections, for example, a procedure. (For more on defining structures, see Chapter 8, "Information modeling.") However, when you examine similar information products, you find that structures are not consistent from product to product. Structures will vary from author to author, from department to department, from division to division. Even information written by a single author will vary over time. This is a big problem for reuse.

In XML, structure can be defined in a Document Type Definition (DTD) or Schema[1]. A DTD is quite specific; it defines all the elements (XML tags) that can be used in a document. It also defines the relationship of those elements to other elements. You can specify the hierarchy of elements ("a chapter contains…"), the order of elements, or even the number of elements.

---

1 DTDs and Schemas are, from the conceptual perspective, the same thing: an expression of the acceptable and required structure of a document. The difference is that they are written in different languages, and Schemas include additional capability aimed primarily at the e-business uses of XML.

A DTD can be incredibly valuable for the writing process. Many authors take as much time figuring out the structure they need to write to as they do actually crafting the information. Does my presentation need an overview? Does my procedure have an introduction? Do I need to include a title for a graphic? With a DTD, you can mandate the structure that is required. This consistency is also very valuable for the information's users. Consistency leads to predictability. Users learn where information is to be found and can automatically navigate to it, finding what they need quickly and efficiently. In addition, a DTD provides a powerful map for systematic reuse and personalization. When content is systematically reused, the content management system must identify what content can be reused where. The DTD specifies this information. Personalization also requires a map and set of rules to define what information should be provided and in what order. The DTD provides this information.

For structural consistency, having a defined structure in a DTD is half of the solution. The other half is provided by specialized editing tools (called *validating editors*) that can read a DTD and enforce the structural rules defined in it. By providing authors with a validating editor and a DTD, you can ensure that all your information products are structurally consistent.

## Separation of content and format

If there's a single characteristic that impedes the effectiveness of traditional authoring tools—such as word processors—it is their focus on formatting. Traditional tools have been designed to make it easy for authors to make documents look good. In doing so, they have turned authors into desktop publishers. But from the perspective of reuse, this is not a good thing.

First, word processors began life as an alternative to typewriters. They allowed authors to make documents attractive and potentially, more usable. But they were still very typewriter-like because their focus was the current document. Authors entered the characters that formed the content, then selected the characters to apply the formatting. This wasn't very effective for repeating formatting in a document; it relied on authors remembering that a section title was 18 pt. Helvetica Bold centered on a 36 pica line. The result was inconsistent formatting for all but the most dedicated authors. Later software versions allowed authors to create "styles": formatting that was defined and given a name to apply as required. But even now, none of the word processors provide any functionality to ensure that the formatting remains constant. Authors can define new styles, redefine existing styles, or ignore them altogether. Consistency—or more accurately, predictability—in the application of style names is vital for reuse.

Second, all that formatting power comes with a price. Simply put, you end up with big, bloated data files that contain not only the content, but also all the details of the formatting. Further, that formatting is specific to the output that the tool is designed to support. Most word processing applications, not surprisingly, have a bias toward paper. What makes this a complication for reuse is that you need a way to remove this formatting to make the content independent of output. To reuse the content, authors must apply formatting that is appropriate for each output. Stripping and reapplying formatting is tricky and usually not 100% effective. Format conversions always require correction by hand or complicated scripting.

For reuse, XML has a significant advantage over traditional word processors. XML stems from the originating goal of making documents transportable across systems and applications. The proponents of markup languages knew that the embedded formatting commands and binary file formats were the main impediment to cross-platform transportability. The solution was to separate the format from the content. XML focuses on the structure of a document, not the presentation. The presentation information (styles) is maintained in separate files that are associated with the document when it is published or used.

The separation of content and format offers immense flexibility. For example, the example XML procedure includes a `<note>` element. Traditionally, this is formatted for output something like what is shown in Figure 14.2.

> **NOTE:** If you do not know your your USERID or
> Password, consult your System
> Administrator.

**Figure 14.2   Simple formatted note.**

The signal word "NOTE" is not part of the actual content; it has been provided
through the style sheet. The keyword could easily be replaced by an signal icon,
again through the style sheet (see Figure 14.3).

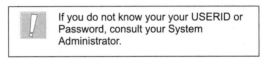

> If you do not know your your USERID or
> Password, consult your System
> Administrator.

**Figure 14.3   Note with signal icon.**

## Built-in metadata

As you've seen, HTML is a defined set of markup tags, whereas XML is a set of
rules for creating markup tags. So what does that mean? Compare the two variations of markup presented earlier. The files contain the same information.
However, to authors the tag names themselves offer additional detail about the
information. The tag names become metadata.

For occasions where additional information is required to describe content,
attributes can be used to further define metadata. An attribute is a name and a
value that can be associated with a tag. For example, a common use for metadata
in a reuse environment is to indicate who the intended audience is for a specific
piece of information. Consider the procedural example. Using attributes, you
can identify the audience for each specific step, option, or even word. Listing
14.3 shows the same procedure but with a step added. The step is tagged like all
the other steps, with the addition of an attribute (`product="extended"`). This
attribute functions as metadata in that it indicates that this step is applicable
only in the extended version of the product.

## Listing 14.3    XML with attribute metadata

```
<procedure>
<title>Logging On to AccSoft </title>
<paragraph>The first time you click on a component in AccSoft you are
required to log on to the system before you can complete any tasks.
</paragraph>
<intro>To log on to AccSoft:</intro>
<procedure_steps>
<step>Double-click the AccSoft application.</step>
<step>Select Accounts Payable from the Explorer.</step>
<step>Type your USERID into the Name field.</step>
<step>Type your password into the Password field.</step>
<step product="extended">Select the customer to update.</step>
<step>Click the OK button to log on to AccSoft.</step>
</procedure_steps>
<exercise>Log onto the training database using the USERID and password
provided by your course facilitator.
</exercise>
<note>If you do not know your USERID or Password, consult your System
Administrator.
</note>
<warning>This database contains personal information about our clients.
Do not let anyone else use your password at any time.
</warning>
</procedure>
```

Using traditional document and content management systems (CMS), authors add metadata through a selection window when they check in a file. The best CMS products include search tools that enable users to search by metadata. But the metadata is only associated with the file; it is not part of the file. You can't email the file to someone and have the metadata go along because the metadata is part of the CMS data. In XML, the metadata travels with the XML file. It is entered as the file is authored or updated. It remains part of the content and can be easily searched.

## Database orientation

If there's a common theme running through the XML references available on the market, it's probably that XML makes you look at information in a different way: as data. The process for determining the structure of your information and the resulting DTD is very similar to the analysis that a developer goes through to design a database. Database designers are not concerned with the actual data values in design; they are interested in the type of information, the hierarchy of that information, and the relationship of the pieces.

A similar approach is taken when designing the structure of XML. The result is a structural format that can be stored very easily in databases. It can be stored as a series of elements rather than as a whole document, and those elements can be extracted and assembled in any order, based on your needs.

## Use of XSL

Separating format from content is all well and good, but sooner or later you need to format information for presentation. XML by itself is not acceptable for display to the average user. The technology for formatting XML presentation is XSL (eXtensible Stylesheet Language). Unlike traditional style sheets, which provide only formatting commands, XSL is a powerful mechanism for both transforming and formatting XML documents.

XSL is an XML markup language itself and as such, can

- Format content for online display or for paper-based delivery
- Add constant text or graphics (such as the icons in the "warning" example)
- Filter content
- Sort or reorder text

There are actually three parts to XSL:

- XPath
- XSL Transformations
- XSL-FO (formatting objects)

Traditional style definitions are very restricted in the way they identify elements for formatting. XPath is a mechanism for identifying and formatting specific elements in an XML document. XPath enables you to apply logic to your formatting. In the XSL style sheet, you can identify and apply specific formatting or transformation to elements, such as a title following a chapter, the first paragraph in a section, and every other bullet in a list.

Other style sheets enable you to describe all your formatting needs, including fonts, colors, sizes, margins, bullets, list numbers, and so on, in a WYSIWYG editor.

But rather than simply formatting the information in a document, XSL gives you the capability to transform it into something else. That is, you can manipulate the information to reorder, repeat, filter out information, or even add information based on details in the file. This is where XSL transformations, also known as XSLT, fit in. XSLT enables you to transform an XML document into another markup language. The most common use of XSLT is to transform information to HTML for display on the Web. But XSLT can also be used to convert information from XML into markup for wireless display, for transmission to PDAs and Web-enabled cell phones.

The flexibility of XSL and its pieces is extremely valuable for information publication and presentation. Unlike traditional tools, which associate one style sheet with one document, you can create any number of style sheets for a single XML document or information type. If you want to post the document on the Web, create an XSL style sheet to HTML. For wireless, create an XSL style sheet to WML.

Despite the unstoppable growth of the Internet and display technologies, paper will continue to be a required output for information. XSL-FO has been designed for that purpose. If you want paper, create an XSL-FO style sheet. XSL-FO (XSL Formatting Objects) provides style sheet capabilities for converting XML to paper-based formats such as PDF. It provides for all the required formatting, including page layouts, headers, footers, recto/verso (odd/even) pages, portrait and landscape pages, and so on.

When the information is ready to publish, you can process the file against all style sheets simultaneously and get all required outputs at the same time.

## Personalization

Personalization is very popular for web delivery of content. Personalization, simply defined, is information that can be manipulated to serve the needs of a specific user. It can be user defined, or it can be managed by software, based on a user's login information. Personalization that is "managed by software" may be controlled by observing user behavior, and/or combined with preferences to create a personalized experience.

With XML, documents can be broken down, stored as separate physical pieces in a database, and then assembled in any order to meet user demands.

# Summary

XML is not the only technology solution for reuse, but it is the most powerful by far. XML combines the best functionality of SGML with the ease-of-use of HTML, which is the best of both worlds.

XML provides powerful support for a unified content strategy through

- Structured content

  A Document Type Definition (DTD) or Schema defines all the elements and their associated tags for a document. The DTD/Schema provides a roadmap to help authors create consistently structured content.

- Separation of content and format

  XML tags focus on a document's structure, not its format. An XSL style sheet can interpret the XML tags to produce any desired format.

- Built-in metadata

  Semantic XML tags (tags that have meaning) can automatically be used to provide metadata (information) about the content. Additional metadata (in attributes in the XML) can also be included in the XML file, which means that when the file is transferred to someone else or a different system, the metadata goes with it.

- Database orientation

  XML describes the content's structure. The structure can easily be stored in a database as a series of elements rather than as a whole document, and then extracted and assembled in any order to meet users' needs.

- XSL style sheets

  XSL is a powerful mechanism for both transforming and formatting XML documents. XSL style sheets let you manipulate the information to reorder it, repeat content, filter out information, or even add information. You can use XSL style sheets to convert XML to any desired format (such as, HTML, PDF, or wireless).

- Personalization

  With XML, documents can be broken down, stored as separate pieces in a database or CMS, then assembled in any order to meet users' needs.

# Chapter 15

## Authoring tools

Before content can be managed, manipulated, or reused, it must be created. Authoring tools enable authors to create that content. To support a unified content strategy, authoring tools must allow content to be written so that it can be structured and reused according to the content life cycle you identified earlier. This chapter describes the different types of authoring tools that are available and their pros and cons for use in a unified content strategy. For more information on the process of selecting tools, see Chapter 13, "Evaluating tools."

# An overview of authoring tools

Authoring tools are among the oldest and most mature tools available for the desktop. The most dominant authoring tool on the market is Microsoft Word, which has become almost ubiquitous. However, there are still many other tools, all with different capabilities, strengths, and weaknesses. An increasing number of XML tools (for the creation of output text, XML stylesheets, and DTDs and Schemas) is also on the market. Additionally, many of the traditional tools are adding or have added XML capabilities. For the purpose of this discussion, authoring tools are broken into two types:

- Traditional word processing and page layout tools
- Structured editors

## Traditional word processing and page layout tools

If you expect to stay with traditional tools, you should understand what they are, as well as what they're capable of doing. There are really three types of traditional tools: word processing tools, page layout tools, and hybrids that combine the functionality (to some degree) of both word processor and page layout tools.

- Word processing tools were originally designed as memo and letter authoring tools; they are focused on authoring. They have been designed to make it easy to enter and edit text and apply formatting.
- Page layout tools typically have had weak text entry capabilities; instead, they rely on importing text from word processors. Their focus has been on formatting content for page layout. Page layout tools are the tools of professional typesetters: they have tremendous typographical control for exacting output standards.
- Hybrids are a cross between word processors and page layout tools, typically designed to manage long documents or series of documents. Their text editing capabilities are better than page layout tools, but not always as complete as word processors. Their formatting capabilities are better than word processors, but not as good as the page layout tools.

## Structured editors

If XML is part of your authoring environment, you have the option of using structured editors as your authoring tool. Structured editors enforce the structure of content, typically based on a model such as a DTD. (For more information on structured authoring, see Chapter 14, "The role of XML.") There are XML-aware tools (traditional tools with integrated XML), Native XML/SGML editors (editors that work natively in XML/SGML), and other editors that enforce structure in different ways.

There are four types of structured editors:

- **Full-function editors**

  A full-function editor is based on XML as its data format and provides the equivalent functionality of something like Microsoft Word, but for XML. It includes spell checkers, table tools, book building tools, and all the usual functions that authors expect to see, but it uses XML and enforces the content's structure as the content is entered. Typically, full-function editors provide a WYSIWYG view of the text that is familiar to most authors, a view that shows the structure of the content (displays tags and hierarchy), and a full XML view that displays the XML.

- **Simple XML editors**

  A simple XML editor is a capable editor, but includes only the functionality for the basic entry of text and XML markup. It does not include any of the book building tools of traditional or full-function tools. It might be better suited to programmers than to authors.

- **XML-aware tools**

  XML-aware tools attempt to combine the ease of use of a traditional word processor or desktop publishing tool with the power of XML. They embed XML functions directly in the familiar authoring tool so the interface looks much like the one authors are used to, but provides XML as the output.

- **Forms-based authoring systems**

  Forms-based authoring tools are usually provided as optional functionality on XML-based content management systems. They are used to create web-based HTML forms that provide text entry capabilities. They are most effective for simple structures. Form-based authoring can also provide benefits to geographically dispersed content creation teams or individuals with special remote access needs.

# Capabilities and requirements for unified content

When deciding what you want an authoring tool to do, it is vital that you consider the needs of authors, not just the interests of the tool evaluators. Typically, tool evaluations are done by people who may not use the tool, such as IT personnel, and may apply a priority to features or characteristics (technology or price) that, although important, are not essential to functionality. Too often, solutions are chosen based on an incomplete interpretation of what authors need. That means that you have to talk to the authors and determine their real authoring needs (see Chapter 5, "Analyzing the content life cycle"). You also have to look at your unified content life cycle vision to determine what kind of authoring functionality you need to support the vision.

When you evaluate authors' needs, you may find that you need different tools for different groups throughout the enterprise. You are likely to have casual authors who submit content occasionally, authors who submit content on a continuous basis, and authors who compile and configure content into multiple information products. Even authors who submit content frequently have different needs; some contribute small pieces of information with simple structures, and others create large, complex information products.

## Familiarity

Given that people do not always accept change easily, there can be an advantage to sticking with the tools they know. The main advantage to traditional word processing tools is that they are familiar to most employees. Tools such as Word are very common on the corporate desktop and authors have become accustomed to their look and their functionality.

Structured authoring tools, on the other hand, have been around for many years, but have not gained the same popularity. The tools with embedded support have a familiar interface, but the technology and the technological concepts behind the interface are new. For other XML tools, both the interface and the concepts will be new to authors.

If you are dealing with casual, non-technical authors, there may be an advantage in sticking with a traditional tool.

**Technical complexity**

Traditional authoring tools are typically more suitable for the lowest common denominator. That is, they are easy for even casual authors to use. That is not the case with most structured editors. In selecting a structured editor, a key factor to consider is how much of the underlying technology is exposed to authors. Can users choose the level of complexity presented to them?

Of course, if you do choose XML, you have additional options. Because XML is an application-independent form of markup, you can select different authoring tools for different groups of authors in your organization. Authors with very simple authoring tasks can use an editor with simple editing functionality. Authors who perform more complex authoring tasks need a more capable tool. Structured editors range from simple file editing tools (that is, tools that are used for editing a file but have no capacity for book building) to full function tools that include all the usual capabilities of standard authoring tools.

## Vendor questions

You must be able to hide or expose technical complexity to suit the needs and skills of your users. Ask vendors the following questions:

- Can the interface be customized to present only the functions that authors need to use?
- Is the interface configurable for groups?
- Is the interface configurable by profile?

**Functional maturity**

Traditional tools tend to be mature tools. They all have things that they do well or not so well, but they also have very rich and complete functionality, including capabilities, such as spelling and grammar checkers, autocorrect and autoinput, change tracking, and macros.

Tools such as spell checkers and grammar checkers are often taken for granted until they are not available. A non-traditional tool may be less mature and may not include the functionality that authors have become accustomed to. Even though such items as spelling and grammar checkers may not be on *your* selection criteria, they may be critical for your authors to have.

Some structured authoring tools have reached the same level of maturity as traditional word processors; others have not. Many of the full-function tools include spell checkers, grammar checkers, table functions, math functions, table of contents tools, index tools, and others that simplify the authoring task.

## Vendor questions

You can ask quite a few vendor questions about functionality in a number of different areas, including the following:

- Does the authoring tool support the full functionality normally found in authoring tools?
  - Spell check/thesaurus?
  - Search and replace?
  - Hypertext links?
  - Bullets?
  - Numbered lists?
  - Tables?
  - Footnotes?
  - Scientific equations/notation?
  - Global search and replace?
  - Autocorrect and autoinput?
  - Macros?
- How are graphics handled?
  - Are images linked or embedded? (static and dynamic?)
  - Does the authoring tool include a preview mode?
  - How are images linked in? Drag and drop?
  - Can you revise graphics in the tool?
  - Can the images be manipulated for size, position, resolution, and orientation in the authoring tool?
- What kind of support is there for tables?
- Is the tool wizard driven?
- Is there embedded support (in the tool)?

- Can tables be generated from links to external data sources (CSV files, XML tagged data, ASCII files, and so on)?
- Can the authoring system track changes in a document?
  - With change bars? With color?
  - Can you track changes for multiple authors with visual differentiation?
  - Can authors turn change indications on and off?
  - Can the system produce change reports?
  - Does the vendor support change management such as change reports, change bars, and version comparisons?
  - Can change bars automatically turn off after a period of time has passed?
  - Can you compare two versions of one document to identify all differences?

## Book-building capability

Word processing tools are the most mature of the traditional tools. They started life as tools for letters, memos, and short reports. Longer documents—not the original focus of the tools—need what are traditionally known as book-building tools. Book-building tools generate:

- Tables of contents
- Indices
- Lists of figures and tables

Most, if not all, of the traditional tools now have book-building capabilities, which is both good and bad. They started off as simple editors, but the book building tools have been added on, and their effectiveness can be debated. There are exceptions: products that were built specifically as long document tools. As a result, their book building functions work very well.

As noted previously, structured editors may or may not support book building; they range from simple file editing tools (that is, tools used for editing a file, but with no capacity for book building) to full-function tools that include all the usual capabilities of standard authoring tools. The full-function tools include spell checkers, grammar checkers, table functions, math functions, table of content tools, index tools, and so on.

When it comes to book building needs, structured editors offer an additional advantage. With XML-based authoring, it is easy to move book building out of the authors' hands and automate the generation of TOCs, indices, and so on. You don't need TOC or list functionality; it can be provided for in style sheets.

## Vendor questions

If you cannot automate book building functions, you must make sure that they are included in the tool. Ask vendors the following questions:

- What book building functions are included in the tool?
  - TOC?
  - Index?
  - Glossary?
  - Lists of figures, tables, and so on?
- Are these structures automatically updated or must they be manually regenerated?

### Structural and stylistic control

The biggest disadvantage to traditional word processing and page layout tools is that they offer too much flexibility. They do not prevent authors from creating new styles or applying formatting to suit their own views of how information should look on the page. The result is inconsistent formatting and style names. There is also no built-in functionality to ensure that authors include all the elements required for the information product they are writing. In other words, there is nothing to enforce structure. Style names only imply structure. Users can easily ignore the styles and format directly. The documents might all look alike on the surface, but may not look alike "under the covers," with authors manually creating the look and feel rather than using consistent style tags. This is inefficient for authors and has a major negative impact on conversion to other formats; content that is not consistently formatted (tagged) cannot be automatically converted to another format. It requires manual cleanup. An alternative is to enforce formatting and structure through policy and procedure (editorial or review), but such reviews are never 100% effective. The result is inconsistency. Inconsistency means unpredictability, which is a killer for reuse and multi-channel output.

Structured editors do not have the same problems with format. As the name suggests, structured editors focus on the structure of the document. Most structured editors enable users to attach a style sheet to documents, which serves primarily to provide a certain comfort level for authors. The obvious advantage to structured editors is that they use XML, with great advantages for reuse (see Chapter 14. More important, structured editors are capable of reading and enforcing a DTD or Schema. At their simplest, structured editors allow authors to validate a document's structure: they identify any structural errors in the document, including when elements are not allowed or when they are missing.

Some editors do not allow authors to insert invalid elements of structure. For example, they would not allow authors to insert a table in a title. The most capable tools provide authors with drop-down lists or menus of elements that are valid in the document. As authors move the cursor around the document, from element to element, the drop-down list changes to show the valid elements. This prevents authors from entering tags where they are not allowed. This type of structured editor does not allow authors to make structural mistakes.

## Vendor questions

Structured tools should provide an efficient authoring environment. Ask vendors the following questions:

- Does the authoring system support structured content templates? How does it handle template versioning?
- Does the authoring tool enforce structure as defined in a DTD or Schema?
- Does the tool indicate what XML tags are valid at the cursor's current position? Does the authoring tool allow authors to make tagging errors?
- How do authors enter XML tags, if at all? Do they pick from a list or menu?

## Separation of format and content

Traditional tools make it easy for authors to make documents look good, and in doing so, they have turned authors into desktop publishers. But from the perspective of reuse, this is not a good thing for many reasons.

Word processors and desktop publishing tools helped to make documents very attractive and, potentially, more usable. Authors enter the characters that form the content, then select them and apply the formatting. For reuse, you need to remove this formatting to make the content output-independent, then apply format that is appropriate to each intended use. Stripping and reapplying formatting always requires correction by hand or complicated scripting.

XML does not have this problem. The presentation information (styles) are maintained in separate files that can then be associated with the document when it is published or used.

## Vendor questions

Styles should be controlled to maintain consistency. Ask vendors the following questions:

- Does the tool use discrete stylesheets or are style commands embedded in the document files?
- If styles are embedded, can they be locked?

### Conversion

A key factor to consider when choosing an authoring tool is conversion. The current pattern of delivery for information is that the same information is delivered in different formats. To move information from one format to the other, the materials must be converted. Ideally, the conversion should be automated so it can be done "on the fly." If you plan to share content authored in many tools, it will be necessary to convert the content from each of the authoring tools into a common format that can be managed and then converted back to another format for reuse.

All the traditional tools have some sort of conversion capability. Some have "save as" functionality, which allows you to save the current document in other formats. The conversion utility converts the native formatting codes into the equivalent codes in the target output format. For example, most (if not all) word processors allow you to save documents as HTML. However, what you get is HTML with formatting characteristics that are more suited for paper output than browser display. The output is not usable in a browser.

Some traditional authoring tools use third-party applications to provide style conversions. These types of conversion tools tend to place more emphasis on defined styles in the document, specifically on style names. They enable you to define format transformations based on the names of styles in the source document. In these transformations, you can ignore the paper-based formatting and apply format characteristics that are better suited to your output medium.

Traditional authoring tools offer no real control over styles. Authors can create, change, or delete styles at will. This is a major problem for conversion. It is very difficult to automate conversion if you cannot predict the styles used in source materials. Where styles and structures in source information are inconsistent, conversion must be done manually. Manual conversion eliminates the option of automatic reuse. For any large enterprise, this is not acceptable: It is simply too expensive.

For conversion, there is a clear advantage to XML tools. The separation of content and format is invaluable. To convert XML content to another format requires only a new stylesheet.

## Vendor questions

Whatever tool you pick must support import from legacy data. Ask vendors the following questions:

- Does the tool support conversion from other formats? Which formats? What level of support?
- What output formats does it support?

## Dynamic/virtual documents

If you need to assemble output documents from pieces of content, whether on the fly or as static output documents, structured authoring has a clear advantage. XML is very easy to assemble and reconfigure into new outputs (see Chapter 14).

The effectiveness of traditional word processors is entirely dependent on the ability of authors to create consistently formatted and tagged files. Files can be reassembled, but you need extensive programming support to build the utilities to strip out and reapply formatting.

## *Vendor questions*

Dynamic documents bring their own requirements for authoring tools. The tool must be capable of assembling pieces into a cohesive whole for authors to work with. Ask vendors the following questions:

- Does the tool support virtual or dynamic documents?
- Can you easily link fragments of documents together?

### Support infrastructure

Traditional tools are already in place in most enterprises. They have been purchased, installed on the desktop, and have been in use for many years. Users have templates in place, and the IT infrastructures are in place to support the tools on the desktop. Extensive training is available for authors not already trained in the use of the tools. In addition, there are individuals who are experts in their use. In a corporate climate where the bottom line is carefully monitored, a solution that uses tools that have already been paid for can be very difficult to argue against.

New tools and technologies do not have the same immediate support. Changing enterprise tools can mean you need to build all the support infrastructure. But, the additional implementation overhead is not necessarily seen as a detriment when the new technology adds new functionality such as structure.

See Chapter 13 for the general questions that you should ask of vendors.

### Integration with a content management system

Although authors can create content, save the content, then check the file(s) into a content management system, it is preferable to have the authoring tools directly integrated into the content management system. This means that when authors select File, Open, the authoring tool automatically goes to the content management system to select content. When authors do a File, Save, the content is automatically saved to the content management system and any version control information is gathered. In addition, if your organization has decided to use systematic reuse, it is important that the content be automatically populated to the document open in the authoring tool.

## *Vendor questions*

The tool that you choose must fully and seamlessly integrate with your content management system. Ask vendors the following questions:

- With what CMS does your authoring tool integrate?
- What functionality of the CMS is available directly from the authoring tool?
- Can I use my desktop authoring tool, but integrate with the web-based version of the CMS?

# Criteria for selection

The usual procedure for selecting authoring software differs from organization to organization. Too often it involves people downloading evaluation copies until they find an application they like. Although selecting appropriate authoring tools may seem like a lesser problem than picking a content management system, it is not. Authoring tools are just as critical to the success of your unified content strategy as the other software components.

To pick authoring tools, whether for department use or for enterprise use, you must start by developing a list of criteria against which to match prospective solutions. The authoring tool that you choose for your department, division, or company should be picked based on its ability to meet specific criteria. Those criteria should definitely include functionality, but must also take into account broader concerns such as price, environment, and the capabilities of your authors. For more information on selecting tools, see Chapter 13.

## Summary

Although authors can create content and convert it to the format of choice, it is preferable for them to use a tool that will minimize the amount of conversion required and will aid them in the authoring process. There are two types of authoring tools for your system:

- Traditional word processing or page layout tools
- Structured editors

There are three types of traditional authoring tools: word processing tools, page layout tools, and hybrids that combine the functionality (to some degree) of both word processor and page layout tools.

There are also different kinds of structured authoring tools. There are XML-aware tools (traditional tool with integrated XML), Native XML/SGML editors (editors that work natively in XML/SGML), and other editors that enforce structure in different ways.

Here are some of the things to consider when selecting a tool:

- Does the tool support conversion from other formats? Which formats?
- Does the authoring tool support the full functionality normally found in authoring tools?
- Does the authoring system support structured content templates?
- What is the support for graphics?
- Does the authoring tool enforce structure as defined in a DTD or Schema? Does the tool indicate what XML tags are valid at the cursor's current position? Does the authoring tool allow authors to make tagging errors?
- For XML editors, how do users enter XML tags? Do they pick from a list or menu?
- What is the support for tables?
- Can the authoring system track changes in a document?
- Can you customize the interface to hide the complexity of the tool or technology?

# Chapter 16

## Content management systems

Content management is an integral component of a successful unified content strategy, and selecting the right content management system can be a lengthy investigational process. This chapter provides you with an understanding of what a content management system does so that you can make the correct decision when selecting your own. One of the hardest decisions is selecting the type of content management system to use. To help you make this choice, this chapter outlines the many types of content management systems and their advantages and disadvantages.

Throughout this chapter, we also provide questions you should ask vendors when selecting a content management system. For general information on how to select an appropriate tool, see Chapter 13, "Evaluating tools."

## The content management process

Content management is, of course, a complex topic, but the overall process can be described rather simply. Content is created in an authoring tool, then saved into the content management system (repository). Content is saved into the repository as individual elements and the metadata is added (see the "Metadata section" later in this chapter). Within the repository, content is managed and then delivered to the appropriate media. Figure 16.1 illustrates this process.

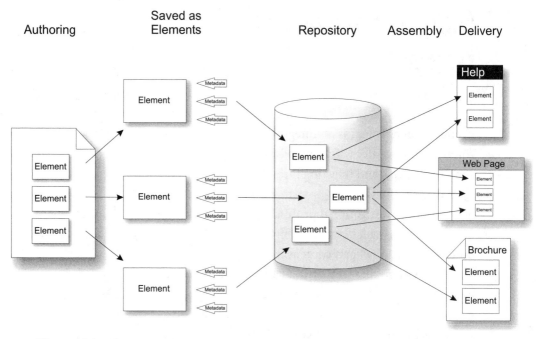

**Figure 16.1    Content management process.**

The basic functionality of a CMS is described as follows.

A content management system must save content so that it can be reused. There are two parts to saving content. First, the content itself is divided into elements of the appropriate sizes for intended reuse. Second, metadata is added to the elements to define these elements for effective reuse, retrieval, and tracking.

However, a content management system does more than save content. The content needs to be accessible for various projects or people; archives need to be built to allow access to previous versions and to track changes over time; security is required to control access to various authors and content users. Management functionalities include access control, version control, updates, archives, and translations.

## "Saved as" elements

As content is saved into the system it is "saved as" individual elements in the repository and the metadata is added. To assist authors in writing contextually, content is usually authored in documents or large components (for example, a complete procedure), although content may be reused at a much more granular level (such as in a step or paragraph). Before being stored in the repository, content is broken apart into its individual elements and then saved. The process of breaking content into its element parts is called *segmentation* or *bursting*.

You define the level of segmentation in a segmentation or bursting map. For example, you may decide that a long section should be saved as a series of elements defined by the third level heading, such that content deeper than the third level heading is kept contained (not broken down further through segmentation). Alternatively, you may decide that content needs to be broken down at each element, such as a step. Organizations typically have different segmentation maps for different types of content.

If you have chosen to create some content following a nested reuse model (see Chapter 2, "Fundamental concepts of reuse") you may decide to keep all the nested content together in one larger element because the content is only reused within itself. For example, using the nested example of the B-Brother product description first introduced in Chapter 2, you probably wouldn't want to break the content at the sentence level and store the sentence-level content separately in the CMS. Rather, you would store the B-Brother product description as an element and use a filter (see Chapter 12, "Implementing your design") to take out the pieces (sentences) that are not relevant in a given information product. In this case the segmentation map would identify that the content should not be segmented (stored as individual elements); it should be stored at the paragraph level (unsegmented) (see Figure 16.2), not the sentence level. Segmentation at the sentence level would look like the example shown in Figure 16.3.

<The B-Brother model 1984 is a device that connects directly to a consumer's television to track their television watching habits.>
<It can be programmed to track the channels they flip to, what programs they record and what commercials they skip. The information is instantly transmitted to the cable or satellite provider.>

**Figure 16.2     Content stored as a paragraph element (not segmented).**

The B-Brother model 1984 is a device that connects directly to a consumer's television to track their television watching habits.

It can be programmed to track the channels they flip to, what programs they record and what commercials they skip. The information is instantly transmitted to the cable or satellite provider.

**Figure 16.3     Content stored as separate elements (segmented).**

For more information about segmentation and granularity see Chapter 12.

### Vendor questions

Flexible segmentation maps are important to a unified content strategy to ensure that content can be stored at an appropriate level for retrievability, reuse, and management. Ask vendors the following questions:

- Does the CMS support segmentation or bursting?
- Can you define the level of granularity? Can you define multiple levels of granularity depending on the type of content? Can you change the level of granularity at a later date?

## Metadata

Metadata can be applied to the content in the authoring tool, or it can be applied as the content is checked into the CMS. Wherever possible you want metadata automatically applied to the elements of content. For example, if you have a container element that is broken into sub-elements like the Contact container (see Figure 16.4), and you add metadata to the Contact container to indicate this contact is for Widget Y, then all the sub-elements will automatically have the metadata Product = Widget Y applied to them as well (inherited). When meta-data is inherited to all sub-elements, it ensures that metadata is applied appropriately and saves the author time.

| Semantic | Element type | Metadata |
| --- | --- | --- |
| Contact | Container | Widget Y  (applied) |
| Name | Container | Widget Y (inherited) |
| First | Element | Widget Y (inherited) |
| Last | Element | Widget Y (inherited) |
| Contact Phone | Element | Widget Y (inherited) |
| Contact Email | Element | Widget Y (inherited) |

**Figure 16.4   Contact container with inherited metadata.**

## Vendor questions

Metadata is the key to effective retrieval and reuse of content in a unified content strategy. It needs to be easy to create and easy for authors to apply to ensure that metadata is applied correctly. Ask vendors the following questions:

- Can metadata be applied in the authoring tool? Is metadata applied as content is checked in? How simple is it for authors to select and apply metadata?
- Can sub-elements of a container element automatically inherit the metadata of the container element?
- What types of metadata can be automatically applied?
- How easy is it to create a new metatag?
- Can the facility for creating/changing metatags be secured so that only the system administrator can make changes?

## The management system

The management portion of the CMS manages the content through such features as access control, check-in/check-out, and version control. This functionality is described in the following sections.

## *Access control*

Access control secures content and identifies who can read, create, modify, and delete content. Access is based on roles. For example, you may determine that authors have permission to create, modify, and delete their own content; editors only modify content; designers modify only templates but not content, and others can only view (read) content.

Certain elements may be accessible only to a certain group (for example, marketing can access all content, but engineering can access only their own materials). Check to ensure you can set access control at any level of granularity. If the information product is secured at a specific level, then all the content in the information product should be secured at the same level. If content is reused and it is secured at one level in one document, the access control should automatically be the same level wherever it is reused. You may decide to have individual element access control levels and container and information product model access control levels. For example, the company logo has no security restrictions associated with it. In the case of an audit report that is restricted to senior management viewing only (restricted viewing at the information product level), the company logo is restricted within that document. In an information product where the viewing of the logo is not restricted (for example, in a brochure) anyone can view that element. The logo element takes on the restriction of the information product where it is reused.

### Vendor questions

When content is being reused it is important to secure the content so that only appropriate individuals can create or modify content. Content may also need to be secured so only certain individuals can view it. Ask vendors the following questions:

- What security features are provided to protect sensitive documents from unauthorized access and modification?
- What levels of security are provided (for example, create, read only, modify)?
- At what level of granularity can content be secured?
- Is an element's level of security maintained wherever it is reused?

## Check-in/check-out

When authors want to work on content they check it out (sign it out) and check it back in again when they are finished with it. This ensures that only one person is working on the same content at any one time and that multiple people cannot concurrently change (or save) the content and create a conflict (which version is correct?) or even destroy the version that was saved by the first person. It is possible to check out previous and current versions of content. When changes occur to both versions, the content branches. This should be discouraged unless it is required (for example, if a product that starts off as one product then splits into two products) because it could cause confusion or inaccuracies if the wrong version of the content is used.

### Vendor questions

Check-in/check-out ensures that only one person modifies content at any point in time. Ask vendors the following questions:

- How easy is it to check-in/check-out content? Is content then locked so other authors cannot also check it out and change it?
- Can the system administrator check in content that is checked out by someone else (useful, for example, if an author is sick)?

## Version control

Version control ensures that each time content is checked in, another version (copy) is created and it is assigned a new version number. This ensures that every change to content is saved and that every change can be tracked. It also enables you to use multiple versions of the same content in different situations. For example, someone might want to use more recent versions of products where the previous version is still being supported. Reviewers like to look at previous versions of content to see what has changed and to ensure that changes have been correctly incorporated.

If for some reason you cannot use the current version of content (for example, you planned to announce something but it has been delayed or there is a problem with the functionality of a piece of content on the web site), you can select a previous version of content and reuse it.

It is important to be able to version each element, not just at the container level or information product level. It is also important to be able to version an entire approved information product as it is delivered (for example, an instance of the web site as it was posted on a particular date, the final version of a report, or the latest version of the brochure). In this way you can easily identify the information product with all its individual elements as it existed on a specific day for tracking or legal purposes, retrieval purposes, or to enable users to go back to that version rapidly. Sometimes this version is called a *released version*, the *delivered instance*, or in the case of a web site, an *edition*.

Versions can be saved as complete new versions (previous version plus changes) or as deltas (changes only). Saving versions as deltas helps to save space in your content management system. However, when a delta version is retrieved the delta (change) is applied to the original content so the author sees a complete element, not just a fragment of an element.

### Vendor questions

Version control enables you to ensure that every time content is changed, not only is the current version available, but all the previous versions are available as well. This enables you to compare versions, track changes to versions, and go back to a previous version if desired. Ask vendors the following questions:

- Is every element versioned individually?
- What types of versioning are provided?
- Are changes stored as complete new versions of an element or does the CMS store the deltas (changes only) from the current/original version?

## Updates

Reused content can be updated in a number of ways. Authors who reuse content can select which type of update they want the reusable content to have. Three types of updates are available:

- **Automatically update**

  Automatically updates the reused element when the original (source) element is changed. This means that authors who reuse the content are not notified; instead, the content is automatically updated. Automatic update can save a lot of time for authors because they do not have to check and verify that they want to reuse the updated content. However, an automatic update could cause problems. The update may not be relevant or correct in the reuse situation. Automatic update could then result in incorrect information.

- **Optionally update**

  The CMS notifies authors of the changes so that they can decide whether they want to update the element or not. This helps authors ensure that the update is relevant to them, because it requires them to review the update and decide to accept or reject it.

- **No update**

  If the original component is updated, the reused element is not updated and authors are not notified if the original element changes. The reused element now exists as a separate element (similar to copy and paste). This option should be discouraged unless there is a good reason for the choice (for example, branching of information) because content will diverge and become inconsistent over time.

For example, a medical devices company has chosen to optionally update all content except corporate branding (for example, logo and product name) for safety reasons. If an author updates a caution for a particular product, it should not automatically update the caution for all other products because the change may not be applicable to all products and could result in a safety hazard. However, the company has recently gone through a merger, so they want the logo to automatically update when the new logo has been defined. In another situation, a software development company has chosen to automatically update all its elements. Now they have developed a new product where 40% of the functionality is in common, but 40% is new and 20% is a modification of existing product functionality. In this case, they keep the automatic update for the 40% in common, but select no update for the 20% that is going to vary from the previous functionality. In this way, the content that will vary becomes the source and can be used to derive new or modified content.

Authors reusing the content are responsible for determining what type of update they want on the reused elements. The system default is usually optionally update. However, different elements can have different update options.

### Vendor questions

Update options enable your authors to control how reusable content is updated. Ask vendors the following questions:

- What are the update options (automatically update, optionally update, no update)?
- How easy is it to change a selected update (for example, "automatic update" to "no update")?

## Repository

The CMS' repository manages the content. It is usually built using a relational database, but some also use object-oriented databases. CMS typically use relational databases because they are the most common type of database and have the greatest adoption (such as, Oracle, Microsoft SQL server). The repository manages the content and the metadata associated with each content object. It also manages other types of objects such as graphics and media (such as, video).

### Vendor questions

The repository is the heart of the content management system and manages your unified content. Ask vendors the following questions:

- What content formats does the CMS support, and at what level of granularity does it support them (for example, file, section, paragraph)?
- What type of database does the content management software use?

- Can the CMS accommodate the demands of enterprise implementations (for example, the number of users and the volume of documents)?

## Search and retrieval

Good search and retrieval functionality is important in ensuring that authors can easily find and retrieve content for reuse and delivery. It should be possible to search and retrieve content based on individual elements, containers, and whole information products. Authors should also be able to find edits, find edits made by particular people or at particular times, search for comments, and search and retrieve on any type of information contained in the content management system. Full-text retrieval searches on the text of the content. Metadata can be used to narrow the search's focus.

### Vendor questions

Search and retrieval facilitates the retrieval of content. Ask vendors the following questions:

- What type of search engine is available? Can you add your own?
- What types of searching are supported (Boolean, natural language, index, keyword, structural, metadata)?
- Can search criteria be restricted based on user security profiles?

## Archive

Previous versions of content that are finalized and approved but no longer current should be archived (stored). Content is archived based on a set of rules that specify the period of time in which the content is considered to be valid or accurate. The CMS can automatically delete expired content or can prompt a manager to review the content and determine whether it should be archived.

### Vendor questions

The capability to store content after it is no longer in use, yet ensure that it is still accessible, is an important component of a unified content strategy. Questions for vendors might include:

- How is archiving, obsoleting, and deleting handled? How do you set the rules?

- How can you reinstate an archive? How can archives be searched? Can archives be summarized or commented for easy access later?

## Translation

Managing content in multiple languages becomes important if you translate your content. It is not enough to just store the multiple language versions of your content; it is very important to ensure that the content management system can create a relationship between your source language (original language) and the translated content. A relationship between the source language and the translated content ensures that when the source language changes, the localized content is identified (through metadata) as requiring new translation. Without a relationship between the source language and the translated content, managing the identification of change is very time consuming and error-prone.

Many organizations use memory translation tools to assist in the translation process. It is advantageous for the content management system to directly integrate with a translation memory tool to further facilitate the translation process (for example, the translators can retrieve content directly from the CMS rather than having to extract the content, send it to the translation firm, then reintegrate the translated content).

### Vendor questions

Effectively managing localized content is important to satisfying all your customer needs. Ask vendors the following questions:

- Can the CMS create a relationship between the source language and multiple translated versions of the content?

- Can the CMS integrate with a memory translation tool? With what memory translation tools can it integrate? Can the CMS be modified to integrate with other memory translation tools if necessary?

## *Workflow*

Workflow functionality is often provided with a content management system. See Chapter 17, "Workflow systems," for more information on workflow.

# The types of content management systems

One of the hardest decisions to make about content management is which type of content management system makes the most sense to purchase. There are many different types of content management systems, and they focus on many different content life cycles. Web content management is the most familiar type of CMS but there are a number of other types of content management. Each type of content management system has its advantages and disadvantages. This section describes the types of content management.

## Web content management system

The term "content management system" has become synonymous with web content management systems. There have been document management systems (see the section "Integrated document management systems") for over a decade, but it was the advent of the Web and the issues of managing large web sites that popularized content management and content management systems.

Web content management systems (WCMSs) assist an organization in automating various aspects of web content creation, content management, and delivery. Delivery to the Web is its primary format, but many WCMS systems also deliver to wireless devices.

## *Advantages*

The interface and functionality of a WCMS are designed to support the web site creation and management content life cycle and provide strong support for collaborative authoring, testing, and controlled delivery of content to the web site.

Typically, a WCMS includes its own authoring tool: either an HTML editor or web-based forms. Some provide an automatic conversion of content from traditional authoring tools into HTML that can be processed by the WCMS.

Authoring and management is managed in stages with authors working in their own content work areas to create content, view and review the content, and test functionality. When content has been approved, it is moved into a staging area, where it is assembled according to your design and integrated with content from other work areas. When content in the staging area is approved, an edition (version) of the content is created. This edition can then be posted to the site to replace existing content. The editions can be archived so that if there is a problem (for example, an error is introduced to the site), content can be rapidly rolled back (returned) to a previous edition. Support of the web content life cycle is very valuable to organizations because it ensures that content is thoroughly reviewed and tested before it is delivered to the site, and only content that meets certain criteria is posted to the site, thus preventing problems of incorrect content or content that does not function (for example, pages that yield error 404). A WCMS can also hold content until a specific date when it becomes effective, and automatically remove content from the web site when the content has expired (is no longer current or relevant).

Personalization is also a strong component of many WCMS systems supporting dynamic content creation. Personalization enables the WCMS to provide personalized content to users. For more information about personalization see Chapter 10, "Designing dynamic content." Delivery to the Web, and often to wireless devices, is directly integrated in the WCMS, unlike paper-oriented CMSs, where an additional publishing tool is often required.

## Disadvantages

WCMSs are designed to create, manage, and deliver web-based content only. In an enterprise environment where paper, and the complexities of paper (for example, sophisticated page layout and support of a TOC and index) is also required, WCMSs fail to meet these needs. Interestingly, many of the WCMSs that exist today were designed first to handle paper publications and then moved to web content management and abandoned paper.

In addition to the lack of support for other types of content, the level of granularity of reuse may be insufficient for your requirements. Granularity of a web page is supported, and often granularity of components within a web page is supported, particularly if the WCM also provides personalization functionality. However, functionality such as nested reuse and granular content that can be exchanged among different types of content is rarely supported.

If the WCMS relies on an HTML editor or forms for input, the complexities of other types of content will not be supported.

### Transactional content management systems

A number of CMSs have been specifically designed to manage e-commerce transactions. Transactional content management systems (TCMSs) are focused on managing the exchange of money through web-based product e-catalogs. They typically integrate with legacy systems for inventory, pricing, and shipping. In addition, they provide shopping cart functionality that enables customers to select products for purchase and track the cost of their potential purchases. A key component of TCMSs is security—providing a secure environment for customers to purchase product and ensure that their credit information remains confidential and secure. Many provide personalization features and provide personalized product recommendations to customers, as well.

Most TCMSs manage transactional information and provide full WCMS capability.

## Advantages

The greatest strength of transactional CMSs is their strong support of e-commerce interactions and their capability to interface with legacy systems for the transfer of product information.

## Disadvantages

Like web-based content management systems, transactional CMSs are web-based only and do not support the requirements of enterprise content.

### Integrated document management systems

Integrated document management systems (IDMSs) have been around much longer than WCMSs. Document management systems have traditionally managed enterprise documents (such as correspondence, reports, and publications).

Initially they were document management systems, not content management systems; they managed whole documents (such as an entire report) rather than individual elements of content. However, in recent years the majority of these systems have moved to the management of elements of content.

IDMSs can interface with multiple types of authoring tools to manage multiple types of content. However, unless the content is converted internally to a common format, it cannot be reused among different types of content.

IDMSs can deliver content in the original source format (for example, Word in, Word out), frequently convert to other formats (for example, Word in, HTML out), and produce PDF versions of content.

A common function of many IDMSs is imaging of content. Many organizations require the capability to image (scan) paper-based content that comes into their organization from an external source (for example, customer correspondence, patient records), then manage that image as they would their other content.

IDMSs have gained widespread acceptance in organizations where security of content and strong control of content is required (such as organizations that produce products regulated by government or agencies). To support this usage, many IDM systems have very robust audit trails (clear history of what has occurred for every piece of content, who made the change and why, and the series of authorizations the content has gone through). They may also include electronic signatures to securely verify authorization of content.

Some IDM systems may have CRM (customer relationship management) and web content management components.

## Advantages

IDM systems have been around much longer than any other type of CMS, so the interface is stable and, because of the products' longevity, the vendors that sell them tend to be financially secure.

IDMSs are very strong on traditional content management (check-in/check-out, version control, access control, workflow, archiving, and audit trails).

Some provide the capability to deliver publications and web content.

## *Disadvantages*

The longevity of these tools is also a negative. For some products, the interface was designed before the Windows graphical user interface, and although they have been modified over time to be more consistent with the Windows interface, they retain some of their original unique interactivity, which can be confusing. Sometimes the interface is hard for users to use and changes to customize the interface and functionality of the system can be expensive.

Because IDMS tools have come from the document management world, they do not always provide effective content management. Granularity of the elements they manage may be only at the section or sub-section level, not at the paragraph or sentence level. Many do not support nested reuse or systematic reuse.

Although IDMSs can output HTML, not all support the web content life cycle.

### Publication content management systems

Publication-oriented content management systems (PCMSs) have served the needs of the technical publication industry and book publishing industry for years. Many began as SGML-based systems and are now XML-based. Others support more traditional authoring tools such as Word.

PCMSs systems were designed to handle the complexities of paper with automated TOC generation, indexes (based on author tags), and cross-references among elements. Most have supported compound documents or virtual documents (documents that consist of pointers to content rather than actual embedded content) since their inception.

Although some do not support granular reuse, the majority do, enabling authors to create reusable elements at the paragraph or smaller level. Systematic reuse is supported in XML-based systems.

Because many PCMS were created to support the technical publications industry—which has published to multiple media for years—they support delivery to a large variety of media such as HTML, DHTML, XHTML, WinHelp, HTML Help, Java Help, WAP, PDF, and XML.

## *Advantages*

PCMSs provide standard CMS capabilities (check-in/check-out, version control, access control) and provide robust content management for publications-oriented content (TOC, index, cross-references).

PCMSs support multiple levels of granularity of content and compound documents. They can support most types of reuse, though systematic reuse is available in only some of the tools.

They have strong multiple media delivery capabilities, enabling publication of customized reusable content to a large variety of media.

## *Disadvantages*

Although they can output to HTML, they typically do not support the web content management life cycle.

### Learning content management systems

Learning content management systems (LCMSs) are content management systems that support the web-based learning materials content life cycle and the components of learning content (such as text, graphics, simulations, and multimedia). The majority of these products are now SCORM-compliant (see Chapter 2), which makes it possible to reuse and share content.

LCMSs support text-based content, but they also support multimedia components (sound, video, animation). Many of these tools are actually web-based authoring tools combined with a content management system that handles traditional CMS functionality, reuse, and delivery. In addition to standard web-based authoring, the LCMSs may include tools for the creation of simulations, animations, and multimedia.

Most LCMSs support opportunistic reuse and locked or derivative reuse, but few support systematic reuse. Some support nested reuse.

Some LCMSs contain Learning Management System (LMS) functionality such as registration, course tracking, and evaluation, but most integrate with a separate LMS.

## Advantages

LCMSs were specifically designed to manage the web-based learning content management life cycle. No other CMS can currently effectively handle this life cycle. LCMS vendors have been working hard to implement SCORM to ensure that their customers can create reusable e-learning materials.

LCMSs deliver the functionality of an e-learning authoring tool with the added functionality of a content management system.

## Disadvantages

Like WCM systems, LCMSs have been specifically designed to manage web-based content. A few provide paper output, but it is very rudimentary.

The LCMS is a closed environment. The vendors assume that authors will author in only the tool and will not need to accept content from other systems, nor share content with another type of content management system. Therefore, this means that it is very difficult to share reusable content with other content areas in the organization, such as technical publications.

### Enterprise content management systems

Many WCMS and some IDMS vendors have started to use the phrase "Enterprise Content Management" (ECM) to describe their products. Organizations have looked around and said web content management is good, but that they need to manage other types of content as well, so vendors have begun to respond with ECM systems.

The meaning of enterprise content management varies from vendor to vendor, with vendors approaching ECM in different ways. Enterprise content management systems have grown to manage more and more unstructured content such as email. In addition they often include records management, digital asset management, enhanced security and compliance capabilities and assist organizations in managing content in all facets of the organization.

## *Advantages*

ECM vendors support a broader-based content management life cycle.

## *Disadvantages*

There is currently no consistency in systems that are called enterprise content management systems. The increased functionality may or may not meet your enterprise content management needs.

### Other

There are other types of content management systems, but they usually do not address the requirements of enterprise content management and a unified content strategy.

- **Knowledge Management**

  Knowledge Management Systems (KMSs) are designed to manage both structured and unstructured knowledge within the enterprise, such as e-mail, databases, memos, and web- and publication-oriented content. Their focus is on the discovery (for example, data mining) and synthesis of information (for example, reports based on results of data mining), and on collecting together all the knowledge in the organization and indexing it for fast retrieval. Frequently they make organizational information accessible through a portal. They typically manage documents and data, not elements of content. However, they may interface with a content management system and make both structured and unstructured content available through a portal.

- **Customer Relationship Management**

  Customer Relationship Management Systems (CRMSs) collect and integrate customer information. They manage information such as customer contact information, products and configurations of products they have purchased, the kinds of questions they have asked, and buyer profiles. When integrated across an enterprise, CRM systems can allow the company to consistently present one face to the customer and work toward improving customer retention. These systems tend to manage data, but they often need to share data and content with other systems in the organization.

- **Application server/development tools**

  A number of CMS tools are built from traditional application server development tools. Vendors of these products indicate that they can provide content management functionality. Typically the functionality provided is that of web content management.

## Database versus CMS

Content management systems use a database for storing content. Frequently, organizations consider whether a database alone is sufficient for their requirements.

You could use a database for storing your content and many organizations do, but a database provides only a portion of the functionality of a content management system. A database begins life as a "blank slate"; there is no structure, no functionality, no interface until you create it. Think of the CMS as an intelligent layer on top of the database that provides both a user interface and adds business logic. A CMS provides a tremendous amount of functionality out of the box, such as:

- Predefined content repository model
- Support for content relationships
- Built-in reports (such as where used, history, or relationships)
- Simplified creation of metadata
- Pre-configured system triggers (for example, notification of change)
- Version control
- Access control (security)
- Integration with authoring tool(s)
- Workflow

To re-create and maintain this functionality could be more costly then purchasing an off-the-shelf product.

## Can one CMS do it all?

Can one content management system meet all your enterprise content requirements? Unfortunately, the answer to this question is "maybe." As you can see by the description of the many types of content management systems available, they each have their advantages and disadvantages. And, each type of CMS supports different content life cycles.

However, this doesn't mean you can't support your unified content strategy with a single CMS. A good publications content management system in conjunction with detailed workflows for each content management life cycle can deliver high-quality publications, high-quality web content, and even e-learning. Your organization may want to use multiple authoring tools to create content, save the content in the CMS in a common form, and share elements.

Unfortunately, supporting your unified content strategy is not as easy with a web content management system. A WCMS can provide high-quality web content and high-quality e-learning (given different authoring tools and shareable content), but it is very difficult to produce high-quality publications. A WCMS is designed around the web-page paradigm, not a publication (for example, a TOC or index) paradigm. You could, however, use the WCMS for content management as you would a database, and use the publication authoring tool to publish the content. You would not be able to do systematic reuse into the publication's information products, but you could do opportunistic reuse. This should not be an issue for those WCMSs that have moved toward enterprise content management with the integration of paper publication functionality, but a transactional content management system may not be as capable for publications. Alternatively, a good web content management system that can support XML can provide robust web support, integrate with print publication tools, and provide systematic reuse.

However, the key to a single solution is the capability to share content among the CMS, the authoring tools, and the delivery tools. If your organization has chosen to use XML, this can greatly facilitate the sharing of information. If you haven't chosen to use XML, but your CMS can import content from a variety of authoring tools, combine the content appropriately (for example, convert into a common format), and then provide appropriate reusable content back to the authoring tools, you might be able to use a single solution.

If your organization decides to go with "best of breed" tools, such as a web content management tool that is really good at creating web content but poor at creating paper content, you still have to share information among content management systems. After all, the key to a successful unified content strategy lies in the capability to share content. Effective sharing of content requires the systems to interpret content as it moves from system to system. Interpreting content is dependent upon

- Common information models (structures)
- Common ways of tagging content (style/structure tags)
- Common metadata

## Summary

Content management is an integral component of a successful unified content strategy. You need to understand the basic functionality of a content management system and the many types of content management systems that exist.

You should understand the following about CMSs:

- Segmentation or bursting is the process of breaking content into its element parts.
- Metadata is applied to the content in the authoring tool, or it may be applied to the content as it is checked into the CMS.
- Access control secures content and identifies who can read, create, modify, and delete content.
- Version control ensures that each time content is saved, another version (copy) is created and is assigned a new version number.
- Authors who are using reusable content are notified of change in any of three ways (automatically update, optionally update, no update)
- Check-in/check-out controls content so that only one author can modify the content at any one point in time.
- The content management repository manages the content and the metadata associated with each content object.

- Search and retrieval enables authors or reviewers to search and retrieve content based on individual elements, containers, and whole information products.

- Archiving stores previous versions of content that are finalized and approved but no longer current.

- Translation support ensures that relationships can be built between the source language and multiple translation versions of the content. Memory translation tools integrated with the CMS facilitate the localization process.

There are many different types of content management systems:

- Web content management systems (WCMSs) assist an organization in automating various aspects of web content creation, content management, and delivery. Delivery to the web is its primary format, but many WCM systems also deliver to wireless devices.

- Transactional content management systems (TCMSs) assist an organization to manage e-commerce transactions.

- Integrated document management systems (IDMSs) assist an organization in managing enterprise documents and content.

- Publication-oriented content management systems (PCMS) assist an organization in managing the publications (manuals, books, help systems) content life cycle.

- Learning content management systems (LCMSs) assist an organization in managing the web-based learning content life cycle.

- Enterprise content management systems (ECMSs) vary in their functionality. Enterprise content management systems manage structured and unstructured content and they often include records management, digital asset management, enhanced security and compliance capabilities and assist organizations in managing content in all facets of the organization.

# Chapter 17

## Workflow systems

Workflow systems are critical in a unified content strategy because they help to ensure that content flows smoothly through the content life cycle. Workflow systems make sure that everybody contributes the required content, that content is reviewed and approved at the necessary stages, and that it is delivered to its various outputs. Rather than relying on manual processes, workflow systems automate them, handling the interrelationships among processes and tracking the status of the project at any given time.

Workflow systems allow work to be assigned, routed, approved, acted upon, and managed with system-controlled rules that you set up when you design your workflow. (For more information about designing effective workflow see Chapter 11, "Designing workflow.")

Workflow systems may be included as part of the content management system you select, or they may be stand-alone systems. If your content management system (CMS) has workflow included, it is particularly important to ensure that it meets your needs. Sometimes embedded workflow systems are specific to only one application of content, or they may be very rudimentary in their functionality.

Suggested vendor questions are included throughout the chapter. For more information on selecting an appropriate vendor see Chapter 13, "Evaluating tools."

This chapter describes what workflow systems should be able to do to support a unified content life cycle. Workflow systems consist of three major components, as shown in Figure 17.1: creation, processing, and administration. All are critical in managing a unified content life cycle.

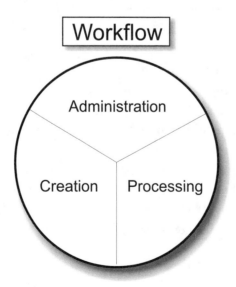

**Figure 17.1.    Workflow components.**

# Creation

The creation component enables workflow authors (for example, information architects or business analysts) to create and test workflow processes. Creation typically consists of:

- **Process flow creation**

  Workflow authors create graphical representations of the workflow, selecting from predefined interactions (for example, print) or creating new interactions if required.

- **Process testing**

  Workflow authors can use test data to simulate a process. Testing workflow under a variety of circumstances before implementing it can be extremely beneficial.

- **Ability to learn**

  Some workflow tools learn from user interactions, creating new workflows based on their analysis of user processes. Your organization can review the automatically created workflows for validity and usefulness. This capability is not the norm in most workflow systems, and it is not a "must have," but it is "nice to have." By identifying repetitive processes, the workflow system can help to point out areas where workflow could be automated.

## Vendor questions

When you're evaluating a workflow system, consider what you want it to do in relation to your unified content life cycle and who is going to perform these tasks. Ask vendors the following questions:

- How easy is it to create the process flow (for example, can a business analyst easily create workflow or is a technical specialist required)?

- Is the user interface graphical? Is drag-and-drop of workflow elements supported?

- How easy is it to create a workflow (that is, what is the methodology)?

- Are there any predefined workflows (templates) that can be used or modified as necessary? Is integration provided for other modeling tools or business process re-engineering tools?

- How easy is it to simulate and test the workflow processes? Can you set up multiple test data scenarios to test exceptions and conditions?
- Can the system learn from user interactions and create new workflow based on its analysis of user interaction?

## Processing

The processing component of a workflow system activates and manages workflow, handling such things as routing work based on rules you set up when you design workflow.

### Routing

Routing moves work through the workflow system. For example, after content is identified as ready for review, it is automatically routed to the reviewers, or reviewers are notified that the content is ready for review so they can link to it. Work can be routed in a number of ways:

- **Sequential**

  Sequential routing moves work through the workflow in a linear fashion. As a step is completed, work is automatically routed to the next step in the process. For example, content that is identified as ready for review is automatically routed to reviewers. Sequential routing is the simplest form of workflow.

- **Rules-based**

  Rules-based routing enables the system to determine how to route content based on logic. For example, if this is content for Product X it should be routed to the Product X reviewers, but if it is for Product Y, then it should be routed to Product Y reviewers. Rules-based workflow enables the system to make intelligent decisions about how to handle work based on certain conditions. Rules also assist in handling exceptions. For more information, see the "Rules" section later in this chapter.

- **Parallel**

  Parallel routing routes work simultaneously, so one part of the work isn't delayed while another part is completed. For example, content for a new brochure can be assigned at the same time as the graphics; the graphics don't have to wait for the content to be finished. However, you may want to include a "wait" step at the end of the parallel processes before the work continues through the flow. For example, if graphics are completed before the content, you could include a wait step to hold the graphics until the content is complete so they can be integrated for review.

- **Ad hoc**

  Ad hoc workflows do not follow a set of rules. Instead, they involve human decisions. Ad hoc workflow is the least used, but can be useful to assist in one-time or unplanned situations. For example, if you have to issue an addendum immediately to announce a change in staff, or to correct a problem users are having with a product, ad hoc workflow lets you route content only to where it's needed immediately, bypassing those people or processes that don't need to be involved. Ad hoc workflow is also useful when it is not possible or necessary to apply a rule to a decision.

## Vendor questions

In assessing what kind of routing you need a workflow system to support, refer to your unified content life cycle and review your workflow design. After you decide what you need, ask vendors:

- What types of routing are supported? Can the system provide ad hoc workflow if you need it?
- Does the system allow steps to be completed simultaneously? Are wait steps supported?
- How easily can a workflow of one type be changed to a workflow of another type?
- Can you have different types of routing for different projects? How easy is it to create the different types of workflow routing?
- Can multiple routing types be supported simultaneously? For example, can you have rules-based and ad hoc workflows working in parallel?

## Rules

Rules define what happens under what circumstances. They determine how content and tasks are routed through workflow. For example, when content has been identified as "ready for review" (that is, the author has selected "ready for review" metadata), that content is either routed automatically to the reviewers, or reviewers are notified that content is ready for them to review. The rule may look something like:

> if metadata = "ready for review" then step 3

Rules should also include exceptions to the normal situation. An exception to the rule tells the system how to process a task when it does not meet all the requirements to continue through the workflow. For example, what happens if three reviewers have been assigned to review some content, two reviewers have completed the review, and the third is on vacation? The exception tells the system to automatically route the content to an alternate reviewer. What happens if that reviewer is off sick and no one else is identified as a reviewer in the workflow processes? If the rule states explicitly that content must have three reviews completed before it can move to the next stage in the workflow process, the content will be delayed until a third reviewer is available. An exception could state that if a third reviewer is unavailable, to route the content as though it had three reviews, or to route the content to a manager to decide whether the two reviews suffice.

For example, the rules may look something like:

> If reviewer3 = "not available" then "alternate1"
>
> If alternate1 = "not available" then "alternate2"
>
> And so on.

## *Vendor questions*

Rules are critical in a workflow system; they determine what happens to content at any given stage in the workflow processes. Remember that workflow should not always be "carved in stone" and may need to accommodate exceptions. Ask vendors:

- What types of business rules are supported?
- How easy is it to create a business rule (for example, predefined elements from which to select, simple rules language, visual)?

# Administration

The administration portion of the workflow system is where all activity is tracked. Administration matches roles to tasks, assigning who—or which system—does what, and it manages security (who can see or do what), deadlines, and reporting when tasks are done.

## Players (role assignment)

In a unified content strategy, different people (players) perform various tasks at different stages in a process, and the workflow system must keep track of who is responsible for what. For example, some players create content whereas others review and approve it. In a workflow system, the system itself is also a player (for example, after the content is approved, the system may initiate an action to deliver the content to the web site automatically or to "fill in" systematic content before delivery to a reviewer).

Although players perform many of the steps in the process, it is important to be able to assign a role to an action or a step rather than a person. Many players can then be assigned to a role and a change in a player will not require a change to the workflow. For example, Fred Turnbull is responsible for the final approval for all Product X information. He has been promoted to general manager and is now responsible for final approval of the entire product suite. Rather than changing the workflow to indicate his changed title, he is just removed from the Product X approver role and assigned to the Product X Suite approver role. His replacement within the department, if any, is then assigned the Product approver role. If there is not a replacement, the workflow won't have to be redesigned, although those already assigned to the Product X approver role will have a larger workload. The tasks stay with the role, not the person.

To move workflow along, it's also beneficial to assign more than one player to a role. That way, if the first person is unable to perform a task, workflow moves the task to the next person whose role is assigned to that task. For example, Nancy Smith is the senior graphic artist who creates graphics for all Product X's web-based information products. If she is on vacation or if she declares herself unavailable for a temporary period of time, such as if she's swamped with other work when a request comes through for some new graphics, the workflow system identifies that she is unavailable and routes the request for graphics to Michael Hotley, another graphic designer associated with that role.

### Vendor questions

Assigning tasks based on roles is important in keeping the work flowing through the system. When you're assessing workflow systems, ask vendors:

- Can roles be assigned to a task rather than to individuals? Can a group be assigned to a role? Can alternates to individuals in a role be assigned?
- Under what circumstances can a role be bypassed (such as by management), and an alternative workflow be applied?
- What possibilities exist for balancing workload responsibilities among redundant or co-existing reviewers in teams?
- Are exceptions easy to create?
- Are temporary exceptions (for example, declaring oneself absent for the next two hours or days) easy to create?
- How easy is it to create or change a role?

## Security and electronic signature

Just like content, workflow should have security assigned to it. It should be possible to apply a security level to any part of a workflow to control who can create, modify, delete, and view a workflow.

## How and where does security apply?

Security can apply to:

- Players
- Groups
- Roles
- Workflow
- Steps
- Tasks
- Objects

Security controls who can start a workflow process, handle an exception, view reports, or change priorities.

Electronic signatures may be a part of security. An electronic signature, like a traditional signature, indicates that work has received some level of sign-off or approval. The ability to use an electronic signature should be strictly controlled. Electronic signatures are particularly important in regulated industries.

## *Vendor questions*

Maintaining control of processes is critical in a unified content strategy because workflow shouldn't be altered to eliminate certain tasks. Eliminating certain tasks or reviews can compromise the consistency of the content as well as the processes intended to create and manage it. When assessing security, ask vendors the following questions:

- What security levels are provided? How easy is it to set security levels?
- Are electronic signatures supported? How are they supported? How are electronic signatures verified (for example, password protected)?
- Can a manager or administrator override the security with appropriate permission?
- How are security changes, administration, and any violations tracked and/or reported?
- How easy is it to set up new controls or to manage new, transferred, or departing employees? How much work is the daily maintenance task to maintain security, permissions, roles, and so on?

## Deadlines and escalation

Within a workflow system, each step or activity has a deadline assigned to it. If the deadline is missed, a series of actions should occur (for example, reminder messages or escalation). Escalation actions can route the issue to a supervisor or manager to ensure the action is completed and does not hold up the process. For example, imagine that content has been routed to three reviewers, and two of the reviewers have completed their reviews and returned their comments. The third has not. The system sends the reviewer reminder messages that get increasingly demanding. After the third reminder, the reviewer's manager is notified that the review has not been completed, and is informed of the number of days the review has been delayed. The manager speaks directly to the reviewer and the reviewer completes the review that day. Alternatively, if the reviewer is actually on vacation and forgot to inform the system of that, the manager can then activate a request for the review to be routed to an alternate list.

Deadlines can be defined to occur after a certain period of time elapses (duration), or in response to external events (as with parallel workflow, managerial discretion, or administrative changes/shifts/reprogramming), or the user can be prompted to enter a deadline. A workflow system can define different deadlines at different levels, including:

- **Step**

    The step is assigned a duration deadline (such as three days) or a specific date of completion.

- **Task**

    The entire task can be assigned a duration or date of completion. This means that the individual steps do not have a specific duration, but the entire task must be completed after a certain period of time has elapsed or by a specific date.

Sometimes you may find that one workflow process needs to take precedence over another process. It is important to be able to change the deadlines to reprioritize the processes.

## *Vendor questions*

Deadlines are critical in keeping content moving. When assessing a workflow system, ask vendors:

- Is there a way to notify users of deadlines (for example, by e-mail or an electronic calendar)?

- Can users choose to add an alarm to a deadline to assist in reminding them of due dates?

- Do missed deadlines trigger actions such as reminders and escalation procedures? Can priorities be changed?

- How can deadlines be affected by external events, such as internal reprogramming, managerial discretion, and so on? How can you ensure that deadlines do not get "lost in the shuffle" when reorganization of some kind takes place?

- How can deadlines be changed mid-stream? How are people notified?

- Can schedules of deadlines be prepared in advance of workflow tasks? Are there ways to notify people of deadlines that are coming up, even if they can't actually start the work yet (such as a notification that their review is scheduled to start in a few days)? Can reports be written to allow for ad hoc managerial inspection?

- When a deadline is missed, can someone insert a comment explaining why, or that it was investigated by appropriate people/managers?

## Reporting

You can create reports to monitor the status of a process, as well as individual and group performance (for example, how long it takes to create a new web page). Reports can also be automatically generated at a specific point in the workflow. For example, a report detailing who worked on a document, how long it took at each stage, and any missed deadlines, could be automatically generated and routed to management as soon as a document is signed off. Reports like these can assist your organization in collecting detailed metrics to be used to better manage your processes and determine return on investment.

Workflow systems typically provide a variety of reports. Sample reports include the following:

- Deadline reports identify upcoming deadlines and deadlines that have been missed.

- Work-in-process reports track what steps have been completed, the location of outstanding items, and whether or not a process is on schedule. Work-in-process reports can also determine the volume of work and any backlog in processes.

- Exception reports identify where exceptions have occurred, the frequency of their occurrence, and who made them. Repeated exceptions may indicate that the workflow needs to be revised to avoid further exceptions.

- Workload balance reports identify how much work a player in the process has waiting to be addressed. The report can assist managers in identifying whether one player has too much work while another has insufficient work, so the workload can be rebalanced. If the workload is frequently out of balance, the reports can help you identify that new rules need to put in place to avoid these problems in the future.

## Vendor questions

Having a unified content strategy means being in control of your content all the time. You can do this only if you know the status of all your work and who is doing what, when, and how much they have to do at any point in time. Make sure you can get the information you need through the reports the system generates. When assessing a workflow system, ask vendors:

- Can comments be added to the resulting workflow to add information about various parts of the process, such as reasons for delays, postmortem notes, and so on?

- Can report generation itself be tracked? Can permissions to create reports be limited to specific individuals or roles?

- How can reports be characterized? By person, task, date, department, keyword, exception, and so on?

- What standard reports are provided?

- Can customized reports be created? How simple is it to create a report? Can customized report templates be built for reuse?

# Other considerations

Traditionally, workflow has been used to manage document life cycle processes, but workflow is now being used to manage many processes within enterprises. Although there are some stand-alone workflow tools, the majority are integrated with existing systems (for example, web content management and integrated document management systems). Like many other software applications vendors, workflow software application vendors have developed their own customized products to meet market needs. This may mean that embedded workflow systems meet the needs of the specific application very well, but may not be extensible to other uses. If the embedded workflow is flexible enough for you to extend the standard workflow to accommodate your additional needs, this may not be an issue; however, if it is not, you may need to integrate with other applications and associated workflow components. If you plan to share your workflow processes with other applications, or you plan to retrieve information from other applications, it is important to be able share information. The use of standards helps to facilitate information sharing.

Standards tend to lag behind market requirements and cannot address all customer needs, so vendors often ignore them and build what they believe will meet customer needs. In the context of a specific customer requirement (for example, web content management) this may not be a problem. However, when integrating with enterprise requirements and potentially multiple workflow systems, the lack of standards can be a problem.

The non-profit Workflow Management Coalition (WfMC) was founded in 1993 by workflow vendors, users, and analysts. Its two main goals are to define standards for workflow and disseminate information about workflow and workflow systems. A standard was defined in 1995, and modified in future years to adopt XML (Wf-XML) and address a broader base of customer requirements. The Wf-XML model is focused on coordinating process data. There are concerns that this standard will not be widely adopted.

An alternate standard, RosettaNet, is gaining wider adoption. RosettaNet is an XML standard. RosettaNet was not specifically designed as a workflow standard; rather, it has been designed to facilitate B2B (business-to-business) interactions. It defines business exchanges for specific business processes and provides a framework that allows multiple application processes to exchange data. To accomplish the sharing of data, RosettaNet provides a framework and XML dictionaries of properties. This standard is getting more interest from vendors.

### Vendor questions

It's important to figure out what you need a workflow system to do, based on your new unified content life cycle. Assess workflow systems against the criteria defined in your content life cycle, asking vendors questions such as the following:

- Does the embedded workflow meet all your organization's requirements, or is it specific to one application of the content life cycle (such as the web)? If it was designed for one application, is it extensible to accommodate the enterprise content life cycle? How easy is it to extend the workflow functionality?

- What standards—if any—are used to exchange data among applications? With which systems does the workflow system integrate? How is integration accomplished? Is there an API that would allow the workflow to be customized to integrate with systems not currently integrated?

## Summary

Workflow systems consist of three major parts: creation (enables you to create and test a workflow), processing (activates and manages workflow), and administration (tracks workflow).

The creation component of a workflow system enables you to create graphical representations of the workflow and to use test data to test the workflow, and it may provide the ability to learn from user interaction and automatically create automated workflow.

In the processing component of a workflow system, work is routed using sequential, rules-based, parallel, and ad hoc workflow routings. Rules define what actions should be taken at each step.

The administration component of a workflow system provides the capability to define roles, assign security to different components of a workflow, and set deadlines for each action in a workflow. Reports enable you to monitor the status of a process as well as individual and group performance.

If work and information from workflows are to be shared among applications, standards can facilitate this process. However, standards have not readily been adopted by the industry.

Here are some of the things to consider when selecting a tool:

- How easy is it to create and test workflow? Are there any pre-defined templates?

- What types of routing are supported (sequential, rules-based, parallel, ad hoc)? How easy is it to create the different types of routing?

- Can roles be assigned to a task rather than to individuals? How easy is it to create or change a role?

- What security levels are provided? Are electronic signatures provided and how are signatures verified?

- What types of deadlines and escalation procedures can be created?

- What standard reports are provided? How easy is it to create a custom report?

- What standards are used for the exchange of data among applications?

# Chapter 18

## Delivery systems

The design and organization of information is a key factor in creating a unified content strategy. But without a capable delivery engine, a unified content strategy is just an exercise in data collection. To turn your data into usable content, you must assemble it, format it, and deliver it to your user community, whenever and however they need it.

Delivery systems have many different capabilities. The content management system may have built-in facilities for delivering content, or you may have to integrate a delivery system with your content management system. Some delivery systems will enable you to deliver to a variety of outputs (such as web, HTML, or PDF), whereas others may be restricted to a single output.

Some delivery mechanisms reside on users' desktops; others are server-based and are available to everyone. Some delivery systems can interface with content management systems, web servers, portal servers, and other systems. This chapter describes the range in capabilities of delivery systems, including considerations to guide you in figuring out what you need your delivery system to do.

## Capabilities

To determine the type of delivery system you need, you must first understand the range of capabilities available in current products. Products may have all or some of the following capabilities:

- Aggregation
- Transformation
- Conversion
- Distribution and output management
- Assembly
- Automation

You need to ask the correct questions when you are selecting a delivery system that will meet the needs of your authors and the requirements of your unified content strategy. This section describes some of the considerations for selecting a tool that best suits your needs. However, each organization's requirements are different, so you will need to identify criteria to meet your specific needs.

For more information on determining your needs and the criteria to meet them, see Chapter 13, "Evaluating tools."

# Aggregation

One of the goals of a unified content strategy is to eliminate multiple occurrences of the same data. But in today's enterprises, where the information that comprises content typically exists in multiple, frequently incompatible systems, that raises complications. Often, data must be maintained in legacy systems for access by specialized applications. Data may also be required in outputs (such as catalogs and specifications) and must therefore be collected from either a single system or multiple systems for delivery. In other circumstances, multiple content management systems may be used as information repositories. Again, information can then be collected from the multiple systems for publication.

Consider the following:

- With which authoring tools does the delivery tool interface?
- With which CMS tools does the delivery tool interface?
- With which databases does the delivery tool interface?

# Transformation

In the past, information was typically delivered in a single format. It was designed for that format and republished each time the information changed. That is no longer the case. With the popularity of web-based publishing, information is typically output to multiple formats, including HTML, paper, and sometimes wireless. The content may be identical, with format optimized for the output. Or, the content may be tailored for use in the output format. Whatever the output, a key function of any delivery system is the transformation of information from its stored format to the required output. Delivering unified content requires the ability to publish not only to traditional outputs (such as paper and web), but also to XML, PDF, and WAP devices (such as PDAs and cell phones).

## Output support

An obvious first question is to ask what output formats are supported by the delivery system. Some possible formats include the following:

- PostScript
- PDF
- HTML
- XML
- Microsoft Word
- Wireless

The next question to ask is whether the tool supports output to multiple formats for a single publishing request. For example, can you create a PDF version of a product specification sheet and an HTML version with a single request?

## XSL support

Most—if not all—of the big delivery systems support some form of XSL, the XML formatting and transformation language (See Chapter 14, "The role of XML"). It is actually their support of XSL that gives many engines their apparent power. There are two questions to be asked of a delivery engine. First, how much of the XSL standard does the tool support?

- XSLT?
- XSL Formatting Objects?
- XPath?

Second, how compliant to the XSL standard is the engine? In the rush to get market share, companies frequently develop their products in advance of the standard: They develop a product based on what they think the standard will be. Sometimes their interpretation is not correct. Or, vendors support part of the standard—the part that's easiest to implement—and save the complicated stuff (frequently the most valuable functionality) for later versions.

You should think carefully about any delivery engine that supports just a part of the XSL standard or that supports the product developer's own version of the standard. XSL is growing in popularity by leaps and bounds. Systems that do not fully support XSL now will be forced to play catch-up with functionality, assuming that XML and XSL maintain their current growth in popularity.

You should also think twice about a delivery engine that does not support XSL. There are processing engines that support other style languages, but they are usually limited in flexibility.

## Book building

In publishing models of the past, authors created the "navigation structures" that are part of a book or web site. The structures include Tables of Contents (TOCs), indexes, lists of figures, lists of tables. For example, the author would embed index entries in a file. They would then need to generate the index and insert it in their document. In today's models, systems can be designed to assemble and locate these structures as part of the automated publishing functions. Therefore, can the tool automatically create TOCs, indexes, and linked lists (for example, of figures) from the content without any intervention from the author?

## Partial or full publishing

On other occasions, you might need to publish just parts of a document, such as updated procedures in an intranet-based policies and procedures guide. Does the tool include support for publishing pieces of a document or just full documents?

## Collection publication

In the case of large volumes of information, it may be necessary to process or publish a collection of discrete information products, such as a series of departmental policy guides to a corporate intranet.

Does the tool include support for publishing collections (groups of documents)? For example, can the tool take a series of input files and build a complete web site, with full hypertext linking? Can the tool compile the TOCs and indexes for these collections?

### Full graphics support

Graphics designed for one media (such as paper) do not display well on another (such as the Web), or may not even be in a compatible format. Graphics must be transformed to match the requirements of each output.

Will the tool perform automatic conversion based on targeted output? Can selected content be flagged to preserve maximum fidelity of graphics?

## Conversion

Conversion is similar to transformation, except that conversion is usually on the input side. The engine takes content in a specific format and converts it to the neutral format required for publishing. For example, it might take a Word document and convert it to XML. After the document is in XML, the delivery engine might transform it into HTML and PDF.

Does the tool support conversion of content? What formats does it support? How clean (that is, problem-free) is the conversion?

## Distribution and output management

There are many potential output formats for information, including PDF for paper and HTML for pure web access.

Enterprise information must be managed throughout its full life cycle. That includes the actual physical outputs from the delivery system. That is, if you create PDF files as your output, they must be fully managed to ensure that the complete, up-to-date versions are available, and that you don't have old versions being distributed. Or, if your output is an HTML file or series of files, they must be managed. Ideally, the publication engine should help to automate this management. Generated files should be copied to web servers, copied to output directories, or checked into content management systems automatically. For the delivery engine:

- Are published documents (outputs) automatically checked into the repository for tracking?

- Can outputs be automatically associated with source documents (through metadata)?

- Are metadata from contributing documents (files) automatically assigned to published output for check-in?
- Are publication directories automatically populated (both internal and external to the repository)?

Any publishing actions that cannot be accomplished automatically must be addressed manually in your processes. In situations where the actions are complicated or involve large numbers of files, human error becomes a risk.

# Assembly

With the increasing capabilities of content management systems has come a building-block approach to output creation. The information exists in the content database as discrete chunks that an assembly engine assembles into complete output entities. Content that is assembled in chunks is often referred to as a *virtual document* or *compound document*.

Does the tool include support for virtual or compound documents (assembled in response to a publishing event or request)?

## Dynamic content

Dynamic content is content that is assembled only when it is requested. It does not exist as a document; rather, it exists as a series of content objects that are assembled on demand. Dynamic content can be delivered to both users and authors (systematic reuse). For more information about dynamic content see Chapter 10, "Designing dynamic content."

Dynamic content can be delivered to the users in multiple ways:

- **Multi-channel format**

  With an assembly engine, appropriate content can be extracted and assembled in the requested format (for example, web page, wireless, or PDF) and delivered to users.

- **ASP (Active Server Page)**

  An ASP is a web page that is created by using Microsoft products. These pages are identified by an .asp extension (file ending). When a browser requests content, the web server for the page dynamically generates an ASP page with HTML code and sends it back to the browser. As far as users are concerned, they are looking at a standard web page.

  An ASP is typically set up as a framework (sometimes called a *wire frame*) that has physical regions on the page for the dynamic content to fill. The ASP can draw the content to fill the page from a database or a content management system.

- **Portal**

  A portal is a web site that is commonly used as a gateway to specific web content or other web sites. Personalization techniques make it possible to dynamically configure a portal to show users only the content that is relevant to them. Users can then navigate from the portal page to the desired content.

The content shown to users is based on metadata, which are derived from:

- **User profiles**

  A user profile consists of explicit information about users. The information is contained in metadata.

- **User selection**

  Users can specifically identify the type of information they want to view. They usually do this by selecting options on a form or selections from a web page. The options are then used as explicit metadata and added to the user profile.

- **Behavior**

  Behavioral information is implicit information gathered about how users navigate the web site, the information they view, and the product or service they buy. This implicit information is then interpreted and the results added to the user profile.

The user content metadata are then interpreted by the business rules that control what content is appropriate at what time, for which user or author, and in what location in the document. The business rules then match and extract content from the content management system. Finally, the assembly engine assembles the content appropriately and delivers it to the user interface. Figure 18.1 illustrates how the metadata from the user profile, user selection, and behavior are matched with the business rules to identify the appropriate content, assemble the content, and deliver it to the user interface.

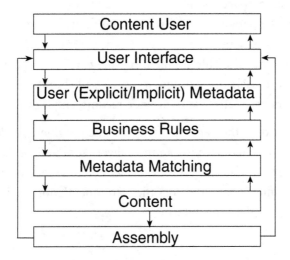

**Figure 18.1    How dynamic content happens.**

Can the delivery tool support dynamic content? How is dynamic content delivered (multi-channel, ASP, portal)? How is it supported? How do you enter user profiles? Can the delivery tool update the user profile based on user selection? How are business rules entered (code or user scenarios or plain language interface)?

## *Personalization*

Personalization is an extension of dynamic content. Personalization engines provide dynamic content to users, but they also recommend related content (for example, products and services). Many web content management systems provide personalization engines. Personalization engines have typically been provided to improve the user experience and to support sales and marketing campaigns. Personalization engines also collect information about the user for the system to use (such as usage reports, login/logout data, navigation reports, history, customized newsletters, and so on.) In addition to the components for dynamic delivery of content, personalization engines typically provide a recommendation engine. A recommendation engine uses the user profile, user selection, behavior, and business rules to identify what content (usually a product or service) to display to users. In addition, it can use collaborative filtering (looking at what other users have selected) to provide recommendations.

What functionality does the personalization engine provide? How do you enter user profiles? How are they saved? Can the delivery tool update the user profile based on user selection? How are business rules entered (code or user scenarios or plain language interface)? How does the recommendation engine work (analytics, algorithms, collaborative filtering)?

## Automation

Gone are the days of big publishing departments, which took files from authors, cleaned them up, and published them to the required output. Today's enterprise model features centralized automated publishing. Authors submit a file directly or by setting a workflow flag, and the required output is generated automatically. Therefore, the question that you need to ask is whether the publishing system supports automated publishing (batch mode, without operator support), triggered by author request, workflow event (check-in, status changes), or end-user request.

## Summary

The delivery engine is an integral component of a successful unified content strategy. You need to understand the basic capabilities of the systems that exist.

Basic capabilities include:

- Aggregation
- Conversion
- Distribution and output management
- Assembly
- Transformation
- Automation

Key questions to ask of potential delivery engine vendors include:

- What output formats are supported? Can you publish to multiple formats with a single request?
- Does the tool support conversion of content? What formats will it support? How clean (that is, without problems) is the conversion?
- Is delivery automated? Can it be triggered by workflow?
- Does the system support XSL? How complete is that support?
- Can the delivery system help to automate the management of the output? Can it automatically check output into content management and apply metadata?
- Can the system build TOCs, indexes, and other navigation structures automatically?
- Can the system build navigation structures for collections of information?
- Does the system support partial publishing, to deliver only changed information, or must you republish everything?
- Can the system assemble chunks of information into virtual documents?
- Can the system convert graphics from one format into another format more appropriate for the output?
- Can the delivery tool support dynamic content?
- How is dynamic content delivered (multi-channel, ASP, portal)?

- How do you enter user profiles? Can the delivery tool update the user profile based on user selection?

- How are business rules entered (code or user scenarios or plain language interface)?

- Does the CMS or delivery tool support personalization? How does the recommendation engine work (analytics [a method for analyzing information], algorithms, collaborative filtering)?

# *Part V*

# Moving to a unified content strategy

So, you've analyzed your content and figured out how it's being used and how it could be reused, you've mapped out a new content life cycle, built information models, designed workflow processes, and selected tools that will support your unified content strategy. However, moving to a unified content strategy takes more than just good design, new processes, and nifty tools! Moving to a unified content strategy also means that you change the way you work. The chapters in Part V discuss some of the organizational issues you'll need to address when implementing a unified content strategy, starting with how groups within your company will need to work together.

In Chapter 1, "Content: The lifeblood of an organization," we introduced you to the concept of the Content Silo Trap, which is caused by authors working in isolation from other authors within the organization. Walls are erected among content areas and even within content areas, which leads to content being created, and recreated, and recreated, often with changes or differences at each iteration. Chapter 19, "Collaborative authoring: Breaking down the silos," suggests strategies for authors working together to create unified content. Collaborative authoring goes beyond having tools that support sharing of information. Collaboration is a human endeavor and requires everyone working together towards a common goal. Chapter 19 describes the human efforts that collaborative authoring requires.

Another significant organizational change is in the way authors create content. A unified content strategy requires that content remains separate from format, so that the same content can be used in different media. Separating content from format means implementing structured writing, in which a structure based on principles of clear communication, information analysis, and cognitive psychology is defined for every element that makes up an information product. Chapter 20, "Separating content from format," describes how and why you should write structured content, including how to write to an information model and how to structure content for different uses by following a building block approach. We also show you examples of how the same content is used in different outputs, as specified by the information models.

Chapter 21, "Managing change," moves from authoring issues to change management ones. Implementing a unified content strategy means big changes, including some new and some modified roles. Even if you adopt a unified content strategy in only one area of your organization, you are still likely to encounter some resistance. Chapter 21 describes some of the issues and offers some suggestions for overcoming resistance. We also provide descriptions of the new and modified roles you will require.

Finally, Chapter 22, "Transition plan" addresses the many issues often involved in moving towards new processes and technology including scoping out your project, working with a restricted budget, implementing your project in phases, and implementing structure without structured authoring tools.

# Chapter 19

## Collaborative authoring: Breaking down the silos

A key concept of a unified content strategy is the sharing of content and collaborating on its development. Collaboration ensures that the content elements, such as product descriptions, are consistent and can be reused wherever they're required—in a printed brochure, on the Web, on an intranet, in user guides, and so on. To ensure content elements will meet all needs, everyone involved in creating content must work together to figure out exactly what the needs are and make decisions about how elements are to be reused, structured, and written.

As discussed in Chapter 1, "Content: The lifeblood of an organization," content is often created by authors working in isolation from other authors. Silos are erected between departments and even within departments, which leads to content being created, re-created, and re-created, causing extra work and introducing inconsistencies. Individual authors working in isolation is not possible in a unified content environment. When content is compiled into its various information products, it must appear to be completely unified; there is no room for different "colors or textures." The finished product must be seamless. The goal of collaborative authoring is to break down the silo walls so that authors can create content consistently.

Collaboration, however, is harder than you might imagine. Collaboration, regardless of the tools in place to support it, is a human endeavor and must be supported by strong teams willing to undertake collaborative efforts. Collaboration requires everyone working together toward a common goal—unified content. To realize this goal, organizations have to change the way content is authored, starting from the modeling process and continuing through each new project.

This chapter discusses collaborative authoring and explores potential strategies for collaborative authoring in your organization.

## What is collaboration?

Collaboration is not a new concept. Think of the many books authored by more than one writer or the albums produced by more than one musician. The common element in successful collaborations is a goal that all players are aware of and support. People involved in the collaboration know what the goals are, know their roles, know others' roles, and know how to invoke change or address issues. Players should also have a stake in the outcome, whether it's content that's easier to access and use, a more productive authoring environment, or even a share of company profits. With all those requirements, figuring out a way to make collaboration work in an organization, especially a large one, can be problematic. But, in a unified content strategy, it's necessary.

More and more, effective information requires many people, often with varying skills and backgrounds, and often from different departments and even different professions, working together on the same project, or more accurately, working together on different aspects of the same project. Authors cannot work in isolation from subject matter experts and users; marketing cannot work in isolation from product documentation and support; product developers and engineers cannot work in isolation from authors. This is certainly true in a unified content environment. Yet, collaboration in relation to writing is often misunderstood. Collaboration involves more than different authors creating content for different aspects of a project.

## Exploring collaboration further

Doing a search for collaborative authoring or collaborative writing on the Internet turns up thousands of hits, most with one thing in common: the human element implicit in collaboration. For example:

- On the web site for the University of North Carolina at Pembroke, a law professor posted guidelines for collaborative writing, with the number one guideline being:

  "Take time at the start of your project to build cohesion. Begin your project by developing a shared understanding of your assignment and discussing basic procedural and logical issues. Build group cohesion and establish good interpersonal relations among members."[1]

- In a thesis on computer-supported collaborative writing, the author defines collaborative writing as follows:

  "In a true co-authoring process, the peers collaborate on every task as opposed to the situation in co-publishing [and] co-responding...In co-publishing the individuals produce a collaborative text based on individual texts. Interaction in a co-responding environment takes place only during the revision process...In peer collaboration, the group assignment is a truely [sic] joint task, all members contribute to the interaction most of the time and each of the peers has equal control over the text as well as within the interaction."[2]

---

1 http://www.uncp.edu/home/vanderhoof/syllabus/colab-rt.html, accessed on March 3, 2002

2 http://infolab.kub.nl/pub/theses/w3thesis/Groupwork/collaborative_writing.html, accessed on March 3, 2002

- In the OII Guide to Workflow Management and Collaborative Authoring, collaborative authoring is defined as follows:

  "Collaborative authoring can be defined as 'the use of workflow techniques to manage the creation of integrated data sets by more than one author.' However, collaborative authoring is normally seen to include more than simply the application of workflow. It also requires facilities for defining how data created by different, parallel, processes is to be combined or linked."[3]

  For an effective collaborative authoring environment to be set up, the team must define how information is to be written, linked, and unified. The tools then support what the team decides.

- In another paper on collaborative authoring of web content, the authors state:

  "Information content publishing may also be performed collaboratively, where multiple geographically dispersed authors contribute to the publishing of semantically related pieces of information…The authors bring together expert knowledge needed to provide parts of the content. Collaboration enables the authors to work together on the authoring tasks by sharing the knowledge needed in the process of producing content."[4]

## What does collaborative authoring require?

From an organizational perspective, collaborative authoring requires that all authors have an understanding of how content is used in multiple situations and the ability to work together to create it. This normally requires organizational change, specifically in the way content is authored. Authors must be involved in development teams (so they can plan for reuse from the beginning); they must have solid information models (that they have helped to create and have been trained to follow); they must have usable authoring tools that assist them in following models and sharing information; they must have a stake in the outcome; and most of all, they need an understanding of what they are trying to accom-

---

3 http://www.diffuse.org/oii/en/workflow.html, accessed on March 3, 2002

4 Kovse, J., Harder, T., Ritter, N., Steiert, H., Mahnke, W. "Supporting Collaborative Authoring of Web Content by Customizable Resource Repositories." Department of Computer Science, University of Kaiserslautern, Kaiserslautern, Germany. Available as PDF at http://www.tu-chemnitz.de/informatik/webdb/020.pdf. March 3, 2002.

plish and the support and resources to do it. Collaborative authoring also requires technology's assistance with some things, such as access to shared information, workflow routing, version management, check-in and check-out, as well as tools to assist authors in writing to models. Although tools are important, they play a supporting role; the focus of this chapter is on the organizational strategies for collaboration. Further information on tools and technologies as they relate to collaboration can be found in Part 5, specifically, Chapter 15, "Authoring tools," Chapter 16, "Content management systems," and Chapter 17, "Workflow systems."

## Strategies for organizational change

Many companies are not structured to support collaboration. Their structure is hierarchical and as a result, many of their projects come together vertically and in isolation. When a company introduces a new product or service, many of the people involved in the project don't even know who the other people are or what aspect of the project they're working on. And the bigger the company, the more true this is. The technical publications people may be aware that the marketing people are "doing their thing," creating the brochures and writing the scripts for television spots, but they see it as separate from what they're working on, which may be the user guides. Likewise, the training people may be creating web-based tutorials, but they see the technical publications group's efforts as separate from theirs. Once you've developed information models—especially if you've developed them by looking beyond the content that your group creates—you'll be more aware of the content that other groups create. Yet the information models themselves are a collaborative effort, and they need collaborative revisiting at the start of new projects to ensure that they still accommodate the information needs of the new project. For example, is the granularity still sufficient to enable you to deliver content dynamically over the Web? For collaboration to occur, change must occur at many levels:

- How groups are organized and managed
- How groups work together
- How individual authors work
- How models are implemented and used

## How groups are organized and managed

For authoring to be collaborative, project members must know and understand each others' roles, even if they perform different functions. The information model will indicate what information products are required (for example, product catalog, user guide, internal support documentation) and based on your knowledge of who does what in your organization, you organize your team around the information products being developed. For example, if you are creating documentation for medical devices, the authoring team will consist of everyone involved in creating any type of documentation (brochures, doctors' manuals, patients' guides, press releases) for the medical device: medical writers, marketing writers, public relations specialists. A unified content strategy requires that all groups collaborate on their efforts so they can complement each other. As groups become more familiar with each other, they can also work together to make sure models continue to meet their needs. Use these techniques to ensure collaboration and a shared vision:

- When you're documenting a new product or service, hold a project "kick-off" meeting (you can do this virtually if you're geographically dispersed) at the project's inception. Discuss the information requirements, ensure that the current information models support them, and establish how you will share information that is reusable. Get questions from everyone involved. Make sure the writing standards for elements are explicit and understood by everyone in the group. However, with that said, use the meeting as an opportunity to share, not to lecture. Additionally, open a line of communication to the project head that anyone can use if concerns pop up later (such as from those who couldn't attend the meeting).

- When you're working on updates to existing content, revisit the information model to make sure everyone on the team understands what information is being reused and what the writing standards are for the elements being revised. Don't assume that your group is the only group involved in an update; check the elements requiring revision against the information model to see who else is involved. As a group, you can make sure the model is still effective as elements are updated; you can also keep it current with what you've learned from users, so you continue to deliver what readers really need, not just what the models say they needed five iterations ago.

## Organizing based on content requirements

Collaboration also implies a change in the way work is organized. In many organizations, individual groups handle a number of projects, separate from each other. A marketing group, for example, will often work on a number of different projects for a variety of other groups in the organization. Those projects are, for the most part, independent of each other in how they're staffed, funded, and managed. It's difficult for groups to collaborate with an independent, project-oriented organizational structure in place.

In a unified content environment, organizations need to be resource-based, focusing on content requirements across the organization, not just for one project. A content database becomes an integrated source of definitive information, contributed to and used by everyone in the organization. When planning the information products required for a project, departments should think about what they will add to and use from the definitive source. As they develop their content, they should plan for its other uses as well. Consider allocating budgets for content development across an organization, not just to individual departments. This enables you to move to a resource-based content development model rather than a project-based one. In a resource-based model, budgets are developed for all the content your organization produces across the organization, thus replacing individual department budgets for content creation.

Resource-based project planning also reduces content creation time and costs. Because content is developed across an organization, fewer resources are needed to re-create content that may already exist elsewhere. The technical publications department doesn't have to write a product description that has already been developed by marketing. When content is tagged and stored for easy retrieval, authors can retrieve it and either incorporate it into their information products as is or modify it for their own purposes (based on their information model). The model will tell the marketing group that technical publications also needs the product description and that it must be written and structured in a certain way so it's usable for both purposes. To get to this understanding of the product description, technical publications and marketing must collaborate.

## How groups work together

Even in a collaborative environment, authors don't have to work together in groups the whole time. Plenty of work can be done on an individual basis. But crucial decisions must be made together and reaching consensus is key to successful collaboration. One author may find that the current level of granularity is insufficient, but before changing it, everyone who is affected by the change must agree. Collaborative teams, when they work, do not proceed by democratic vote. Instead, they struggle to reach consensus, even though it takes longer than voting. Consensus means that everyone agrees to a change, not just the seven out of ten who vote for it. With consensus, everyone buys into the change and will support it in their writing.

Furthermore, collaboration is significantly different from cooperation. When we cooperate, we work together, but we each produce and "own" our individual projects. We retain our separate styles and in the finished product, we can usually tell which portions are "ours," and we can certainly tell which information products we created in their entirety. This kind of independence doesn't work in a unified content environment, when information products are compiled from a number of different elements, often written by a number of different authors.

### Relinquishing ownership

In a unified content environment, the concept of ownership becomes irrelevant. For instance, in an "independent but cooperative" environment, my colleague writes a procedure, which I edit. I write another procedure, which my colleague edits. But, ultimately, my colleague is in charge is his or hers, and I'm in charge of mine. We negotiate changes and we (often delicately) suggest improvements. But we "live with" what the other person produces. We do not really merge our thoughts so that it becomes transparent who wrote what. However, if a particular author's style is discernible, the content may not be reusable in different information products. Independence often leaves documentation uneven, which is unacceptable in a unified content environment.

Instead of the usual, cooperative approach to writing that many groups use, a unified content strategy requires true collaboration, which means working together so thoroughly that you no longer own any part, any chapter, any sentence, any procedure. Elements are truly unified, based on the information model, and authors can't tell who did what. This is difficult for many authors to get used to; they claim it takes away their creativity. We, in our role as consultants, frequently dispute this belief, emphasizing that the real creativity comes in analyzing users' needs and figuring out the best way to meet those needs, often dynamically. The creativity also lies in building strong models, based on possible uses and potential users for content. In this way, authors truly become information architects, with more and more emphasis on the analysis and design that drive the content. Collaboration is critical in creating and sharing the information design and the standards that everyone follows.

## How individual authors work

In the past, many technical writers became technical writers because technical writing is—or used to be—a solitary profession. Many technical writers are accustomed to working independently, with little collaboration. A single writer would be assigned a single document, retreat to his or her office to complete the assignment, sometimes interrupting the day to make phone calls to subject matter experts to clarify understanding of the content. When the document was complete, it was published and distributed to those who needed it and authors continued with their next project. This would often result not only in disparities in a single author's work, but in disparities in the documentation produced by the entire work group.

Collaboration requires not only that authors work with each other within their own departments, but also with authors from different departments. In a collaborative environment, authors work together to ensure that content is not written more than once by more than one author, and more importantly, that similar content is not written about differently. The information models must be clear about what the information requirements are; the organizational structure must be clear about which department authors which elements.

**Developing new skills**

What does this mean in the workplace? It means that authors may need new skills, such as information analysis, design, modeling, structured writing, and conflict management to help them in the transition from independent to collaborative work. Strategies for helping authors switch to a collaborative authoring environment include:

- Training authors in analysis, information modeling, and design; emphasizing analysis of information and users' needs so authors learn to model based on needs
- Involving authors from across the organization in developing models and in reviewing them on an ongoing basis
- Training authors in following models
- Training authors in structured writing

Also, often overlooked in favor of the more "technical" skills of analysis, design, and writing is the ability to handle conflict. A certain amount of conflict is necessary to motivate change and encourage creativity. However, unmanaged conflict can quickly turn to chaos. Conflict will certainly be present as groups try to reach consensus, and it's important for team members to understand conflict responses and how to deal with them. Furthermore, in collaborative efforts across departments and even within departments, there are likely to be "turf" wars. Departments or individual authors may feel they are being compromised, and when this happens, conflict is imminent. Jean Richardson and Lisa Burk's paper, "Conflict Management in Software Development Environments,"[5] provides a good description of conflict management techniques, as well as a thorough bibliography.

## *How models are implemented and used*

Models are the key to a successful unified content strategy. Although not everyone in your organization can get involved in the modeling process, you should have representatives from every area that creates content. Their input is critical in defining information requirements and potential reuse. Once models are developed to accommodate needs across the organization, anyone involved in authoring content must learn how to follow them. We advocate the following:

5 Burk, Lisa and Jean Richardson. Conflict Management in Software Development Environments. Available from www.bjr.com, June 25, 2002.

- Run workshops introducing the concept of models and how to use them not only to authors, but to reviewers of content and to managers of content creation groups. Stress the importance of models to unified content, and the importance of different groups contributing to and following models. Make the models available for reference, so that everyone who needs to use them can access them. Revisit models regularly to ensure they continue to support your information requirements.

- Usability test new authoring tools and authoring scenarios with all the groups that will be using them. Provide real authoring scenarios to each group, including such things as their ability to:

  - Follow the model (whether it's supported by a tool or referenced in a writing guide or spreadsheet)
  - Identify and retrieve reusable information
  - Populate a document with reusable information
  - Create elements
  - Publish elements
  - Store elements

  Refer to Appendix A, "Checklist for implementing a unified content strategy," for more information on conducting a usability test. There are also some references to usability testing in the bibliography.

## Strategies for technological change

Although tools by themselves are not the key to implementing collaborative authoring (change must occur at the organizational level), their role is a critical supporting one. They don't replace the teamwork, the understanding, or the cohesion that collaborative authoring requires. In fact, tools can make collaboration easier, but they do not guarantee success. In working with a tool that is not conducive to the creative process, authors often feel like they're submitting rather than creating.

The tools required for collaboration involve more than giving everyone access to the same directories on the same file server, regardless of how user-friendly the file server may be! Tools for collaboration are described in Chapters 15, 16, and 17, but some factors critical for effective collaboration include the following:

- Access to shared information
- Check-in and check-out
- Locking and version control
- Transparent authoring to support models
- Managed workflow
- Event notification

## Summary

Collaborative authoring is key to breaking down silo walls. Collaboration means everyone working together to achieve the common goal of unified content that is truly seamless. Collaboration sounds easier than it is, though. Some elements necessary for successful collaboration include the following:

- Know everyone involved in creating content and what each person's role is; look to models to provide advice about information requirements; consider including a "responsible party" for each information type in your model so that you know what information is required as well as who is responsible for creating it. Hold "kickoff" meetings at the beginning of projects.

- Think about how your organization is structured. Does your structure allow for collaboration across departments? How do departments know what other departments are working on?

- Provide authors with a stake in the outcome and an understanding of how collaborative authoring will benefit them.

- Consider moving to a resource-focused approach to developing content; develop budgets based on content requirements across the organization, rather than department-specific budgets.

- Start with strong models; introduce models to everyone in the organization who creates content; revisit models iteratively.

- Make any changes to models, authoring processes, and standards by consensus and not by democratic vote; train authors in conflict management techniques.

- Encourage authors to relinquish ownership of their content; content with a discernible style is not necessarily reusable.
- Train writers in information analysis, modeling, design, and structured writing so they all have the same understanding of how to create and how to write to information models.
- Provide usable tools that support collaborative processes, not impede them.

# Chapter 20

## Separating content from format

Once you take on a unified content strategy, authors will create content for a number of different purposes, but with greater integration and far less duplication of effort. An author may create a product description that will be used in a printed brochure, in a product catalog that forms part of the external web site, on an intranet that mirrors the external web site but provides additional details, in the user guide, and in training materials. In some cases, the same author may reuse the content that he or she creates, but other authors may also retrieve it and use it for their purposes. The whole idea behind reuse is to avoid "reinventing the wheel," but for reuse to occur, authors must focus on the content's meaning as opposed to its format. That is, they write it independent of where or how it may appear. This is a difficult concept for some authors to adopt, but separating content from format provides your organization with ultimate flexibility in how the content is used and displayed, both today and into the future. After all, even though you model the potential uses for your content, you never know when new uses may arise.

This chapter discusses why it's a good idea to separate content from format and describes the structured writing principles that allow authors to focus primarily on content. It also challenges the belief that for content to be effective, authors must know exactly how it will be used. To that end, this chapter provides some guidelines for writing the same content so it works in different media and for different uses.

## Why separate content from format?

When implementing a unified content strategy, it's critical that authors structure and write their content consistently. Well-structured content leads to more opportunities for reuse across product lines, audiences, and information products, as well as to greater return on investment. Not only can content be reused more effectively if it is structured consistently, it can also be *used* more effectively. Well-structured content is more usable content, potentially reducing support calls from customers and staff who need assistance finding or interpreting information.

In "traditional" environments, authors write the content, then format it to accommodate the media in which it is being delivered. Authors will often spend hours and hours adjusting such things as font size, kerning, paragraph and line spacing, as well as margins—anything to make the information fit its particular format. In addition to format changes, authors will often make content changes if they decide to use the same content elsewhere. They may change the focus of the content slightly (to make it more marketing-oriented, for example), or they may shorten content to make it fit into a smaller space, such as a package label or brochure.

In a unified content strategy, authors are not required to format the content; style sheets automatically format it based on the content's desired context and medium. Instead, authors focus on the information—specifically, its meaning and structure. Structure is critical because it unifies the content, regardless of who is writing it. When content is structured consistently, it is transparent that a number of different authors may have worked on it. In this way, structured writing enables collaborative authoring and prepares content for reuse, regardless of who writes it, enhancing authors' productivity. In a structured writing environment, whoever writes a warning—or an overview, or a procedure, or a copyright notice—writes it the same way. Plus, when similar types of content are always structured the same way, users quickly learn how to read or find information which can potentially reduce your support costs.

The degree to which you break down (and enforce) the structure of your content depends on the "granularity" of your material and your desire for consistency. (Granularity refers to the smallest piece of information that is reusable. For more information on granularity, see Chapter 8, "Information modeling.") The structure of the various information products is defined in an information model and, depending on the authoring environment, authors may be prohibited from including content that is not defined in the model.

For instance, if the model is supported by a Document Type Definition (DTD), the DTD will allow authors to create documents only according to the structure defined in the DTD. If the model is not supported by a DTD, authors may select from style tags, complete areas within a form, or enter text into a template that tells them what content must appear in the document. In an authoring environment not supported by a DTD, authors would rely on the model itself for the hierarchy.

Many problems arise when content is not structured. Some procedures include results within a step; some don't. Some procedures include an introductory or stem sentence; some do not. Sometimes steps are numbered; sometimes they are not. Sometimes warnings are included; sometimes they are not, and when they are they might contain inconsistent types of information. If the structure for writing a procedure (and for writing all the components within a procedure) is standardized, then authors can focus on the content that belongs in each step, not on how to put the procedure together. Also, readers get used to reading information in the same way, reducing their cognitive load.[1]

# Writing structured content

Before getting into the concepts of structured writing, it's beneficial to understand the meaning of structure. According to Merriam-Webster's online dictionary, the noun "structure" has the following five definitions:

- the action of building
- a: something (as a building) that is constructed; b: something arranged in a definite pattern or organization
- manner of construction
- a: the arrangement or particles or parts in a substance or body; b: organization of parts as dominated by the general character of the whole
- the aggregate of elements of an entity in their relationship to each other

Merriam-Webster's also lists a definition for "data structure" that is applicable to information: "Any of various methods of organizing data items (as records) in a computer." Applied to information, this could easily read, "Any of various methods of organizing content in an information product."

In fact, all these definitions lend themselves well to writing, in particular, the manner of construction (that is, how content is put together), the arrangement of parts (that is, the hierarchy of elements), and the aggregate of elements of an entity in their relationship to each other (that is, how certain elements relate to other elements).

## What is structured writing?

So, you know what structure is, but what is structured writing? "Structured" writing, as its name implies, is the way pieces of information or content are put together to form an information product—a whole sentence, a whole paragraph, a whole procedure, or a whole book. Structured writing is based on information theory, as follows:

---

1 For more information on how consistent structure facilitates comprehension, see Dr. Robert Horn's studies on structured writing, available at `http://www.infomap.com` and `http://www.stanford.edu/~rhorn`.

- **Structured writing is based on cognitive psychology.**

  Structured writing is based on how people read, process, and understand information. Within a structured writing environment, authors follow standards developed for certain types of content, ensuring content is always presented consistently. For example, principles of cognitive psychology guide us in determining how many steps a procedure should contain before providing users with a break. In a structured writing environment, the size of a procedure becomes a guideline, or even a rule, ensuring the consistency of the procedure for both authors and users.

- **Structured writing follows standards.**

  Information standards, once defined, are consistent. Once you define the structure of the content (for example, the structure of a procedure), whoever writes a procedure must follow that structure. Not only do you define how many steps there should be in a procedure, you define what the structure for a step is. The standard tells authors such things as "A step must always contain the condition under which the step is performed, the action, and the result of the action…in that order." Whoever writes the step writes it in this way, so ideally, that step can be reused in any other related procedure. The structure can apply to individual steps, to the whole procedure, or to individual elements within a step, which brings us to our next point…

- **Structured writing applies at numerous levels, depending on your needs.**
  For example:

  - sentence/step

  - paragraph

  - chapter

  - document, volume, set, and more

  In a structured writing environment, standards apply at the level where you want consistency and reuse. If you plan to reuse information at the sentence level, then sentences must be structured consistently; likewise, if you plan to reuse information at the paragraph level, then paragraphs must be structured consistently. The granularity will dictate the level of structure you must define. Chances are, if you're reusing information in user guides, marketing materials, press releases, external web sites, and intranets, the granularity will be at the paragraph level. To accommodate all uses, a paragraph must be structured in a similar fashion, following guidelines for the type of information it conveys. When paragraphs are structured consistently, they can come together to form a unified information product, regardless of who has written each paragraph. Without structure, information products can take on "ransom note" characteristics, similar to the appearance many publications had in the early days of desktop publishing. Without structure, elements also read dissimilarly, resulting in a lack of cohesion. The more granular your information, the more structure you will need, as well as more adherence to structure.

## Principles of structured writing

Structured writing is governed by principles that describe how people process information:

- **Chunking**

    People can best hold 5 to 9 chunks of information in short-term memory. Accordingly, structured writing groups information into small, manageable units, and compiles those units into larger structures, also based on the 5-to-9 principle. Each chunk is an independent unit of information that can either stand on its own or contribute to a larger unit. If a procedure contains more than 10 steps, it's likely that those steps can be broken down further. Imagine having to read 32 steps just to program the stations on your car radio. That much information is not only intimidating, it's also difficult to follow and still keep track of where you are. Four smaller procedures—each with 8 steps—categorized according to subtopic would be much more usable, not to mention user friendly.

- **Labeling**

    Chunks of information are labeled to identify the type of information they contain. To be effective, labels (for example, titles, headings, and subheadings) are substantive, indicative of the information they contain. For instance, rather than calling a procedure "Radio Stations," you could call it "Tuning Your Radio Stations." Substantive labels give users a clear indication of what to expect when they select a particular piece of content. Clear labels also make it much easier for users to scan for the correct information. Every chunk of information should have a substantive label. In fact, if you can't think up a good label, you may not need the chunk itself.

- **Relevance**

  Only information that relates to one main point is contained in a chunk, eliminating "nice to know" information. If authors want to include "nice to know" or "commentary" information, they can include it in an appropriately labeled chunk, allowing users to decide whether it's relevant for them. According to the relevance principle, the chunk labeled "Tuning Your Radio Stations" would contain information that describes how to tune radio stations—and nothing else. Commentary about various radio stations is not relevant. If authors wish to include commentary, it must be in a separate chunk and labeled accordingly, something like "Jazz Radio Stations on the Eastern Seaboard." Relevance is important from both reuse and usability perspectives. If procedures, for example, contain only relevant details (as defined in an information model), then procedures and parts of procedures can be reused effectively because they are consistent from procedure to procedure. Their usability is also enhanced because relevancy teaches users to always expect the same type of information in a procedure, overview, recipe, and so on.

- **Consistency**

  For similar subject matters, use similar words, labels, formats, organizations, and sequences. If you decide that procedures should always be in numbered lists (with a certain type of numbering), then procedures should always appear in numbered lists. If cautions are to be worded in a certain way (again, as defined in the information model), then cautions should always be worded that way. If you decide that proposals should be organized in a particular order, then they should always be organized in that order. Note, however, that even though the consistency principle also applies to format, authors still separate content from format during the writing process. Instead of being part of the writing process, format is usually defined in a style sheet that formats content according to the rules that authors develop for each type of content, for each user group, for each information product, and for each medium. When determining format rules, authors analyze information to figure out the best way to present it; style sheets are then developed for the content outputs, so even though format is applied after content is written, it is still based on content.

Consistency, like relevancy, is critical for both reuse and usability. If you are reusing steps from procedure to procedure, then the steps must be consistent in style, format, and wording, or the reuse will be jarring and the procedure potentially unusable. Likewise, if a caution from one document will be used in several other documents, then it must be consistent with the other cautions that appear in those documents. From a usability perspective, when information is presented consistently, readers form expectations about what it contains, which reduces their learning curve as well as their cognitive load. They may decide to always skip a certain type of procedure because it is not applicable. If writers change what that type of procedure contains, users may miss relevant information.

- **Reuse**

Building on the consistency principle, the reuse principle dictates how a chunk of information can be reused in similar information products, so that wherever it is repeated, it is the same. The reuse principle also ensures that when a chunk is updated, it is updated in all places it appears, guaranteeing ongoing consistency. Reuse is indicated in the information models (and supported by authoring and content management tools), along with writing standards that address all the principles of structured writing, such as how big that element should be (chunking), how it must be labeled (labeling), what type of information it must contain (relevance), and how it is to be structured (consistency). In this way, elements are both reused consistently and written soundly.

## Basing structure on information type

In a structured writing environment, chunks of content are assigned "rules" about their structure, based on how that chunk will be used and the type of information it contains. Rules are based on the belief that not all information is created equally and that it should be treated differently. Accordingly, if information is conceptual, it will follow the structure rules for conceptual information. And, if information is procedural, it will follow the structure rules for procedural information.

Ideally, authors consider information types when applying the principles of structured writing to their content. How each type is structured is then documented in the information model and supported by a style sheet that applies a design suitable to the information type. For example:

- Procedures and processes are best presented in sequentially numbered action tables and lists.

- Concepts and principles often comprise text-based information chunks, with examples and illustrations included to support the concept.

- Classifications are often presented in lists and tables.

- Comparisons are best presented in tables that directly compare one component with another.

Table 20.1 provides an example of writer guidelines for semantic model.

**Table 20.1    Authoring and structure guidelines for a warning**

| Element | Authoring and structure guideline |
| --- | --- |
| Icon/Signal word | The signal word (for example, Warning) lets the user know that the related information is important. Using the icon in conjunction with the signal word enables the reader to locate them both quickly. Both these elements are automatically inserted by the style sheet. |
| | For a list of warnings or precautions, one signal word at the head of the list is sufficient. Presenting the list in a bulleted fashion helps reduce the "information overload" that would otherwise be experienced if a series of individual alerts were to be presented one after another. |
| Title | Identify the hazard with a title. This gives users an easy way to identify the different types of hazards that may apply to them. |
| Alert body | Tell users how to avoid the hazard or tell them how to identify the potential problem. Include specific information on what not to (or what to) do. |

*continues* ▶

**Table 20.1    Continued**

| Element | Authoring and structure guideline |
|---------|-----------------------------------|
| | This is usually in the form of "Do not…," Never…," and so on, and is followed by the specific actions that will enable the reader to avoid the hazard. Where appropriate, add hazard identification information that will enable users to identify the hazard or problem so that they may avoid it. |
| | Tell users the consequences of ignoring the warning. Explain the problems, limitations, or effects that may occur as a result of ignoring or disregarding the warning. |

# Applying the model

As described so far in this chapter:

- Content must be structured so that it can be reused.

- Structuring content not only makes it consistent for reuse, it also enhances its usability.

- The guidelines for creating structured content are contained in models.

Depending on your need for control and precision in your unified content strategy, and on the tools you're using, you can provide explicit models that guide authors through the process of creating structured content (for example, DTDs, authoring templates, or forms), or you can provide written guidelines that authors follow manually (instead of being guided by a tool).

Writing to a model is critical in adopting structured writing because the model contains the rules that govern not only what elements belong in which information product, but also how each element is structured (based on the type of information it contains). When implementing structured writing, models serve three purposes:

- **Provide guidelines for authors.**

  Authors use information models to determine what information goes in which information product, as well as how to structure each element. Referring to the information model, they can, for example, determine that an information product requires error codes, determine the structure of an error code, and get hints or rules about how to write an error code. Models should also contain examples of elements as they should be written; these "best practices" help authors to compare their elements against what they should be, whether they're writing from scratch or revising existing elements.

- **Provide guidelines for architects.**

  Information architects use models to build the DTD or template that authors must follow. Instead of referring to written guidelines, authors are guided by the tool through what to include and how to structure it. Some tools even allow architects to include examples or help that shows authors samples of completed elements. Even in a structured writing environment supported by tools, authors still need to understand the model to follow what the tool is asking them to do.

- **Provide guidelines for reviewers.**

  Model reviewers check information models to ensure they support customer and information requirements. Documentation reviewers use models to review authors' drafts. They compare the draft against the information model to ensure it contains all the necessary elements.

## Reading the model

Figure 20.1 shows the information elements for a product description model and how they are reused to accommodate different needs. In writing to this model, authors know that a product description must contain a product name, a product description (divided into long, short, and medium components), and a graphic, in that order. Each element within the product description must be structured this way to accommodate its different uses. If this model is supported by a DTD (or other automated authoring tool), the DTD would guide the authors through the product description, prohibiting entries that are not included in the model. If the model is not supported by an authoring tool, authors would refer to the model to know how to put each element together. The model would go on to provide writing guidelines and an example for each element, showing authors such things as how the long product description should be structured and written, based on the type of information it conveys.

| | A | B | C | D | E | F | G | H |
|---|---|---|---|---|---|---|---|---|
| 1 | | | Base element | | | Reuse Map | | |
| 2 | Semantic | Element type | XML | Product Sheet | Brochure | Press release | Web Site | E-catalog |
| 3 | Product Name | Element | title | L | L | | L | L |
| 4 | Product Description | Container | container | L | | | L | L |
| 5 | Product Desc. Short | Element | para | L | L | L | L | L |
| 6 | Product Desc. Med. | Element | para | L | | | L | L |
| 7 | Product Desc. Long | Element | para | L | | | L | L |
| 8 | Graphic | Element | figure | L | L | | L | L |

**Figure 20.1    Product description information model.**

For further information on models, refer to Chapter 8, "Information modeling."

## Using the building block approach

Another way of separating content from format is to use the building block approach. The building block approach allows you to identify a core of information that is applicable for all information products and users, then build on it to customize information for different uses and users. You start with core information and then build on it, as follows:

- Identify the core information (the information that is applicable for all uses).

- Identify what has to be added to the core to meet other needs, such as training or different audiences.

- Tag additional elements according to where they belong, as in a patient guide or programming guide.

For example, you might start with a product description that contains the elements in the model shown above in Figure 20.1. That entire product description becomes your core information, to which you then add elements to create the following materials:

- User guide information

  To the product description, you add specifications.

- Training materials for the product

  You might add instructions for getting started with the product.

- Internal staff support materials

  You might add frequently asked questions about the product so staff can respond to customers' questions.

Table 20.2 shows a building block approach for creating the documentation accompanying a software package. The online user guide contains the core information, and the internal support and training materials build onto the core.

**Table 20.2    Building blocks for software documentation**

| Online user guide (attached to application) | Internal support materials (intranet) | Internal training materials (classroom) |
|---|---|---|
| Field definitions | Field definitions | Field definitions |
| Screen-level information (details about each field on the screen) | Screen-level information as part of an overall task | Screen-level information as part an overall task |
| Screen images | Screen images (optional) | Screen images |
| Overviews (optional) | Overviews | Overviews |
| User tasks | User tasks | User tasks |
| | Troubleshooting for tasks | Troubleshooting for tasks |
| | | Objectives |
| | | Task context |
| | | Examples |
| | | Exercises |

In the building block approach, each element is identified by the information product in which it belongs (for example, training, user guide, intranet), and supported by style sheets that format it for the appropriate media. In this way, authors create content elements, augmenting the core sequentially. The format is applied after the content is published to its output. (Different media have different requirements for displaying content effectively. For example, the Web has different display requirements than a printed user guide, and a printed user guide has different display requirements than a printed training guide. Hence, different format requirements are required for each output.)

# Same content, different uses?

So, what about using a product description in a number of different places and publishing it to a number of different media. Can the same content really be written so that it's appropriate for all its potential uses? Can a product description that is used in a brochure really be reused in training materials? Shouldn't the brochure have a different tone?

We believe that content can be reused effectively, simply by following writing guidelines that are applicable to all the potential uses for the content. In addition, the building block approach allows for content to be augmented as required, so the core is written in a style that is applicable for all uses and the augmented parts are written to accommodate their specific uses. Training materials, for example, can use the same product description as the brochure, but where they differ is in the exercises and explanations that characterize training materials. Likewise, the brochure can use the same product description as the user guide and the training materials, but where the brochure differs is in the addition of "marketing" details that explain to potential customers why they should buy the product. But, the product description is the same, regardless of where it is used. The writing guidelines for each reusable component are documented in the information model (along with the structure guidelines) and are based on the type of information each component contains, as well as its potential users, uses, and reuses. Where the difference occurs is in how much information is provided and how it is presented. Figures 20.3 and 20.4, in the section "The Finished Product," provide excellent examples of how the content can be reused in many different places.

## Writing guidelines for different uses

After developing content for both online and print media for more than 20 years, our experience has taught us that well-written online documentation also makes good paper documentation and vice versa. Consequently, we've developed guidelines to ensure that content really can be used in a number of different ways. Many of these guidelines are simply guidelines for clear communication and make for better content, regardless of reuse. Some sample guidelines (not all-inclusive) are summarized in Tables 20.3 and 20.4 and are described in detail in Appendix B, "Writing for multiple media."

The guidelines for online documentation (such as online help) and web materials are very similar:

**Table 20.3   Guidelines for online documentation and the Web**

| | Online documentation | Web | Wireless (such as, PDAs) |
|---|---|---|---|
| Write succinctly | ✓ | ✓ | ✓ |
| Write so users can scan | ✓ | ✓ | ✓ |
| Layer information | ✓ | ✓ | ✓ |
| Write useful titles | ✓ | ✓ | ✓ |

However, if you look at these guidelines closely you will find that they are just as valid for paper.

**Table 20.4   Same guidelines applied to paper**

| | Paper | Reasoning |
|---|---|---|
| Write succinctly | ✓ | Clear concise content can greatly improve the quality of paper materials. |
| Write so users can scan | ✓ | Long passages of text that extend down a page or over pages is hard to read. Chunking that information can make it much easier for a reader to comprehend. |
| Layer information | ✓ | This is a bit harder on paper. You don't want to have a lot of "gotos" in the text that take the reader back and forth. However, layering of content is appropriate for things such as overviews, summaries, and check lists, as opposed to the detail of the body. |

*continues* ▶

**Table 20.4   Continued**

| | Paper | Reasoning |
|---|:---:|---|
| Write useful titles | ✓ | Useful titles make it easier for users to find what they want. |

Note that these guidelines also relate to the principles of structured writing:

- Writing succinctly relates to chunking and relevance; only relevant content is included in "bite-size" chunks.

- Writing so users can scan is handled through labeling, chunking, and relevance.

- Layering information is achieved through chunking, labeling, and relevance (layering according to hierarchy of relevant information).

- Writing useful titles is accomplished by following the labeling principle.

All guidelines help writers to achieve consistency and reusability, especially when standards accompany each guideline.

## Example: Same content, different uses

The Reo Auto Company is preparing for the annual auto show and launch of its new vehicles. This year they are launching their first sports utility vehicle (SUV)—the Tsai. They require a variety of information products: a press release to announce their new lineup, brochures to hand out at the show and dealer showrooms, updates to the web site, and a show catalog. The web site team and marketing group sit down to figure out a unified content strategy for the materials. They determine that the information products are to be provided in three media: paper (show catalog, press release, brochure), web (web site, press release), and email (press release). Each information product requires different content and design:

- Show catalog for the entire line-up (photo, short description, and key features, three cars to a page)

- Brochure for the Tsai only (photo, long description with all the features and benefits)

- Press release for the Tsai only (no photo, short description, features and benefits)

- Web site for entire line-up (home page for each car with photos, list of full features combined with a pricing calculator)

## The information model

Figure 20.2 shows a portion of the information model for the Tsai product description.

|  | A | B | C | D | E |
|---|---|---|---|---|---|
| 1 |  | Reuse Map | | | |
| 2 | Semantic | Show catalog | Brochure | Press release | Web Site |
| 3 | Product Name | L | L | L | L |
| 4 | Product Description | L | L | L | L |
| 5 | Product Desc. Short | L | L | L | L |
| 6 | Product Desc. Med. |  | L |  | L |
| 7 | Product Desc. Long |  | L |  | L |
| 8 | Graphic | L | L |  | L |
| 9 | Features | L | L | L |  |
| 10 | Feature title |  | L | L |  |
| 11 | Feature item | L | L | L |  |
| 12 | Benefits |  | L | L | L* |
| 13 | Benefit item |  | L | L |  |
| 14 | Tag line |  | L | L | L |
| 15 |  |  |  |  |  |
| 16 | *Not shown in illustration, but included on additional web pages. |  |  |  |  |

**Figure 20.2   Information model for Tsai product description.**

Working with the model, the web site team and marketing group proceed to develop the content, as shown in Table 20.5. (The metadata column indicates in which information product the content will appear.)

**Table 20.5   Content development for Tsai product description**

| Element | Content | Metadata |
|---|---|---|
| Product Name | Tsai | All |
| **Product Description** | | |
| Product Desc. Short | The new Tsai is a totally new experience in SUVs. The revolutionary Tsai combines a gas engine with an electric motor, resulting in a fuel-efficient and environmentally conscious SUV. Yet none of the features like roominess and ruggedness are lost. The best of all worlds, the Tsai. | All |

continues ▶

**Table 20.5    Continued**

| Element | Content | Metadata |
|---|---|---|
| Product Desc. Med | The Tsai features an all-wheel drive with an inline four-cylinder engine. The powertrain includes a five-speed automatic transmission and has a towing capacity of 1,000 pounds. Integrated light-weight roof rails and fold-down rear seats with 70/30 split make carrying loads a breeze. | Brochure |
| Product Desc. Long | The revolutionary light-weight body is manufactured with dent-resistant polymer. Front and side air bags add to safety and security. The car-friendly height makes it easy to get in and out of and to load all your essentials on top. | Brochure |
| Graphic | TBD. | Show catalog Brochure Web site |
| Graphic | TBD. | All[2] |
| **Features** | | |
| Feature title Press release | Features. | Brochure |
| Feature item | 2L engine. | All[2] |
| Feature item | Anti-lock brake system. | |
| Feature item | Power brakes. | |
| Feature item | Stabilizer bars. | |
| Feature item | Low emission Vehicle Standards. | |
| **Benefits** | | |
| Benefit item | The only SUV that is truly environmentally friendly from its construction to its operation. | Brochure Press release Web site[2] |
| Tag line | Practicality of a car, power of an SUV. | Brochure Press release Web site |

2 Not shown in illustration, but included on additional web pages

## *The finished product*

After the content is written, it is published to each information product; the format is applied based on the content's use. Figures 20.3 and 20.4 show how the same product description is reused effectively, in each medium.

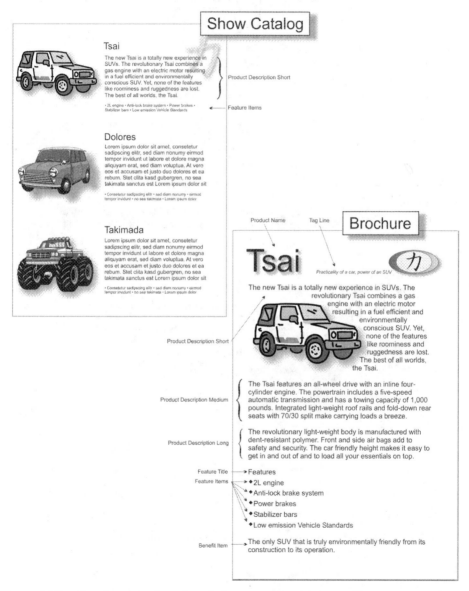

**Figure 20.3     Reusing a product description across multiple media.**

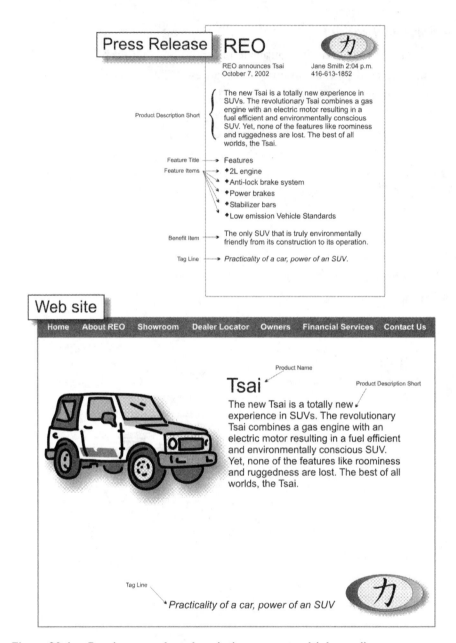

**Figure 20.4    Reusing a product description across multiple media.**

## Summary

In a unified content strategy, structure is critical because it unifies the content, regardless of who is writing it. Information is chunked and written in elements, which are then assembled—according to a predetermined hierarchy—into information products. Each element, and each information product, is structured in a consistent way, which both enables it to be reused and allows for consistency. The information models specify how information products and information elements are put together to ensure that consistency.

To structure information effectively, you need to separate content from format, which means you need to:

- Define standards that focus on meaning rather than format.
- Think about what you want the information to *do* rather than what you want the information to look like.
- Create standards for each element, so wherever the element appears, it is consistent, and so it is also consistent with the other elements contained in the information product.
- Define standards to identify what content an element contains and how it should be put together, as well as an example.
- Create a writing environment that enables authors to structure their content consistently, by either supporting them with tools or providing comprehensive models for them to follow.
- Decide how the elements should appear in their various outputs and develop style sheets that are applied when the content is published to its various formats.
- Follow writing guidelines to ensure content is written effectively for all media and all uses.

# Chapter 21

## Managing change

In today's world, change is inevitable. Business has to change to stay competitive. Small changes have become part of the daily business culture, but larger changes can be more problematic. Adopting a unified content strategy across the enterprise is a big change. Even if you adopt a unified content strategy in only one area, you will experience some resistance to the change. A unified content strategy requires authors to go through a paradigm shift. This paradigm shift requires change management.

This chapter describes some of the issues to consider when planning your change management strategy, including suggestions for overcoming resistance and descriptions of new and modified roles.

# Change management

Never underestimate the impact change will have on your organization. If you have change management personnel in-house, get them involved in your project as soon as you make the decision to adopt a unified content strategy. If you don't have change management personnel, consider hiring consultants who specialize in change management. This section provides suggestions to help you effectively manage the change associated with a unified content strategy.

## Identify the pain, issues, and consequences

People are unwilling to change unless there is a very good reason for that change and they can see the benefits. Identifying the benefits means first identifying your pain, issues, and consequences. What are the real issues facing your organization? What is the impact of not addressing these issues? (Refer to Chapter 4, "Where does it really hurt?," Chapter 5, "Analyzing the content life cycle," and Chapter 6, "Performing a content audit" for information about identifying the pain, issues, and consequences.) After you have identified your reasons for change, communicate your findings to everyone involved.

Reach out to people within the organization and listen to what they have to say about the issues and the solutions. Be sure to thank them for their input. When you have summarized their input, go back to them and verify that you understood them correctly. Then as you move into design, testing, and implementation, involve them and ask them to assist you in determining whether your design correctly addresses their issues and needs. If you involve people early on, really listen to what they have to say, then show them that you are addressing their requirements; they will be among your strongest supporters.

## Communicate

Communication is critical to the success of change. You need to communicate the reasons for change, your plan, and the project's status. Projects that are developed "under wraps" are viewed with suspicion. Lack of communication results in anxiety and starts rumors. The longer that information is withheld, the more anxious people become and the harder it becomes to convince them of the need to adopt the change. Plan to communicate as early in the project as possible and continue to communicate throughout.

You need to communicate:

- **Why change?**

  Frequently communication plans tell people only what is happening and what they have to do; they don't tell people why they have to do it. When some people don't understand the "why," they have a tendency to ignore or resist the change. Other people need simply to know that the important and influential decision-makers have bought into the idea. (There are the two personality types according to Meyers-Briggs[1]: those who need the champion and those who need a reason.) Ensure that you indicate that the important and influential decision-makers in the company have embraced the idea.

  Use the results of your analysis, summarize your findings, and present your findings in a clear manner. Don't play down the current issues or the dangers that face the organization; lay them on the table so that people see the reasoning behind the change. Take care not to scare people with the issues and dangers, but be honest in your presentation; they will appreciate the honesty and clarity. Emphasize the current issues are no one's fault and that the change is possible with their help.

- **The plan**

  Explain your plan, including an approximate timeline for implementation. This gives people an understanding of the scope and timeline for the project. Informal lunch-time sessions provide a non-threatening atmosphere and allow people to ask questions.

- **Ongoing status**

  Keep everyone who has a direct involvement in the unified content strategy now or in the future up to date as the project progresses, even if only specific groups are involved in the beginning. A newsletter is a good vehicle to communicate ongoing progress and answer commonly-asked questions.

---

1 The MBTI is based on Carl Jung's notions of psychological types. The MBTI was first developed by Isabel Briggs Myers (1897-1979) and her mother, Katharine Cook Briggs.

- **Successes**

  Ensure that you communicate the successes you have achieved. This enables people to understand that it is possible to achieve a unified content strategy.

- **Problems**

  No project is without its problems. As you start to implement the unified content strategy in additional areas, point out the problems you encountered, how they were addressed, and how they will be avoided as you move forward. Admitting problems brings them into the open and ensures that people understand that problems are inevitable and solvable.

## Elicit the help of "change agents"

Communication will help people to understand what is going on and why, but it will not necessarily convince them to participate. The best way to convince people of a change's value is to have "one of their own" communicate the excitement and possibilities. To do this you need "change agents." A change agent is someone who is not necessarily part of the assigned implementation team, but who will be a user of the new system and methodologies.

The best way to create change agents is to bring together a group of representative users who have shown an early understanding of the problems or who are open to change. Help them to clearly understand the pain, issues, and dangers you are aware of, and have them voice their own ideas. Take them through a short content audit exercise to help them to see the possibilities. Discuss their specific opportunities and the ways in which this change will apply to them. Discuss how they can share their learning with others on their teams. Make sure you address all their questions and concerns. When they have an understanding of why this change should happen and are excited about the change, they will begin to communicate this to others on their teams, easing the transition to the unified content strategy. Make sure that you help the change agents to prepare a consistent message to take back to their teams. A consistent message reduces the possibility of misinterpretation.

## Get a champion

The broader the scope of your unified content strategy, the more likely you are to have disagreement. A champion (someone high enough up in the organization to effect change) needs to endorse the cause and ensure that different content areas understand the need for change and buy into it. If a group resists the change despite having their concerns and questions addressed, the champion may have to insist on them adopting the change or make a change in personnel to facilitate adoption.

# Overcoming resistance

Many of the challenges of a unified content strategy are common to any new process or system, whereas others are unique to a unified content strategy. The following are some of the more common challenges associated with a unified content strategy as well as suggestions for how to overcome them.

## "These ideas come from a different kind of company."

People find it hard to believe that content somebody else created could possibly meet their needs. After all, it was written for a different purpose and media, and the author couldn't possibly know their customers/audience/requirements.

In some ways, this is true. If content is written for a different purpose, audience, or media without considering how the content can be reused, it won't work. However, content can be reused if it is:

- Written according to models
- Written in the form of building blocks so that content can be selectively used as required
- Written with good writing principles
- Written without format in mind

In some cases, the content can be reused identically; in other cases, it must be modified, resulting in derivative reuse. But regardless of the type, reuse is possible.

So how do you convince people of that? The best solution is to trust that "seeing is believing." Bring together different groups who create similar content and work through a mini-content audit exercise with them. It's a good idea if you have an understanding of where reuse is possible and select appropriate materials in advance so that the analysis can be rapid. Having different groups identify the potential areas of reuse is an eye-opener. Many people are unaware of just how much content is reused or could be reused. After they see the volume of potential reuse they are usually convinced that reuse is possible.

The media issue may be more of a hurdle. Prepare for this one in advance. Create an example using some material that was written differently for different media, but that could be written the same for all media. Show the group the original materials. Show how the content could be written for multiple media. Show them the content in each medium (for example, in paper, then on the web) as it follows your current design templates. See Appendix B, "Writing for multiple media," for more information.

## "That's not how we do things here."

It's not unusual for different departments and different business units to have their own values and ways of doing things. Many organizations even encourage different parts of the organization to compete with each other. They may not talk to each other and cooperate.

In this case, the enterprise content coordinator needs to find a balance between similarity and diversity. The overall business needs must be identified and communicated to the different areas. They are all in business together and the focus should be on their businesses' competitors rather than on competition with other departments.

However, even when departments compete with each other, find out what their commonalities are and share them. Let each department or business unit focus on what is unique and optimize those unique qualities.

You might also consider adopting variations on the solution to meet the needs of different areas. For example, one area may use a full authoring tool, another area may use templates and forms, and yet another may use modified traditional authoring tools. This makes it easier for each area to author in a way that supports its own processes.

It's okay that processes may be different in different areas. As long as the result of these processes is the same—effective reusable content—different areas can continue to follow different processes. It is not necessary to create one unified process for the whole organization.

## "I can't be creative under these conditions."

Authors often feel that they will lose their creativity if they are forced to write structured content and write to models. First you need to identify what they consider creativity and what value is being added to the content through that creativity. Frequently, creativity is the work authors put into the layout rather than the content. It is true that in a unified content environment, authors no longer have creative control over format and layout. However, authors who enjoy layout and design may want to participate in the design of templates and style sheets in addition to creating content.

For authors who enjoy the content creation process, point out that they can be more creative in their writing because they no longer have to worry about format and layout. Their creative efforts can be put into designing the most effective information products possible and ensuring that content is readable and usable.

Others may greatly welcome the structured content and models, because doing so frees them up to do what they do best: creating content, which some consider to be their "real" job.

For teams such as marketing, where unique design and layout are integral to the effectiveness of information products, consider enabling authors to modify the style sheets. Take care to ensure that the structure of the content remains consistent with the models so content can be reused, but give authors the flexibility to change their style sheets and develop materials to meet their customers' needs. Alternatively, consider enabling authors to pick from a series of format elements so they can specify to a certain extent the "look and feel" of the content, by media.

### "It's not worth all this extra work."

Developing a unified content strategy is a lot of work. However, the work comes at the beginning, not throughout the content life cycle. After your strategy is implemented, the average author will have a reduced workload. When speaking with authors, don't overemphasize the amount of work it takes to implement the strategy. Instead, emphasize what they will save in working this way, and how much time will be freed up when they don't have to create everything from scratch.

For management, who should be concerned about the amount of work a unified strategy requires, emphasize that all new methods and systems require up-front work, but the investment is returned later in benefits and reduced costs.

### "You're making my job obsolete."

Companies and departments never have enough time, money, or resources to do all the work they need to do. Less work in one area means more time and resources are available to do work in another. Rarely are jobs lost. More frequently, organizations reorganize the workload and pursue projects and initiatives that they didn't have the time, money, or resources to do before. You can do more with the same resources.

## Why some projects fail

Failure is always a possibility when organizations change the way they do business. The following list includes some of the reasons projects fail or falter and some ways you can address these issues.

- **Resistance to change**

    Failing to address peoples' concerns during implementation can result in the project's failure. This is addressed in detail in "Overcoming resistance," earlier in this chapter.

- **Failure to address both technical and non-technical issues**

    Focusing on non-technical issues alone may obscure the issues of technology. Yet focusing on only the technological issues may result in failing to realize the impact a unified content strategy will have on the organization, its culture, its people, and its political processes. Ensure that you address all the issues, both technical and non-technical.

- **Failure to recognize that analysis and design take time**

  Implementing a unified content strategy and realizing the benefits does not happen overnight. It is important to recognize that time must be spent up front to produce an efficient, flexible, and robust unified information architecture. Departments or business units that recognize the opportunities for a unified content strategy and spend the time to develop an effective one should be rewarded for their efforts.

- **Lack of a champion**

  Starting a unified content strategy at the grass roots of an organization then gradually extending it to address the enterprise may succeed in meeting only the immediate needs. You need a champion to endorse your project and to make sure that different areas understand the need for unified content and buy into it.

- **Biting off more than you can chew**

  Organizations that try to do it all at once may fail due to the complexities of the content, the technology, or the organizational issues. It is more effective to develop in phases. Start with a prototype, implementing in one area, then move into other areas. Implementing in phases provides small-scale successes that allow developers and managers to build the necessary skills and confidence. And it provides you with the opportunity to work out the bugs in a small, controlled environment.

- **Economic needs**

  Different departments or business units may operate as different cost centers. Reusing content could be a disincentive. You may need to develop a new way of identifying the cost of creating and maintaining reusable content that is distributed fairly across the organization.

- **Cataloging too many reusable elements**

  It is hard to catalog (for example, add appropriate metadata) and retrieve reusable content across multiple business units or departments. Authors often find it hard to locate suitable reusable components outside their own areas.

Employing systematic reuse can reduce this issue. Information architects who have a thorough understanding of the entire domain of content can also help through the effective categorization of content (metadata).

- **Lack of core competencies**

  The organization may lack the core competencies necessary to design, create, and integrate reusable components. Implementing a unified content strategy means you should be thinking about content in a new way, and many in your organization may lack the skills or perspective to recognize the opportunities unified content offers.

  Key personnel should receive appropriate training, and where necessary, consider using consulting resources at the beginning of the project to help you get started. Develop the strategy in stages to ensure that appropriate skills are gained and that lessons learned are implemented with the next phase of the project.

- **Lack of communication**

  Lack of communication breeds rumor and resistance. It is important to communicate what is happening, why it is happening, and what is going to happen to ensure that everyone is aware of the project. Change is not as great a shock when information is communicated over time.

- **Failure to involve others**

  Often when teams are assigned, they go off and do their jobs on their own. Their results depend on how clearly they've identified the full scope of the project and its issues. To be successful, they must involve all the parties affected by the issues and the change.

  Perform a thorough analysis to ensure you understand the scope of the issues and goals, invite people to participate in the design and testing process, communicate how you have implemented their suggestions, and employ the people who have assisted in the process and are convinced of the value of the unified content strategy to act as change agents (see "Change management," earlier in this chapter).

- **Using only one type of reuse**

  The most common form of reuse is opportunistic, which results in the lowest incidence of reuse because it puts the responsibility on the authors to decide to reuse content, then find the content they want to reuse. Alternatively, systematic reuse ensures that content is reused and reduces the onus on authors to know that reusable content exists, to find it, and reuse it appropriately. However, authors may perceive systematic reuse as overly restrictive. Using a combination of reuse types provides the greatest results and the most flexibility.

- **Project-by-project reuse**

  Although it is a good idea to start small and work in phases, it is not a good idea to develop a unified content strategy on a project-by-project basis. This can lead to a lack of awareness of how content needs to be structured and modeled for optimum reuse, resulting in a lot of rework later on. You can implement project by project or area to area, but design for the entire scope of the unified content strategy.

- **Selecting the wrong first project**

  Selecting the correct first project to begin your unified content implementation is very important. Picking the wrong one can lead to failure. Don't pick a mission-critical project with a very short deadline, because developing an effective unified content strategy takes time. You need the time to do it properly. You also need the opportunity to make mistakes and learn from them. The pressure to perform quickly may sabotage the development team's desire to do it properly.

  Pick a project that will show return on investment, but is not a "make or break" proposition. You should also pick a project where content already exists, but where it requires a major revision to meet current needs. The changes required for a unified content strategy will be less onerous if the content has to change anyway. Using existing content also enables the analysts and architects to have a "real" rather than abstract example to work with.

- **Reusing everything you can**

  Reusing content for the sake of reusing content or to show high levels of reuse may not be effective. You could compromise the quality and effectiveness of your materials. Reuse content only where appropriate and effective and always ensure that the reuse will not compromise the quality of your materials or make the reusable content difficult to create, find, or manage.

- **No facility for change**

  Some organizations may implement their unified content strategy and then either fail to support ongoing change or discourage change. They do this to ensure the greatest use of the system and most effective implementation of the strategy, but situations change and models, processes, and even technology need to be revised. Ensure that there is open communication between the authors and the business owners to enable your organization to adopt change when required and to respond to unique needs where appropriate.

## Changing roles

Implementing a unified content strategy together with the designated tools requires new roles, a modification to existing roles, and new skill sets. Part of managing change is getting new roles in place and adjusting others to meet the new requirements. Each organization has different requirements, but the following sections cover a few of the commonly required roles.

Two new roles you may need to create in your organization to implement your unified content strategy include enterprise content coordinators and information technologists. In addition, many of the other roles that may already exist within your organization will require modifications; those jobs include business owners and analysts, information architects, authors, content owners, and editors. The following sections provide insight into the kinds of responsibilities expected from each of these roles.

## Enterprise content coordinator (new role)

The traditional role of a project manager is to identify the project requirements, create a plan and schedule to meet these requirements, identify and manage resources, and manage the project from idea to implementation. Typically project managers work within one area of the organization, on one project. As such, they are responsible for and measured against the success of their project and their project alone, and they are therefore likely to veto anything that is not on their critical path. They have not had to take into account the requirements of other projects, nor has it been their responsibility to ensure the success of other projects. Instead, they stay focused on their own project to ensure its success.

In a unified content environment, you need an enterprise content coordinator to work with each of the project managers to ensure that the unified content strategy is being effectively addressed. In particular, the enterprise content coordinator needs to communicate the concepts and advantages of reuse on an ongoing basis to facilitate agreement among project teams.

The enterprise content coordinator must also be able to oversee many projects and determine the unified content strategy required to address both the needs of all the project owners and the needs of the organization as a whole.

The enterprise content coordinator requires a skill set that includes the following:

- A broad-based understanding of business needs
- The ability to determine an effective unified content strategy
- The ability to manage diverse requirements
- Negotiating techniques
- Strong people management skills

## Information technologist (new role)

In a traditional authoring system, many authors are responsible for creating the multiple media output for their content. In a unified content strategy, the system handles this automatically. An information technologist is required to handle the system technology.

An information technologist is skilled at implementing content models in the various tools, including programming and supporting style sheets to meet specifications provided by the information architect.

Information technologists should be well-versed in a wide variety of tools and technologies, including XML. Specifically, they should understand the tools and technologies you choose for your system. The role of the information technologist can be assumed by an existing author or a member of the IT team.

Their skill set includes designing and developing:

- DTDs or other supporting content frameworks
- Authoring and publishing style sheets
- Authoring templates
- Workflow
- Repository design

## Business owners or analysts (modified role)

Business owners or analysts are very important to an effective unified content strategy. They determine the requirements of the business and frequently the customers' needs as well. Their role is to ensure that products, services, and content are designed to effectively meet the customers' needs. However, they must also ensure that any strategies and solutions meet the needs of the employees, the individuals tasked with creating the products, services, and content.

Too often organizations bring in a technological solution to business problems. It is critical that business owners or analysts participate in the effective design of your unified content strategy. Their role is to ensure that content meets the customers' needs and that the unified content strategy meets the authors' needs.

To support a unified content strategy, business owners or analysts should expand their skill set to include:

- A broad-based understanding of business needs
- The ability to determine an effective unified content strategy
- In-depth understanding of customer needs and the ways in which the unified content strategy can support those needs.
- In-depth understanding of the unified content life cycle and the authors' requirements for success

## Information architects (modified role)

Information architects play a key role in analyzing and designing content. They are responsible for building the information product models, element models, metadata, reuse strategies, and architectural models. They may also be responsible for designing the information retrieval for both authors and users. Accordingly, they should have a keen ability to design information for ease of use by content users and ease of reuse by authors.

The role of the information architect can be assumed by an existing author or business analyst; in fact, information architects are becoming more common on web site development teams. Existing web site information architects can expand their role to include the architecture of reuse and content for multiple media. New graduates of information science and library science programs also make good candidates for this role, as do senior technical writers with an extensive background in information design.

Regardless of who assumes the role of information architect, their skill set must expand to include:

- Analysis
  - Analytical problem-solving
  - Information analysis
- Design
  - Information product and element models
  - Metadata
  - User interface
  - Information retrieval
- Standards
  - Usability
  - Information

## Authors (modified role)

Creating materials in a unified content strategy separates the creation of the input (content) from the output (media or information type). This means that authors, as proficient communicators, can now rely less on the tools that are used to display the final information.

Authors no longer have to worry about applying styles or becoming involved in the formatting of the information; now the authoring and delivery systems handle the formatting automatically. Instead, authors can concentrate exclusively on the content they create and combine.

Authors identify the building blocks of information and how the blocks will fit together. They also identify opportunities for content reuse and write applicable content elements for single sourcing. Accordingly, their skill set must expand to include:

- Working in a collaborative environment (see Chapter 19, "Collaborative authoring: Breaking down the silos")
- Creating structured content and writing to models
- Writing reusable content

## Content owners (modified role)

In a traditional authoring environment, authors own the content they create because they are also responsible for creating a specific information product. However, in a unified content strategy, content can be used in many different information products. The concept of the content owner needs to change to accommodate this.

In a unified content strategy, the person who authors the content still owns it; however, that person may not own all the content that comes together to create an information product. There may be many authors, all of whom may not be responsible for creating an entire information product. Rather, they may be responsible for creating content about a certain subject that goes into many different information products.

In addition, the unified content needs an owner, someone who can oversee the creation of all the content related to a particular product, service, product family, or any other associated content set. The unified content owner facilitates the collaborative authoring process and ensures consistency and quality of the materials.

The role of the unified content owner can be assumed by an existing author, a business owner or analyst, or a project manager, reporting to the enterprise content coordinator. The skill set required by the unified content owner includes:

- Information analysis
- Information design
- Ability to determine an effective unified content strategy
- Ability to manage diverse requirements
- Negotiating techniques
- Strong people management skills

## Editors (modified role)

Standards and consistency are important in creating seamless unified materials. In a unified content environment, it is particularly important that editors not just look at the words, but look at how the information is used to ensure it is written effectively for reuse.

To support a unified content strategy, editors must expand their skill set to understand:

- The unified content strategy
- The information product models and element models
- Editorial techniques
- Writing for multiple media, information products, and audiences
- Structured writing techniques

## Summary

Implementing a unified content strategy requires a number of changes in an organization, specifically in how people think about content and the way they create, manage, and deliver content. This kind of change requires a change management plan that includes:

- Identifying the pain, issues, and consequences of continuing to do business the way you currently do and listening to and addressing others' issues
- Communicating on an ongoing basis such things as:
  - Why change needs to happen
  - The plan for implementing the change
  - The ongoing status of the change
  - The successes you have achieved in early implementations
  - The problems you have encountered and how you fixed them or plan to avoid them in the future
- Involving "change agents" (people from the areas being affected by the change) to help you implement the change
- Using a champion to endorse your project
- Overcoming resistance to such things as
  - The "not invented here" and "we do it differently" syndromes
  - Authors' perceived loss of creativity
  - The perception that reuse is good, but too much work
  - The fear of people losing their jobs if more can be accomplished with less
- Understanding why projects fail and addressing issues in advance
- Implementing the following new roles:
  - Enterprise content coordinators
  - Information technologists
- Modifying the following roles:
  - Business owners or analysts
  - Information architects
  - Content owners
  - Authors
  - Editors

# Chapter 22

## Transition plan

The long-term goal of a unified content strategy is to provide for the sharing of consistent content across the organization. However, content silos and disparate technologies can pose challenges to this goal. It may be unrealistic to implement a completely unified strategy from the beginning. However, you can implement your strategy in a modular fashion that can be built upon as you achieve small successes.

This chapter provides guidance on scoping your unified content strategy so that it is not too small, limiting your growth in the future, or too large, potentially making the implementation unmanageable. If you are working with a tight budget, this chapter provides some ideas on how you can implement your unified content strategy at as low a cost as possible. Creating structured content is integral to the success of your unified content strategy, but if you decide not to adopt a structured authoring tool, don't despair: structured writing is still possible and this chapter tells you how. Finally, this chapter explains how to implement your unified content strategy in a phased approach.

## Scoping your unified content strategy

Implementing your unified content strategy in a small controlled way can help you to introduce the concepts and methodologies successfully. It may be appropriate to implement your unified content strategy in one area, or start in one area and expand.

- **Implementing in one area**

  Frequently, implementing a unified content strategy across the enterprise is not possible now or in the future. There may be barriers associated with cost, organizational structure, logistics, or implementing across the organization may not be appropriate for you. If you see an opportunity to implement a unified content strategy in one area, identify the return on investment for that area (see Chapter 3, "Assessing return on investment for a unified content strategy" for details). If you do see the potential in one area but you do not see the potential of taking the strategy across areas or across the enterprise, then do it in that one area. A unified content strategy does not have to be enterprise-wide. It can be just as effective on a very small scale (even as small as a one-person "shop"). The only thing that changes is the size of your technological implementation; your analysis and modeling processes remain the same and the benefits remain the same. However, if you think there might be an opportunity to expand the unified content strategy into other areas of your organization in the future, you should "act small, but think big."

- **Act small, think big**

  If your decision is to focus on a specific area within your department, division, or enterprise, but grow your unified content strategy to other areas in the future, you need to "act small, but think big." Thinking too small can result in a solution that will not meet your ongoing needs. Thinking big means considering the larger needs of the organization so your solution will meet future needs and encompass a broader unified content strategy.

  To ensure your unified content strategy can grow with your organization, conduct a substantive audit –(see the chapters in Part 2, "Performing a substantive audit: Determining business requirements") across the areas that may participate in the future. Without this big picture, you can implement a solution that is too narrowly focused and that will be very costly if you want to adapt it to others' needs. You should also model for future reuse. Take the time to think through how your models will address future opportunities for reuse. Modeling for future reuse doesn't mean you have to model content for all the areas from the beginning, but it does mean that you should model the reusable components.

- **Manage widespread implementation**

  Sometimes the excitement, enthusiasm, and return on investment convince many people in your organization that a unified content strategy should be implemented in multiple areas as soon as possible. This is very exciting, but can also be very problematic. As many IT professionals will tell you, implementing in multiple areas at the same time can result in a number of logistical issues, a resource "crunch," and potential implementation in consistencies that can cause problems in the future. No one wants to wait for new processes and technology that show the potential for improving your business, but moving too quickly can jeopardize the results. If your organization would like to simultaneously implement in multiple areas, the following will help you avoid the most common pitfalls:

- Start with a proof-of-concept and pilot

  A proof-of-concept (small controlled test of the functionality) and pilot (small implementation in one area within the organization) helps your organization test ideas, test multiple technologies, and work through your design and processes in a small, controlled environment. Developing an understanding of what is going to work best for design and implementation will make more rapid implementation possible in other areas. See "A phased approach," later in this chapter, for more information about this topic. Companies and employees can learn by making mistakes in a small contained test such as a proof-of-concept or pilot. A proof-of-concept or a pilot can also help you to delay your tools decision and the full cost of that decision as you test the tools' effectiveness with an evaluation copy in a small implementation (see Chapter 13, "Evaluating tools," for more details).

- Consider using outside resources

  Consider using outside resources to supplement your IT staff or consultants and facilitate the coordination of the analysis and modeling process. Using your resources where it is critical and supplementing where it makes sense can help you to effectively implement a unified content strategy.

- Create a top-level cross-functional team

  A top-level cross-functional team can co-ordinate the information modeling, metadata, workflow, and technological implementation. A cross-functional team will ensure that information is effectively shared across the implementation teams, which is critical for a truly unified content strategy. The cross-functional team requires participants from all the involved areas as well as IT. In addition, the cross-functional team requires a project manager who is accepted by all areas.

- **Implement across the organization**

  Sometimes you may find that you have the opposite problem to the issue of
  everyone wanting to implement at once: you may find it difficult to convince others to adopt a unified content strategy. The best answer to concerns expressed in other areas is proof of the effectiveness in the first area.
  Adopt a unified content strategy in one area. Validate the expected return
  on investment through ongoing collection of metrics (see Chapter 3, for
  details). Share your results to help others understand the benefits that can
  be accrued from a unified content strategy.

# Structure without structured authoring tools

Structure is an integral part of a successful unified content strategy. Structure
provides consistency between materials, making reuse transparent to the reader
and improving readability. However, your organization may not want to change
your current authoring tool for a structured authoring tool, because of either
costs or existing technology standards. The use of models and structured writing
principles can be adopted without unstructured editors. It is more difficult to
enforce structure without a structured editor, but it can be encouraged with a
detailed authoring style guide.

A structured editor guides authors through the models by presenting appropriate tags; an unstructured editor does not do this. In the case of an unstructured
editor, you need to formalize the structure of your models in a style guide. A
style guide typically includes the following elements:

- **Semantic model**

  To implement structure without a structured editor, you need a semantic
  model as described in Chapter 8, "Information modeling." The process of
  modeling remains the same whether you use a structured editor or not.

- **Base elements**

  As described in Chapter 8, base elements guide authors in selecting the correct tag for the model. A structured editor automatically presents authors with the next appropriate element to use, and restricts the number of elements that can be selected based on the container element selected. However, in a traditional authoring tool this type of feature is not available. The result is that you have to use a large number of semantic tags, which results in large volumes of style tags. It can be an onerous task for authors to select the appropriate tag from a large list. Therefore, you should still have a semantic model that tells your authors what they need to put into the content, but you also need to tell them which non-semantic style tag (base element) to use in their editor.

- **Reuse map**

  The reuse maps identify where content can—and should—be reused in your information set. Using these maps, authors can determine whether a reusable element is likely to exist and whether the elements they are writing are likely to be reused elsewhere.

- **Writing guidelines**

  No matter how clear the model, you should always include writing guidelines to assist authors in understanding what they should create. Provide any tips or rules about how to write an element.

- **Example**

  Always provide a sample of completed content that uses the model. The sample should be a "best practices" example that illustrates how the desired content should be written.

## Working with a limited budget

Budgets are always more limited than required. Even if your return on investment (ROI) indicates considerable cost savings that would outweigh the costs, the cost of a unified content strategy may still be difficult to justify. If you are working with a limited budget, you can still do a number of things to implement a unified content strategy, or to position yourself to adopt a unified content strategy in the future. Here are a few guidelines for working with a limited budget:

- **Adopt structured writing.**

  Regardless of whether you can afford new technology or are ready to adopt a unified content strategy, you should adopt structured writing principles as identified in Chapter 20, "Separating content from format." Moving your organization toward structured writing principles will improve the quality of your materials and position them for reuse.

- **Write to models.**

  Go beyond just structured writing and adopt information models for your materials. See "Structure without structured authoring tools," earlier in this chapter, for information about this task.

- **Adopt an authoring tool that supports reuse with or without the addition of a content management system.**

  Some authoring tools provide the functionality to reuse content with or without a content management system. This functionality is provided through features such as conditions or user profiles that enable you to "mark" text to be shown or hidden in specified circumstances. Also look for functionality that lets you import text by reference. Text by reference "points" or links to external content, so you don't have to cut and paste it into your document. Using text by reference means that when the imported element is changed, it will be updated the next time a document that uses the imported element is opened for editing. Refer to the accompanying web site for authoring tools that support these features.

- **Investigate low-cost content management options**

  Sometimes the cost of the content management system is the most daunting financial hurdle to overcome. Vendors know this and are starting to become quite creative in their offerings. Some offer an ASP service (hosting a web-enabled, secured version of their product), others offer a lease-to-own system, and yet others offer modular versions of their product so you can get started at a reasonable price and purchase additional modules when you need the additional functionality. See the accompanying web site for details on some of these vendors.

If you can't bring in a content management system initially, consider creating a database to store your content or adopting a source code management tool. The software industry has been managing code in this way for years. These tools are fairly reasonable in price and although they don't offer the same functionality of a content management system and are not document "intelligent" (they don't understand the structure of content), they do provide check out/check in and version control, which are the rudiments of content management.

If source code management software is not an option, build yourself a really good tracking spreadsheet and develop some strict guidelines for content reuse and storage. You'll need to reinforce these guidelines on an ongoing basis to enforce them.

## A phased approach

The best way to implement any new methodology or technology is through a phased approach. Implementing in phases ensures that you incrementally design, test, and implement in a controlled fashion. You can get the "bugs" out of the implementation on a small scale before implementing on a large scale. To implement in phases:

- **Conduct a proof-of-concept.**

  A proof-of-concept tests design decisions and tools. It is a very small test used to make sure that you can address some of the issues identified in the substantive audit, and to test the tools. Talk to the tools vendors to get an evaluation copy of their product for use in the proof-of-concept. An evaluation copy can be "free" or provided for a limited time period at a low cost. It is an excellent way to "try before you buy." For more information about conducting a proof-of-concept, refer to Chapter 13.

- **Conduct a usability test.**

  A usability test verifies the usability (effectiveness) of your processes and technology. It is imperative to conduct usability testing before the pilot or full implementation. During a usability test, users with different roles (for example, authors and reviewers) test the processes and technology to identify any problems so they can be addressed before widespread implementation. After implementation, problems have a much larger impact, so it's best to catch them first. The value of usability testing has been validated in numerous other areas of design, such as web design and software design; your unified content strategy can be significantly improved by usability testing too.

Usability testing involves testing representative tasks in as real-life a scenario as possible. Multiple users should participate in the usability test to ensure you get a good representative sample of results. Modify your implementation based on the results of the usability test.

- **Conduct a pilot.**

  To create a pilot, you select the group, department, or area where you plan to roll out a scaled-down version of the solution. A pilot allows for thorough testing of the unified content strategy processes and infrastructure.

  A pilot is conducted over a period of weeks or months. Participants perform their tasks using the new system. They must be working on real content for real projects with real deadlines. In the beginning a pilot can be disruptive as people get up to speed with new ways of doing things, but eventually this disruption will disappear as long as your implementation is working effectively.

  Monitor the pilot to gather information and provide support throughout; ensure that participants have the help they need with questions and implementation problems. For more information about conducting a pilot, refer to Appendix A, "Checklist for implementing a unified cntent strategy."

- **Roll out to one or many departments.**

  After you have thoroughly tested your processes, design, and technology, you are ready to start rolling out your implementation to other departments. You can choose to roll out to departments successively or concurrently. Remember that departments or areas need a lot of design work to complete their models, metadata, and workflows, even though the system configurations should be similar.

## Summary

A successful unified content strategy requires an effective transition plan to guide you through implementation in a phased approach. Begin by determining the scope of your project. If it makes sense to implement in one area only then do so, but if you plan to eventually implement your strategy across the organization, conduct a substantive audit for all concerned areas. However, if you plan to implement in only one area at first and then implement in additional areas, ensure that you design for reuse across the areas.

If you do not plan to implement with a structured authoring tool, create a detailed style guide for your authors that provides:

- Semantic models to clearly identify how to create elements
- Base element guidelines to guide authors in selecting the appropriate style tags
- Reuse maps to clearly identify where content should be reused and to help authors identify whether a reusable element should exist
- Writing guidelines to help authors understand how to create content
- Examples to illustrate "best practices" content

If you are working with a limited budget, investigate vendors who provide options such as ASP services, lease-to-own systems, or modular components. You can also consider using source code control software to provide rudimentary content management, such as check-in and check-out and version control. At a minimum, implement processes that tell people how to track and reuse content. Even if you don't use a content management system, consider using an authoring tool that supports reuse.

Implement your unified content strategy in a phased approach by:

- Conducting a proof-of-concept
- Conducting a usability test
- Conducting a pilot
- Implementing your unified content strategy in a single area and then progressively to other areas or concurrently to multiple areas after you have conducted a thorough proof-of-concept, usability test, and pilot to ensure that your decisions and design are appropriate

# *Part VI*

## Resources

# Glossary

**Access control**—Secures content and identifies who can read, create, modify, and delete content.

**Access permissions**—Access authorization permitting authors and editors, reviewers, and users the right to create, edit, and view content.

**Architectural information**—A component of an information model; provides information on how content should be reused (for example, systematic), guidelines for how you want the content formalized in your DTD or templates (for example, use semantic tags or not), where content is reused, and how it is reused, for example, locked (L) or derivative (D).

**Attribute**—See *Metadata*.

**Audit**—See *Content Audit*

**Author**—A creator of content. Authors identify the building blocks of information and how the blocks will fit together. They also identify opportunities for content reuse and write applicable content elements for reuse.

**Authoring forms**—HTML forms with individual fields to capture content model elements. The is used to write only a controlled chunk of content, such as a concept, feature, policy, or procedure.

**Authoring tool**—A tool that enables authors (content creators) to create content.

**Auto-population**—Automatic insertion of reusable content into the appropriate locations in the document. See also *Systematic reuse.*

**Base information**—A component of an information model; describes the common naming of each element within a container and uses generic tags or "base elements".

**Baseline**—A starting point for developing metrics.

**Building block approach**—Allows you to identify a core of information that is applicable for all information products or users, then build on it to customize information for different uses and users

**Bursting**—See *Segmentation.*

**Categorization metadata—**
Organizes content into logical categories (groupings) of content that aid in the retrieval of content. Categorization is utilized by content users to retrieve content.

**Change agent—**An individual recruited prior to implementation of a change; must be representative of the user population, understand the reasoning behind the change, and help to communicate the excitement, possibilities, and details of the change to others within the organization.

**Change management—**Managing the process of implementing major changes in IT, business processes, organizational structures, and job assignments to reduce the risks and costs of change, and to optimize its benefits. Change management is focused on the issues of managing the resistance and discomfort experienced by people in an organization when new processes or technology is introduced.

**Check-in—**Act of putting content previously checked out of a content management system back into the content management system. Content is versioned when it is checked back in.

**Check-out—**Act of signing out content from the content management system. When content is checked out, no one else can modify that content; it is locked.

**Chunk—**An element of information, sized according to principles of cognitive psychology; the ideal size of a chunk (for users to comprehend and retain) is 5 to 9 units of information, for example, 9 steps instead of 32.

**Collaborative authoring—**The process of collaborating on content creation to ensure that content elements are consistent and can be reused wherever they're required. See also *Structured writing*.

**Container element—**A content element that contains other elements (sub-elements) within it. There can also be containers within containers. See also *Element* and *Sub-element*.

**Content—**Content is what authors create (words, phrases, sentences, charts, graphs). Information products are made up of content. See also *Dynamic content*.

**Content audit**—An accounting of the information in your organization. Requires analyzing representative materials, looking for similar/identical information, as well as information that is distinct but can be similar or identical.

**Content life cycle**—The various phases that content moves through, such as creation, review, management, and delivery.

**Content management**—A system or the capability to manage and track the location of, and relationships among, a firm's content at an element level in a repository.

High-end content management systems apply workflows, and enable the use and reuse of content and content collections.

Content management systems can manage entire binary files (documents), components of files, or XML/SGML data.

**Content owner**—The person who authors the content. However, the content owner may not own all the content that comes together to create an information product. There may be many authors, none of whom is responsible for creating an entire information product. Rather, each author may be responsible for creating content about a certain subject that goes into many different information products.

**Content reuse**—Writing content once and reusing it many times; reusable content is written as objects or elements. See also *Reusable content* and *Reuse.*

**Content Silo Trap**—A situation created by authors working in isolation from other authors within the organization. Walls are erected among content areas and even within content areas, which leads to content being created, and re-created, and re-created, often with changes or differences at each iteration.

**Controlled vocabulary**—A list of metadata terms in which each concept or subject has a specific term to be used. A controlled vocabulary reconciles all the various possible words that can be used to identify content and differentiates among all the possible meanings that can be attached to content.

**Core information**—In a building block approach, information that is applicable for all uses. See also *Building block approach.*

**Customer Relationship Management (CRM)**—Tracking and acting upon everything you need to know about your customers, including their buying history, budget, timeline, areas of interest, and their future requirements. Ensuring that customers have exactly the right information at exactly the right time and in exactly the right form.

**Customization**—The design and creation of content that meets a customer's specific needs. Customized content is not delivered dynamically (as with personalization, for example); it is created by an author for a specific requirement and is static until changed.

**Delivery**—The automatic assembly, formatting, and delivery of content to your user community, whenever and however they need it, using a delivery system.

**Derivative reuse**—Derivative reuse occurs when a reusable element is modified. The resulting element is a "child" of a "parent" element.

**Document type definition (DTD)**—A DTD is the form of document definition used to support and effectively describe XML file structures, providing the vocabulary and allowable structure of the elements in an XML document. See also *Extensible Markup Language (XML)*.

**DTD**—See *Document Type Definition*.

**Dynamic content**—Content that is assembled to meet users' specific needs, providing them with exactly what they are looking for, when they are looking for it, and in the format they need.

**Element**—A unique, discrete module of information. An element is an information container (for example, Summary, Procedure); container elements can contain other elements. In a content reuse environment, documents are made up of elements. Elements may be as granular as required to support your reuse strategy. For example, an element may contain one chunk or a portion of one chunk, but it may also contain numerous chunks. See also *Chunk* and *Granularity*.

**Element metadata**—Identifies content at the element level. Element metadata is used by content authors to identify content for reuse, retrieval, and tracking.

**Enterprise project coordinator**—Role of an individual in the organization who oversees many projects and determines the unified content strategy required to address both the needs of all the project owners and the needs of the organization as a whole.

**Extensible Markup Language (XML)**—XML is a markup language for documents containing structured information.

XML is a successor technology to the markup language SGML, which authors use to prepare content in small chunks, or elements. These elements can then be mixed and matched when the content is displayed online.

XML is a data format for structured document interchange that is more flexible than HTML. Whereas HTML tags are predefined, XML tags can be defined by the content type designer. Thus, XML-defined web pages can function like database records.

A metalanguage, XML contains a set of rules that expand the amount and kinds of information that can be provided about the data held in documents. XML is a subset or restricted form of SGML, the Standard Generalized Markup Language. A goal of XML is to enable generic SGML to be served, received, and processed on the Web in the way that is now possible with HTML. XML has been designed for ease of implementation and for interoperability with both SGML and HTML.

**Extensible Stylesheet Language (XSL)**—A language used to create style sheets for XML, similar to Cascading Style Sheets (CSSs) that are used for HTML. In XML, content and presentation are separate. XML tags do not indicate how they should be displayed.

An XML document has to be formatted before it can be read, and the formatting is usually accomplished with style sheets. Style sheets consist of formatting rules for how particular XML tags affect a document's display on a computer screen or a printed page.

In XML, different style sheets can be applied to the same data to hide or display different parts of a document for different users.

**Forms**—See *Authoring forms.*

**Generalized Markup Language (GML)**—Developed in 1969 by Charles Goldfarb; focused on the structure of a document, not the formatting, and was the first text processing language to view and formalize the hierarchical nature of information. It was also the first language to define the hierarchy of documents in a Document Type Definition (DTD). GML was implemented in mainframe-based text processing systems.

**Generated text**—Text that is not supplied by authors but that the structure generates or mandates. Examples are the numbers in a numbered list, numbers in headings, numbers in numbered tables or figures. Also, labels or keywords that are required for presentation, but are not authored. Examples are "Note," "Caution," "Warning."

**GML**—See *Generalized Markup Language*.

**Granularity**—Granularity refers to the smallest element of information that is reusable. See also *Element* and *Physical granularity*.

**HTML**—See *Hypertext Markup Language*.

**Hyperlink**—An electronic path from one object to another.

**Hypertext**—Any text that contains links to another object—words, phrases or images—that, when clicked by the user, retrieves and displays the linked object.

**Hypertext Markup Language (HTML)**—Created in the early 90s by Tim Berners-Lee at CERN (the European Laboratory for Particle Physics) as a way for scientists to share information. HTML is the best-known application of SGML for the Web.

**In-depth analysis**—Part of a content audit; involves examining common information found in the top-level analysis further to see how or whether it can be reused. See also *Content audit* and *Top-level analysis*.

**Information architect**—Role of an individual in the organization who analyzes and designs content. They are responsible for building the information product models, element models, metadata, reuse strategies, and architectural models. They may also be responsible for designing the information retrieval for both authors and users.

**Information architecture**—The blueprint that describes how content is organized, structured, and reused to make up the various information products in your organization.

**Information element model**—Breaks down an information product model down; describes each element within an information product model. See also *Element*.

**Information model**—A formalized framework on which a reuse strategy is based. See also *Information product model* and *Information element model*.

**Information product**—A collection of content that is processed as a unit. Consists of a series of elements in a defined order and structure. Examples include user guides, brochures, press releases, web site content, and technical specifications.

**Information product model**— Defines all the elements that make up an information product, including the content's elements, attributes, and metadata, and the relationship among elements.

An information product model provides a formal description of the structure of a document; it may also provide some content information.

**Information technologist**—Role of an individual in the organization who implements content models in the various tools, including programming and supporting style sheets to meet specifications that the information architect provides.

**Lifespan (of a document)**— The time before a document needs to be changed.

**Locked reuse**—Locked reuse is reusable content that cannot be changed except by an authorized author.

**Mandatory elements**—Elements are specified in an information model as either mandatory or optional; mandatory elements are those that must be included for an information product to be considered complete. See also *Optional elements.*

**Markup language** —A mechanism to identify structures in a document. See also *Hypertext Markup Language (HTML), Standard Generalized Markup Language (SGML),* and *Extensible Markup Language (XML).*

**Metadata**—Data that describes other data. Metadata is often referred to as an attribute. Metadata is the encoded knowledge of your organization.

Metadata includes descriptive terms attached to an object (element) that allow for additional information about the element and accurate indexing and querying of the element.

XML elements are indexed by metadata that is described in the DTD or in the XML document itself, enabling other applications to interact with it.

**Metadata crosswalk**—Maps the structure and semantics of one set of metadata to the structure and semantics of another set of metadata. Usually a table is used to map one set of metadata to the other.

**Metric**—Measurement of a particular characteristic of a task (for example, duration, effort, quality, cost, value delivered, or customer satisfaction).

**Modular content**—See *Reusable content.*

**Modular style sheet**—Style sheets that are built in layers so that layers that are common across multiple style sheets can be shared.

**Module**—A collection of functions or data implementing one idea or concept.

**Nested reuse**—Nested reuse is content that has a number of reusable elements contained within a single element.

**Opportunistic reuse**—Reuse occurs when the author makes a conscious decision to find an element, retrieve the element, and reuse it.

**Opportunity cost**—The amount of money lost if an opportunity (such as quick time-to-market) is not achieved. Opportunity cost is usually calculated based on the potential amount of money lost for each day an opportunity is delayed.

**Optional elements**—Elements are specified in an information model as either mandatory or optional; optional elements are those that authors can choose to use, based on the information's context. See also *Mandatory elements.*

**PDF**—See *Portable Document Format (PDF).*

**Persona**—A profile of a typical user represented with a description of a "real" individual.

**Personalization**—Delivery of personalized content (content that specifically meets the content users' needs). Uses dynamic content to automatically assemble appropriate content. Learns from content user actions and requests, and predicts the user's content requirements.

**Physical granularity**—The physical chunk of information stored in the CMS, as opposed to the size of a reusable element (granularity).

**Players**—Everyone involved in the content life cycle, such as users, authors, reviewers, publication staff, Information Technology staff.

**Portable Document Format (PDF)**—A cross-platform file format developed by Adobe Systems, Inc. PDF documents are created with Adobe Acrobat software and the PostScript language.

**Portal**—Special web page that organizes access to all online resources about a topic, providing a one-stop shop of sorts.

**PostScript**—A page description language from Adobe Systems, Inc. PostScript translates the text and graphic images that appear on the computer screen into instructions for the printer. PostScript must be used with a printer that can interpret it.

**Process**—Part of workflow; the flow of tasks, as performed by the various players, showing the interactions and interdependencies among players. See also *Workflow* and *Task*.

**Production information**—A component of an information model; guides the information technologist in creating the style sheets or templates.

**Publishing**—The process of rendering, or outputting, files from the content management system into the required output format (for example, PDF, HTML).

**Return on investment (ROI)**—The anticipated savings that can result after the cost of implementing a unified content strategy is subtracted. ROI is used to help determine whether the adoption of new technology, systems, and processes will be worthwhile.

**Reusable content**—Self-contained components of content that can be used in combination with other components.

**Reusable learning object**—An element of reusable content intended for learning materials.

**Reuse**—Content reuse is the practice of using existing components of content to develop new "documents"; the process of linking to an element of reusable content. See also *Reusable content*.

**Reuse map**—Identifies which elements are reusable, where they are reusable, and how they should be reused (for example, identically, derivatively).

**Rich Text Format (RTF)**—A way of formatting text designed by Microsoft, and intended as a universal standard for exchanging documents between different programs. Special symbols indicate such characteristics as bold, italic, the formatting of paragraphs, and so on. Microsoft Word files can be saved in Rich Text Format.

**RLO**—See *Reusable Learning Object*.

**Roles**—Part of workflow; the people who do the tasks, identified by their role. See also *Workflow* and *Task*.

**RTF**—See *Rich Text Format (RTF)*.

**Schema**—A defined structure for a document or type of document. Sometimes used synonymously with Document Type Definition (DTD).

**SCORM**—See *Shareable Content Object Reference Modelm(SCORM)*.

**Segmentation**—The process of breaking content into element parts before storing the content in a content management system.

**Semantic information**—A component of an information model; uniquely identifies the content of that element, making it easy for authors to identify exactly what content they should include. Semantic information also enables the identification and reuse of specific content.

**SGML**—See *Standard Generalized Markup Language (SGML)*.

**Shareable Content Object Reference Model (SCORM)**—A model for sharing learning objects; developed by the ADL (Advanced Distributed Learning) network to provide a standard for reusing learning objects.

**Single-sourcing**—Activity of identifying all information requirements for a particular document set up front, then developing them from a single source. Single-sourcing can include multi-channel publishing (publishing to multiple outputs), as well as publishing to multiple information products (for example, brochure, manual, learning product).

**Smart template**—A template that not only prompts the author for the type of information required, but also automatically inserts reusable content.

**Standard**—A rule, principle, or measure established as a model or example by authority, custom, or general consent. In the computer industry, standards are rules that encourage open systems and provide the basis for portability, interoperability, and manageability.

**Standard Generalized Markup Language (SGML)**—"A language for document representation that formalizes markup and frees it of system and processing dependencies" (ISO 8879 4.305).

SGML is the parent language for XML and HTML.

**Static content**—Information created in a specific way for a specific purpose and that remains the same until the author deliberately changes it.

**Structural templates**—Templates that clearly define the structural composition of output products. They can include hierarchical elements such as chapters, sections, and subsections, as well as provide generic or required text.

**Structure**—Organized framework of information.

**Structured content**—Content in which the organizational hierarchy of information has been identified in a systematic, consistent manner.

**Structured writing**—The practice of writing content following structured writing guidelines, so that information can be effectively reused and still fit the "style" of each document. Authors write to the content models, using document definitions to guide them in creating elements consistently.

Following a method of structured writing means that all contributors to a document have a standard template (or outline) to follow when providing, writing, and editing information. This approach also assists readers in finding similar types of information and in interpreting it consistently.

**Style sheet**—Structured, controlled content needs to be formatted before it can be read, and the formatting is usually accomplished with style sheets. Style sheets consist of formatting rules for how particular semantic tags affect the display of a document on a computer screen or a printed page. See also *Modular style sheet* and *XSL style sheet*.

**Sub-element**—A smaller component of information contained within an element. See also *Container element* and *Element*.

**Swimlane diagrams**—A diagram that shows processes in "lanes" (like the lanes in which you swim laps) to depict tasks that occur concurrently, illustrating who does what, and when. Used to design workflow. See also *Workflow*.

**Systematic reuse**—Systematic reuse is automatic reuse. Reuse is planned before authoring begins. Systematic reuse uses dynamic content functionality to dynamically assemble content to meet content authors' needs.

**Tag**—A code within a data structure that identifies content elements, or otherwise provides information about the data. Content is either labeled with a single tag or delimited by starting and ending tags.

In HTML, tags serve various functions, such as controlling the styling of text and placement of graphic elements and providing links to interactive programs and scripts. In XML and SGML, tags are limited to defining content and semantic structure.

**Tagged PDF**—PDF files that are enhanced with the addition of metadata. Adobe Acrobat Reader interprets the metadata to repaginate the display of content based on the device on which the content is being displayed (for example, Palm OS devices, the Web, or print).

**Task**—A unit of work within a workflow. Workflows are composed of multiple tasks, which can be executed serially, in parallel, or on a conditional basis.

Examples of tasks include creation and editing of a variety of content types, approval of a set of modified content, automatic link-checking of content, automatic e-mail reminders, and publishing. See also *Workflow*.

**Taxonomy**—A type of hierarchical representation of your metadata in which every element within the structure can exist in only one location within the structure; no ambiguity of placement, no cross-references. The top level is the category, and each subsequent level provides a refinement (detail) of the top-level term.

**Template**—A collection of boiler-plate text, tags, and structure rules, used as a guide or pattern for a document. May also provide examples of well-written content (best practices).

**Time-to-market**—The time it takes an organization to get its product from conception through implementation and delivery to the customer.

**TOC**—Table of contents.

**Top-level analysis**—Part of a content audit; involves scanning representative information products to find common information. See also *Content audit* and *In-depth analysis*.

**Unified content strategy**—A repeatable method of identifying all content requirements up front, creating consistently structured content for reuse, managing that content in a definitive source, and assembling content on demand to meet your customers' needs.

**Valid**—In the context of XML, *valid* refers to information elements in a document that are allowable, based on the structure that the DTD has defined.

**Variables**—Values that can be assigned names and used by reference to the name. Variables are an excellent mechanism for using small elements of content (such as product names or versions) that are used in large numbers of places and that are subject to frequent or last-minute change.

**Version control**—Each time content is changed and checked back into a content management system, a copy of the content is saved and its identifier (version number) is incremented to indicate its difference from the previous copy.

**Workflow**—A set of interdependent tasks that occur in a specific sequence. Examples of workflow include automated routing of content for authoring, review, approval, and publishing, from one department or individual to another, or to the system itself for the execution of automated tasks.

Components of workflow are roles, responsibilities (tasks), and processes.

**XML**—See *Extensible Markup Language (XML)*.

**XSL**—See *Extensible Stylesheet Language (XSL)*.

**XSL style sheet**—A style sheet written using the eXtensible Stylesheet Language, which is an XML markup language that can define transformations from one markup language to another, as well as standard formatting (fonts, colors, margins, and so on).

# Bibliography

"A Manager's Introduction to Adobe eXtensible Metadata Platform, The Adobe XML Metadata Framework." Retrieved from `http://www.adobe.com/products/xmp/pdfs/whitepaper.pdf` on May 31, 2002.

"How Much Information." Retrieved from `http://www.sims.berkeley.edu/how-much-info` on April 24, 2002.

"Information mapping, structured writing information." Available from `http://www.infomap.com`.

Albers, Michael and Kim, Loel. "Information Design for the Small-Screen Interface: An Overview of Web Design Issues for Personal Digital Assistants." *Technical Communication*, vol. 49, no. 1. February 2002.

Baca, Murtha Editor. "Introduction to Metadata: Pathways to Digital Information." Retrieved from `http://www.getty.edu/research/institute/standards/intrometadata/index.html` on February 13, 2002.

Beer, Valorie. *The Web Learning Fieldbook: Using the World Wide Web to Build Workplace Learning Environments*. Jossey-Bass/Pfeiffer, 2000.

Blicq, Ron S. *Guidelines for Report Writing*. second edition. Prentice-Hall, 1990.

Boiko, Bob. *Content Management Bible*. Hungry Minds, 2002.

Boumphrey, Frank; Direnzo, Olivia; Duckett, Jon; Graf, Joe; Hollander, Dave; Houle, Paul; Jenkins, Trevor; Jones, Peter; Kingsley-Hughes, Kathy; McQueen, Craig; and Mohr, Stephen. *XML Applications*. Wrox Press Ltd., 1998.

Burk, Lisa and Jean Richardson. "Conflict Management in Software Development Environments." Available from `http://www.bjrcom.com`.

Clark, Ruth Colvin. "Four Architectures of Instruction." *Performance Improvement*, vol. 39, no. 10. November/December 2000.

Cleveland, Donald B. and Cleveland, Ana D. *Introduction to Indexing and Abstracting.* Englewood, Colorado: Libraries Unlimited, Inc., 2001.

Collins, Heidi. *Corporate Portals.* New York: American Management Association, 2001.

Davenport, Thomas H. and Beck, John C. *The Attention Economy: Understanding the New Currency of Business.* Boston: Harvard Business School Press, 2001.

DoD Software Reuse Initiative, "Software Reuse Executive Primer." April 15, 1996. Retrieved from `http://dii-sw.ncr.disa.mil/reusic/pol-hist/primer/` on January 1, 2002.

Duck, Jeanie Daniel. *The Change Monster.* New York: Crown Business, 2001.

Fayad, Mohamed and Laitinen, Mauri. *Transition to Object-Oriented Software Development.* John Wiley & Sons, 1998.

Flottemesch, Kim. "Building Effective Interaction in Distance Education: A Review of the Literature". *Education Technology*, May/June 2000.

Fung, Khun Yee. *XSLT: Working with XML and HTML.* Addison Wesley, 2001.

Glaze, Geoff. "Personas," October 18, 1999. Retrieved from `http://www.cs.utexas.edu/users/almstrum/cs373/general/personas.html` on May 1, 2002.

Goldfarb, Charles F. and Prescod, Paul. *The XML Handbook, Third Edition.* Prentice Hall, Inc., 2001.

Goodwin, Kim. "Perfecting Your Personas", *Newsletter Cooper Interaction Design,* July/August 2001. Retrieved from `http://www.cooper.com/newsletters/2001_07/perfecting_your_personas.htm` on May 1, 2002.

Graham, Ian S. *HTML Stylesheet Sourcebook.* John Wiley and Sons, 1997.

Hackos, JoAnn T, and Janice C Redish. *User and Task Analysis for Interface Design.* John Wiley and Sons, Inc., 1998.

Hackos, JoAnn T., and Dawn M. Stevens. *Standards for Online Communication.* Wiley, 1997.

Hayhoe, George. "From Desktop to Palmtop: Creating Usable Online Documents for Wireless and Handheld Devices." In International Professional Communication Conference 2001 Proceedings.

Instone, Keith. "Information Architecture and Personalization," 2000. Retrieved from `http://argus-acia.com/white_papers/personalization.pdf` on Jan. 22, 2002.

Maler, Eve and El Andaloussi, Jeanne. *Developing SGML DTDs, From Text to Markup.* Prentice Hall, Inc., 1996.

Marchand, Donald, editor. "Competing with Information". West Sussex, England: John Wiley & Sons Ltd., 2000.

Marco, David. *Building and Managing the Meta Data Repository: A Full Lifecycle Guide.* New York: Wiley Computer Publishing, 2000.

Marsh, C. Hugh and Eric C. Morris. "Corporate Memory and Technical Communicators: A Relationship with a New Urgency." In International Professional Communication Conference 2001 Proceedings.

Myers, Kenneth L. "Is There a Place for Instructional Design in the Information Age?" *Educational Technology,* November/December, 1999.

Nakano, Russell. *Web Content Management: A Collaborative Approach.* Addison-Wesley, 2002.

Nielson, Jakob. *Designing Web Usability.* New Riders Publishing, 2000.

Perfetti, Christine. "Personas: Matching a Design to the Users' Goals." Retrieved from `http://world.std.com/~uieweb/Articles/Personas.htm`.

Pfaffenberger, Bryan. *Web Publishing with XML in 6 Easy Steps.* Academic Press, 1999.

Rockley, Ann. "Information Modeling for Single Sourcing" in *Content and Complexity: The Role of Content in Information Design.* Michael J. Albert Beth, Mazur, editors. Lawrence Erlbaum Assoc., ISBN 0805841407 (July 2002)

Russell, John. "Discovering the Information Model." In International Professional Communication Conference 2001 Proceedings.

Sharp, Alec and Patrick McDermott. *Workflow Modeling: Tools for Process Improvement and Application Development.* Boston: Artech House, 2001.

Tannenbaum, Adrienne. *Metadata Solutions.* Upper Saddle River, NJ: Addison-Wesley, 2002.

Taylor, Arlene G. *The Organization of Information.* Englewood, Colorado: Libraries Unlimited, Inc. 1999.

Tessmer, Martin and Rita C. Richey. "The Role of Context in Learning and Instructional Design". *Educational Technology Research & Development,* vol. 45, no. 2, 1997.

Tozer, Guy. *Metadata Management for Information Control and Business Success.* Norwood, MA: Artech House, 1999.

# Appendix A

## Checklist for implementing a unified content strategy

Throughout the book, we have described the various phases of implementing a unified content strategy, starting from analysis and working through to selecting tools and managing the change. This appendix provides a checklist for implementing a unified content strategy. Some portions of the checklist apply to processes that are unique to a unified content strategy and refer to the chapters in the book where you can find more information. We've also included some processes (such as usability testing) that are common to many implementation projects and should be part of your unified content implementation. However, because these processes are not explained in the book, there are no references to chapters where you can read up on them further. You can find additional references in the bibliography.

## Phase 1—Analysis

Starting with a thorough analysis is key to a successful unified content strategy. Thorough analysis ensures that your strategy addresses your organization's specific needs and goals.

The analysis phase has four stages, as described in Table A.1.

**Table A.1    Analysis**

| Stages: What's involved | Tasks: What to do | Deliverables | Refer to... |
|---|---|---|---|
| Identify the "pain" in your organization. | Ask the following questions:<br>• What are the top three dangers your organization is facing or will face if you don't meet your goals?<br><br>• What are the top three opportunities are you hope to take advantage of?<br><br>• What are your organization's greatest strengths?<br><br>• What are your organization's goals for the next year?<br><br>• What are the challenges your organization must overcome to meet those goals? | Analysis report | Chapter 4, "Where does it really hurt?" |
| Analyze the content creation life cycle. | Identify your current content life cycle.<br><br>Identify who does what within that life cycle; learn what their issues are. | Analysis report | Chapter 5, "Analyzing the content life cycle" |
| Conduct a content audit. | Examine the content in your organization to determine how it's used and how it can be reused<br><br>Establish the scope of the audit.<br><br>Select representative samples of content. | Analysis report | Chapter 6, "Performing a content audit" |

*continues* ▶

**Table A.1    Continued**

| Stages: What's involved | Tasks: What to do | Deliverables | Refer to... |
|---|---|---|---|
| | Conduct a top-level analysis of samples, looking for structural similarities that indicate where to analyze further. | | |
| | Look at selected samples closely, making observations about how content is used and how it can be reused. | | |
| | Create a reuse map, illustrating potential content reuse and the type of reuse. | | |
| Formulate your vision for a new, unified content life cycle. | The new content life cycle is based on the issues you identified in the first three stages: identify pain, analyze content life cycle, and conduct content audit to form the basis for implementing the unified content strategy. | Recommendations report | Chapter 7, "Envisioning your unified content life cycle" |
| | Identify how to address issues. | | |
| | Document a new life cycle, addressing each phase of the life cycle, such as create, review, manage, and deliver. | | |

# Phase 2—Design

Design is one of the most critical phases of implementing a unified content strategy. During the design phase, you figure out how you will address the issues you discovered during your analyses—how you will realize your vision for a new content life cycle. You design information models that specify how information will be used and reused; you define metadata to ensure that every element of content can be tracked, retrieved, and reused; you design dynamic content to suit users' unique needs; you design workflow to ensure that content moves through the content life cycle; and you plan the change management processes (including security) you'll need to help the changes take place.

The design phase has six stages, as shown in Table A.2:

**Table A.2 Design**

| Stages: What's involved | Tasks: What to do | Deliverables | Refer to… |
|---|---|---|---|
| Create information models. | Identify all possible uses for the information. | An information model spreadsheet that outlines the elements for each information product and indicates how each element is structured and reused. The spreadsheet also includes the metadata for each element. | Chapter 8, "Information modeling" |
| | Identify the level of reuse required. | | |
| | Create detailed audience profiles including their objectives for the information. | | |
| | Determine the granularity of the information. | | |
| | Identify the structure of the information product, showing how all the elements fit together. | | |
| | Build models for each information product and each information element within the product. | | |
| Define metadata. | Identify and evaluate industry metadata standards. | The metadata specification. | Chapter 9, "Designing metadata" |
| | Define your taxonomy and controlled vocabulary. | | |
| | Define your metadata for reuse. | | |
| | Define your metadata for retrieval. | | |
| | Define your metadata for tracking. | | |

| Stages:<br>What's involved | Tasks: What to do | Deliverables | Refer to... |
|---|---|---|---|
| Design dynamic content (if appropriate). | Create personas for your key customer types. | Revised information model spreadsheet. | Chapter 10, "Designing dynamic content" |
| | Design metadata and user profiles. | User personas. | |
| | Identify dynamic elements in models. | Business rules. | |
| | Define rules for the assembly of dynamic content. | | |
| Design workflow. | Select start and end points for all the tasks within your content life cycle. | Swimlane diagrams illustrating your desired workflow. | Chapter 11, "Designing workflow" |
| | Determine everything that has to happen in between, assigning tasks to roles. | | |
| | Identify all the interactions and dependencies, notifications and approvals. | | |
| | Figure in the "what ifs." | | |
| | Document your workflow in swimlane diagrams, showing players' roles in the appropriate swimlanes. | | |
| | Examine your documented workflow to simplify where possible. | | |

*continues* ▶

**Table A.2    Continued**

| Stages: What's involved | Tasks: What to do | Deliverables | Refer to... |
|---|---|---|---|
| Develop organizational change management plan. | Though not part of design, you should begin to address change management during the design phase.<br><br>Tasks include:<br><br>• Identify areas where you should focus your change management efforts.<br>• Analyze barriers to effective change.<br>• Identify change success factors.<br>• Identify role of stakeholders.<br>• Select a change management strategy.<br>• Identify change management team members.<br>• Identify a communications strategy.<br>• Create change management plan. | The organizational change management plan. | Chapter 21, "Managing change" |
| Define your security model. | Define groups and individual users; identify who gets access to what.<br><br>Create the Access Control List (ACL).<br><br>Configure the security in the selected tools. | Security model.<br><br>User and group security profiles.<br><br>Access control list.<br><br>Security configured for the system. | Chapter 16, "Content management systems" |

# Phase 3—Selecting tools and technologies

Evaluating and selecting tools is a large part of implementing a unified content strategy. There are many types of tools available and you need to select ones that meet your organization's needs, your authors' abilities, and what you've decided to do with your information (established during the design phase). Using everything you learned in the analysis and design phases—and referring to your new content life cycle—evaluate tools and technologies as described in Table A.3.

**Table A.3    Tools and technologies**

| Stages: What's involved | Tasks: What to do | Deliverables | Refer to… |
|---|---|---|---|
| Evaluate tools and technologies. | Identify your criteria for selection. | Tool selection criteria | Chapter 13, "Evaluating tools" |
| | Develop a weighting system for your criteria. | RFI/RFP (if applicable) | |
| | Develop a list of vendors to investigate. | Tools to support your various authoring, content management, workflow, and delivery needs | Chapter 14, "The role of XML" |
| | Request a custom demonstration from vendors that interest you. | | Chapter 15, "Authoring tools" |
| | Send out an RFI/RFP to selected vendors that includes your detailed criteria and ask them to respond to your questions. | | Chapter 16, "Content management systems" |
| | Evaluate the responses or compare the custom demonstration against your criteria. | | Chapter 17, "Workflow systems" |
| | Pick three vendors that most effectively meet your criteria (best ranking). | | |

| Stages: What's involved | Tasks: What to do | Deliverables | Refer to... |
|---|---|---|---|
| | Ask vendors to use a sample of your content to create a content specific demonstration for you. | | Chapter 18, "Delivery systems" |
| | Narrow your selection down to one or two vendors. Conduct a proof-of-concept to test the required functionality and determine whether the product meets your needs. | | Appendix C, "Vendors" |
| | Purchase the product if it performs well in the proof-of-concept. | | Appendix D, "Tools checklist" |

# Phase 4—Development

Moving forward with your unified content strategy means changing the way you work. As you develop your proof-of-concept and pilot, you need to help your authors to collaborate, provide them with guidelines and training on how to write and structure content in the same way, and roll out your strategy throughout your organization. You also need to put together your change management plan, implement your models, and install and configure your software and hardware. Table A.4 summarizes the stages of developing your strategy.

**Table A.4   Development**

| Stages: What's involved | Tasks: What to do | Deliverables | Refer to... |
|---|---|---|---|
| Implement collaborative authoring. | Identify everyone involved in creating content and what their role is; hold "kickoff" meetings at the beginning of projects. | Project plans and kickoff meetings | Chapter 19, "Collaborative authoring: Breaking down the silos" |
| | Design collaboration into workflow. | | |
| | Develop resource–focused budgets based on content requirements across the organization, rather than department-specific budgets. | Budgets based on content requirements | Chapter 20, "Separating content from format" |
| | Introduce models to everyone in the organization who creates content; revisit models iteratively. | Information models | Chapter 11, "Designing Workflow" |
| | | "Buy-ins" from authors | |
| | | Training in information analysis, modeling, design, and structured writing | |
| | Make changes to models, authoring processes, and standards by consensus and not by democratic vote; train authors in conflict management techniques. | Authoring and collaboration tools | Chapter 15, "Authoring tools" |
| | Encourage authors to relinquish ownership of their content; content with a discernible style is not necessarily reusable. | | |

*continues* ▶

**Table A.4    Continued**

| Stages: What's involved | Tasks: What to do | Deliverables | Refer to... |
|---|---|---|---|
| Implement structured writing. | Train writers in information analysis, modeling, design, and structured writing so they all have the same understanding of how to create content and how to write to information models. | Structured writing standards (and possibly templates or DTDs) | Chapter 8, "Information modeling" |
| | Provide usable tools that support collaborative processes, not impede them. | Information models | Chapter 15, "Authoring tools" |
| | Define writing standards that focus on meaning rather than on format. | Format style sheets for each output | Chapter 20, "Separating content from format" |
| | Create standards for each element, so wherever the element appears, it is consistent, and so it is also consistent with the other elements contained in the information product. | Authoring tools | |
| | Train authors in structured writing and support them with tools and with comprehensive models to follow. | Structured writing, documentation and training | |
| | Create style sheets that are applied when the content is published to its various formats. | | |

| Stages: What's involved | Tasks: What to do | Deliverables | Refer to... |
|---|---|---|---|
| Address organizational change. | Communicate the following on an ongoing basis; communicate:<br><br>• Why change needs to happen.<br><br>• The plan for implementing the change.<br><br>• The ongoing status of the change.<br><br>• The successes you have achieved in early implementations.<br><br>• The problems you have encountered and how you fixed them or plan to avoid them in the future.<br><br>• Involve "change agents" to help you implement the change.<br><br>• Get a champion on board to help ensure that everyone understands the reason for change and buys into the process. | Organizational change plan | Chapter 21, "Managing change" |

*continues* ▶

**Table A.4    Continued**

| Stages: What's involved | Tasks: What to do | Deliverables | Refer to... |
|---|---|---|---|
| Implement your design. | Create templates. | | Chapter 12, "Implementing your design" |
| | Create web forms (if using). | | |
| | Create DTDs. | | |
| | Develop style sheets. | | |
| Install and configure hardware/software. | Write configuration specification. | System specification | N/A (not covered in book) |
| | Configure tools. | Installed and configured system | |
| | Write scripts. | | |
| Create workflows in CMS. | Create workflows using CMS functionality. | Workflows created in the CMS | Chapter 11, "Designing workflow" |
| | | | Chapter 17, "Workflow systems" |

| Stages: What's involved | Tasks: What to do | Deliverables | Refer to... |
|---|---|---|---|
| Develop a prototype. | Select short sample (existing content) for prototype testing. | A working prototype | N/A (not covered in book) |
| | Convert/restructure content according to your new models. | Prototype gap analysis report | |
| | Publish (deliver content) using the system. | | |
| | Analyze gaps (prototype against requirements). | | |
| | Create prototype report. | | |

# Phase 5—Testing and system modifications

During this phase of the project, you use your prototype to extensively test the system's functionality, the information models, business processes, and the workflows. Although many of these tasks are required for most project implementations, they are not specific to a unified content strategy and are not covered in the book. Table A.5 describes the stages of testing and making system modifications.

**Table A.5   Testing and system modifications**

| Stages: What's involved | Tasks: What to do | Deliverables | Refer to… |
|---|---|---|---|
| Conduct usability test. | Define the objectives of the test (what you want to learn). | Usability test plan | N/A (not covered in book) |
| | Define success criteria. | Usability test questionnaires | |
| | Define the test questions. | List of usability test participants | |
| | Develop any necessary information or training to support the test participants in understanding their tasks. | Usability test | |
| | Identify the usability test participants. | Usability test report | |
| | Develop the pre- and post-usability test questionnaires and coordinate times with participants. | Possibly, a modified system | |
| | Conduct the usability test. | | |
| | Summarize the usability test findings. | | |
| | Create a usability test report covering results and recommendations. | | |
| | Revise the user interface and processes where necessary. | | |

*continues* ▶

**Table A.5    Continued**

| Stages: What's involved | Tasks: What to do | Deliverables | Refer to... |
|---|---|---|---|
| Conduct verification test. | Create verification test plan. | Verification test plan Problem reports | N/A (not covered in book) |
| | Test functionality. | | |
| | Identify problem areas. | Engineering Change Notices | |
| | Document problems (bugs). | | |
| | Determine appropriate changes and create Engineering Change Notices for system changes. | | |
| Revise specification. | Update specification Review. | Revised specification | N/A (not covered in book) |
| Implement system modifications. | Revise information frameworks. | Revised style sheets | Chapter 12, "Implementing your design" |
| | Revise style sheets. | Revised batches | |
| | Revise all batches and scripts. | Revised scripts | |

| Stages:<br>What's involved | Tasks: What to do | Deliverables | Refer to… |
|---|---|---|---|
| Implement process modifications. | Identify modifications to processes. | Revised process descriptions | N/A (not covered in book) |
| | Update process descriptions | | |
| | Update process maps. | Revised process maps | |
| | Communicate changes to authors. | | |
| Implement workflow modifications. | Update workflow diagrams. | Revised workflow diagrams | Chapter 11, "Designing workflow" |
| | Update workflows in the system | Revised workflows in the system | Chapter 17, "Workflow systems" |
| | Communicate changes to authors | | |

# Phase 6—Pilot

A pilot is required to selectively roll out and test the new tools and processes in a controlled environment that will not impact key deliverables. To conduct a pilot, you select a group, department, or area you will use to roll out a scaled-down version of the unified content strategy so you can thoroughly test the processes and infrastructure. Again, although conducting a pilot is critical, it is not unique to a unified content strategy and accordingly, there are no chapter references provided.

After the pilot is complete, the rest of the process can be prioritized for implementation. Table A.6 describes the stages of conducting a pilot.

**Tabled A.6    Pilot**

| Stages: What's involved | Tasks: What to do | Deliverables |
|---|---|---|
| Create pilot plan. | Create a pilot plan. | Pilot plan |
| | Create pilot monitoring plan. | Pilot monitoring plan |
| | Create a pilot schedule. | Pilot schedule |
| | Create a pilot participant agreement. | Pilot participant agreement |
| Select and brief participants. | Create pilot selection criteria. | Pilot selection criteria |
| | Evaluate plans against criteria. | Selected documents |
| | Select one or more documents for inclusion in the pilot process. | Signed pilot participant agreement |
| | Meet with the teams to communicate the vision and pilot plan. | |
| | Get signatures of all parties on the pilot participant agreement. | |
| Install pilot on pilot server and participants' machines. | Configure pilot server. | Configured pilot server |
| | Install tools. | Configured author interface |
| | Configure tools. | |

*continues* ▶

**Tabled A.6    Continued**

| Stages: What's involved | Tasks: What to do | Deliverables |
|---|---|---|
| Develop preliminary training plan and materials. | Perform task analysis. | Training plan |
| | Identify roles to be trained. | Preliminary training materials |
| | Identify learning styles. | |
| | Identify learning objectives. | |
| | Determine the delivery mechanism. | |
| | Write training plan. | |
| | Write training materials. | |
| Conduct pilot training. | Train staff. | Trained staff |
| | Collect feedback. | Feedback report |
| | Create feedback report. | |
| Develop pilot user documentation. | Define user documentation requirements and deliverables. | User documentation deliverables report |
| | Create information product models for each deliverable. | User documentation information product models |
| | Develop preliminary user documentation based on the models. | First draft user documentation |

| Stages: What's involved | Tasks: What to do | Deliverables |
|---|---|---|
| Monitor pilot. | Conduct pilot kickoff meeting. | Pilot kickoff meeting |
| | Monitor pilot. | Pilot summary report |
| | Summarize pilot. | |
| | Create pilot summary report. | |
| Revise specification. | Update models. | Updated specifications (models, maps, descriptions, workflow diagrams) |
| | Update process maps and descriptions. | |
| | Update workflow diagrams. | |
| | Communicate changes to stakeholders. | Informed stakeholders |
| Implement changes. | Update work processes. | Updated system, processes and workflows |
| | Update system work flows, templates, interface, system configuration. | |
| | Communicate changes to stakeholders. | Informed stakeholders |

*continues* ▶

## Phase 7—Implementation

Proper planning and training are essential to the successful implementation of your unified content strategy. Table A.7 describes the various stages of implementation, as applicable to any project.

**Table A.7    Implementation**

| Stages: What's involved | Tasks: What to do | Deliverables |
|---|---|---|
| Develop rollout plan. | Identify all users involved. | Rollout plan |
| | Identify hardware and software requirements. | |
| | Identify training needs. | |
| | Develop rollout schedule. | |
| | Create rollout plan. | |
| Develop final training plan and materials. | Perform task analysis. | Training plan |
| | Identify roles to be trained. | Training materials |
| | Identify learning styles. | |
| | Identify learning objectives. | |
| | Determine delivery mechanism. | |
| | Write training plan. | |
| | Write training materials. | |
| Conduct training. | Train staff. | Trained staff |
| | Collect feedback. | Feedback report |
| | Create feedback report. | |

*continues* ▶

**Table A.7    Continued**

| Stages: What's involved | Tasks: What to do | Deliverables |
|---|---|---|
| Develop technical support plan. | Identify required technical resources. | Technical support plan |
| | Identify tools resource. | |
| | Identify process resources. | |
| | Write technical support plan. | |
| Finalize user documentation. | Review user documentation and edit. | Final user documentation |
| | Finalize user documentation | |
| Roll out solution. | As defined in your rollout plan. | The rolled-out system |

# Phase 8—Post-implementation

After your strategy has been successfully implemented, you need to ensure that it continues to run smoothly, and that you keep up to date on the latest technological advances. It is also important to analyze your recently completed unified content project to determine how you can leverage the experience for future projects. Table A.8 describes the stages of post-implementation.

**Table A.8    Post-implementation**

| Stages: What's involved | Tasks: What to do | Deliverables |
|---|---|---|
| Develop migration/upgrade plan. | Determine migration/upgrade criteria. | Migration/upgrade plan |
| | Contact vendors about upcoming product release functionality and schedule. | |
| | Develop migration/upgrade plan. | |
| Conduct post-project audit. | Identify review topics. Suggested topics include: | Post-project audit meeting |
| | • Did the final product match the one designed in the project plan and outline? | Post-project audit report |
| | • Did the scope of the project remain the same? | |
| | • Did the project dependencies remain the same as originally predicted? | |
| | • What went as it should? | |
| | • What went wrong? | |
| | • How can you build on actions that lead to success? | |
| | • How can you change actions that caused problems or failures? | |
| | Conduct post-project audit meeting. | |
| | Create post-project audit report. | |

# Appendix B

## Writing for multiple media

When creating unified content, writers sometimes struggle with the idea that content written for one medium can be appropriate for another. This appendix explains how to write for multiple media, ensuring that content can be written once and used as required, regardless of the medium in which it appears. It includes writing guidelines for various electronic formats, as well as for paper. Then it compares them to show how the guidelines are applicable, regardless in which medium the content appears.

In our experience, following guidelines for clear, effective writing makes content usable, regardless of the medium or format in which it appears. If you need to add or remove detail to make content more applicable to a certain user group, or a particular product, or for a particular medium, you can do so through nested or derivative reuse (see Chapter 2, "Fundamental concepts of reuse"), or through the building block approach (see Chapter 20, "Separating content from format").

## Writing online documentation

Online documentation (initially, help files and later, HTML-based documents) was the first new medium—beyond paper—for which authors struggled to write effectively. Guidelines[1] for writing effective online documentation include:

- **Write concisely.**

  Users of online documentation do not read; instead, they scan or browse. Because reading is 25% slower from the screen, text should be short and to the point. Don't be chatty or verbose. Remove excessive adjectives, compound sentences, and compound phrases.

- **Make writing easy to scan.**

  It is difficult to read large volumes of information online. Users tend to visually scan the text to pick out important pieces of information. To assist them, use:

  - Bulleted or numbered lists instead of "burying" lists or steps in the body of paragraphs

  - Short tables or columns to display relationships of information (for example, comparisons or "if/then" situations)

  - White space (don't tightly pack information, but don't leave too much blank on the screen either; use screen real estate wisely)

  - Sub-headings to break up information and make it easy to scan

  - Short paragraphs (3-6 sentences)

---

1 First appeared in Rockley, Ann. "Putting Documents Online: A Manager's Guide" (European Conference on Hypertext ECHT'94, Edinburgh, Scotland).

- A consistent design for similar types of information so that users become accustomed to always seeing certain types of information presented in the same way, for example, comparisons might always appear in short tables. See Chapter 20, for more information on consistent designs for different types of information.

- **Layer information.**

  Online information should be short and precise. However, sometimes you need to provide more information than can be covered in one screen or topic. You can layer information with one level presented and subsequent levels linked through additional windows.

- **Write useful titles.**

  Titles are a key access point for users into the information. Titles form the table of contents and are often used as keywords for searching. Titles must be substantive and indicate to users exactly what the document contains. Avoid titles such as "General," which are...well...too general!

- **Provide continuity/connection.**

  Chunks of information in an online environment are short and discrete. In continuing processes, users may have difficulty identifying what has gone before and what comes after. Explicitly refer to preceding or following processes and provide links to the processes. Write all "see" and "see also" references consistently.

- **Use specific references.**

  Avoid using references such as "See figure below/beside/above/in this section." Instead, refer to figures, graphics, or tables explicitly by name or link to them in secondary windows.

## Writing for the Web

With the explosion in popularity of the Internet (followed by intranets and extranets), authors needed to find effective ways to write for the Web. Jakob Nielsen (author of *Designing Web Usability*, New Riders, 2000), a recognized leader in the field of web usability, provides these guidelines (available on his web site at `http://www.useit.com`). Note how similar they are to the guidelines for writing online documentation, discussed previously.

- **Be succinct.**

  Write no more than 50% of the text that you would have used in a hard-copy publication.

- **Make information easy to scan.**

  Users scan text and pick out keywords, sentences, and paragraphs of interest. Don't make your user read long continuous blocks of text. Ensure paragraphs contain one main idea. Use bulleted and numbered lists to draw attention to important points.

- **Make use of hypertext structure.**

  Rather than sacrificing the depth of information, split information up into multiple pages. Use secondary pages for long and detailed information.

- **Write simple sentences.**

  Convoluted writing and complex words are even harder to understand online.

- **Use effective headings.**

  Make sure that headings clearly indicate the content of the sections.

## Writing for wireless devices

Online and web-based information is also available (and becoming more popular) on wireless devices such as PDAs and cellular telephones. Guidelines for effective content are only beginning to be developed for these devices. The major problem is the small screen size. A PDA has an average screen size of 160×160; a cellular phone's screen is even smaller. This means that writing concisely is even more important.

There are a number of other issues in writing for wireless devices, such as ensuring that users can find the correct content and navigate through content. These issues and many others require more research before they can be effectively addressed with guidelines. But using clear, concise writing, and providing short, yet substantive, headings are still critical.

# Writing for paper

Writing for paper adheres to principles of clear communication, just as writing online documentation and writing for the Web do. Some guidelines for clear communication include:

- **Make the document's purpose obvious and clear.**

  Make sure your document has a clearly defined purpose, audience, and context. Include only information that supports the defined purpose based on the users' needs.

- **Express only one central idea per paragraph or section within the document (based on the users' needs) and make the central idea clear—right away.**

  Write a topic sentence for each paragraph or section; the topic sentence must state the central idea you are expressing. If supplementary information is available, tell users where to find it, but be careful that you don't send them searching all over the document for related information.

  Linking users to related information is much easier online, but even then, you run the danger of sending users off into hypertext, often forgetting where they started from. On paper and online, always make your reason for including references to supplementary information very clear, and make it an option. If content is necessary for the understanding of a particular topic, include it in one place, with all other relevant content.

- **Chunk information into manageable pieces.**

  Content should be grouped into small pieces that are easy for users to scan, read, and comprehend. A manageable chunk consists of five to nine pieces of information.

- **Use headings that tell readers the purpose of the information in the paragraph.**

  Choose specific headings (for documents, sections, paragraphs, lists, and so on) that enable users to tell, at a glance, whether the information is relevant to them. Include only information that supports the stated purpose, as indicated by the heading.

- **Use clear, concise language.**

  Use words with common meanings and use them consistently. Avoid jargon, legalese, foreign phrases, and pompous expressions. Always match vocabulary and style of writing to the users' needs.

These guidelines also apply to online documentation and to the Web. All information, regardless of the medium in which it appears, should have a clearly stated purpose, should contain only information that supports that purpose, should provide clear references (links) to related information, should be chunked into manageable pieces, with headings to indicate the content's purpose, and should be written in language best suited to the users' needs.

## Summarizing the guidelines

As shown in Table B.1, the guidelines for online documentation and the Web are very similar.

**Table B.1    Writing guidelines for online documentation and the Web**

|  | Online documentation | Web | Wireless devices (such as PDAs) |
| --- | --- | --- | --- |
| Write succinctly | ✓ | ✓ | ✓ |
| Make information easy to scan | ✓ | ✓ | ✓ |
| Layer information | ✓ | ✓ | ✓ |
| Write useful titles | ✓ | ✓ | ✓ |

The guidelines in Table B.1 were developed to address the differences between paper and online/web and to ensure usability. However, if you look at these guidelines closely you can see that they are just as valid for paper. Table B.2 explains how the guidelines for online documentation and the Web also apply to paper.

**Table B.2   Online documentation and web guidelines applied to paper**

| | Paper | Reasoning |
|---|---|---|
| Write succinctly | ✓ | Clear, concise content can greatly improve the quality of paper materials. |
| Make information easy to scan | ✓ | Long passages of text that extend down a page or over pages are hard to read. Chunking that information can make it much easier for a reader to comprehend. |
| Layer information | ✓ | This is a bit harder for paper. You don't want to have a lot of "gotos" in the text that take the reader back and forth. However, layering of content is appropriate for things such as overviews, summaries, and checklists. They provide information that is further explained in the body of the document. |
| Write useful titles | ✓ | Users should be able to tell, at a glance, whether content is relevant to them. Useful titles make it easier for users to find what they want. |

## Accommodating different media, levels of detail, and styles

Even though the guidelines of clear communication apply to online documentation, the Web, and to paper, there are still distinct differences in how people write for paper versus how they write for the web. However, after developing content for online media for more than 20 years, our experience has shown that well-written online documentation also makes good paper documentation and vice versa. Where the difference occurs is in how much information is provided in each medium and how it is presented. Content should be optimized for the medium in which it appears and presented in the most appropriate manner. For example, definitions can be presented as pop-ups in online documentation, but as in-line text on paper. But, the definition must still be written clearly, following guidelines for effective writing. In addition, there may be less detail online and more detail in paper documentation. The level of detail and the way content is presented may not just depend upon the medium; it may also depend upon the information product and the audience.

Training materials, for example, can use the same product description as the brochure, but where they differ is in the exercises and explanations that characterize training materials. Likewise, the brochure can use the same product description as the user guide and the training materials, but where the brochure differs is in the addition of "marketing" details that explain to potential customers why they should buy the product. But the product description is the same, regardless of where it is used. Where the difference occurs is in how much information is provided and how it is presented. This is a perfect opportunity for nested reuse.

There are also differences in style, such as marketing versus technical documentation and user documentation versus learning materials. Although the same information can be used in a number of different places, authors may want to customize it by adding details, examples, or exercises. In some cases, authors may want to rewrite material to accommodate a particular need, while maintaining a link to the source so they know when it's updated. This is a perfect opportunity to employ derivative reuse.

## Conclusion

Well-written content that is created with good writing principles in mind, and that follows models designed for reusable content, means that you can write material once and use it many times, regardless of the media.

# Appendix C

## Vendors

Sample products and vendors are provided for each of the key technology areas. However, products and vendors change on an ongoing basis, so refer to the accompanying web site for current information. For a better understanding of the types of technology these vendors provide, see the chapters in Part IV, "Tools and technologies."

# Authoring systems

The tools presented in Table C.1 represent authoring tools that can support a unfied content strategy. They are categorized as follows:

- **XML**—Native XML tools
- **XML Aware**—Tools that provide structural authoring and XML output from a traditional authoring interface
- **Non XML**—Tools that provide authoring functionality but not XML output.

**Table C.1   Authoring systems**

| Vendor/<br>Product | Description | Category<br>information | Contact |
|---|---|---|---|
| Adobe | | | |
| • FrameMaker 7.0 | Adobe FrameMaker is a desktop publishing tool that provides a structured authoring environment with output to XML.<br><br>FrameMaker includes Quadralay Webworks Standard Edition, which provides delivery to XML, HTML, XHTML, DHTML, and all industry-standard Help formats. | XML Aware | Adobe Systems, Inc.<br><br>345 Park Avenue<br>San Jose, CA<br>95110-2704<br><br>http://www.adobe.com |
| Altova | | | |
| • XML Spy | Altova XML Spy provides native XML authoring, as well as XSL, DTD, and Schema authoring.<br><br>XML Spy can also provide output to PDF HTML, and other formats from the desktop. | XML | Altova, Inc.<br><br>900 Cummings<br>Center, Suite 306-T<br>Beverly, MA<br>01915-6181<br><br>978-927-9400<br><br>http://www.xmlspy.com |

*continues* ▶

**Table C.1    Continued**

| Vendor/ Product | Description | Category information | Contact |
|---|---|---|---|
| Arbortext<br>• Epic Editor | Arbortext Epic Editor provides native XML authoring. Functionality includes tag view and formatted view. Epic Editor can also provide output to PDF, HTML, and other formats from the desktop. | XML | Arbortext, Inc.<br><br>1000 Victors Way<br>Ann Arbor, MI 48108<br><br>734-997-0200<br><br>http://www.arbortext.com |
| Blast Radius<br>• XMetal | Blast Radius XMetal provides native XML authoring. Functionality includes tag view and formatted view. | XML | Blast Radius<br><br>594 Broadway, Ste. 206<br>New York, NY 10012<br><br>1-212-925-4900<br><br>http://www.blastradius.com/ |

| Vendor/<br>Product | Description | Category<br>information | Contact |
|---|---|---|---|
| HyperVision<br>• WorX | HyperVision WorX provides a structured authoring environment with output to XML as an add-on to Microsoft Word. Users get editing functionality with a structural view. | XML | HyperVision, Ltd.<br><br>230 East Ohio Street<br>Suite 210<br>Chicago, IL 60611<br><br>312-274-1206<br><br>http://www.hv1td.com |
| i4i<br>• x4o | i4i x4o provides a structured authoring environment with output to XML as an add-on to Microsoft Word. Users get editing functionality with a fully validating parser. | XML | i4i<br><br>116 Spadina Avenue<br>Fifth Floor<br>Toronto, Ontario<br>Canada M5V 2K6<br><br>416-504-0141<br><br>http://www.i4i.com |

*continues* ▶

**Table C.1    Continued**

| Vendor/<br>Product | Description | Category<br>information | Contact |
|---|---|---|---|
| TIBCO<br>Extensibility<br>• TurboXML | TIBCO Extensibility TurboXML provides native XML authoring, as well as DTDs and Schema authoring. | XML | TIBCO Software, Inc.<br>World Headquarters<br><br>3303 Hillview Avenue<br>Palo Alto, CA 94304<br><br>650-846-1000<br><br>http://www.tibco.com/ |

# Content management systems

The tools presented in Table C.2 represent content management systems that can support a unified content strategy. They are categorized as follows:

- **ECMS**—Enterprise Content Management System
- **IDMS**—Integrated Document Management System
- **PCMS**—Publication Content Management System
- **TCMS**—Transactional Content Management System
- **WCMS**—Web Content Management System

**Table C.2    Content management systems**

| Vendor/Product | Description | Category | Contact information |
|---|---|---|---|
| Astoria Software | | | |
| • Astoria | Astoria Software provides XML-based content management. Astoria integrates with many XML-based authoring tools and delivery tools. Astoria includes workflow and dynamic content delivery. | PCMS WCMS | Astoria Software, Incorporated 66 Bovet Road, Suite 280 San Mateo, CA 94402 650-357-7477 http://www.astoria software.com/ |
| AuthorIT | | | |
| • AuthorIT | AuthorIT provides an end-to-end solution for creating, managing, and delivering reusable content. AuthorIT includes workflow. An optional module provides project management. AuthorIT outputs to Word, PDF, WinHelp, HTML, XHTML, Microsoft HTML Help, Sun JavaHelp, and Oracle Help for Java. | ECMS | AuthorIT Software Corporation P.O. Box 300-273 Albany, Auckland New Zealand +64-9-915-5070 http://www. authorit.com |

| Vendor/ Product | Description | Category | Contact information |
|---|---|---|---|
| EMC Documentum | | | |
| • Documentum | EMC Documentum provides many different versionsof Documentum to meet the needs of web content management, enterprise content management, transactional content management, and integrated document management. Reusable content can be created in Word, FrameMaker, HTML, or XML. All versions of the product include workflow. Documentum also includes dynamic content delivery and personalization.<br><br>4i uses XML to deliver content to multiple channels, including HTML, print, CD, and wireless. | ECMS<br><br>IDMS<br><br>TCMS<br><br>WCMS | EMC Documentum<br><br>6801 Koll Center Parkway<br>Pleasanton, CA 94566<br><br>925-600-6800<br><br>http://www. documentum.com |
| Ektron | | | |
| • CMS400.NET | Ektron CMS400.NET is a full-function, but low-cost web content management system. CMS400.NET works equally well with HTML or XML. CMS400.NET includes workflow and dynamic content delivery. | WCMS | Ektron<br><br>5 Northern Blvd. Building 6<br>Amherst, NH 03031<br><br>603-594-0249<br><br>http://www. ekton.com/ |

*continues* ▶

**Table C.2    Continued**

| Vendor/Product | Description | Category | Contact information |
|---|---|---|---|
| Interwoven | | | |
| • TeamSite | Interwoven TeamSite provides web content management. TeamXML provides XML-based content management. Both versions include workflow. Interwoven products also provide dynamic content delivery and personalization. | WCMS | Interwoven |
| • TeamXML | | ECMS | 803 11th Avenue Sunnyvale, CA 94089 |
| | Interwoven delivers to HTML and wireless. PDF is supported but only through the XML version made available through the integration of the Xyenterprise XPP delivery system (see the "Delivery systems" section). | | 408-774-2000 |
| | | | http://www.interwoven.com |
| Oracle | | | |
| • ECM | Oracle ECM is an upgrade to the company's Collaboration Suite. Oracle ECM is a mid-range ECM solution with increased security, collaboration, and workflow functionality. | CMS | Oracle Corporation |
| | | | 500 Oracle Parkway Redwood Shores, CA 94402 |
| | | | 1-800-ORACLE-1 |
| | | | http://www.oracle.com |

| Vendor/ Product | Description | Category | Contact information |
|---|---|---|---|
| Vasont Systems | | | |
| • Vasont | Vasont Systems provides XML-based enterprise content management. Vasont integrates with many XML-based authoring tools and outputs to paper, HTML, CD-ROM, and wireless. Vasont includes workflow and dynamic content delivery. | PCMS<br><br>WCMS | Vasont Systems<br><br>315 Busser Road Emigsville, PA 17318<br><br>800-673-2500<br><br>http://www.vasont.com |
| Siberlogic, Inc. | | | |
| • SiberSafe | Siberlogic SiberSafe provides XML-based content management. SiberSafe integrates with many XML-based authoring tools and delivery tools. SiberSafe includes workflow and dynamic content delivery. | PCMS<br><br>WCMS | Siberlogic, Inc.<br><br>7700 Pine Valley Dr. PO #72007 Woodbridge, Ontario, Canada L4L 8N8<br><br>877-742-3754<br><br>http://www.siberlogic.com |

*continues* ▶

**Table C.2    Continued**

| Vendor/ Product | Description | Category | Contact information |
|---|---|---|---|
| Stellent | | | Stellent, Inc. |
| • Universal Content Management | Universal Content Management provides content management for multiple authoring tools (can convert content from 250 different formats) and outputs to HTML, XML, cHTML, and PDF. | ECMS | |
| | | WCMS | 7777 Golden Triangle Dr. Eden Prairie, MN 55344 |
| | Stellent CMS includes workflow and personalization. | | 952-903-2000 or 800-989-8774 |
| | | | http://www. stellent.com |
| XyEnterprise | | | Xyvision Enterprise Solutions, Inc. |
| • Content@ | XyEnterprise Content@ provides XML-based content management. Content@ integrates with many XML-based authoring tools and delivery tools. Content@ includes workflow and dynamic content delivery. | PCMS | |
| | | WCMS | 30 New Crossing Rd. Reading, MA 01867 |
| | Content@ integrates with XML Professional Publisher for output to PDF from XML. | | 781-756-4400 |
| | | | http://www xyenterprise.com |

# Workflow systems

The tools shown in Table C.3 represent workflow systems that can support a unified content strategy. They are categorized as follows:

- **Integrated**—Integrated within a content management system
- **Standalone**—Interfaces with an existing content management system

**Table C.3    Workflow systems tools**

| Product | Description | Category | Contact information |
|---|---|---|---|
| AuthorIT | | | |
| • AuthorIT | See Table C.2 | Integrated | See Table C.2 |
| EMC | | | |
| • Documentum | See Table C.2 | Integrated | See Table C.2 |
| J.D. Edwards | | | |
| • Enterprise Content Manager | See Table C.2 | Integrated | See Table C.2 |
| Interwoven | | | |
| • TeamSite • TeamXML | See Table C.2 | Integrated | See Table C.2 |
| Vasont Systems | | | |
| • Vasont | See Table C.2 | Integrated | See Table C.2 |
| Stellent | | | |
| • Universal Content Management | See Table C.2 | Integrated | See Table C.2 |

| Product | Description | Category | Contact information |
|---|---|---|---|
| XyEnterprise • Content@ | See Table C.2 | Integrated | See Table C.2 |
| IBM • MQSeries Workflow | MQSeries Workflow provides complete business process support. It can be integrated with many applications, including content management. | Standalone | IBM Corporation<br><br>1133 Westchester Avenue White Plains, NY 10604<br><br>1-800-IBM-4YOU<br><br>http://www.ibm.com |

*continues* ▶

**Table C.3    Continued**

| Product | Description | Category | Contact information |
|---|---|---|---|
| TIBCO Software, Inc. | | | |
| • iProcess Suite | Staffware Process Suite provices complete business process support. It can be integrated with many applications, including content management. | Standalone | TIBCO Software, Inc. World Headquarters<br><br>3303 Hillview Avenue Palo Alto, CA 94304<br><br>650-846-1000<br><br>http://www.tibco.com/ |

# Delivery systems

The tools shown in Table C.4 represent delivery systems that can support a unified content strategy. They are categorized as follows:

- Multi-channel delivery
  - Enterprise—Available across the enterprise
  - Desktop—Available from a single desktop
- Dynamic Content Delivery
  - Integrated—Integrated within a content management system
  - Standalone—Standalone system that interfaces with an existing content management system

**Table C.4    Delivery systems**

| Product | Description | Category | Contact information |
|---|---|---|---|
| **Multi-channel Delivery** | | | |
| Arbortext | | | |
| • E3 | Arbortext E3 provides enterprise conversion from XML to PDF, HTML, and other formats. | Enterprise | Arbortext, Inc. |
| • 3B2 | Arbortext 3B2 provides a high-end composition and pagination software. | | 1000 Victors Way Ann Arbor, MI 48108 |
| | | | 734-997-0200 |
| | | | http://www.arbortext.com |
| Quadralay | | | |
| • WebWorks Professional | Quadralay WebWorks Professional provides desktop and batch conversion to XML, HTML, XHTML, DHTML, and all industry-standard Help formats from FrameMaker. | Enterprise | Quadralay Corporation |
| | | | 9101 Burnet Road Suite 105 Austin, TX 78758 |
| | | | 512-719-9700 |
| | | | http://www.quadralay.com |

| Product | Description | Category | Contact information |
|---|---|---|---|
| **Multi-channel Delivery** | | | |
| XyEnterprise<br>• XML Professional Publisher | XyEnterprise XML Professional Publisher (XPP) provides conversion from XML to Postscript and PDF formats | Enterprise | Xyvision Enterprise Solutions, Inc.<br><br>30 New Crossing Rd. Reading, MA 01867<br><br>781-756-4400<br><br>http://www.xyenterprise.com |
| **Dynamic Content Delivery** | | | |
| EMC<br>• Documentum | See Chapter 16 | Integrated | See  Chapter 16 |
| Interwoven<br>• TeamSite<br>• TeamXML | See Chapter 16 | Integrated | See  Chapter 16 |
| Vasont Systems<br>• Vasont | See Chapter 16 | Integrated | See  Chapter 16 |

*continues* ▶

**Table C.4    Continued**

| Product | Description | Category | Contact information |
|---|---|---|---|
| **Dynamic Content Delivery** | | | |
| Stellent<br>• Universal Content Management | See Chapter 16 | Integrated | See Chapter 16 |
| BEA<br>• WebLogic Personalization Server | BEA WebLogic Personalization Server is a component of BEA WebLogic Portal. The portal provides personalization functionality for web sites on multiple platforms. | Standalone | BEA Systems, Inc.<br><br>2315 North First St. San Jose, CA 95131<br><br>408-570-8000<br><br>http://www.bea.com |
| IBM<br>• WebSphere Personalization | IBM WebSphere Personalization provides personalization functionality for web sites on multiple platforms. WebSphere Site Analyzer can be used to report on the effectiveness of the personalization strategy. | Standalone | See Chapter 16 |

# Appendix D

## Tools checklist

Part IV, "Tools and technologies," described the process of selecting tools and technologies, as well as the capabilities required for a unified content strategy. This appendix provides a concise checklist for the tools required to implement a unified content strategy.

This appendix is a summary of the questions for vendors provided in Part IV. It is not designed to be used until you have completed a thorough analysis of your requirements. Some of the questions provided here may not be appropriate for your project, company, users, or budget. Use the checklist to assist you in developing your questions for the vendors.

## Authoring tool functionality

Table D.1 summarizes the questions you should ask of an authoring tool vendor.

**Table D.I   Authoring tool criteria**

| Criteria | Definition |
|---|---|
| **User interface** | |
| User friendly, author-intuitive graphical user interface (GUI) | Does the system have a GUI that is designed for use by writers/authors and that facilitates efficiency of their tasks? |
| Web interface | Does the authoring tool include a web-based interface? |
| **Functionality** | |
| Good/powerful text handling capabilities | Does the authoring tool support the following:<br><br>• Spell check/thesaurus?<br>• Search and replace?<br>• Hypertext links?<br>• Bullets?<br>• Numbered lists?<br>• Tables?<br>• Footnotes?<br>• Scientific equations/notation?<br>• Global search and replace?<br>• Document preparation and creation capabilities?<br>• Automatic creation of headers/footers?<br>• Automatic generation of tables of contents?<br>• Automatic generation of index? |

*continues* ▶

**Table D.1 Continued**

| Criteria | Definition |
|---|---|
| Template support | Does the authoring system support structured content templates? |
| | How does the authoring system handle template versioning? |
| Graphics support With user-managed | Are images linked or embedded? (Static and dynamic status?) |
| | Does the authoring tool include a preview mode? |
| | How are images linked in? Drag and drop? Can the images be manipulated for size/position/resolution in the authoring tool? |
| | Can callouts be added? Can they exist as a layer for translation and multi-product labeling purposes? |
| Complexity filter | Can the interface be customized to present only the functions that the authors need to use? Is it configurable for groups? By profile/user login? |
| Standard window functionality | Does the authoring tool support standard windowing functionality? |
| | • Cut and paste? |
| | • Split panes? |
| | • Drag and drop? |
| | • Multi-level undo? |

| Criteria | Definition |
|---|---|
| Conversion | Does the tool support conversion from other formats?:<br>• FrameMaker?<br>• Quark?<br>• Others? |
| Indicate changes to users | Can the authoring system track changes in a document?<br>• With change bars?<br>• With color?<br>• Can change indications be turned on and off by the author?<br>• Can the system produce change reports?<br>• Does the authoring tool support change management such as change reports, change bars, version comparisons?<br>• Can the user turn change bars on and off?<br>• Can change bars automatically turn off after a period of time has passed? |
| Indicate standard (signed-off) content | Can the authoring system identify content that is "locked" (not available for change)? If yes, describe how (for example, with color or with a locked symbol). |
| Link within documents | Does the authoring tool support linking within elements or documents?<br>Drag and drop? |
| Link to external documents | Does the authoring tool support linking outside of elements/documents?<br>Drag and drop?<br>Links to specific file versions or most recent? |

*continues* ▶

**Table D.1    Continued**

| Criteria | Definition |
| --- | --- |
| Indicate changes to users | Can the authoring system track changes in a document? |
| | • With change bars? |
| | • With color? |
| | • By another customizable method? |
| | • Can the author turn change indications on  and off? |
| | • Can the system produce change reports? |
| | • Does the authoring tool support change management such as change reports, change bars, version comparisons? |
| | • Can the user turn change bars on and off? |
| | • Can change bars turn off automatically  after a period of time has passed? |
| | • Is it possible to compare multiple versions of content and see the changes between the versions? |
| **XML/SGML support (if applicable)** | |
| Enforce structure/Full rules checking | Does the authoring tool enforce structure as defined in a DTD or schema? |
| | Does the tool indicate what tags are valid at the cursor's current position? |
| | Does the authoring tool enable the author to make tagging errors? |

| Criteria | Definition |
|---|---|
| DTD Support | Describe the authoring tool support for the following:<br>• DTDs<br>• Schemas |
| Controlled access to DTDs | Can authors change the DTD, or can access be restricted via Access Control List (ACL) permissions or by requiring the use of a compiled DTD? |
| Customized DTDs | Does the authoring tool support the use of customized DTDs? |
| Multiple and flexible DTD support | Is the system designed to support multiple DTDs and flexible DTDs so that the system can grow as content and use evolve enterprise-wide? |
| Validated parsable output | Is the output validated against the DTD or schema? |
| Non-validated output handling | Does the system allow the author to override the system and process "invalid" content instances if needed? |
| Easy tag entry | How do users enter XML tags?<br>• Do users pick tags from a list?<br>• Do users pick tags from a dropdown menu?<br>• Is there some other mechanism? |
| Easy metadata (attributes) entry | How do users enter attributes?<br>• Users pick predefined metadata (attribute) values from a picklist?<br>• Users are prompted for required metadata?<br>• Some other way? |

*continues* ▶

**Table D.1    Continued**

| Criteria | Definition |
|---|---|
| Tables | Describe the table support for the authoring tool:<br>• Wizard driven?<br>• Embedded support (in the tool)?<br>• Can tables be generated from links to external data sources (CSV files, XML tagged data, ASCII files, and so on)? |
| Multiple authoring views, including "What You See Is What You Get" (WYSIWYG) | Does the authoring tool support multiple (author selected) authoring views?<br>• Formatted (no code)?<br>• Content and codes (no formatting)?<br>• Other? |
| Language support | Does the system support double-byte languages for authoring and display?<br>• How do authors enter accented characters?<br>• Does the system support multiple language dictionaries, or dictionaries for different industries? |
| Interfaces to CMS | With which CMS systems does the tool interface? |
| Cost | What is the cost? |
| Implementation time | What is the typical analysis, development, and implementation time? |

# Content management

Table D.2 summarizes the questions you should ask of a content management
tool vendor.

**Table D.2    Content management criteria**

| Criteria | Definition |
|---|---|
| Repository | What content formats does the CMS support, and at what level of granularity does it support them (for example, file, section, paragraph)? |
| | What type of database does the content management software use? |
| | How much effort is required to set up and maintain the database? |
| | Can the CMS accommodate the demands of enterprise implementations (for example, the number of users and the volume of documents)? How scalable is the database? |
| | How well does it grow to meet growing content? |
| | How is growth accomplished? |
| Segmentation/Bursting | Does the CMS support segmentation or bursting? |
| | Can you define the level of granularity? Can you define multiple levels of granularity depending on the type of content? Can you change the level of granularity at a later date? |
| User interface | How easy is the tool to learn and use? |
| | • What are its limitations? |
| | • Can the interface be customized? |
| | • Is there an "offline" mode? |
| Version control | Is every element versioned individually? |
| | What types of versioning are provided? |
| | Are changes stored as complete new versions of an element, or are just the deltas (changes only) saved from the current/original version? |

| Criteria | Definition |
| --- | --- |
| Check-in/Check-out | How easy is it to check-out/check-in content? Is content then locked so other authors cannot also check it out and change it? |
| | Can the system administrator check-in content that is checked-out by someone else (useful, for example, if an author is sick)? |
| Security | What security features are provided to protect sensitive documents from unauthorized access and modification? |
| | What levels of security are provided? |
| | What capabilities are available at each level? |
| | At what level of granularity can content be secured? |
| | Is the level of security of an element maintained wherever it is reused? |
| | Can security admin functions be delegated or distributed? |
| | Do all security changes have audit trails? |
| | If access is granted to groups of users, can a user belong to multiple groups? |
| | Are there automatic timeout features that protect content from access when a user leaves a workstation unattended for a specified period of time? |
| | Are invalid attempts to access secured content tracked? Managed? |
| | Do users see only the info (content or metadata) they are privileged to see, or can they see more info (metadata) but not content that is restricted? |
| | Does this system allow delegated authentication (access common LDAP directory or other remote authentication service)? |

*continues* ▶

**Table D.2    Continued**

| Criteria | Definition |
|---|---|
| Web-enabled | Is the "In-box" web-enabled? Does it have the same functionality as client version? |
| | Can the in-box be integrated into a corporate portal? |
| **Metadata** | |
| Creation | Can metadata be applied in the authoring tool? Is metadata applied as content is checked in? How simple is it for authors to select and apply metadata? |
| | Can sub-elements of a container element automatically inherit the container element's metadata? |
| | What types of metadata can be automatically applied? |
| | How easy is it to create a new metatag? |
| Storage | How is metadata stored? |
| Security | Can the facility for creating/changing metatags be secured so that only the system administrator can make changes? |
| **Managing elements** | |
| Tracking | Can the system identify and track all occurrences of specific information so that all occurrences are easily updated? |
| History | Does the system display a history of revisions? |
| | • Can the system generate history reports? |
| | • What information is available in the history? |
| | • What can the user track? |

| Criteria | Definition |
|---|---|
| Status of each component/ element | Can the system indicate whether a component has been checked out or is shared? |
| Update options | What are the update options?<br><br>• Automatically update the element selected to reuse when the original (source) element is changed?<br><br>• Notify authors of the changes so that they can decide whether they want to update the element or not?<br><br>• No update. Can authors choose to copy a component rather than reuse it? This means that if the original component is updated the copied element will not be. They exist as two separate components. |
| Content history mapping to source | Can the CMS keep a history trail that maps elements, when reused, to their original source? How is this done?<br><br>• Accomplished systematically?<br>• Accomplished with metadata? |
| Ability to sever the relationship | Can the author sever the relationship between a shared component so that the reused element now becomes a copied element? |
| Ability to merge components that diverged previously | Can you merge components that diverged previously? |
| Search and retrieval | What type of search engine is available? Can you add your own?<br><br>What types of searching are supported (Boolean, natural language, index, keyword, structural, metadata)?<br><br>Can search criteria be restricted based on user security profiles? |

*continues* ▶

**Table D.2    Continued**

| Criteria | Definition |
|---|---|
| Virtual documents | Does the system support virtual documents? <br>• How do you link the parts together? (Drag and drop?) |
| Authority tables | Does the system support the use of "authority tables" to contain master metadata and master content across (for example, global information that any element or document can access)? |
| Link control | Does the system provide automatic link checking? <br><br>Does it automatically detect changed/moved/broken links and correct problems? <br><br>Can it maintain or hide links when not relevant in dynamic documents? |
| Archive | How are archiving, obsoleting, and deleting handled? How do you set the rules? |
| **Structure** | |
| Automatic structure identification/ structural view | Does the system provide a visual, structural representation of documents or virtual documents? |
| Level of structure supported through metatags | What level of structure is supported for control or reuse? <br>• File? <br>• Paragraph? <br>• Sentence? <br>• Word? <br>• Special character? <br>• Graphic? <br>• Table? |

**Table D.2   Continued**

| Criteria | Definition |
| --- | --- |
| Are variables allowed? | Does the system support variables for small components of information (for example, at the word level)? |
| Translation | Can the CMS create a relationship between the source language and multiple localized versions of the content? |
| | Can the CMS integrate with a memory translation tool? With what memory translation tools can it integrate? Can the CMS be modified to integrate with other memory translation tools if necessary? |
| Integrated workflow | Is workflow integrated into the content management system, or is a separate work flow tool required? |
| | Is it configurable on the fly or must it be predetermined? |
| | Is the actual workflow audit-trailed? |
| | Can users share a common in-box so that you route work to a department or team as opposed to individuals? |
| Importing content | Can you import content by batch or by script? |
| | Is automatic conversion "into" the system supported from any file types (for example, are there built-in filters for data coming from Frame, RTF, Quark, and so on)? If not, do you have plug-ins available to handle this, or would this be a customization option? (Explain.) |
| Remote access | Is the system designed and constructed with remote access users in mind? Can it perform "real-time" and with adequate processing speed when accessed as follows: |
| | • Via web? |
| | • Via dial-in, modem (56K) connection? |

*continues* ▶

**Table D.2    Continued**

| Criteria | Definition |
|---|---|
| Reporting | What are the reporting features? Can the user generate:<br>• Status reports (of document elements)?<br>• Relationship reports (parent/child)?<br>• Where-used reports indicating where an element is being reused?<br>• A list of changed modules for reviews? |
| Metrics measuring and reporting | Does the system capture "use/reuse" measurements and provide reports? Can "use/reuse" be captured by different criteria (for example, reuse in one category of content versus reuse in another category of content)? |
| Audit trails/offline security | Does the tool provide any audit trails or other reporting to track content edited offline? |
| Interfaces to other tools | To which authoring tools does the CMS interface?<br>To which workflow tools does the CMS interface? |
| Cost | What is the cost? |
| Implementation time | What is the typical analysis, development, and implementation time? |

# Workflow

Table D.3 summarizes the questions you should ask of a workflow tool vendor. If the workflow is integrated in the content management system, ask these questions of the content management tool vendor.

**Table D.3    Workflow criteria**

| Criteria | Description |
|---|---|
| Interface | What is the interface?<br>• Web-based?<br>• Windows-based?<br>• Other? |
| Integration | Where is workflow integrated?<br>• With the content management system?<br>• With the email system? |
| Workflow creation | How easy is it to create the process flow (for example, can a business analyst easily create workflow or is a technical specialist required?) Is the user interface graphical? Is drag and drop of workflow elements supported?<br><br>Are there any predefined workflows (templates) that can be used or modified as necessary? Is integration provided for other modeling tools or business process re-engineering tools?<br><br>How easy is it to simulate and test the workflow processes? Can you set up multiple test data scenarios to test exceptions and conditions?<br><br>Can the system learn from user interactions and create new workflow based on its analysis of user interaction?<br><br>Are different workflows definable for each user at different levels? For example, can different workflows be created to accommodate different groups within the organization and their different work or review cycles? |

| Criteria | Definition |
|---|---|
| Business rules creation | How easy is it to create a business rule (for example, pre-defined elements to select from, simple rules language, visual)? |
| Administration | Can roles definitions be linked with existing roles and responsibilities software (for example, content management system, logon profiles)?<br><br>• Individual roles?<br><br>• Group?<br><br>• Can roles be assigned to a task rather than to individuals? Can a group be assigned to a role? Can alternates to individuals in a role be assigned?<br><br>• Would the system support a user-level (for example, author-level) administration role for certain admin activities that do not require a "system administration" level of support? |
| Security and electronic signature | What types of security are provided? Individual?<br>• Group?<br>• Shared?<br><br>• What security levels are provided (author, editor, team lead, and so on)? How easy is it to set security levels?<br><br>• Are electronic signatures supported? How are they supported? How are electronic signatures verified (for example, are they password protected)? |
| Support of automatic monitoring of status | Does the workflow system display the status of documents? |

*continues* ▶

**Table D.3    Continued**

| Criteria | Description |
|---|---|
| Reports | What standard reports are available? |
| | • Length of time to complete process |
| | • Status? |
| | • Workloads? |
| | • To do lists? |
| | • Can users define their own custom reports and create them "on the fly" (that is, ad hoc)? |
| Pull technology | Does the system include the capability to submit something to the system and have it automatically handled (for example, new publication)? |
| Push technology | Does the system include the capability to automatically perform a task (or trigger other processes, such as publishing, for example) at a given time or a given status? |
| **Types of workflow** | |
| Support of collaborative | Does the system support processes that workflows may change given appropriate security access? |
| Support of administrative | Are standard workflows enforced for workflow repeatable processes (for example, review and sign-off)? |
| Embedded workflow enabling | Can workflow be integrated with the content management system for transparent usage? |
| Complex workflows | Does the system support the following: |
| | • Branched workflows (based on metadata)? |
| | • Multiple branching? |
| | • Simultaneous review and automatic merging? |

| Criteria | Definition |
| --- | --- |
| Notification | Does the system support the following:<br>• Notification of tasks or requirements from members of the workflow?<br>• Ability to view status (for example, in progress, complete)? |
| Deadlines and escalation | Is there a way to notify users of deadlines (for example, by email, with an electronic calendar)?<br><br>Can users choose to add an alarm to a deadline to assist in reminding them of due dates?<br><br>Do missed deadlines trigger actions such as reminders and escalation procedures? Can priorities be changed? |
| Routing | What types of routing are supported? Can the system provide ad hoc workflow if you need it?<br><br>Does the system allow steps to be completed simultaneously? Are wait steps supported?<br><br>Can you have different types of routing for different projects? How easy is it to create the different types of workflow routing? |
| Other considerations | Does the embedded workflow meet all your organization's requirements, or is it specific to one application of the content life cycle (such as web, for example)? If it was designed for one application, is it extensible to accommodate the enterprise content life cycle? How easy is it to extend the workflow functionality?<br><br>What standards, if any, are used to exchange data among applications? With which systems does the workflow system integrate? How is integration accomplished? Is there an API that would allow the workflow to be customized to integrate with systems not currently integrated? |

continues ▶

**Table D.3    Workflow criteria**

| Criteria | Description |
|---|---|
| Cost | What is the cost? |
| Implementation time | What is the typical analysis, development, and implementation time? |

# Delivery

Table D.4 summarizes the questions you should ask of a delivery tool vendor. If the delivery tool is integrated in the content management system or the authoring tool, ask these questions of these vendors.

## Table D.4    Delivery criteria

| Criteria | Definition |
|---|---|
| Aggregation | With which authoring tools does the delivery tool interface? |
| | With which CMS tools does the delivery tool interface? |
| | With which databases does the delivery tool interface? |
| Output support | What output formats are supported by the delivery system? |
| | ● PostScript? |
| | ● PDF? |
| | ● HTML? |
| | ● XML? |
| | ● Word? |
| | ● Does the tool support output to multiple formats for a single publishing request? For example, can you create a both a PDF version and an HTML version of a product specification sheet with a single request? |
| Book building | Can the tool automatically create TOCs, indexes, and linked lists (for example, lists of figures)? |
| Partial or full publishing | Can the tool include support for publishing pieces of a document or just full documents? |
| Collection publication | Does the tool include support for publishing collections (groups of documents)? For example, can the tool take a series of input files and build a complete web site, with full hypertext linking? |
| | Can the tool build the TOCs and indexes for these collections? |

| Criteria | Definition |
|---|---|
| Full graphics support | Can the tool perform automatic conversion based on targeted output? |
| | Can selected content be flagged to preserve maximum fidelity of graphics? |
| Conversion | Does the tool support conversion of imported content? What formats does it support? How clean (that is, problem free) is the conversion? |
| Output management | Are published documents (outputs) automatically checked into the repository? |
| | Can outputs be automatically associated with source documents (through metadata)? |
| | Is metadata from contributing documents (files) automatically assigned to published output for check-in? |
| | Are publication directories (both internal and external to the repository) automatically populated? |
| Assembly | Does the tool include support for virtual or compound documents (assembled in response to a publishing event or request)? |
| Dynamic content | Can the delivery tool support dynamic content? |
| | How is dynamic content delivered (multi-channel, ASP, portal)? |
| | How is it supported? |
| | How do you enter user profiles? |
| | Can the delivery tool update the user profile based on user selection? |
| | How are business rules entered (code or user scenarios or plain language interface)? |

*continues* ▶

**Table D.4   Delivery criteria**

| Criteria | Definition |
| --- | --- |
| Personalization | What functionality does the personalization engine provide? How do you enter user profiles? |
| | Can the delivery tool update the user profile based on user selection? |
| | How are business rules entered (code or user scenarios or plain language interface)? |
| | How does the recommendations engine work (analytics, algorithms, collaborative filtering)? |
| Automation | Does the publishing system support automated publishing (batch mode, without operator support), triggered by: |
| | • Author request? |
| | • Workflow event (check-in, status changes)? |
| | • End-user request? |
| Language support | Does the system support double-byte languages in output? |
| Scripted publishing | Can publishing be managed through defined scripts? |
| Cost | What is the cost? |
| Implementation time | What is the typical analysis, development, and implementation time? |

# Appendix E

## Content Relationships

When creating unified content, it can be difficult to track versions of content and select the correct content if multiple versions exist. As authors create and modify information elements, whether revising for new information, or revising to make information more appropriate for a specific output product or customer, they create layers of content and complexity. Understanding the relationships between content elements and tracking the use of content versions is vital to effective reuse.

## Basic relationships

The basic relationship for versions of content is a simple parent-child relationship. The originating version is the parent, the revised version of the content is the child. In the simplest relationship, the child replaces the parent. For example, imagine a production description for a piece of hardware. For clear identification, the part includes an identification number. When the part is replaced by a newer part, a new version of the product description is released with the new part number. To actually create the new product description, the author would retrieve the original description from the content management system and revise it. Assuming the new part replaces the old, the new description (the child) effectively replaces the old description. The old version still exists in the content management system. It may or may not be used or updated after the newer version is created.

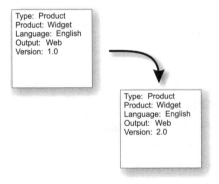

**Figure E.1    Parent-child relationship.**

You can also build relationships between original and translated content. For example, the sample part might be distributed globally. To sell in foreign markets you need to localize the information. In this case, the translated versions of the content are considered children of the original. In Figure E.2, the English version of the description is the parent, and the French and Spanish versions are the children. Some systems refer to the translated versions as siblings or peers of each other. Unlike the earlier example, in this case, the children do not replace the original. The original is used in English-language publications, the French description in French-language publications, and so on. However, it is still important to maintain the links between the versions. If the original version is changed, the child versions must be changed. If not, they are out of sync.

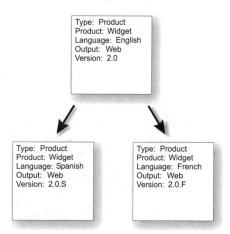

**Figure E.2    Sibling relationships.**

Whenever you create derivative content for an element, the derivative element is a child. Multiple children of the same parent are siblings.

## Complex relationships

Where outputs are more numerous and complex, the relationships between versions can become more complicated. For example, continuing the previous scenario, the part description might be used in several different outputs. It could be used in help, on the web site, and in a paper-based brochure. If the description is modified for each of the outputs, variants of the description must be tracked.

The relationship in this case starts as a simple relationship. The original description is used in the web site, and two derivative versions of the description are created for the help and the brochure, as illustrated in Figure E.3. In this case, the derivative versions are children of the original.

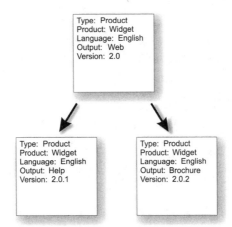

**Figure E.3    Sibling relationships for output version.**

If the materials are translated for global distribution, a third level of versioning is created, as shown in Figure E.4.

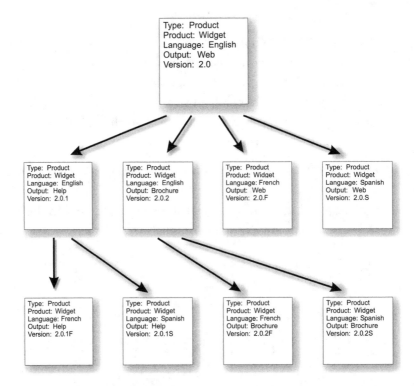

**Figure E.4    Complex relationships.**

In this example, the translated versions of the descriptions are children of the original. The translated versions of help and the brochure can also be considered grandchildren of the original description; they are once removed from the original.

This is not an unusual level of complexity in reuse systems. However, it does place certain strains on your content management systems and processes. Any time an information component is changed, you must ensure that all children/grandchildren/descendants of that component are evaluated to ensure that they are also changed if required.

## Managing the complexity

There are only two ways to manage version complexity: The first is to select a content management system that can track and report all the variants and relationships in your information models; second, you can choose reuse techniques that limit the number of variations that you create. For example, for this product description, a single element can be created that includes all information for the web site, help, and brochure (nested reuse), and output filtering can be used to ensure that only the required information appears in each output.

To further simplify your management, you need to determine when content becomes "obsolete" or no longer used. For example, in the case of the new part, the part description for the old part becomes obsolete if the old part is no longer being supported. Then the child becomes the source (parent), and the other elements can be archived.

Finally, you can use systematic reuse. Systematic reuse automatically identifies the correct reusable object for the author, relieving authors from having to determine which version of the content they want to reuse. Your content management still needs to manage the versions and relationships effectively, but some of the burden of understanding the relationships and selecting the correct element to reuse is removed from the author.

## Conclusion

Content relationships can be complex. Take care to think through how you want to reuse content, update content, and track content as you develop your system to ensure you develop your content reuse strategies effectively and select an appropriate content management system.

# Index

# G

Generalized Markup Language (GML), 282

generalized tools versus specialized tools, 279-280

generated indexes and TOCs (tables of contents), 355

generated text, style sheets for, 262

generic versus semantic elements for unified content strategy implementation, 254-259

GML (Generalized Markup Language), 282

goals
  organizational goals, 65-66
    *challenges, identifying, 73-75*
    *dangers, identifying, 67, 69*
    *identifying, 44-45, 72-73*
    *opportunities, identifying, 69-70*
    *qualifying, 46-47*
    *quantifying, 47-52*
    *and ROI (return on investment), 44-52*
    *role of unified content strategy in achieving, 75*
    *strengths, identifying, 70-71*
  of XML, 284-285

Goldfarb, Charles (history of SGML), 282

granularity, 165-166
  unified content strategy implementation, 248-249

graphics, supported by delivery systems, 356

group organization/management (collaborative authoring), 370-371

# H

hierarchies versus taxonomies, 187

history of content reuse, 26-29

history of XML, 282
  HTML, 283-284
  SGML, 282-283

HR department as content source, 4

HTML (Hypertext Markup Language)
  history of, 283-284
  sample document (listing 14.1), 285
  versus XML, 285-288

Hysell, Deborah A. (OCLC information modeling example), 177

# I

identifying needs (evaluating software tools). *See also* user needs
  general criteria, 270-271
  specific criteria, 268-269
  weighting the criteria, 272-273

IDMSs. *See* integrated document management systems

implementation of unified content strategy. *See also* transition plans
  with authoring forms, 252-253
  checklist for, 474-476
  factors affecting, 246-247
  granularity, 248-249
  metadata, 259
  overcoming resistance to change, 408
  requirements
    *ease of use, 247*
    *finding information quickly, 247-248*
    *scalability, 247*
  semantic versus generic elements, 254-259

VOICES THAT MATTER

## VISIT OUR WEB SITE

WWW.NEWRIDERS.COM

On our Web site you'll find information about our other books, authors, tables of contents, indexes, and book errata. You will also find information about book registration and how to purchase our books.

## EMAIL US

Contact us at this address: **nrfeedback@newriders.com**

- If you have comments or questions about this book
- To report errors that you have found in this book
- If you have a book proposal to submit or are interested in writing for New Riders
- If you would like to have an author kit sent to you
- If you are an expert in a computer topic or technology and are interested in being a technical editor who reviews manuscripts for technical accuracy

- To find a distributor in your area, please contact our international department at this address. **nrmedia@newriders.com**

- For instructors from educational institutions who want to preview New Riders books for classroom use. Email should include your name, title, school, department, address, phone number, office days/hours, text in use, and enrollment, along with your request for desk/examination copies and/or additional information.
- For members of the media who are interested in reviewing copies of New Riders books. Send your name, mailing address, and email address, along with the name of the publication or Web site you work for.

## BULK PURCHASES/CORPORATE SALES

The publisher offers discounts on this book when ordered in quantity for bulk purchases and special sales. For sales within the U.S., please contact: Corporate and Government Sales (800) 382-3419 or **corpsales@pearsontechgroup.com**. Outside of the U.S., please contact: International Sales (317) 428-3341 or **international@pearsontechgroup.com**.

## WRITE TO US

New Riders
1249 Eighth Street
Berkeley, California 94710

## CALL US

Toll-free (800) 571-5840. Ask for New Riders.
If outside U.S. (317) 428-3000. Ask for New Riders.

New
Rider

# Peachpit

*Essential books for the creative community*

# Visit Peachpit on the Web at www.peachpit.com

- Read the latest articles and download timesaving tipsheets from best-selling authors such as Scott Kelby, Robin Williams, Lynda Weinman, Ted Landau, and more!

- Join the Peachpit Club and save 25% off all your online purchases at peachpit.com every time you shop—plus enjoy free UPS ground shipping within the United States.

- Search through our entire collection of new and upcoming titles by author, ISBN, title, or topic. There's no easier way to find just the book you need.

- Sign up for newsletters offering special Peachpit savings and new book announcements so you're always the first to know about our newest books and killer deals.

- Did you know that Peachpit also publishes books by Apple, New Riders, Adobe Press, Macromedia Press, palmOne Press, and TechTV press? Swing by the Peachpit family section of the site and learn about all our partners and series.

- Got a great idea for a book? Check out our About section to find out how to submit a proposal. You could write our next best-seller!

**You'll find all this and more at www.peachpit.com. Stop by and take a look today!**

VIEW CART

search

▸ Registration  already a member? Log in.  ▸ Book Registration

# Publishing the Voices that Matter

OUR AUTHORS

PRESS ROOM

| web development | design | photoshop | new media | 3-D | server technologies |

EDUCATORS

ABOUT US

CONTACT US

You already know that New Riders brings you the **Voices that Matter**.

But what does that mean? It means that New Riders brings you the

Voices that challenge your assumptions, take your talents to the next

level, or simply help you better understand the complex technical world

we're all navigating.

## Visit **www.newriders.com** to find:

- ▸ **10% discount** and **free shipping** on all purchases
- ▸ Never before published chapters
- ▸ Sample chapters and excerpts
- ▸ Author bios and interviews
- ▸ Contests and enter-to-wins
- ▸ Up-to-date industry event information
- ▸ Book reviews
- ▸ Special offers from our friends and partners
- ▸ Info on how to join our User Group program
- ▸ Ways to have your Voice heard

New
Riders

WWW.NEWRIDERS.COM

0735712026
Jesse James Garrett
US$29.99

0735712506
Christina Wodtke
US$29.99

0735710627
Kelly Goto and Emily Cotler
US$45.00

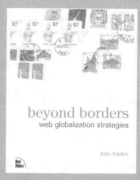

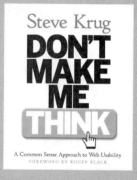

0735712085
John Yunker
US$39.99

0789723107
Steve Krug
US$35.00

0735711518
Jonathan and Lisa Price
US$40.00

VOICES
THAT MATTER™

New
Riders

WWW.NEWRIDERS.COM

www.managingenterprisecontent.com companion web site at

# Web Site for:

## *Managing Enterprise Content:*
## *A Unified Content Strategy*

The accompanying web site provides a return on investment (ROI) calculator to assist you in calculating potential savings and expenses, links to potential vendors, a bibliography, a glossary of terms, and an electronic version of all the significant examples used in the book.

## Other Content Management Resources:

www.aiim.org

www.asis.org

www.contentworld.com

www.horton.com

www.ieeepcs.org

www.stc.org

www.kmworld.com

www.intranetjournal.com/km/

www.managingenterprisecontent.com

New
Riders

www.newriders.com